LAW

for the

Pharmacy Student

LAW

for the
Pharmacy Student

WILLIAM E. HASSAN, Jr., Ph.D., LL.B.

Adjunct Professor of Hospital Pharmacy and
Pharmacy Law

Acting Chairman, Department of Pharmaceutical
Administration, Massachusetts College of Pharmacy

Director, Peter Bent Brigham Hospital

Member, Massachusetts Bar

LEA & FEBIGER • Philadelphia 1971

ISBN 0-8121-0320-3

Library of Congress Catalog Card Number 78-135682

Published in Great Britain by Henry Kimpton Publishers, London

PRINTED IN THE UNITED STATES OF AMERICA

Preface

PRIOR to World War II, pharmacy, like many other professions, operated within its own enclave. The pharmacist was required to meet the obligations imposed upon him by the Board of Registration in Pharmacy, federal narcotic and alcohol regulations and some state statutes and local ordinances. His relationship to the business world was generally limited to purchase and sale transactions. Clearly, a broad knowledge of the law, although desirable, was not essential then for the successful conduct of his business.

Within the past decade there has been a marked proliferation of federal laws that have a direct bearing upon the practice of pharmacy. These include a revised Federal Food, Drug, and Cosmetic law, and regulations governing drug labeling, drug experimentation and drug control. In addition the Medicare law, the Public Information Act and the Truth in Lending Act have been passed.

During the same period of time, the various states have enacted and adopted new laws such as the Uniform Commercial Code. The laws of agency, contract and tort have been updated to reflect a modern economy as well as changes in social, moral and legal attitudes.

The purpose of this text, therefore, is twofold—to aid practicing pharmacists to understand their legal responsibilities and thereby avoid the pitfalls that lead to litigation, and to serve as a textbook for courses in pharmacy law which will provide the student with some insight into the legal aspects of the practice of his profession.

In the preparation of this book, I have consulted many teachers of pharmacy administration and law. For their guidance and advice I am grateful.

Special appreciation is hereby extended to my wife and children, whose patience and understanding were instrumental in my decision to prepare this volume and to all organizations, publishers and authors whose publications have been consulted for ideas and materials which have been included in this text-book.

WILLIAM E. HASSAN, JR.

Boston, Massachusetts

Contents

CHAPTER 1

The Forms
of Law

The course in law for the pharmacy student is designed to introduce him to basic elements of the legal theory of that part of the law that is pertinent to conducting his business and practicing his profession. The materials hereinafter presented represent but a fragment of the total body of law. Therefore the student must realize that to master these introductory materials does not make him a lawyer. Furthermore, the student should understand at the outset that the practice of law is a specialty unto itself and that consultation with a competent attorney *before* entering into negotiations for a sale of the business, the negotiation of a lease or the purchase of fixed assets from another party will often save time and money and eliminate later misunderstanding and grief.

Case Law and Legislation Compared

American law is found in two forms: case law and legislation. The differences between them are complex and numerous. For the purpose of this text, it is necessary to indicate three formal characteristics which will identify them.[1]

a. Political Origin

Case law has its origin in the decisions that are rendered by judicial or administrative tribunals which are authorized to hear and determine particular controversies. Legislation originates in a legislative body the function of which is to make rules; a prime example is the state legislature.

b. Bibliography

Case law is published in "reports" of judicial or administrative decisions and relates to determinations that have been reached in a particular controversy or some phase thereof. An example of this is the *Massachusetts Decisions* series or the decisions of the Internal Revenue Service.

1

Legislation, as one might expect, is to be found in statute books and is called "laws" or "acts." In Massachusetts, they are referred to as *The Acts and Resolves of the General Court;* the "general court" in this instance is the state legislature.

c. Textual Form

Case law consists of the propositions of law which acquire authoritative status because they are inferred from judicial or administrative precedents based upon the facts, official determinations and subsequent opinion. These propositions of law are not collected and reduced to an official text but remain in the various "reports" that comprise part of the law library of the practicing attorney.

Legislation, once enacted, is reduced to an official textual form representing an exclusive official wording of the rule.

In summary, case law is flexible; legislation is textually rigid.

Types of Case Law

a. Judicial Decisions

Laymen generally consider case law to be the by-product of the settling of a controversy in court. In reality, case law represents the general rule(s) for which the case stands. Of nearly equal significance is whether the decision was rendered by a "higher" court or a "lower" court and whether the decision was accompanied by an official "opinion of the court" which expressed the court's reasoning in reaching the decision.

b. Administrative Decisions

An administrative tribunal is a body of officials ("commission" or "board") having authority by statute to make decisions about the rights or privileges of individuals. For example, the official body which grants licenses to practice pharmacy is the Board of Registration in Pharmacy. This board confers on a pharmacist, by the license which it grants, the privilege of practicing pharmacy, which would be illegal if done without such a license.

Some administrative tribunals may reach a decision yet refuse to make known the opinion which sets forth the reasons. This is quite common with the various licensing bodies such as the boards of registration in medicine, pharmacy or nursing. Others have a more formal type of procedure and give opinions or explanations in connection with their decisions. Included in this group are the Interstate Commerce Commission and the Federal Trade Commission. Their decisions, when published, have the status of precedents.

Court Hierarchy

In the discussion on judicial decision, it was pointed out that one of the factors affecting the significance of case law was whether the decision was rendered in a higher court or a lower court.

The Supreme Court of the United States is the nation's highest tribunal with respect to certain types of controversies: namely those requiring an interpretation and application of a provision of the Constitution of the United States. In such a controversy, its case law is the supreme authority. The Constitution provides that the power of the Supreme Court "shall extend to all cases, in law and equity, arising under this constitution, the laws of the United States, and treaties made, or which shall be made, under their authority; to all cases affecting ambassadors, other public ministers and consuls; to all cases of admiralty and maritime jurisdiction; to controversies to which the United States shall be a party; to controversies between two or more States, between a state and citizens of another state;—between citizens of different States, between citizens of the same state claiming lands under grants of different States, and between a state, or the citizen thereof, and foreign States, citizens or subjects."

In general, the states have one high court usually called the Supreme Court the precedents of which are binding on all the lower courts in the state; examples of such courts include the Court of Appeals of New York, the Supreme Judicial Court of Massachusetts and the Supreme Court of Maine.

Immediately below these high courts there are, in some states, intermediate appellate courts; the decisions of these courts are authoritative precedents unless they conflict with the case law of a supreme court of the same state. Examples of such courts are the Pennsylvania Superior Courts and California Appellate Courts.

Trial courts are below the intermediate appellate courts. It is at this level that all controversies must be tried and determined before they can be appealed. The decisions of these courts are not officially published and ordinarily they serve as judicial precedents only within that court.

There are, of course, other courts such as land courts, small claim courts for civil matters and municipal courts and magistrate or police courts for minor criminal offenses. Decisions reached at this level are generally not relied upon as case law.

Types of Legislation

The word "legislation" is commonly used as if it were synonymous with the word "statute." Within the context of this broader meaning, the student will not find it difficult to include all forms of law that are characterized by the rigidity of fixed wording. Incidentally, it is this fixed wording of a statute or other piece of legislation that makes the problems of its interpretation substantially different from those of the interpretation and application of case law.

Because it is not the intent of this text to make a law student of the pharmacy student, the following types of legislation are presented with relatively little comment.

a. The Constitution of the United States

The Federal Constitution is the supreme law of the country. This view is supported by the following passage from Article VI (second paragraph) of that document:

> This constitution, and the laws of the United States which shall be made in pursuance thereof; and all treaties made, or which shall be made, under the authority of the United States, shall be the supreme law of the land; and the judges in every state shall be bound thereby, any thing in the constitution or laws of any state to the contrary notwithstanding.

The primary functions of the Constitution are to prescribe the powers of the several branches of government—judicial, executive and legislative—and to prescribe the parameters of authority of officials over the private citizen.

b. Treaties

The Federal Constitution states that treaties made under the authority of the United States shall also be the supreme law of the land. This is understandable when one realizes the significance of a formal agreement that is entered into by two or more nations and is concerned with peace, alliance, trade, nuclear energy or world health.

c. Federal Statutes

These are the statutes enacted by the Congress of the United States. They are of a higher authority than any state constitution or statute. Examples of this type of statute include the Social Security Act, the Harrison Narcotic Act, the Federal Food, Drug, and Cosmetic Act, and the National Labor Relations Act.

d. Federal Executive Orders and Administration Regulations

The Constitution of the United States in Article II, Section 1 confers upon the President "executive power"—a power of broad scope which, if they prescribe general rules of conduct, are laws, legislative in form.

Federal administrative officials or bodies have power to make general rules which are usually referred to as "regulations." These are legislative in character and, when issued according to a Congressional statute, are superior to all forms of state law. Examples are the regulations of the Secretary of the Treasury (e.g. tax-free alcohol) and the Food and Drug Administration.

e. State Constitutions

A state constitution is, within the jurisdictional boundaries of the state, the "supreme law" of the state subject to the operation of the Federal Constitution, treaties and statutes. State constitutions generally differ from the Federal Constitution in that in addition to prescribing the framework of government within the state they often contain rules of conduct for private citizens such as the prohibition of gambling and lotteries.

f. State Statutes

The commonest type of legislation is the statute of the state legislature. This body of law can be varied and deals with complex subjects in view of the fact that the state legislature has all of the powers not excluded by the Federal Constitution, treaties and statutes or by the state constitution.

g. State Administrative Regulations

Administrative regulations are forms of law and must be so recognized. Although many of these regulations relate merely to the operation and function of the particular agency, there are administrative regulations that do concern the private citizen. Good examples for the pharmacy student are the regulations emanating from the Board of Registration in Pharmacy, the Board of Registration in Medicine or the Department of Public Health.

h. Municipal Ordinances

Municipal corporations (cities, towns and villages) have limited legislative powers with respect to matters of local concern such as zoning laws and building construction codes. The general rules enacted by these municipalities are called municipal ordinances.

i. Rules of Court

The rules of court do not regulate the life of a private citizen but are of importance to him as a possible litigant. In general, rules of court are developed and adopted by a court; they regulate pleading and other steps in the litigation procedure or they direct the internal organization of the court. This body of law is, of course, of primary interest to the practicing attorney and is cited here only to alert the pharmacy student as to its existence.

Court Jurisdiction Over Drug Cases

The failure of a pharmacist to comply with a city ordinance may result in a case which would be tried first in the local municipal court from which there is an appeal to a higher state court.

If the pharmacist violates a state statute, the case will be tried in the state trial court of general jurisdiction. These courts are known by various names some of which are district court, circuit court or superior court. Litigants may appeal the decisions of these trial courts to the supreme court of the state if there is basis upon which such an appellate procedure can be invoked.

Because of the increasing number of federal statutes that affect the practice of pharmacy, it is possible for the pharmacist to violate a federal law and thus be prosecuted in a federal court. In general, a case brought up for the violation of a federal statute, or one involving diversity of citizenship of the litigants will be tried in the United States District Court, with the right to appeal to the United States Circuit Court of Appeals or, if warranted, to the United States Supreme Court.

Sociology and the Law

In modern society, there is very little that is not covered in one way or another by our system of law. This may come as a surprise to the student because he invariably labors under the misconception that law only applies to and governs criminal behavior.

If one were to reassess objectively the role played by law in his daily life he would inevitably conclude that all aspects of everyday living are controlled by or subject to rulings of the legal system. The doubter should consider the ownership of real and personal property, tax laws, traffic laws, domestic relations laws, sales law and labor relations laws.

Some of these laws are expressed by statutes, judicial decisions or regulations of administrative bodies. Indeed any fact situation may be brought under the scrutiny of the legal system simply by initiating a legal proceeding on the issue.

The law is therefore all encompassing. It makes no distinction between social strata or sociological ramifications. It is a system that must be understood and not merely recognized. Law is a mechanism of social control; there is a place for it as a major institutional complex within society.[1]

References

1. H. JONES: LEGAL METHOD, 2nd Ed. (Text originally by N. DOWLING, E. PATTER-SON, and R. POWELL), The Foundation Press, Brooklyn, New York, 1952.

CHAPTER 2

Contracts

A general knowledge of the law of contracts is important to the pharmacy practitioner regardless of whether he becomes the proprietor of a community pharmacy or of a chain of pharmacies, or chooses to be an institutional practitioner of his profession. This becomes patently clear when the many facets of the daily practice of pharmacy are considered. The pharmacist-manager is frequently involved in the purchase of the inventory, supplies and equipment; he negotiates service arrangements with cleaning companies, air conditioning firms and burglar alarm specialists; he may participate in the acquisition of personnel and in the termination of their employment; and finally he may become engaged in plans for remodelling or even acquiring another outlet. Throughout all of the above transactions the word *contract* might very well serve as the common denominator. In each, the pharmacist is "contracting" for the purchase of a service or of merchandise. Even when he is dismissing personnel he is, in effect, terminating an employment contract.

Thus, it is of paramount importance that the pharmacist have some knowledge relative to such aspects of contract law as offer, acceptance, consideration, capacity of the parties and breach of contract. No attempt will be made to go into great detail on such complex matters as joint and several contracts, illegality, duress, fraud and the statute of frauds. The wise pharmacist will consult with his attorney relative to the resolution of contractual problems involving them.

Definition

Despite popular belief, there are many definitions of a contract. Typical of these are the following:

A contract is a promise, or set of promises, for breach of which the law gives remedy, or the performance of which the law in some way recognizes a duty.[1]

* * * * *

A promissory agreement between two or more persons that creates, modifies or destroys a legal relation.[2]

* * * * *

An agreement upon sufficient consideration, to do or not to do a particular thing.[3]

* * * * *

An agreement between two or more parties, preliminary step in making of which is offer by one and acceptance by other, in which minds of parties meet and concur in understanding of terms.[4]

* * * * *

A deliberate engagement between competent parties, upon a legal consideration, to do, or abstain from doing, some act.[5]

* * * * *

It is agreement creating obligation, in which there must be competent parties, subject matter, legal consideration, mutuality of agreement, and mutuality of obligation, and agreement must not be so vague or uncertain that terms are not ascertainable.[6]

Analytical dissection of the foregoing definitions of a contract reveals that the following elements are essential to a contract:

1. competent parties,
2. mutual assent—offer and acceptance,
3. legal consideration, and
4. the act to be done or abstained from must in itself be legal.

A simple illustration of a contract containing all of these elements is the following:

I, John Doe, in consideration of $1500, herewith paid to me by Tom Doe, do hereby promise to refrain from operating a retail drugstore in the town of Redville for one year beginning with the date of the signing of this agreement.

Kinds of Contracts

Briefly, contracts may be described as express contracts, unilateral or bilateral contracts and as implied contracts. Implied contracts are further subdivided into implied contracts in fact and implied contracts in law.

An *express contract* is an agreement between two or more competent parties based upon a consideration to do or not to do a lawful thing.

A *unilateral contract* is one in which a promisor receives no promise as consideration for *his* promise and differs from a *bilateral contract* in that in the latter there are mutual promises between two parties to the contract; each party being both a promisor and a promisee. This is illustrated by the following case[7]:

An insurance company agreed, through its adjuster, to pay the plaintiff's claim if he would execute a release. The plaintiff complied however the defendant's insurance company refused to pay and claimed that no binding contract was ever completed.

The judge found that an agreement was made to settle and releases were given in accordance with the agreement and were accepted by the defendant. The promises of the plaintiff to settle and the promise of the defendant to pay if releases were given were consideration–one for the other. If the agreement be taken as unilateral, on the offer to pay if releases were given, the result is the same. Releases were given before the offer was withdrawn.

A *contract implied in fact* is a genuine contract. The only difference between a contract implied in fact and an express contract is the method by which the actual mutual understanding of the parties is manifested. In the latter, the mutual understanding is manifested by express words; in the former, it is inferred, implied or presumed from the circumstances surrounding the conduct of the parties. In other words, the source of the obligation in both express contracts and contracts implied in fact is the intention of the parties, there being merely a difference in the character of the evidence by which the contract in either case is proven.[8]

While contracts implied in fact possess all the essential elements of express contracts, with the exception of the written or oral expression of the terms of the contract, *contracts implied in law* are not contracts at all but are obligations imposed by law irrespective of consent, and in many cases, in spite of actual dissent. The term "contract implied in law" merely denotes the source of the obligation. It is generally said that contracts in law are founded upon the doctrine that no man shall be permitted to enrich himself *unjustly* at the expense of another.

Offer and Acceptance

The first requisite of a contract is that there must be a manifestation of an intent to contract. This results in a meeting of the minds relative to the same subject at the same time. This takes the form of *offer* and *acceptance.*

Generally an offer possesses the following three elements: (a) the intent to contract must be present, (b) the offer must be definite and certain in terms and (c) it must be communicated to the other party. Thus, a contract entered into in jest by both parties is no contract at all nor is an offer intended and understood as loose conversation to be taken as the basis for the formation of a contract.

Each day the practicing pharmacist is besieged by advertisements, catalogues and trade circulars containing price quotations; these may not be considered to be offers because they contain no manifestation of present intent to contract. These materials are properly classified as trade announcements.

On other occasions, the pharmacist may request a firm to submit a bid on various propositions of interest to him. Upon submitting these bids, some companies infer that the next step is the consummation of a contract on the basis that they have complied with the pharmacist's request for submission of the bid. There is no obligation to accept the most favorable proposal received or to accept any proposal at all. Any or all may be rejected for any reason or without any reason. A mere indication of a willingness to receive proposals is not an offer which can lead to a contract upon the submission of the proposal.[9]

An *option* is an offer accompanied by consideration. It is in fact a binding contract not to withdraw an offer.

a. Termination of Offer

An offer will continue and be binding on the offeror until (a) the time specified in the offer has expired, (b) a reasonable period of time has expired, if no time were specified, (c) it is accepted or (d) it is rejected by the offeree or other legally effective means including counter-offer, death of the offeror, insanity and illegality. From the above, it is clear that a counter-offer destroys the original offer forever therefore one must be ready to distinguish between an inquiry and a bona fide counter-offer. An inquiry will not destroy an offer.

b. Acceptance

Acceptance of an offer is the expression by the offeree of his assent to the terms of the offer; or the performance by the offeree of that which is called for by the offer, if the offer required more than the assent of the offeree.[10] An acceptance must be unequivocal and must comply with the terms of the offer.

The acceptance must be transmitted by the means authorized by the offeror however, where none are specified, the means customarily used in such transactions is acceptable. With regard to the acceptance, it is the general rule that a contract is complete when the letter of acceptance or when any other invited mode of acceptance leaves the hands of the offeree. In some states a uniform commercial code has been adopted; this provides that an acceptance can be made in any manner and by any medium reasonable in the circumstances prevailing.

Consideration

Consideration is the relinquishment of or promise to relinquish a legal right, at the request of another. As a general rule, courts will not inquire into the adequacy or fairness of consideration except that where there is a liquidated sum due presently without dispute, a promise to accept a less sum in full satisfaction is *nudum pactum.*

In any discussion of consideration it is necessary to point out that *moral* consideration is insufficient as legal consideration; nor is doing what one is already legally bound to do sufficient consideration; on the other hand, *contingent* consideration is sufficient so that a promise to do an act upon condition is acceptable.

Capacity of the Parties

A contract cannot be made by and it cannot be enforced against a party who does not possess the capacity to contract. An example of this class of individual is a person who is adjudicated insane. However, a contract made by a person having the power to contract is valid, even though such person has a power to avoid or disaffirm the agreement. Examples of individuals in this category are unemancipated infants and a person who is inebriated when he enters into the contract.

In the above discussion, reference is implied to situations which might create *voidable* and *void* contracts. A *voidable* contract is a perfectly good contract and is enforceable until it is legally disaffirmed by the other party. This situation generally applies when a contract is entered into with an unemancipated infant who later disaffirms. However, having avoided the contract, the same party may still be liable in *quasi* contract for the reasonable value of the goods or services if they are in the categories of necessaries. This situation usually develops when an infant purchases groceries on credit and later disaffirms his agreement to pay for them.

It should also be remembered that a contract that is ordinarily voidable may not be set aside when it is clearly fair to both parties and it has been so far executed by one party that he cannot be put back into the same status as existed prior to the contract.

A contract that is *void* as to one of the parties is one which imposes no liability on such party. A voidable contract can be ratified; a void contract cannot be ratified.

Privity of Contract

The general rule is, and apparently has always been, that a plaintiff in an action on a simple contract must be the person from whom the consideration of the contract actually passed, and that a stranger to the consideration cannot sue on the contract. One court has stated that "there must be a privity of contract between the plaintiff and defendant, in order to render the defendant liable to an action by the plaintiff on the contract."[11]

Exceptions to the above rule include those where promises have been made to a parent for the benefit of a child; beneficiaries of insurance policies; in certain partnership cases where partner Adam sells his interest in the partnership to Brown (later a plaintiff creditor can sue Brown for earlier debts of the partnership); and under the Uniform Commercial Code where there is an assignment of a contract for the sale of goods, the promise of the assignee to perform the duties of the assignor is enforceable by either the assignor or the other party to the original contract.[12]

Statute of Limitations

The Statute of Limitations may run for different periods of time in the various states. In Massachusetts, on ordinary informal contracts, the statute runs for six years. A judgment is presumed to have been paid in twenty years. This presumption is rebuttable. Under the Uniform Commercial Code, contracts for the sale of goods have a time limitation of only four years.[13]

Assignment of Contracts

Contracts may be assigned unless they are of a strictly personal nature or unless the contract specifically prohibits assignment. The assignor of a contract is still liable under it and if the assignment is in writing, the assignee may sue in his own name.

Statute of Frauds

All jurisdictions possess a Statute of Frauds that generally provides that no action shall be taken on the following unless there is a written statement signed by the party sought to be charged or by his authorized agent:

1. A promise by an executor or administrator to pay out of his own estate a claim against the deceased.
2. A promise by the promisor to pay for the debt of another.
3. A contract which is made in consideration of marriage or a promise to marry, other than mutual promises to marry.
4. A contract for the sale of an interest in land.
5. A bilateral contract, any segment of which cannot be performed within a year from the making thereof, and has not been fully performed by one of the parties.
6. A contract for the sale of goods—of a value above that stated in the State's Statute unless the purchaser accepts and actually receives the goods—or part thereof or makes part or entire payment therefor.

Some states have added to their Statutes of Frauds and require a writing signed by the party to be charged if (a) the contract cannot be performed during the lifetime of the promisor, (b) the contract has been barred by the statute of limitations and (c) the contract is authority for an agent to sell real property.

Where the Statute of Frauds is pleaded by the defendant as a defense, the burden of proving compliance therewith or of proving a contract to which the Statute does not apply rests upon the plaintiff.[14]

Accord and Satisfaction

An *accord* is an agreement whereby one of the parties undertakes to give or to perform and the other party agrees to accept in *satisfaction* of the claim something other than or different from what he considers himself entitled to. For example, Adam purchased a preserve from Brown. Adam later claimed that the preserves were not as specified in the contract. Brown replied that he would take back the merchandise and refund Adam's money. This he did. Later, Adam sued Brown for breach of contract. Adam was entitled, in this instance, to merchantable preserves and, not having received same, he could have sued for breach of contract. However when Brown offered a refund and Adam took the same thus accepting something in place of that to which he was legally entitled, there was satisfaction.

Conditions in Contracts

There are three important conditions in the performance of contracts: condition precedent, condition concurrent and condition subsequent.

A *condition precedent* is one which must be in existence before there is any obligation or liability on the part of the promisor. Another way of expressing this principle is that no obligation arises until after an act or event happens.

The following case[15] clearly demonstrates this principle:

> The plaintiff sold the defendant a piece of equipment for use in his business. The contract of sale provided that the defendant was to pay for the equipment with a product manufactured on this machine. The plaintiff agreed to instruct the defendant on how to manufacture this product on the same piece of equipment. Since the plaintiff failed to instruct the defendant, the machine was not paid for in accord with the terms of the contract. Here, the court held that the defendant was not liable for payment because the doing of the act of instructing the defendant in the manufacture of the product is a condition precedent to the maintenance of an action by the plaintiff for non-performance.

In general, the same situation is created when a pharmacist enters into an agreement to purchase a drugstore with the proviso that he is able to obtain a mortgage on his house from the XYZ Bank. The obtaining of the mortgage is a condition precedent. Until said mortgage is obtained he can not be held liable for non-performance.

A *condition concurrent* is one which must exist simultaneously with the performance of both parties. Seldom does a day pass in the retail practice of pharmacy when such a situation does not exist. For example, merchandise is often shipped to the pharmacy on a C.O.D. basis. At the moment of delivery the seller expects to receive payment for the goods. If payment is not received, the seller is entitled to remove the merchandise because the payment is a concurrent condition to the delivery of the merchandise. The act and the creation of the obligation are simultaneous.

A *condition subsequent* is defined as one which, when it exists or occurs, creates the obligation to perform under the contract. This condition is commonly used in various types of insurance policies. Here, the insurance company will pay the pharmacist if the drugstore premises are damaged by fire. The payment of their liability is based upon the condition subsequent namely the damage, by fire, to the store.

Promises of Performance

Promises of performance under a contract may be either dependent or independent conditions. Generally, dependent promises operate in the same manner as concurrent conditions in that neither party to the agreement has a right to the performance of the other party until he himself is ready, willing and able to tender or offer performance.

Independent promises are categorized as those that the promisor must perform without entitlement to a return performance.

The following case illustrates this principle:

> Brown promises to sell Adam his drugstore in consideration for Adam's promise to pay $500,000 for the business 90 days after Brown delivers and transfers title to Adam. In this fact situation Brown's promise is independent and must be performed without his receiving immediate payment. Adam, on the other hand, does not have to pay one cent until Brown has performed.

Does the above fact situation sound familiar? It happens every day when the pharmacist extends credit to his customer.

Married Women Contracts

For a good many years some jurisdictions permitted a married woman to make contracts with a third party but not with her husband. This prohibition applied to implied as well as express contracts. Any attempted contract was held to be void and not voidable hence it could not be enforced even when coverture ended. This situation created a great deal of difficulty and forced the use of a third party in any contract between husband and wife.

In most jurisdictions the old law has been amended or changed and provides that a husband and wife can now make contracts, oral and written, sealed and unsealed, with each other. In addition, they can sue each other in actions arising out of the contractual relationship. The statutes further provide that private conversations between husband and wife are now admissible in suits involving a contract made between them. It should be noted here that this change in the law is expressly limited to contracts and does not permit actions between husband and wife because of torts committed.

A married woman, in Massachusetts, is liable jointly with her husband for *necessaries* furnished her family with her consent up to $100 in each instance if she has property to the amount of $2000 or more. The prudent pharmacist will seek the law of his state concerning this aspect of his business.

The term *necessaries* is difficult to define. Due consideration must be given to the life, habits and circumstances of the person involved; as a general rule, however, food, clothing, shelter, medical attendance and proper education have been held to come under the term.

Whenever a husband and wife are engaged in separate business ventures, a Business Certificate should be filed by or on behalf of the wife. Whenever such a Business Certificate is filed on behalf of a married woman, it is often referred to as a "married woman's certificate." Unless a married woman's certificate (Figure 1) is filed with the town or city clerk by her or her husband, he will be liable for all debts incurred by her in the operation of her business. Also, her personal property used in the conduct of her business can be attached to pay her husband's debts during his lifetime.

Illegality, Duress, Fraud

In general, a contract may be considered to be *illegal* if its formation or performance is criminal, tortious or contrary to public policy. Contracts falling within these categories include those involving wagering, restraint of trade, creation of monopolies and price fixing.

A *fraud* is an intentional perversion of truth for the purpose of inducing another in reliance upon it to part with some valuable thing belonging to him or to surrender a legal right: a false representation of a matter of fact, whether by words or by conduct, by false or misleading allegations, or by concealment of

The Commonwealth of Massachusetts

....

....19..............

In conformity with the provisions of Chapter one
hundred and ten, Section five of the General Laws, as
amended, the undersigned hereby declare(s) that a
business under the title of ....

....

....

is conducted at Number ....Street

CITY OR TOWN

by the following named persons.

FULL NAME   RESIDENCE

....

....

....

....

Signed

....
(SIGNATURE)   (SIGNATURE)

....
(SIGNATURE)   (SIGNATURE)

The Commonwealth of Massachusetts

....ss.   ...., 19..........

Personally appeared before me the above-named ....

....

....

and made oath that the foregoing statement is true.

(Seal)

....

TITLE

Fig. 1. Typical Form of Business Certificate.

that which should have been disclosed, which deceives and is intended to deceive another so that he shall act upon it to his legal injury.[16]

Duress in relationship to contract law implies that the "agreement" is obtained by force, threats or by putting one of the parties in fear. Such a contract obtained by duress, necessitates that the one so obtaining must return what he has received under the contract. In determining whether a person acted under compulsion, the courts consider and give weight to the conduct which overcame the mind and will of the person in question. It is generally irrelevant to argue that the conduct used was not sufficient to overcome an ordinary person's will and mind.

Mistake

Where parties enter into a contract based upon mutual mistakes as to the existence or identity of the subject matter, as to the nature of the contract itself, or as to some other important fact, there is no meeting of the minds and therefore no contract results.

For example, when two parties agree to the sale and purchase of a house located at No. 10 Winter Street and neither party specifies the city or town; and there is in fact a No. 10 Winter Street located in each of the towns where the buyer and seller come from; and each has in mind the No. 10 Winter Street located in his town—there is no meeting of the minds and therefore there is no contract. There could be no meeting of the minds here because of the honest mistake made by each in referring to a different piece of property.

Sunday Contracts

Secular business on the Sunday, not a work of necessity, charity or mercy is prohibited.[17] However, many jurisdictions allow various types of businesses to operate on a Sunday if they obtain a permit to do so. This trend is becoming more popular particularly in resort areas.

A contract made on Sunday is invalid. It cannot be ratified at a later date. Where negotiations are made on Sunday and the contract is completed on a secular day, the contract is valid.

Margin Contracts

Margin contracts are those transactions whereby one puts through an order to a broker for the sale or purchase of stock with the full knowledge of the parties that the actual sale or purchase is not contemplated. This type of transaction is illegal.

Contracts in Restraint of Trade

It was formerly held that a contract not to engage in business, unlimited in space and time, was void as against public policy; however, if it were limited either as to time or geographical area, the contract was upheld if the restriction were reasonable. Clearly then, the inclusion of a clause which *unreasonably* prohibits another pharmacist from practicing his profession should not be included in the purchase and sale contract of a drugstore.

Breach of Contract

Breach of contract implies the violation of a contractual duty which one party owes to the other.[18] The renunciation or repudiation of a contract *before* the day of performance ordinarily has not been considered to be a breach of obligation; however, where time for the performance of the contract arrives and there is no performance, the injured party may sue for damages on the refusal to perform in the future.

On the other hand, the Uniform Commercial Code provides that in contracts for the sale of goods the plaintiff may treat the renunciation as a breach and bring an immediate action for recovery of damages. It further provides that the party repudiating may retract his repudiation if the other party has not acted on it.

Non-performance of contract is the failure to perform the whole or a material part of a contract, whether or not the party failing to perform was, under the existing circumstances, legally bound to perform.[19] A party may be excused from performing if the other party to the contract has broken it. So too, a subsequent agreement may substitute new terms of performance.

In those instances where one party has endeavored in good faith to complete his performance and fails, his failure is considered to be a breach, however he is allowed to recover for the services rendered on a *quantum meruit* basis not in excess of the contract price.[20]

References

1. Restatement of the Law of Contracts Section 1.

2. Buffalo Pressed Steel Co. v. Kirwan, 138 Md. 60, 113 A. 628, 630.

3. Justice v. Lang, 42 N.Y. 496, 1 Am. Rep. 576.

4. Lee v. Traveler's Ins. Co. of Hartford, Conn., 173 S.C. 185, 175 S.E. 429.

5. Smith v. Thornhill, Tex. Com. App. 25 S.W. 2nd 597, 599.

6. H. Liebes & Co. v. Klengenberg, C.C.A. Cal., 23 F. 2nd 611, 612.

7. Segal v. Allied Mutual Insurance Co., 285 Mass. 106, 188 N.E. 504.

8. Gordon v. Sales, 337 Mass. 35, 147 N.E. 2nd 803.

9. Cronin v. National Shawmut Bank, 306 Mass. 202, 27 N.E. 2nd 717.

10. Benton v. Springfield YMCA, 170 Mass. 534, 49 N.E. 928.

11. Mellen v. Whipple, 1 Gray 317.

12. Clark v. General Cleaning Co., 185 N.E. 2nd 749.

13. Massachusetts General Laws ch. 106, Sec. 2-725.

14. Beaver v. Ratheon Mfg. Co., 299 Mass. 218, 12 N.E. 2nd 807.

15. Caldwell v. Blake, 6 Gray 402.

16. Brainerd Dispatch Newspaper Co. v. Crow Wing County, 196 Minn. 194, 264 N.W. 779, 780.

17. Carton v. Shea, 312 Mass. 634, 45 N.E. 2nd 826.

18. Realty Developing Co. Inc. v. Wakefield Ready-Mixed Concrete Co., 327 Mass. 535, n00 N.E. 2nd 28.

19. *Supra*

20. Douglas v. Lowell, 194 Mass. 208, 80 N.E. 510.

CHAPTER 3

Torts

The pharmacist in his daily practice generally is not as concerned with torts as much as he is involved with the laws of contract and the Uniform Commercial Code. This is due to the fact that tort law is complex and its interpretation and application vary with the slightest change in applicable facts. Actually, most pharmacists do not have a clear knowledge of what constitutes a tort.

Tort is defined as a breach of duty fixed by law for which an action for damages may be commenced. At this point, it is important to cite the fact that a tort is a violation of a legal duty. No action may be instituted for the breach of a moral duty no matter how much suffering and loss may occur.

Causes of Breach

A breach is caused by (a) malfeasance, (b) misfeasance or (c) nonfeasance.

Malfeasance is the doing of an unlawful act whereby another party is injured.

Misfeasance is the doing of a lawful act in a negligent or careless manner so that another is injured.

Nonfeasance is the failure to do an act which one is legally bound to do.

Tort Vs. Crime

A crime is an injury to the public and is punished by the state. A tort is an injury to an individual; the injured party, in this instance, is entitled to damages for the injury. Crimes involving injury to individuals, i.e. assault and battery, are also torts but not all torts are crimes; for example, slander and libel are torts but not crimes. During the course of a trial, the state must prove a crime beyond a *reasonable doubt* whereas the plaintiff in an action of tort proves the tort by a *preponderance* of the evidence.

Tort Vs. Contract

A contract is the result of an agreement between two competent parties. This differs from a tort in the sense that a tort is a violation of a legal duty even though there may not be an agreement in existence between the two parties.

Very often, a breach of contract may also result in an action in tort. For example:

> Defendant had agreed to board plaintiff's horse. One day he rented out the horse to some tourists who in turn drove the horse too hard. This resulted in the death of the animal.
>
> At trial, the judge may find defendant liable in contract for breach of an agreement to keep the horse carefully, or on a count in tort for negligently keeping and using him.

Elements of a Tort

Two elements are essential for a tort to be created. First, there must be a violation of a legal duty owed by one person to another. Second, an injury must result from the violation. Both elements must exist. One without the other will not be enough to institute an action in tort.

Basis of Liability

Tort liability is based on one of three grounds: (a) intentional aggression, (b) negligence or (c) liability without fault.

Intentional aggression may be toward property, personal or real, or toward the person, physical or mental. Sometimes this aggression may take the form of wanton and reckless misconduct. Wantonness is conduct entered into with full knowledge of all the facts. Although this demonstrates an absolute disregard for the probable consequences, the individual has no conscious intent to do harm to anybody. On the other hand, recklessness exists when the individual does not possess the conscious knowledge of all the surrounding facts, the presence of which would serve to transfer his conduct into wantonness.

Negligence is the failure to exercise that degree of attention or care required by the law in the fact situation at hand. Since the attention or care may differ in degree, negligence has come to be described as "slight" negligence, "ordinary" negligence or "gross" negligence. The student must bear in mind that the term negligence refers only to that legal delinquency which results from the failure to exhibit care. Thus, the words *slight, ordinary* and *gross* more appropriately describe the degree of care and not the negligence despite the common usage of the phrases.

As has been previously stated, damages generally arise from the commission of a tort and are described as nominal, compensatory, punitive, special or consequential. These are defined as follows:

Nominal damages are represented by a trivial sum given to a plaintiff where a tort has taken place but no real injury has been demonstrated. For example,

Brown trespasses upon the property of Smith without damaging anything. Since he has committed a tort, he is guilty but because there was no apparent damage, the court may award damages of one dollar. This minimal sum is a payment of nominal damages.

Compensatory damages are usually awarded to the plaintiff to compensate him for the injuries he received.

Punitive damages are assessed as punishment and are in excess of the actual damage caused.

Special damages represent the actual, as distinguished from any presumed, losses peculiar to the particular case; special damages may include those damages that are the natural but not the necessary consequence of the wrongful act.

Consequential damages are those recovered by a parent for the loss of services of a child and for expenses reasonably incurred in the care and cure of the child. Consequential damages are also those that are recovered by a husband for expenses incurred in the care and cure of his spouse in consequence of damage or injury to her.

It is important to note here that mere mental suffering alone which is caused by a wrongful act is not a "damage." Therefore, there can be no recovery for physical injuries resulting solely from mental and emotional disturbances. However, recovery for fright, terror, alarm, anxiety and distress of mind is permitted if they are accompanied by some physical injury to the person "from without."[2]

This point of law is best illustrated by the findings in *Sullivan* v. *Hood*[3]. Here, the plaintiff drank milk from a container in which there was a dead mouse. In the milk was fecal matter of a mouse. The plaintiff brought an action, among others, of negligence against the company. Throughout the presentation of the case, there was no evidence presented that the fecal matter was the cause of her subsequent illness. Accordingly, the court found for the defendant because the plaintiff suffered no injuries "from without." Her injuries were caused solely as a result of psychological and emotional disturbances.

Liability of Infants and Insane Persons for Torts

The liability of infants for torts is practically the same as that governing the liability of an insane person; namely, infants are liable for all torts which they can physically commit; but for those involving a mental element, an infant of tender years will not be held liable if his mind is not sufficiently mature to meet the mental requirement.

Liability of Parent for Infants' Tort

Since there is a rule[4] that every person is liable for his own torts, a parent is not responsible for the torts of his infant. The exceptions to this rule are as follows:

1. Where the act takes place in the presence of the parent and he does nothing to prevent it.

2. Where the minor is acting as a servant or agent of the parent. Under these circumstances, the standard rules of agency apply.
3. Where the parent is negligent in entrusting the child with a dangerous instrumentality.
4. Where the parent permits the infant to retain a nuisance on the premises.
5. Where the parent knows of the propensity of the child to commit torts of a particular nature and takes no precautions to restrain the child in that respect.

Liability of Husband and Wife

Husbands and wives are independently liable for their own torts. However, for reasons of public policy an action of tort for negligence resulting in personal injury cannot be maintained by one standing in either of the above relationships against the other.[5]

Liability of Corporations

Generally, a corporation is subject to an action of tort the same as an individual. If a malicious or fraudulent intent is an essential element of a particular tort, the intent of its duly authorized agents or servants is imputed to the corporation.

Liability of Municipal Corporations

A municipality, in the absence of special legislative provisions imposing liability, is not liable for the tortious act of its officers and agents in connection with the gratuitous performance of strictly public functions imposed by mandate of the legislature or undertaken voluntarily by its permission, and from which it derives no special corporate advantage, no profit and no enforced contribution from individuals particularly benefited by way of compensation for use or assessment for betterment. The same rule applies to towns.

In Massachusetts, for example, a municipality is liable for damages caused through negligent construction, operation or maintenance of its various projects such as defects in highways and bridges. In order to recover against a municipality, the injured party generally must give written notice to the municipality of the time, place and cause of the accident within 30 days, or in case of defects due in part to snow and ice, within 10 days. The time limits vary with the jurisdiction.

Liability of Charitable Corporations—
Doctrine of Charitable Immunity

A charitable corporation performing functions which the municipality itself might perform is, in some states, exempt from liability for the same reason which favors the non-liability of municipal corporations. Furthermore, the funds for the charitable corporation are given for charitable purposes and not for the payment of damages. This concept is often referred to as the *doctrine of charitable immunity*.

Charitable immunity has been defined as the doctrine under which charitable institutions are relieved of liability for injuries resulting from negligence of the institution or its employees. In order that an institution be considered for purposes of the immunity doctrine, it must be organized as a charity—namely, no profit can inure to the benefit of any individuals. If there is an excess of income over expenses, it must be used for the improvement of the institution's facilities and services. Whenever a hospital meets these criteria, it is classified as a voluntary, nonprofit hospital.

Historically, the doctrine was first promulgated in the United States by the Massachusetts court in the case of *McDonald* v. *Massachusetts General Hospital* (120 Mass. 432, 1876). At the present time the doctrine is held in low repute by the legal profession and is continually being attacked by them in the hope that the courts of the various jurisdictions will reject the doctrine.

The explanation of the doctrine is best understood by studying the following five theories which serve as the basis of its existence: trust fund; inapplicability of the doctrine of respondeat superior; implied waiver; governmental function and public policy.

The *trust fund* theory is based upon the assumption that the funds of a charity are held by it in trust and that the payment of these funds to individuals in payment of injury claims constitutes a violation of the trust's purposes and in fact impairs its usefulness to charity and the public at large.

Some jurisdictions have supported the doctrine of charitable immunity on the basis that the *doctrine of respondeat superior* is inapplicable to charitable institutions. They hold that the doctrine of respondeat superior holds as a relationship between parties in a profit making organization and not in a nonprofit institution.

The *implied waiver* theory is based upon the fact that a benefit has been conferred upon the patient by the hospital, thus, the acceptance of any care furnished by the hospital constitutes a waiver of any right to recover from the charity for injury arising from its neglect.

The theory of *governmental function* considers the activities of charitable institutions as supplemental to governmental responsibilities, in that the benefits may be derived by the public at large and public responsibilities are thereby assumed.

The general *public policy* theory relies upon the theme that a charitable institution does a great deal of public good and therefore its funds should be preserved for the good of the public.

In recent years, this doctrine has been rejected by some state courts and legislatures so that today there are only eleven states which uphold it. As the courts proceed with its rejection, some state legislatures have seen fit to enact legislation restricting recovery by a plaintiff from a charity to a specific level e.g. $10,000.

This trend towards the abolition of the doctrine is understandable in view of the fact that in general it is a judicially created exception to the ordinary rules of liability.

Joint and Several Liability of Tort-Feasors

Where two or more individuals are responsible for a wrong, the liability is joint and several. This responsibility can come about by participation, concerted action or authorization. In such case the injured party may sue one or all of the tort-feasors since they are equally responsible.

Some states have adopted the right of reimbursement and contribution by a joint tort-feasor who has paid more than his pro rata share of the common liability. He is now able to recover the excess over his pro rata share from the other joint tort-feasor or tort-feasors. Some jurisdictions have never allowed the degree of negligence or culpability of each participant in a wrong to be weighed in assessing damages. Instead, the principles of equity applicable to contribution generally are applied. That is, in ascertaining the pro rata share the obligation will be assessed against those who are solvent and within the jurisdiction of the court.

Negligence

The one area of tort law that is of major importance to the pharmacist is that of negligence. Because of the subtle nature of negligence, the practitioner, often unknowingly, may become negligent in his daily practice. Unless there is resulting injury to a customer or his property, the negligence goes undetected or, worse still, uncorrected.

Although it will not be possible to explore the many ramifications of the legal aspects of negligence in this limited text, an endeavor will be made to present to the pharmacy student some of its essential elements.

The violation of a legal duty that is owed by one party to another may manifest itself by intentional and willful misconduct, wanton and reckless misconduct or through negligence.

Intentional and willful misconduct occurs when the individual intends to do a wrongful act; negligence, on the other hand, is the omission to do something which a reasonable man, guided by those considerations which ordinarily regulate human affairs, would do, or it is the doing of something which a reasonable and prudent man would not do.[6] The term refers only to that legal delinquency which results whenever a man fails to exhibit the care which he ought to exhibit whether it be slight, ordinary or great.[7]

A pharmacist is responsible if anyone is injured by his negligent act or the act of his agent, provided such act is done within the scope of the agent's real or apparent authority.

Since negligence is the absence of proper care, what is proper care is a question depending on the facts in each case.

The following excerpt from a judicial opinion, rendered in disposition of a damage case resulting from the negligence of a pharmacist when engaged in the practice of his profession, explores this question:

A pharmacist is required by law, in the first place to possess a reasonable and ordinary degree of knowledge and skill with respect to the pharmaceutical duties which he professes to be competent to perform.

In the second place, the law imposes upon the pharmacist the obligation to exercise all reasonable and ordinary care and prudence in applying his knowledge and skill in compounding medicine, filling prescriptions, and performing all the other duties of an apothecary.

'Ordinary care' with reference to the business of a pharmacist must therefore be held to signify the highest practicable degree of prudence, thoughtfulness, and vigilance, and the most exact and reliable safeguards consistent with the reasonable conduct of the business.[8]

In those states where the doctrine of charitable immunity exists a charitable hospital which employs a pharmacist may not be liable for his errors because the pharmacist is and has always been responsible for his own mistakes. His responsibilities for negligence are the same as for any other person functioning in a professional capacity.

A case which illustrates this is the celebrated *Norton* v. *Argonaut Insurance Company*.[9] Here the patient was a three-month old baby with a heart condition. On the doctor's order sheet was written: "Give 3.0 ml. Lanoxin today for one dose only." The assistant director of nursing in checking the ward found the nurse very busy and decided to help her even though she had, over the last few years, been solely engaged in administrative work.

She noted that the 3.0 ml. of Lanoxin had not been given and commenced to administer it. She did think the dose was high for a three-month old infant because she was thinking of Lanoxin Injection and did not know that the physician intended Lanoxin Pediatric Elixir. She asked a student nurse, a registered nurse and another physician on the ward if 3.0 ml. of Lanoxin was too high and, since these three were thinking of the elixir, she was assured it was proper. Shortly after the administration of 3.0 ml. of the injection, the baby died. In holding both the nurse and the doctor liable, the court said,

We are of the opinion that she was negligent in attempting to administer a drug with which she was not familiar—not only was she unfamiliar with the medicine in question, but she also violated what has been shown to be the rule generally practiced by members of the nursing profession in the community and which rule, we might add, strikes us as being most reasonable and prudent, namely, the practice of calling the prescribing physician when in doubt about an order for medication.[9]

Although an action in negligence can be brought against anyone who breaches a duty to another, a large number of suits are brought against practitioners of a profession.

Profession of Pharmacy

It is of interest to note, at this point, some legal definitions of the term "profession":

A vocation, calling, occupation or employment involving labor, skill, education, special knowledge and compensation or profit, but the labor and skill involved is predominantly mental or intellectual, rather than physical or manual.[10]

The term originally contemplated only theology, law and medicine, but as applications of science and learning are extended to other departments of affairs, other vocations also receive the name, which implies professed attainments in special knowledge as distinguished from mere skill.[11]

In the daily practice of the profession of pharmacy, one can easily find situations to serve as examples where a little caution may prevent a charge of negligence. Consider the acts of hiring personnel and compounding prescriptions.

For example, state pharmacy laws, hospital licensing acts, food and drug laws, and state public health laws and their regulations are clear on this point in the majority of the states. The use as pharmacists of pharmacy helpers and others not skilled and experienced in the practice of pharmacy as evidenced by state registration is a criminal offense. In this connection it is pointed out that an owner-pharmacist is not relieved by law of his responsibility where pharmacists are employed yet the work load is so great that non-professionals must perform duties that laws limit to the registered practitioner of pharmacy.

As a reasonable man, the owner-pharmacist knows or should know the relationship between the work load and the number of pharmacists necessary.

When a non-professional person acts in the capacity of a licensed pharmacist with the expressed or implied consent of the owner and as a result there is injury or death, the owner may be civilly liable and the unlicensed person criminally liable.

If a pharmacist fills a prescription according to its terms, ordinarily he is not responsible if the medicine fails to cure or even does harm to the person taking it.

Cases, however, may arise where a pharmacist is under a special duty to guard the patient from harm. Where unusual circumstances show that the physician who wrote the prescription could not have been aware of the dangerous nature of the ingredients prescribed, a duty rests upon the pharmacist to refuse to fill the prescription.

The pharmacist should be especially careful to see that the dosage is safe under the conditions prescribed, as failure to observe this caution would, in all probability, constitute negligence on his part.

The rule is universal that prescriptions may be filled only by a registered pharmacist or by some other person acting under his *direct* and *immediate personal supervision.*

Standards of Duty

Ordinarily, the duty owed the plaintiff is to exercise the care which a reasonably prudent man would exercise under the same circumstances. There are degrees of care, and failure to exercise the proper degree of care is negligence, but there are no degrees of negligence.[12]

The classification of negligence as "gross," "ordinary" and "slight" indicates only that under special circumstances great care and caution, or ordinary care, or slight care is required; but failure to exercise the care demanded is "negligence."[13]

In order to sustain an action based on negligence, the plaintiff must show the following elements:

1. That the defendant owed the plaintiff a duty to use due care.
2. That the defendant breached that duty by being negligent.
3. That the plaintiff was injured.
4. That the defendant's negligence caused the plaintiff's injury.

The fact that the defendant did not intend to injure the plaintiff is not a defense and is otherwise irrelevant.

Gross negligence is the intentional failure to perform a manifest duty in reckless disregard of the consequences as affecting the life or property of another; it is such a gross want of care and regard for the rights of others as to justify the presumption of willfulness and wantonness.[14] Another court has held that it is substantially higher in magnitude than simple inadvertence, but falls short of intentional wrong.[15]

Ordinary negligence is the omission of that care which a man of common prudence usually takes of his own concerns.[16] Ordinary negligence is based on the fact that one ought to have known the results of his acts, while "gross negligence" rests on the assumption that one knew the results of his acts but was indifferent as to the results.

Slight negligence is defined to be only an absence of that degree of care and vigilance which persons of extraordinary prudence and foresight are accustomed to use.[17]

Locality Rule

Until recently, the philosophy of the local reasonable man, often called the "community" or "locality rule," was judicially supported by a holding in a case decided in 1880. In this case, the court held:

> It is a matter of common knowledge that a physician in a small country village does not usually make a specialty of surgery, and however well-informed he may be in the theory of all parts of his profession, he would, generally speaking, be but seldom called upon as a surgeon to perform difficult operations. He would have but few opportunities of observation and practice in that line such as public hospitals or large cities would afford. The defendant was applied to, being the practitioner in a small village, and we think it was correct to rule that he was bound to possess that skill only which physicians and surgeons of ordinary ability and skill, practicing in similar localities, with opportunities for no larger experience, ordinarily possess; and he was not bound to possess that high degree of art and skill possessed by eminent surgeons practicing in large cities, and making a specialty of the practice of surgery.[18]

The community or locality rule has been modified in several jurisdictions. Some courts have emphasized such factors as accessibility to medical facilities and experience[19] whereas others have adopted a standard of reasonable care and allow the locality to be taken into account as one of the circumstances, but not as an absolute limit upon the skill required.[20]

In still another jurisdiction, the court stated:

> Frequent meetings of medical societies, articles in the medical journals, books by acknowledged authorities, and extensive experience in hospital work put the country doctor on more equal terms with his city brother. . . . [W]e are unwilling to hold that he is to be judged only by the qualifications that others in the same village or similar villages possess.[21]

The Supreme Court of Washington has virtually abandoned the "locality rule"[22] ; the Supreme Court of Appeals of West Virginia criticized the "locality rule" and appears to have abandoned it in the case of specialists[23] ; in a similar situation, the Supreme Court of New Jersey abandoned the "locality rule."[24] In a more recent decision, Massachusetts courts have held that a physician's conduct is not to be measured by the standards of other doctors practicing in similar communities and having opportunity for no larger experience and thus overruled *Small* v. *Howard*, the original Massachusetts case which announced the "locality rule."

Based upon the above cited judicial actions, it is obvious that all professional personnel, pharmacists included, may be held to the standards of the profession at large rather than the standards of the local area of practice.

Proximate and Remote Cause

The liability for negligence extends to all those results which proximately flow from the wrongful conduct of the defendant. In actions of this description, the defendant is liable for the natural and probable consequences of his negligent act or omission. The injury may be the direct result of the misconduct charged; but it will not be considered too remote if, according to the usual experience of mankind, the result ought to have been apprehended. The act of a third person, intervening and contributing a condition necessary to the injurious effect of the original negligence, will not excuse the first wrongdoer, if said act ought to have been foreseen. The original negligence still remains a culpable and direct cause of the injury. The test is to be found in the probable injurious consequences which were to be anticipated and not in the number of subsequent events and agencies which might arise.

Contributory Negligence

Contributory negligence is the failure of a person, who is later a plaintiff in the suit, to use the care of a reasonable, prudent man in the protection of himself and his property, which failure is a contributing cause to his damage. Contributory negligence is a complete defense to an action based on negligence.

A classical example of contributory negligence is demonstrated by the following fact situtation:

Defendant offered to drive plaintiff home from the office. During the trip, defendant drove at excessive speeds and was otherwise reckless. As the car entered the turnpike, plaintiff wagered that defendant could not get the car speed up to 100 m.p.h. Defendant accepted the challenge, accelerated the car and after a short distance lost control of the car, thereby causing it to leave the roadway and overturn. Plaintiff was injured. Later he sued defendant for damages and cited defendant's negligence. The defense of contributory negligence was raised by defendant and sustained by the court.

Assumption of the Risk

Whenever a party consents to assume the risk of injury from a particular hazard it generally constitutes a complete defense in favor of the defendant. Assumption of the risk may be by express agreement or implied from the facts. This legal doctrine is best exemplified if the student will recall the common highway sign which one encounters when a roadway is under construction. It reads: "Road Closed—Use at Own Risk." Clearly, the traveler has been warned of possible danger; thus, should he choose to drive over that roadway and become injured, he cannot seek to recover damages for the injury from the municipality because he personally assumed the risk of possible injury.

Res Ipsa Loquitur

Literally translated, the words *res ipsa loquitur* mean "the thing speaks for itself." In law it provides a rebuttable presumption that the defendant was negligent upon proof that the instrumentality causing the injury was in the defendant's exclusive control, and that the accident is one which ordinarily does not happen in absence of negligence.

Defamation

Defamation is a communication which injures another's reputation and good name. Because everyone has a right to acquire, maintain and enjoy a good reputation, any injury caused to it may be the basis of an action of tort for defamation.

Defamation includes both *libel* and *slander*; libel is seen and slander is heard.

In order to sustain a cause of action for defamation, the following elements must be present:
1. The language must be defamatory.
2. The words must be communicated to a third party.
3. The language must be about the plaintiff and so identifies him to a reasonable reader, listener or viewer.
4. The plaintiff's reputation must be injured among a substantial and respectable segment of the community.

There are certain defenses to defamation and these include:
1. Truth.
2. That the publication was made by accident without either negligence or intent to publish.
3. Privilege as during a judicial or legislative proceeding.

Malicious Prosecution

Law suits for malicious prosecution have been based upon malicious criminal prosecution, malicious bankruptcy proceedings, malicious liquidation proceedings, malicious arrest and malicious attachment of property.

A man has a right to protect his freedom, reputation, dignity, honor and financial integrity. However, the law will protect one who acts (a) upon probable cause or (b) in good faith. Thus, one acting maliciously will be protected if there is *probable cause*. The same protection is available if he acts in *good faith* even though it is later determined that there was no probable cause. Therefore, the plaintiff in a malicious prosecution case must prove both (a) no probable cause and (b) malice.

Pharmacists are not generally involved in this type of tort action. However, the tort is encountered as is evidenced by the following case:

> The plaintiff, Frances Kauffman, owner and operator of a drugstore, brought this suit against the A. H. Robins Pharmaceutical Company alleging malicious prosecution. Specifically, the plaintiff charged that the defendant company filed a false and malicious complaint against her with the State Board of Pharmacy, charging that she substituted another preparation for the defendant's product Donnatal. As a result of the complaint, the plaintiff was ordered to appear before the State Board of Pharmacy. After a hearing, the plaintiff was exonerated and she filed suit against A. H. Robins Company.

> The plaintiff alleged that she suffered loss of business, loss of reputation, and that she incurred expense in defending the action. The drug company's defense was as follows: "Under the law of Tennessee no suit for malicious prosecution can be maintained unless there has been a prior judicial proceeding which was alleged to have been falsely or maliciously prosecuted." The trial court entered a judgment sustaining the defendant's demurrer, and the plaintiff appealed. The Supreme Court of Tennessee held that the plaintiff had a cause of action against the drug company since the action before the Board of Pharmacy was a "prior judicial proceeding." The court said that such proceedings need not be conducted in a "court" in the strict and legal sense, provided all the requisite elements of such an action are both alleged and proved. The State Board of Pharmacy is vested with power to conduct investigations and hold hearings in regard to violation of the pharmacy laws. The court noted that the defendant drug company had filed a formal complaint which caused the Court to say that: "If this complaint was indeed false, and filed through malice, the fact that the Board of Pharmacy was the agency which instituted and conducted the investigation and hearing does not excuse the defendant."[26]

Survival of Tort Actions

At common law, torts affecting the person did not survive his death, while torts affecting property rights did survive. Today, by statute, nearly all torts survive except actions for slander or libel, malicious prosecution and deceit.

References

1. Felton v. Nichols, 180 Mass. 245.

2. O'Neil v. Toomey, 218 Mass. 238.

3. Sullivan v. H. P. Hood, 341 Mass. 216.

4. Norlin v. Connolly, 336 Mass. 553.

5. Massachusetts General Laws (Ter. Ed.) ch. 84, Sec. 17-21.

6. Schneeweisz v. Illinois Cent. R. Co., 196 Ill. App. 248, 253.

7. Hazzard v. Chase Nat. Bank of City of New York, 287 N. Y. S. 54, 552.

8. Tombari v. Connors, 85 Conn. 231.

9. Norton v. Argonaut Ins. Co., 144 So. 2nd 249.

10. Maryland Casualty Co. v. Crazy Water Co., Tex. Civ. App. 160 S.W. 2nd 102, 104.

11. Aulen v. Triumph Explosive, 58 F. Supp. 4, 8.

12. Murray v. DeLuxe Motor Stages of Illinois, 133 S.W. 2nd 1074, 1078.

13. Seelig v. First Nat. Bank, 20 F. Supp. 61, 68.

14. *Supra*

15. Young v. City of Worcester, 149 N.E. 204, 205.

16. Ouderkirk v. Central Nat. Bank, 23 N.E. 875.

17. Briggs v. Spaulding, 141 U.S. 132.

18. Small v. Howard, 128 Mass. 131.

19. Tvedt v. Haugen, 294 N.W. 183.

20. McGulpin v. Bessmer, 43 N.W. 2nd 121.

21. Vitia v. Fleming, 155 N.W. 1077.

22. Pedersen v. Dumouchel, 431 P 2nd 973, 978.

23. Hundley v. Martinez, 158 S.E. 2nd 159.

24. Carbone v. Warburton, 11 N.J. 418.

25. Brune v. Belinkoff, 235 N.E. 2nd 793.

26. Kauffman v. Robins, 448 S.W. 2nd. 400.

CHAPTER 4

Law of Agency

Agency includes every relation in which one person acts for or represents another by the latter's authority[1] or in which one person acts for another, either in the relationship of principal and agent, master and servant, employer and employee or independent contractor.[2] It is no wonder, then, that agency is involved in many phases of the practice of pharmacy. An agency relationship exists between the store manager or owner and the staff pharmacists and clerks, delivery boys and even the drug salesman who is asked to do a particular errand.

Generally an agent is a person authorized by another to act for him such as in a contractual relationship or via ratification, estoppel or by necessity. Anyone may be an agent if he has the mental capacity to understand orders, interpret them and execute them. Since agency does not depend solely upon a contractual relationship, a person may be appointed an agent and bind his principal even though the contract between them is not enforceable. Thus an infant may act as an agent.

Under the laws of agency, a *principal* is defined as the employer or constitutor of an agent, the person who gives authority to an agent. Anyone who has the mental capacity to direct the action of another and who may legally bind himself can be a principal. In ascertaining the obligations between principal and agent, one must resort to the law of contracts.

Agency by Necessity

Marriage does not, of itself, create the relationship of principal and agent between husband and wife. However, if he leaves her wrongfully and without means of support, she becomes his agent *by necessity* to purchase food, fuel, clothing and medicines upon his credit.[3]

The relationship of agency does not exist between parent and child unless the child has been appointed the agent of his parent or the child's acts have been ratified by the parent or where the parent neglects to support the child so that agency by necessity arises.[4]

Agency by Appointment

In this situation, the law of contracts applies. The form of appointment may be oral or written, or by a deed.

Agency by Ratification

Ratification is, in a broad sense, the confirmation of a previous act done either by the party himself or by another; it is the confirmation of a voidable act.[5]

Another court has described it as the affirmance by a person of a prior act which did not bind him, but which was done or professedly done on his account, whereby the act, as to some or all persons, is given effect as if originally authorized by him.[6]

Ratification need not be by express words. Any act of the principal showing an intent to ratify is sufficient. However, even though the principal remains silent after learning of the unauthorized act, he will not be bound if he learned of the fact too late to take advantage of the agent's acts. Also, in order to ratify, the principal must have had the power to authorize the act at the time it was done.

Duties of Agent to Principal

Generally, the agent's duties to his principal include those of fidelity, respect, subordination and duty to account.

An agent lacks fidelity when he fails to disclose to his principal any material facts which he has learned about during the course of his agency. An agent is under a duty not to disclose the trade secrets of his employer.

Duty of Respect and Subordination

Insubordination is a willful disregard of express or implied directions as well as a refusal to obey reasonable orders. When this is established, it constitutes such a degree of breach of duty on the part of the servant as to warrant his discharge. Persons holding positions of responsibility which require an exercise of one's judgment are not bound to as strict an adherence to directions of superiors as ones having employment involving less responsibility and discretion.

Duty to Account

An agent owes to his principal the duty to account and a failure to so perform will be sufficient cause to warrant discharge by the principal.

Delegation of Authority

Generally, an agent has no authority to delegate *his* authority. However, he may ordinarily delegate acts of a mechanical or ministerial nature or delegate his duties where they are incidental to the business to be done. For example, a foreman may delegate certain of his duties to others working on a particular job.

Undisclosed Principal

All discussion pertaining to a principal has, to this point, implied that there was knowledge on the part of a third party as to the identity of the agent's principal. Since this is not always true, a principal not disclosed in a contract is categorized as an undisclosed principal. Despite lack of disclosure, an undisclosed principal may hold the third person on the contract made with an agent on behalf of the undisclosed principal.

Power of Agents

An agent has, in addition to the powers actually or expressly conferred, certain implied powers, affixed by custom or reasonably incident to those expressly conferred, or arising because of the conduct of his principal.

Implied authority of an agent to make a warranty depends upon what warranties an agent of that type, in that business and in that locality has authority to make. For example, in an attorney-client relationship, an attorney has implied authority to control the law action and his acts which affect the remedy are binding upon his client.

Liability of Principal for Torts of Agent

The principal or master generally is liable for the torts of his agent or servant who is acting within the scope of his employment. This is so despite the fact that the agent violates express instruction; all that is of importance is that he is acting within the apparent scope of his authority.

On the other hand, a principal is not liable for the acts of his agent if the agent departs from his principal's business and embarks upon a new and independent enterprise.

Liability of Agent

As a general rule, the agent is liable to a third person for misfeasance but not for nonfeasance.[7] In those instances where the master is liable because of the doctrine of respondeat superior and the agent is liable because of his negligence, the liability is several and not joint. However, the practice acts of some states permit them to be joined in one action in separate counts.[8]

Termination of an Agency

It is quite clear that a principal may revoke the authority of his agent at any time. This may happen despite the fact that the revocation amounts to a breach of the contract of agency. If the agent suffers damage by such action he may seek to recover same in a later action. Some of the conditions which terminate an agency are: (a) by the terms of the original agreement, (b) by revocation, (c) by subsequent agreement, (d) by renunciation by the agent, (e) by operation of law, (f) by death of one of the parties, (g) by insanity of one of the parties and (h) by the bankruptcy of the principal.

Independent Contractor

An independent contractor is one who agrees to accomplish a certain result with the power of control over the details of accomplishing it left to him. Thus, there is no master-servant relationship when one contracts with an independent contractor. Instead there is a relationship of *contractor* and *contractee*. In such cases, the general rule is that the negligence of the contracting party cannot be charged to him for whom the work is being done.

Exceptions to the foregoing rule are: (a) where the contract itself calls for the performance of acts which will bring wrongful consequences to pass and (b) where the contract calls for the construction of a dangerous thing or nuisance.

References

1. Saums v. Parfet, 270 Mich. 165, 258 N.W. 235.

2. Gorton v. Doty, 57 Idaho 792, 69 P 2nd 136, 139.

3. Benjamin v. Dockham, 134 Mass. 418.

4. Commonwealth v. Slavski, 245 Mass. 405.

5. Gallup v. Fox, 30 A. 756.

6. Goldfarb v. Reicher, 171 A. 149, 151.

7. Somers v. Osterheld, 335 Mass. 24.

8. Massachusetts General Laws ch. 231, Sec. 4A.

CHAPTER 5

Landlord and Tenant

From the point of view that the conduct of the practice of pharmacy must be from a building and that said building must be purchased, leased or rented, the laws bearing upon these relationships are of major importance to the pharmacy-owner. Throughout the course of one's business life, such matters as termination of the tenancy, non-payment of rent, assignment of the lease, liabilities of the assignee, subleases and eviction crop up from time to time.

It should be readily apparent to the student that the magnitude of the subject matter precludes detailed discussion in one short chapter. However, an attempt has been made to touch upon those facets of the law of landlord and tenant that are more frequently encountered by the retail pharmacy practitioner.

Relationship of Landlord and Tenant

A landlord has been defined as he who, being the owner of an estate in land, has leased it for a term of years, on a rent reserved, to another person called the tenant.[1] Conversely, a tenant is one who holds lands of another or one who has temporary use and occupation of real property owned by another person (called the "landlord"), the duration and terms of his tenancy being usually fixed by an instrument called a lease.[2]

The relationship of landlord and tenant exists whenever there is a contract, express or implied, by which one agrees to give the possession or occupation of land or tenements to another. The contract need not be stipulated in formal words nor is it necessary that a money rent be stipulated.[3]

Tenancy Distinguished from a License

A licensee is one who occupies land by virtue of a contract which spells out a specific occupancy. He occupies the land under the owner and any rights that he may have are only those provided by the contract. This type of relationship occurs when one "rents" or "leases" a hall for two nights for the local church club. This arrangement is not a lease. It simply gives those attending a license to be on the property and only for the purpose spelled out in the license request.

Kinds of Tenancies

Three kinds of tenancies will be discussed; (a) tenancy for years, (b) tenancy at will and (c) tenancy at sufferance.

A *tenancy for years* is one whereby the tenant holds the land by a written lease for a definite period of time. This type of tenancy can be terminated by (a) expiration of the term of the lease, (b) forfeiture and re-entry by the landlord because the tenant has broken the terms of the lease and (c) issuance, by the landlord, of a fourteen-day notice for non-payment of rent (Figure 2).

A *tenancy at will* may be created in various ways. It may arise from a parol agreement, or under a written agreement where there is no fixed or determinable time, or from an implied contract. Under this type of tenancy, the tenant must not commit voluntary waste or through his acts damage the property. If he so does, then he is not only liable to the landlord for the damage but his act(s) terminates his tenancy and gives the landlord the right to treat him as a trespasser. A tenant is never liable for permissive waste such as normal wear and tear.[4]

Formerly a tenancy at will could be terminated at the will of either party, however today such processes are controlled by statute. For example, Massachusetts General Laws Chapter 186 Section 12 provides that "estates at will may be terminated by either party by three months notice in writing for that purpose given to the other party; and if the rent reserved is payable at a period of less than three months, the time of such notice shall be sufficient if it is equal to the interval between the days of payment. The notice must be in writing but it need not be signed personally by the landlord or tenant."

The notice (Figure 3) must follow the terms of the statute and should either specify the exact day upon which the next rental day expires or should state generally that the tenancy will be terminated at the end of the month from the next rent day if the rental period is one month.

A second way to terminate a tenancy at will is non-payment of rent. Again, statutes regulate this activity and generally provide that, "in case of refusal or neglect to pay the rent due from a tenant at will, fourteen days notice to quit, given in writing by the landlord to the tenant, shall be sufficient to determine the tenancy; provided that the tenancy of a tenant who has not received a similar notice from the landlord within the twelve months next preceding the receipt of such notice shall not be determined if, within five days after the receipt thereof, he pays or tenders to the landlord the full amount of the rent due."[5]

Once a tenant receives a fourteen-day notice to quit for non-payment of rent, the tenancy terminates upon the giving of the notice. From that time on, he

[NOTICE TO QUIT FOR NON-PAYMENT OF RENT]

The Commonwealth of Massachusetts

....ss.   .... 19.......

To...

      Your rent being in arrear, you are hereby notified to quit and deliver up in fourteen days from receipt of this notice the premises now being held by you as my tenant namely:—

....

....

....

....

    Hereof Fail Not, or I shall take due course of Law to eject you from the same.

....

....

Fig. 2. Notice to Quit for Non-Payment of Rent. Commonly referred to as a "fourteen-day notice."

[NOTICE TO TERMINATE TENANCY AT WILL]

The Commonwealth of Massachusetts

ss. ....19 .

To ....

      It being my intention to terminate your tenancy you are hereby notified to quit and deliver up at the expiration of that..of your tenancy which shall begin
month or week
next after this date, the premises now held by you as my tenant, namely:—

....

....

Hereof Fail Not, or I shall take due course of Law to eject you from the same.

....

Fig. 3. Notice to Terminate Tenancy at Will.

becomes a tenant at sufferance and the landlord owes him only the duty not to wantonly or willfully injure him.[6]

It should also be noted that where the landlord accepts rent for a time subsequent to the expiration of the notice to quit, he waives the notice unless he expressly reserves his rights.[7]

A third way to terminate a tenancy at will is by the agreement of the parties. Such agreement may provide for the termination at a certain time or at the occurrence of a specific event. In these instances no notice to either party is necessary.

An assignment by the tenant at will terminates the tenancy without notice because the tenant cannot transfer any rights.

Illegal use of the premises constitutes grounds for the termination of a tenancy at will. In general, statutes provide that

> if a tenant or occupant of a building or tenement, under a lawful title, uses such premises or any part thereof for the purposes of prostitution, assignation, lewdness, illegal gaming, or the illegal keeping or sale of intoxicating liquors, such use shall at the election of the lessor or owner annul and make void the lease or other title under which such tenant or occupant holds and, without any act of the lessor or owner, shall cause the right of possession to revert and vest in him, and he may without process of law, make immediate entry upon the premises, or may avail himself of the remedy provided. . . . [8]

Surrender is another means of terminating a tenancy at will. In this instance the tenant's surrender of the premises must be accepted by the landlord otherwise the tenancy has not been terminated.

Finally, a written lease or sale of the premises by the landlord effectively terminates a tenancy at will. Again, in order to avoid the chaos which results from such an action, statutes have been enacted and generally provide that if the premises are occupied for dwelling purposes,

> no action to recover possession of the premises shall be brought nor shall the tenant be dispossessed, until after the expiration of a period, equal to the interval between the days on which the rent reserved is payable, from that time when the tenant receives notice in writing of such termination; but such tenant shall be liable to pay rent for such time during the said period as he occupied or detains the premises at the same rate as theretofore payable by him while a tenant at will.[9]

The third kind of tenancy is the *tenancy at sufferance.* Such a tenant is one who comes into possession lawfully but after his term is ended continues the possession wrongfully by holding over. A tenant at sufferance is not entitled to any regular notice to quit but he must be given a reasonable length of time in which to move.

The Lease

A lease is a contract that creates between two parties the relationship of landlord and tenant. Here, the landlord becomes the "lessor" and the tenant the "lessee."

In some states a lease for more than seven years or for less than seven years with a right of renewal carrying it beyond seven years, must be recorded.[10] A lease should also be recorded where, although for less than seven years, the end of the term is more than seven years from the date of its making; a lease, the term of which is five years but which is not to take effect until three years from the date of making, would come within the statute and should be recorded.

Where the title to the land is registered, the lease must be registered instead of recorded.[11]

Assignment of Leases

In general, a lease may be assigned or sublet in the absence of provisions prohibiting such assignment or sublease. The words "assignment" or "sublease" are not synonymous.

An *assignment* is a transfer or making over to another of the whole of any property, real or personal, in possession or in action, or of any estate or right therein.[12]

A *sublease* or *underlease* is one executed by the lessee of an estate to a third person, conveying the same estate for a shorter term than that for which the lessee holds it.

The distinction between an assignment of a term for years and a sublease or subletting is that if the lessee parts with his entire interest in the term, it constitutes an assignment and not a subletting although the transfer is in the form of a sublease. A transfer of something less than the entire interest or of the whole interest for less than the whole term, amounts only to a sublease. In Massachusetts, an assignment of a lease for more than seven years must be recorded in the district or county where the land is located.

Liabilities of the Assignee

Since the assignee stands in place of the assignor, he is liable to the lessor on all covenants running with the land. This is so only during the term that he holds the legal title to the leasehold estate under his assignment.[13]

Liability of Assignor to Lessor

The assignor of a lease remains liable to the lessor during the term upon the express covenant of the lease through privity of contract. However, whenever the lessor agrees to accept the tenancy of the assignee in place of that of the lessee, there is privity of contract between the lessor and the assignee. Thus, the assignee is bound by the terms of the lease to the lessor and the lessee is then discharged of any obligation.[14]

The receipt by the lessor of rent from the assignee may have some tendency to show substitution of tenants, but it is not conclusive. On the other hand, if the assignee by consent of the lessor is to hold the premises on terms different from those spelled out in the lease, there is then a substituted tenancy and the lessee is discharged.

Liability Under a Sublease

A sublease creates a contract between the parties to it. Since there does not exist any relationship between the lessor and the sub-lessee it stands to reason that since there is a contractual relationship between the lessor and the lessee, the lessee is liable to the lessor for breach of covenants to the lease.

Parties to a Lease

Up to this point, much has been written concerning the lease, its assignability and the liabilities stemming from such. Also of great importance to the student is the matter of the parties to a lease. In other words, who may give a lease and to whom?

The Lessor

Simply defined, a lessor is one who grants a lease. When a lessee subleases the res, he becomes lessor for purposes of the sublease.

Whenever the pharmacist is confronted with the problem of leasing property, he should bear in mind the following few basic rules:

1. A corporation may take or give leases if the right is expressly or implicitly granted in the charter or is necessary in the ordinary course of business.
2. Executors and administrators may lease real estate if they obtain the consent of the heirs.
3. A guardian generally is not empowered to give a written lease of the real estate of the ward except by decree of the court.
4. Where a lease is made in good faith by one having an imperfect title, the lease is valid as between the parties and voidable by those whose rights the lease has infringed.[15]

The Lessee

A lessee is generally the one to whom a lease is granted. One court of law defines a lessee as "one who has been given possession of land which is exclusive even of the landlord, except as the lease permits his entry, and except right to enter to demand rent or to make repairs."[16]

Duration of Lease

If a lease does not contain words indicating the duration of the term, it is ineffective as a lease and only creates a tenancy at will. Oral evidence is not admissible in court to prove that the lease had a different construction.

On occasion, a lease is issued for a definite period of time however no time is named for its commencement. In these cases, the courts have held that the time begins to toll from the time that the lease is delivered to the lessee.

Rent

Rent may be payable in anything of value, tangible or intangible. It is payable up to midnight of the day it is due and, unless otherwise indicated in the lease, rent is payable at the end of the term.

Taxes and Other Charges

The lessor pays taxes and assessments in the absence of any special covenants regarding them in the body of the lease.

When the lease is silent as to which party shall pay water rates, the lessee must pay them.

By statute[17] the municipality may charge taxes to either the owner or the tenant in possession. However, if the tenant is forced to pay, he may retain out of his rent the amount paid by him or he may sue the landlord for this amount.

Repairs

Whether lessor or lessee provides repairs to leased premises has always been controversial. Legally, there is no implied obligation on the part of the landlord to make repairs. The lessee, in the absence of a contrary agreement, must keep the premises in the condition they were in at the beginning of the tenancy, reasonable wear and tear excepted.

In executing a lease, the lessee should protect himself by insisting that the lease contain an exception as to his liability for such damage as by fire. Failure to insert such an exclusion may mean that the lessee must rebuild the leased structure if it is destroyed by fire or by *Act of God.*

Renewal and Extension

Most leases provide for an option to "renew and extend." In these circumstances, the option could be exercised by giving the lessor a notice to extend.

Eviction

Eviction is a positive act of expulsion or some act of a permanent nature which prevents the tenant from getting enjoyment out of the premises. If there is an eviction, the tenant is not liable on his covenant to pay rent.

Fixtures Affixed to the Premises

Tenants are often under the mistaken impression that if a fixture or other similar item is purchased by them, it belongs to them and can, therefore, be removed from the premises when the lease expires. This line of reasoning is inconsistent with legal doctrine.

Legally, the landlord acquires title to articles affixed to his realty. The problem that usually arises is that which tries to ascertain what is and what is not a fixture.

The courts have applied two basic tests:

1. How is the item affixed—can it be easily removed without defacing the property?
2. Is the item peculiar to a certain trade?

Trade fixtures are usually removable.

Clearly then, the best way of coping with a situation of this type is to insert a provision in the lease whereby the landlord disclaims ownership interest in any item that the tenant installs. The landlord may agree to this, however he will generally insist that after the removal of the fixtures, the premises must be put back into its original condition, wear and tear excepted.

At any time during the term of occupancy, the pharmacist should obtain a specific disclaimer from the landlord before he does proceed to install such items as air conditioners, dehumidifiers and refrigeration equipment.

A lease can offer a great deal of peace of mind to the busy practitioner. However, it must be a thorough lease and provide for the specific type of business being conducted.

References

1. Becker v. Becker, 13 App. Div. 342, 43 N.Y. S 17.

2. *Supra*

3. Hooton v. Holt, 29 N.E. 221, 139 Mass. 54.

4. Means v. Cotton, 114 N.E. 361, 225 Mass. 313.

5. Massachusetts General Laws ch. 186, Sec. 12.

6. Margosian v. Markarian, 192 N.E. 612, 288 Mass. 197.

7. Gordon v. Sales, 147 N.E. 2nd 803, 337 Mass. 35.

8. Massachusetts General Laws ch. 139, Sec. 19.

9. Massachusetts General Laws ch. 186, Sec. 13.

10. Massachusetts General Laws ch. 183, 4.

11. *Supra*, ch. 185, Sec. 46.

12. Bostrom v. Bostrom, 60 N.D. 792, 236 N.W. 732, 734.

13. Donaldson v. Strong, 81 N.E. 267, 195 Mass. 429.

14. Carpenter v. Pocasset Mfg. Co., 61 N.E. 816, 180 Mass. 130.

15. 118 Mass. 92.

16. Seabloom v. Krier, 219 Minn. 362, 18 N.W. 2nd 88, 91.

17. Massachusetts General Laws ch. 59, Sec. 11, 15.

CHAPTER 6

Business Law

With the increase in population and the improvement in the socio-economic status of the individual, the number and variety of business transactions handled by the pharmacy practitioner have increased sharply. Thus, it is important that the pharmacist be exposed, in a general way, to the laws of sole ownership, partnership, corporations, the Uniform Commercial Code, taxation, estate planning and insurance. Students desiring further knowledge in these areas are advised to refer to more specialized and comprehensive texts on the various subjects.

SOLE OWNERSHIP

The simplest form of business organization is the sole ownership (sole proprietorship). This simple form of ownership is used by many pharmacists and other small business enterprises because of some of the following advantages:

1. It is very simple to go into business. No legal formalities are necessary other than the procurement of necessary licenses and permits.
2. A statement of ownership is required only if the business uses a name that does not identify the proprietor.
3. Termination of the business is equally simple. All that is necessary is that the sole owner close his door and pay his creditors.
4. A single proprietor may conduct his business as he deems appropriate in view of the fact that there are no partners or stockholders to consult.
5. Sole ownership taxes are not as high or as complex to report as the corporate counterparts.

The simplicity of the above should not mislead the student because there are serious disadvantages that accrue to a sole proprietorship. Consideration should be given to the following:

1. The business assets are not considered to be separate and distinct from his private assets or individual affairs and therefore become interchangeable in the settlement of law suits or debts.
2. A sole owner may not be in a position to raise sufficient capital to conduct the business. Banks are more willing to advance capital to partnerships because of the joint and several liability on the loan.
3. The death of the sole owner may cause the business to come to a close unless other provisions can be made.

For these reasons and others, drugstores generally are not owned by a single proprietor. Since many of them are owned as partnerships and corporations, it is necessary to comment upon these types of business entities.

PARTNERSHIPS

A partnership or copartnership is a legal relationship created by the voluntary association of two or more persons to carry on, as co-owners, a business for profit.[1]

Characteristics of a Partnership

A partnership generally has the following characteristics:
1. It is a voluntary contractual relationship.
2. The partnership provides for the membership to contribute capital, labor or skill either singly or in combination.
3. The parties are associated as co-owners or principals.
4. The partnership is organized as a for-profit organization.

Purposes of a Partnership

A partnership may be formed for any legal purpose. It cannot be created to carry out immoral or illegal acts that are contrary to public policy.

Classification of Partnerships

Partnerships may be classified as general or special or as trading and non-trading partnerships.

A *general* partnership is usually created for the conduct of a particular business, such as a retail pharmacy, whereas a *special* partnership is formed for a single transaction.

A *trading* partnership is organized for the purpose of buying and selling, such as a retail pharmacy, whereas a *non-trading* partnership is one organized for a non-commercial purpose such as the practice of law or medicine.

Firm Name

In the absence of local statute, it is not necessary for a partnership to have a firm name, although it is customary to have one. The partners may adopt any name they desire so long as it does not deceptively conflict with that of an existing firm.

Classification of Partners

1. A *general partner* is one who openly engages in the conduct of the partnership's business.
2. A *silent partner* is one who does not openly engage in the activities of the firm although his association with the firm is known to the public.
3. A *secret partner* is one who is not known to be a partner by the public yet takes part in the affairs of the firm.
4. A *dormant partner* is one who is a secret partner and does not take active part in the transactions of the business.

Composition of Partnerships

Unless statutory provisions prohibit such, any person who is competent to contract may form a partnership. Thus, the principles of contract law apply to partnership situations involving minors and insane persons.

Formation of Partnership

Because a partnership is viewed as an association of two or more persons to carry on as co-owners a business for profit,[2] the courts have ruled that there must exist an intent between the partners to associate themselves as such.[3] The mere participation in profits is insufficient to create a partnership in the absence of an intent to become partners.[4]

Articles of Partnership

Partnership agreements do not have to be reduced to writing unless they fall within the provision of the statute of frauds that a contract which cannot be performed within one year must be in writing. Partnership agreements must also be in writing when a transfer of an interest in land is involved.

Rules for Determining Existence of Partnership

In order to prove the existence of a partnership, one must prove the intent of the parties. The burden of proving the existence of the partnership rests upon the one who claims its existence.

Since this is not always easy to do, the law has developed guides, of which the following are typical:

1. Persons who are not partners as to each other are not partners as to third persons.
2. Joint ownership of property does not of itself establish a partnership, whether such co-owners do or do not share any profits made by the use of the property.
3. The sharing of gross returns does not of itself establish a partnership, whether or not the persons sharing them have a joint or common right or interest in any property from which the returns are derived.

4. The receipt by a person of a share of the profits of a business is *prima facie* evidence that he is a partner in the business, but no such inference shall be drawn if such profits were received in payment:
    a. Of a debt by installments or otherwise.
    b. As wages of an employee or rent to a landlord.
    c. As an annuity to a widow or representative of a deceased partner.
    d. As interest on a loan, though the amount of payment vary with the profits of the business.
    e. As the consideration for the good will of a business or other property by installments or otherwise.[5]

Partnership Property

Unless otherwise indicated, partnership property consists of all property originally brought into the partnership stock or subsequently acquired, by purchase or otherwise, on account of the partnership; property acquired with partnership funds; and any estate in real property acquired in the partnership name.[6]

Relations of Partners to Persons Dealing with the Partnership

Every partner is an agent of the partnership for the purpose of its business, and the act of every partner, including the execution in the partnership name of any instrument, for apparently carrying on in the usual way the business of the partnership of which he is a member binds the partnership, unless the partner so acting has in fact no authority to act for the partnership in the particular matter, and the person with whom he is dealing has knowledge of the fact that he has no such authority.[7]

An act of a partner outside the scope of the partnership does not bind the partnership unless authorized by the other partners.

Unless authorized by the other partners or unless they have abandoned the business, one or more but less than all the partners have no authority to:

1. Assign the partnership property in trust for creditors or on the assignee's promise to pay the debts of the partnership.
2. Dispose of the good will of the business.
3. Do any other act which would make it impossible to carry on the ordinary business of the partnership.
4. Confess a judgment.
5. Submit a partnership claim or liability to arbitration or reference.[7]

Finally, no act of a partner in contravention of a restriction on his authority shall bind the partnership to persons having knowledge of the restriction.[7]

Relations of Partners to One Another

The rights and duties of the partners in relation to the partnership may be determined, subject to any agreement by them, by statutory regulations of which the following are typical:

1. Each partner shall be repaid his contributions, whether by way of capital or advances to the partnership property, and share equally in the profits and surplus remaining after all liabilities, including those to partners, are

satisfied; and must contribute towards the losses, whether of capital or otherwise, sustained by the partnership according to his share of the profits.

2. The partnership must indemnify every partner in respect of payments made and personal liabilities reasonably incurred by him in the ordinary and proper conduct of its business, or for the preservation of its business or property.

3. A partner, who in aid of the partnership makes any payment or advance beyond the amount of capital which he agreed to contribute, shall be paid interest from the date of the payment or advance.

4. A partner shall receive interest on the capital contributed by him only from the date when repayment should be made.

5. All partners have equal rights in the management and conduct of partnership business.

6. No partner is entitled to remuneration for acting in the partnership business, except that a surviving partner is entitled to reasonable compensation for his services in winding up the partnership affairs.

7. No person can become a member of a partnership without the consent of all the partners.

8. Any difference arising as to ordinary matters connected with the partnership business may be decided by a majority of the partners; but no act in contravention of any agreement between the partners may be done rightfully without the consent of all the partners.[8]

Dissolution

The dissolution of a partnership is the change in the relation of the partners caused by any partner ceasing to be associated in the carrying on as distinguished from the process of concluding the business.[9] Upon dissolution, the partnership is not terminated but continues until the winding up of partnership affairs is completed. From the moment of dissolution, the partners lose authority to act for the firm except for the purpose of completing its affairs.

Causes of Dissolution

Dissolution is caused, without violation of the agreement between the partners, by:

1. The termination of the definite term or particular undertaking specified in the agreement.

2. The express will of any partner when no definite term or particular undertaking is specified.

3. The express will of all the partners who have not assigned their interests or suffered them to be charged for their separate debts, either before or after the termination of any specified term or particular undertaking.

4. The expulsion of any partner from the business bona fide in accordance with such a power conferred by the agreement between the partners.[10]

Dissolution is also caused by the following:

1. In contravention of the agreement between the partners, where the circumstances do not permit a dissolution under any other provision of this section, by the express will of any partner at any time.
2. By any event which makes it unlawful for the business ot the partnership to be carried on or for the members to carry it on in partnership.
3. By the death of any partner.
4. By the bankruptcy of any partner or the partnership.
5. By decree of a court of law.[10]

Decree of Dissolution

Generally, on application by or on behalf of a partner, the court will decree a dissolution whenever:

1. A partner has been declared a lunatic in any judicial proceeding or is shown to be of unsound mind.
2. A partner becomes in any other way incapable of performing his part of the partnership contract.
3. A partner has been guilty of such conduct as tends to affect prejudicially the carrying on of the business.
4. A partner willfully or persistently commits a breach of the partnership agreement, or otherwise so conducts himself in matters relating to the partnership business that it is not reasonably practicable to carry on the business in partnership with him.
5. The business of the partnership can only be carried on at a loss.
6. Other circumstances render a dissolution equitable.[11]

Notice of Dissolution

Whenever a partner effects a dissolution of the firm, notice must be given to the other partners unless his act clearly demonstrates his intent to withdraw or effect dissolution.

Whenever dissolution of the partnership is brought about, notice must be given to third persons. Generally, a formal notice is given to those third persons who have been dealing with the firm whereas a newspaper notice is sufficient for all others. When dissolution has been caused by operation of law, notice to third persons is not required.

Distribution of Assets

The general rule is that creditors of the firm have first claim on its assets, and the individual creditors share in the remaining assets, if any are available. Conversely, individual creditors have priority in the distribution of individual assets and firm creditors may be satisfied from the remainder if any exists.

After the firm's creditors have been paid, the assets are parceled out as follows:

1. Each partner receives a refund of any advances he has made to or on behalf of the firm.
2. Contributions to the capital of the firm are returned.

3. If any assets remain, they are divided equally as profits among the partners unless there exists an agreement to the contrary.
4. If the partnership has sustained a loss, the partners share it equally unless there exists an agreement to the contrary.

CORPORATION LAW

A corporation is an artificial person or legal entity created by or under the authority of the laws of a state or nation. It is composed, in some rare instances, of a single person and his successors, being the incumbents of a particular office. Ordinarily a corporation consists of an association of numerous individuals, who subsist as a body politic under a special denomination, which is regarded in law as having a personality and existence distinct from that of its several members, and which is, by the same authority, vested with the capacity of continuous succession, irrespective of changes in its membership, either in perpetuity or for a limited term of years. It acts as a unit or single individual in matters relating to the common purpose of the association, within the scope of the powers and authorities conferred upon such bodies by law.[12]

Classification

According to the accepted definitions and rules, corporations are classified as follows:

a. Public and Private

A public corporation is one created by the state for political purposes and to act as an agency in the administration of civil government, generally within a particular territory or subdivision of the state, and usually invested, for that purpose, with subordinate and local powers of legislation—such as a county, city, town or school district. These are also sometimes called "political corporations."[12]

Private corporations are those founded by and composed of private individuals, for private purposes, as distinguished from governmental purposes, and having no political or governmental franchises or duties.[12]

b. Domestic and Foreign

A domestic corporation is one created by, or organized under the laws of that state. A foreign corporation is one created by or under the laws of another state, government or country.

c. Close and Open

A close corporation is one in which the directors and officers have the power to fill vacancies in their own number, without allowing to the general body of stockholders any choice or vote in their election.[12] An open corporation is therefore one in which all of the members or corporators have a vote in the election of the directors and other officers.[12]

d. Subsidiary and Parent

A subsidiary corporation is one in which another corporation (called the parent) owns at least a majority of the shares and thus has control.

In modern business practices, most businesses are classified as business corporations. These entities are generally formed for the purpose of transacting business in the widest sense of that term, including not only trade and commerce, but manufacturing, mining, banking, insurance, transportation and practically every form of commercial or industrial activity where the purpose of the organization is pecuniary profit; these are in contrast to religious, charitable, educational and other like organizations which are sometimes grouped in the statutory law of the state under the general designation of "corporations not for profit." Thus, an incorporated "family-pharmacy" might well be classified as a private, domestic, close business corporation.

The Incorporators

In order to obtain a corporate charter, the applicants (incorporators) must file a certificate of incorporation with the Secretary of State, the Secretary of Corporations or other duly designated state authority. After the charter* is approved, the incorporators and/or others who have subscribed for the corporate stock become stockholders or, in effect, the "owners" of the corporation.

The minimum number of incorporators required varies with each state and ranges from one to five. No maximum number is set in any of the states.

The incorporators, since they are in reality entering into a "contract" must possess the power to contract; that is, they must be of sound mind and have attained the age of 21 years. In some states married women, aliens and corporations are prohibited from acting as incorporators.

State of Incorporation

Sometimes there may be advantages for a local group of businessmen to incorporate in a state other than their own. Delaware, for example, is a very liberal incorporating sovereignty. Although it does not stand alone in this category, it is the prime example of a "liberal" state.

Since the statutes of the several states vary with regard to incorporation, one must compare their considerations of the following factors:
1. The size of the corporation.
2. The scope of the business.
3. Liabilities imposed upon the directors and officers.
4. Quorum restrictions.
5. Qualifications of the directors.
6. Restrictions as to the amounts of indebtedness or capitalization.
7. Classes of stock that may be issued.
8. Dividend payment regulations.

Clearly the above and many other considerations must be evaluated before the final selection of the state of incorporation.

*Certificate of Incorporation or Articles of Incorporation

Formation of a Corporation

Because of the limited scope of this volume, it is not possible to cover the variations provided by each state for the formation of a corporation. Therefore, the Massachusetts regulations for the creation of a corporation will, hereinafter, be used as the general example.

The incorporators first sign a written agreement of association which provides for the following information:

1. The corporate name.
2. The location of the principal office.
3. The nature of the business to be conducted.
4. The total amount of stock. The par value, if any, of the stock and the classes of stock.
5. The names of the subscribers by whom the first meeting is called.
6. The names and residences of each incorporator and number of shares of stock taken by him.

At the first meeting of the subscribers, of which seven days' notice must be given, unless waived, the incorporators organize, elect officers and adopt bylaws. The majority of the directors elected then sign and attest to the articles setting forth:

1. A true copy of the agreement of association and the names of the subscribers.
2. The date of the first meeting.
3. The amount of capital stock then to be issued, the amount thereof to be paid for in cash or in installments, or in property, or by services with a description of the nature of such property and services.
4. The names and addresses of the officers.
5. A certification that the provisions relative to the calling and holding of the first meeting of the corporation, the election of a temporary clerk, the adoption of the bylaws and the election of officers have been complied with.
6. The final day of the corporation's fiscal year and the date provided in the bylaws for the annual meeting.

Corporate Name

Most states require that the name of the business indicate that it is incorporated. This provision may be complied with by the use of the words "corporation" or "incorporated" or their abbreviations as part of the name.

Although other terms may be used, one must be careful that they do not conflict, as to meaning, with partnerships, joint ventures or limited partnership associations.

Corporate Purpose

The "purpose clause" in the articles of incorporation is intended to state the scope of the line of business to be conducted. Generally, the concluding words used by most attorneys are, "and for any other lawful business or purpose." Clearly then, one must assume that if the purpose does not conflict with the laws of the state or the country, the corporation may conduct its business.

Corporate Powers

Corporate powers may be either expressed or implied. These terms have been discussed previously in Chapter 2.

Ultra Vires Acts

Ultra vires is the modern technical designation, in the law of corporations, of acts beyond the scope of the powers of a corporation, as defined by its charter or act of incorporation.[12]

Corporate Bylaws

The purpose of preparing bylaws is the same for a corporation as it is for any organization: to establish the rules for the operation of the corporation. Generally, the power to make bylaws is vested in the stockholders; the charter or state statute, however, might provide to the contrary and vest the authority in the directors.

The bylaws of most corporations contain many provisions; the following will provide the student with an over view:

a. Officers

Their number, designations, duties, qualifications, powers, term of office, compensation etc.

b. Directors

In addition to the matters outlined under "officers" this section might deal with directors' meetings—such matters as their place, time, order of business, number constituting a quorum and methodology for the appointment of committees.

c. Stockholders' Meetings

Time, place, order of business, quorum, voting, proxies etc.

d. Financial Matters

Fiscal year, authorization of signatures on checks and notes, details of stock issuance etc.

Rights of Stockholders

Stockholders have certain legal rights that may be classified as *collective rights* and *general rights*. However, additional rights may be provided by the corporate charter of state statutes.

Collective rights include the right to amend the charter; to adopt and amend bylaws; to call and hold meetings; to elect directors; to authorize sales of assets, merger, reorganization and dissolution. The student must bear in mind that the above are applicable in some instances only with the approval of the state or where provided for by the bylaws.

General rights of stockholders include the right to receive stock certificates; to transfer stock; to be notified of all stockholders' meetings; to vote; to receive dividends, if declared; to inspect corporate records and to share in the residual assets after dissolution.

Liabilities of Stockholders

The liabilities of stockholders are based upon so many contingencies, limitations and qualifications that any brief statement of them must of necessity be inadequate. For the purposes of this outline, however, they may be briefed as follows:

1. "In some cases (depending on the statutes, charter, bylaws or terms of the subscription agreement), stockholders may be liable to the corporation for the amount of the subscription after the subscription has been accepted by the corporation.

2. "In some states the stockholders of corporations which accept money on deposit carry 'double liability'—that is, liability to creditors for an amount equal to the par value of stock held. National bank stockholders are now exempt from such liability, as are state bank stockholders in some states.

3. "In the absence of any valid provision to the contrary, when stock is originally sold by the corporation at less than par or, if no-par stock, at less than its stated value, the stockholder is liable to the corporation for the difference between the par or stated value and the price actually paid. (Such liability is several, not joint.) Innocent purchasers of such stock for value, however, are not liable, provided the stock was sold as full-paid or was so marked on the certificate.

4. "When stock is issued in exchange for property or services of a lesser value than the par or stated value of the stock, it is said to be 'watered stock.' Stockholders may be liable to creditors for the difference between the par or stated value of the stock and the value of the property or services exchanged for it.

   a. "The question as to whether they are or not liable depends on whether the stock is determined by the court to be watered. Unless it is clear that the directors acted fraudulently or with extreme indiscretion, it may be assumed that, from a judicial point of view, the stock is not watered.

   b. "The same general principles apply to stock issued as a bonus or as a dividend, or for cash of a lesser amount than the par or stated value.[13]

Liabilities of Directors

"Directors are liable to the corporation for any losses sustained by it as a result of their fraudulent acts, ultra vires acts, negligence or errors of judgment resulting from their negligence.

"The statutes of the various states make the directors criminally liable for the doing of certain acts such as the following:

1. "The payment of dividends except from surplus.
2. "Signing of a statement, report or public notice which is known to be false.
3. "Causing or permitting false entries to be made on the books of the corporation.
4. "Refusing to allow the stockholders their proper right of examining the corporation's books and records.
5. "Failure or refusal to make certain reports.
6. "Making transfers of property when the corporation is insolvent for the purpose of defrauding, or preferring creditors.
7. "Embezzlement, larceny, conversion and misapplication of corporate property.
8. "Misstatements of material facts or omission to state any material facts in connection with the sale of securities to the public, unless they had reasonable ground for belief that the statements were true. (This penalty was enacted by the Federal government in the Securities Act of 1933)."[14]

Liabilities of Officers

These are similar to those outlined for the directors.

Classes of Corporate Stock

Stock is distinguished from *bonds* and, ordinarily, from *debentures* in that it gives right of ownership in part of the assets of the corporation and the right to interest in any surplus after payment of debt.

Capital stock is defined as the amount of stock that a corporation issues. Capital stock consists of two types—preferred stock and common stock.

Preferred stock is a separate portion or class of the stock of a corporation, which is accorded by the charter or bylaws a preference or priority in respect to dividends, over the remainder of the stock of the corporation, which in that case is called *common stock*. That is, holders of the preferred stock are entitled to receive dividends at a fixed annual rate, out of the net earnings or profits of the corporation, before any distribution of earnings is made to the common stock.

If the earnings applicable to the payment of dividends are not more than sufficient for such fixed annual dividend, they will be absorbed entirely by the preferred stock. If they are more than sufficient for the purpose, the remainder may be given entirely to the common stock (which is the more usual custom) or such remainder may be distributed pro rata to both classes of stock, in which case the preferred stock is said to "participate" with the common.[12]

Stock Subscriptions

A subscription to corporate stock is an offer even though the corporation has not come into existence; being an offer, the subscription can be revoked at any time before the corporation has come into existence.[17]

On the other hand, if a subscriber under Massachusetts law wrongfully refuses to take and pay for his share after the corporation has been organized the corporation has the choice of suing him for the par value which he agreed to pay and hold the stock for his disposal or it may make demand for payment within 30 days and then sell his rights to some other party; if the rights bring more than he was to pay, he receives the surplus—if less, he is liable for the deficit.[18]

Dissolution

"Dissolution of a corporation means the extinguishment of its franchise to be a corporation; it is the destruction of all rights, powers, duties and privileges it enjoys as a legal entity, together with the termination of its corporate existence."[15]

There are many reasons for the dissolution of a corporation, the following being but a few examples: bankruptcy; assets have been liquidated; purpose has been accomplished; expiration of charter; revocation of charter by the state.

Some states[16] provide that after dissolution, the corporation shall continue to exist for three years for the purpose of prosecuting and defending suits by or against it and/or enabling it gradually to settle and close its affairs, to dispose of and convey its property and to divide its capital stock, but not for purpose of continuing business. As to any suit brought by or against the corporation within this period of three years, the corporation shall continue until 60 days after final judgment in the suit.

Revival

Some jurisdictions[19] authorize the commissioner of corporations or secretary of state to revive a dissolved corporation for all purposes or for a specified purpose with or without limitation of time within five years after dissolution.

Federal Corporate Taxation

Corporations are taxed by both the state and federal government. Because of the complexity of the associated tax law as well as its fluidity, no attempt will be made herein to enter into a discussion of either. However, within the federal tax sphere, there exists some possibility of acquainting the student with some common and elementary principles associated with the preparation of the corporate tax return.

Therefore the following are excerpted from Document No. 5180 (10-66) of the U.S. Treasury Department's Internal Revenue Service. The student must bear in mind that these are *examples only* and are not intended to reflect the latest regulations of the Internal Revenue Service:

> Every corporation, unless expressly exempt, must file an income tax return regardless of the amount of its income.

> For Federal income tax purposes, the term corporation includes associations, joint stock companies, insurance companies, and trusts and partnerships that actually operate as associations or corporations.

An election not to be taxed may be made by a corporation under certain conditions.

Unincorporated organizations having certain corporate characteristics are classified as associations and must be taxed as corporations. The characteristics of such an organization are that it must: (a) have associates; (b) have an objective to carry on business and divide the gains therefrom; (c) have continuity of life; (d) have centralization of management; (e) limit its liability for corporate debt to corporate property; and (f) have free transferability of interests. To determine whether an organization is an association, the presence or absence of these characteristics must be taken into account. Whether the characteristics are present or not is a question of fact in each case. Other factors may be present in some cases which may be significant in classifying an organization as an association. An organization will be treated as an association if the corporate characteristics are such that the organization more nearly resembles a corporation than a partnership or trust.

A corporation is required to file an income tax return if it has not dissolved even though it has ceased doing business and has disposed of all of its assets, except a small sum of cash which it retains to pay state taxes to preserve its corporate charter. The filing of a corporation return may be required for any year following the year in which the corporation has been dissolved, if substantial activities are carried on in connection with the termination of its business affairs, such as the collection of assets or the payment of obligations.

A corporation need not file an income tax return after it has ceased doing business and dissolves, retaining no assets, whether or not under state law it may thereafter be treated as a corporation for certain limited purposes connected with winding up its affairs, such as suing or being sued.

Return form 1120 is the income tax return for ordinary corporations.

All corporation returns must be manually signed by the corporate officer authorized to sign.

. . . .

Due date of return. If a corporation's income tax return is made on a calendar year basis, it must be filed on or before March 15th following the close of the tax year. If a corporation uses a fiscal year, it must file its return on or before the 15th day of the third month following the close of its fiscal year.

Saturday, Sunday, or Holiday. If the last day (due date) for performing any act for tax purposes, such as filing a return or making a tax payment, etc., falls on Saturday, Sunday, or a legal holiday, you may perform the act on the next succeeding day which is not a Saturday, Sunday, or legal holiday.

. . . .

Extension of time for filing. If there is reasonable cause for a corporation's inability to file a return on time, an extension of time for filing may be obtained. An application on Form 7004 may be filed with the district director on or before the original due date of the return to obtain an automatic 3-month extension of time for filing the return. If a corporation requires a longer period of time in which to file, a written request for extension must be submitted, explaining the reasons for the request. Such written application must be submitted to the district director early enough to allow time for consideration and reply prior to the original or other due date of the return. Not more than 6 months beyond the original due date may be allowed for filing the return of a domestic corporation.

3

At least 50% of the balance of the tax still due at the time the extension is requested must be paid on or before the original due date of the return, and the remainder within 3 months after that date, unless a later date for payment is specified by the district director in granting a request for an extension of time to file a return.

. . . .

Rules on income and deductions which apply to individuals also apply, for the most part, to corporations.

Formation of a corporation involves a transfer of either money, property, or both by the prospective shareholders in exchange for capital stock in the corporation.

Where money is exchanged for stock, there is no gain or loss realized by the shareholder or the corporation, and the stock received will have a basis in the hands of the shareholder equal to the amount of money transferred to the corporation.

If property is exchanged for stock, the shareholder who transferred the property to the corporation will usually realize a taxable gain or loss.

The gain or loss on taxable exchanges is determined by comparing the adjusted basis of the property transferred with its fair market value at the time of the transfer to the corporation. This may be a capital gain or loss.

Nontaxable exchange. Where property is transferred to a corporation in exchange for its capital stock by a person or persons who, immediately after the transfer of such property, own at least 80% of the total combined voting power of all classes of stock entitled to vote and at least 80% of each class of nonvoting stock outstanding, no gain or loss will be recognized.

Organizational expenditures. A newly organized corporation may elect to deduct its organizational expenditures ratably over a period of not less than 60 months beginning with the first month the corporation is actively in business.

These expenditures must be incurred before the end of the first tax year in which the corporation begins business. If the corporation uses the cash method, it may amortize all the organizational expenditures incurred within the specified period even though the expenses may not have been paid within the first tax year.

Such expenditures are those directly incident to the creation of the corporation. They also must be of a character which would chargeable to the capital account and which, if expended incident to the creation of a corporation having a limited life, would be amortizable over such limited life.

They include expenses of temporary directors and of organizational meetings, fees paid to a state for incorporation, accounting services incident to organization, and expenditures for legal services, such as for drafting the charter, bylaws, minutes of organizational meetings, and terms of the original stock certificates.

Expenses for issuance or sale of stock or securities, such as commissions, professional fees, and printing costs, may not be deducted or amortized. Neither may the expenses connected with the transfer of assets to the corporation be deducted or amortized.

Time and manner of election. If a corporation desires to amortize organizational expenses, it must elect to do so when it files its return for the first tax year it is actively in business.

The election must be exercised not later than the due date of the return plus any extensions of time which may be granted. The corporation makes the election by attaching a statement to its return indicating it elects to amortize these expenditures.

The statement should show the description and amount of the expenditures, the date incurred, the month the corporation began business, and the number of months (but not less than 60) over which the expenditures are to be deducted. The time over which the corporation elects to amortize the organizational expenses is binding and must be adhered to for the year of the election and for all subsequent years.

A corporation begins business when it commences the activities for which it was organized. In most cases this occurs after the charter is issued. However, a corporation will be considered as having begun business if its activities have advanced to the extent necessary to establish the nature of its business operations, even though it may not have received its charter. For example, if a corporation acquires the assets necessary to operate its business, such acquisitions may constitute the beginning of business activities.

. . . .

Charitable contributions. A corporation may claim a deduction, subject to certain limitations, for any charitable contributions made. However, in order to be deductible as a charitable contribution, the donation or gift must be made to or for the use of one of the following:

A state or possession of the United States, or a political subdivision of either, or the United States, or the District of Columbia, if made exclusively for public purposes.

Community chests, funds, foundations, corporations, or trusts, organized and operated exclusively for religious, charitable, scientific, literary, or educational purposes, or for the prevention of cruelty to children or animals. The organization must have been created or organized in the United States or its possessions, or under the laws of the United States, any state or territory, the District of Columbia, or any possession of the United States.

No substantial portion of the activities of the organization may be devoted to propaganda or attempts to influence legislation.

Contributions to a trust, chest, fund, or foundation are deductible only if they are to be used within the United States or any possession of the United States. This restriction does not apply to contributions made to a qualified organization organized as a corporation.

War veterans' organizations, auxiliary units, and trusts or foundations for such organizations organized in the United States or any of its possessions.

Cemetery companies owned and operated for the exclusive benefit of their members, or corporations chartered solely for burial purposes as cemetery companies.

. . . .

A deduction will not be allowed if any of the net earnings of an organization which receives the contribution are used for the benefit of any private shareholder or individual.

A cash method corporation may deduct contributions only in the year paid.

An accrual method corporation may elect to deduct contributions authorized by the board of directors during the tax year, but not paid, if payment is made within 2½ months after the close of the tax year.

Professional Corporations

Prior to 1961 professional corporations were not in existence. Since that time practitioners of the various professions have brought political and economic pressures upon state legislatures to enact legislation to qualify corporations for the practice of the professions. The major reason for wanting professional corporations was for federal income tax benefits. The Massachusetts Professional Corporations Act, Mass. Gen. Law. Chpt. 156A, enacted in 1963, is typical of this type of legislation.

Section 1 defines a "professional corporation" as one that is organized—for the purpose of rendering professional services which in turn are stated to be the personal service performed by registered physicians and surgeons, chiropodists, physical therapists, dentists, veterinarians and optometrists, all of whom are registered under the State licensure act for health professionals, and by attorneys-at-law admitted to practice in the Massachusetts courts.

Section 2 dealing with the contents of the articles of organization provides that one or more individuals each of whom is licensed to perform the same professional service may organize a professional corporation by filing articles of organization with the State Secretary. Such articles of organization must comply with the requirements established for business corporations and in addition thereto contain the following:

1. The profession to be practiced through the professional corporation.
2. The names and residence addresses of all of the original shareholders, directors and officers of the professional corporation.
3. A certificate by the appropriate regulating board that each of the incorporators, directors and stockholders is duly licensed to practice such profession.

The professional corporation is restricted in the type of service that it can render to only one specific type of professional service. However the corporation may own real and personal property necessary or appropriate for rendering the type of professional services it was organized to render. In addition, it may invest its funds in real estate, mortgages, stocks, bonds and any other type of investments.

Unlike business corporations, the officers, directors and shareholders of a professional corporation are restricted to those persons who are licensed to render the same professional service as those for which the corporation was organized.

Faced with an influx of state professional corporation statutes, the Internal Revenue Service in 1965 promulgated new regulations dealing specifically with professional corporations. These regulations tried to show that the professional corporation was "inherently different" from the relations characteristic of an ordinary business corporation and therefore it does not qualify as a corporation for federal income tax purposes.

However, after continued litigation[20, 21] the Internal Revenue Service announced that "it is conceding that organizations of doctors, lawyers and other professional people organized under state professional association acts will, generally, be treated as corporations for tax purposes."[22]

Pharmacists interested in a group practice arrangement might very well explore the possible formation of a professional corporation.

UNIFORM COMMERCIAL CODE

Commercial Paper

Within the world of commerce there exists a rather unique series of instruments known as commercial paper or negotiable instruments. Some are quite familiar to the average citizen whereas others are not. Consider, for example, the following negotiable instruments:

Bill of exchange, also known as a *draft, a trade acceptance* or with certain modifications, a *check.* (See Figures 4, 5 and 6.)

Promissory notes and *certificates* of deposit.

Negotiable instruments might be considered as substitutes for money; e.g., when a person pays a debt by a check. Negotiable instruments may be used to created credit e.g., if a debtor gives his creditor a promissory note committing him to pay the creditor within thirty days.

Definitions of Commercial Paper

A negotiable promissory note is an unconditional promise in writing, made by one person to another, signed by the maker, agreeing to pay on demand or at a particular time, a sum certain in money to order or to bearer [Section 3-104(1)]. The person making the promise is often called the *maker* and the recipient of the promise the *payee.*

A draft or bill of exchange is an unconditional order in writing from one person to another, signed by the drawer, requiring the person to whom it is given to pay on demand or at a particular time a sum certain in money to order or to bearer [Section 3-104(1)]. Simply stated, it is an order by one person upon a second person to pay a sum of money to a third person.

A check is a bill of exchange drawn on a bank payable on demand [Section 3-104(2) (b)].

A certificate of deposit is an instrument issued by a bank that acknowledges the deposit of a specific sum of money and promises to pay the holder of the certificate that amount when the certificate is surrendered [Section 3-104(2) (c) (d)].

Parties to Commercial Paper

The *maker* and the *payee* are the two original parties to a note whereas a draft or a check has three original parties—the drawer, the drawee and the payee. In addition to these original parties, a negotiable instrument may have one or more secondary parties. These may be known as indorser, indorsee, bearer, and holder.

An *indorser* (endorser) is a person who owns a negotiable instrument and transfers it to another person by signing his name on the back of the instrument and delivering it to the other person.

An *indorsee* (endorsee) is the person to whom an indorsement is made.

A *bearer* is the person in physical possession of a negotiable instrument "payable to bearer."

A *holder* is a person in possession of a negotiable instrument which is payable to him as a payee, an indorsee or bearer.

An individual who becomes a party to a negotiable instrument in order to lend the strength of his credit to the paper is called an *accommodation party*. As such, he is liable on the instrument irrespective of the reason why he signed.

A *guarantor* is a person who signs commercial paper and adds the words "payment guaranteed" or "collection guaranteed." If the words "payment guaranteed" are used, the implication is that the guarantor will pay the instrument when due even though the holder of the paper has not tried to collect from any other party. On the other hand, use of the words "collection guaranteed" means that he will not pay the paper until after the holder has sought to collect payment from the maker or acceptor and has been unable to do so.

Liability of Parties

A person is primarily liable if he is, by the terms of the instrument, absolutely required to pay. For a note, the maker is primarily liable; for a draft, the acceptor or drawee, who has accepted, is primarily liable. A guarantor of payment is primarily liable in any case. Other parties are generally secondarily liable or not liable at all.

Sales—Uniform Commercial Code

A sale of goods is a transfer of title to the goods (the tangible personal property) in consideration of a payment of money, an exchange of other property, or the rendering of a service. The consideration in the transaction is the price. The parties to the sale are the person in whom the title resides and the person to whom the title is transferred. The transferor is the seller or vendor and the transferee is the buyer or vendee.

Although the law of sales has been described as a mixture of common law of England, mercantile practices and statutes, emphasis will be placed upon the Uniform Commercial Code insofar as it relates to sales.

First, consideration must be given to the difference between a *sale* and other closely related transactions.

a. Bailment

A sale is an actual present transfer of title. A transfer of a lesser interest than ownership or title does not constitute a sale but rather a *bailment*. This holds because under a bailment, the bailor retains title to the property but transfers possession to the bailee.

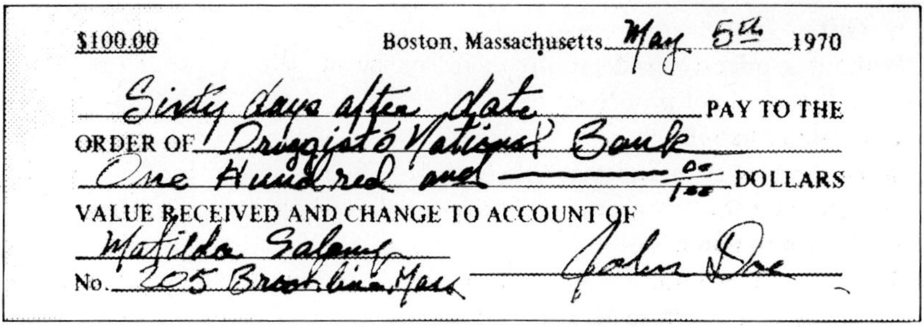

$100.00 Boston, Massachusetts May 5th 1970

Sixty days after date PAY TO THE

ORDER OF Druggists National Bank

One Hundred and 00/100 DOLLARS

VALUE RECEIVED AND CHANGE TO ACCOUNT OF

Matilda Salamy

No. 205 Brookline Mass John Doe

Fig. 4. A Typical Draft (Bill of Exchange). In this sample, John Doe is the "drawer;" the "drawee" is Maltilda Salamy and the "payee" is the Druggists' National Bank.

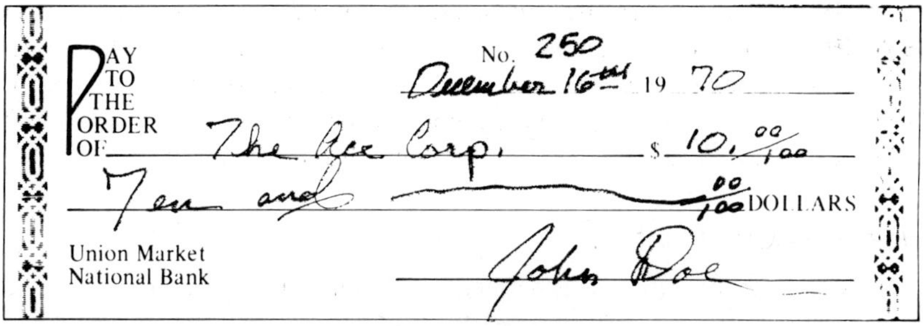

No. 250

December 16th 19 70

PAY TO THE ORDER OF The Ace Corp. $ 10.00/100

Ten and 00/100 DOLLARS

Union Market National Bank

John Doe

Fig. 5. A Typical Check. In this example, the "drawer" is John Doe; the "drawee" is the Union Market National Bank and the "payee" is The Ace Corp.

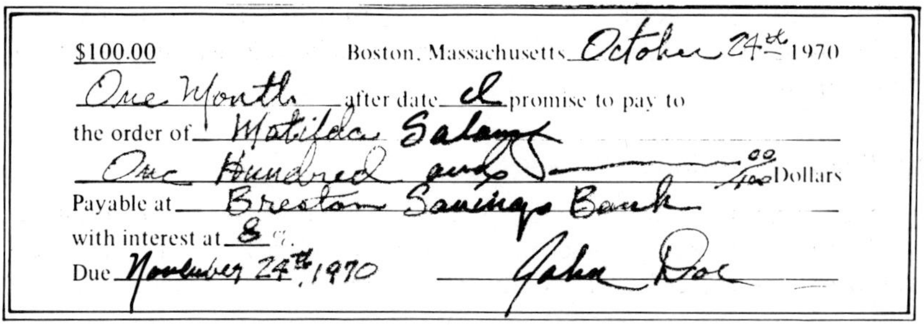

$100.00 Boston, Massachusetts October 24th 1970

One Month after date I promise to pay to

the order of Matilda Salamy

One Hundred and 00/100 Dollars

Payable at Breston Savings Bank

with interest at 8 %.

Due November 24th, 1970 John Doe

Fig. 6. A Typical Promissory Note. In this example, John Doe is the "maker" whereas Matilda Salamy is the "payee".

b. Gift

Without a price (consideration) there can be no sale. A gift is a gratuitous transfer of the title of property.

c. Contract to Sell

When the parties intend that title to goods will pass at a future time and they make a contract for that event, a contract to sell is created.

d. Option to Purchase

This is not a sale nor a contract to transfer title but it is a power to force a sale to be made at a future date.

e. Conditional or Secured Transaction Sale

A conditional sale generally refers to a "condition precedent" transaction whereby title does not transfer to the purchaser until he has paid in full for the property purchased.

f. Furnishing of Labor or Services

A contract for personal services differs from a sale of goods even when some transfer of merchandise is involved in the performing of the services. For example, the contract of a repair man to fix the water still is a contract for services even though in making the repairs he may install replacements parts in order that the still may operate properly. The supplying of the parts is not considered to be a sale because it is incidental to the primary purpose of the contract.

Subject Matter of Sales

The subject matter of a sale is defined in Section 2-105 as follows:

> Goods means all things (including specially manufactured goods) which are movable at the time of identification to the contract for sale. . . .
>
> Goods must be both existing and identified before any interest in them can pass. Goods which are not both existing and identified are 'future goods'.
>
> There may be a sale of a part interest in existing identified goods.

The subject matter of a sale may not be investment securities, such as stocks and bonds; choses in action, since they are generally assigned rather than sold; and real property.[23, 24]

Applicability of Contract Law

Generally speaking, most of the principles of contract law are applicable to a sale, however, commercial practices have modified the strict principles of contract law as is evidenced by the Code. For example, Section 2-204 provides that

> (1) A contract for sale of goods may be made in any manner sufficient to show agreement, including conduct by both parties which recognizes the existence of such a contract.

> (2) An agreement sufficient to constitute a contract for sale may be found even though the moment of its making is undetermined.

(3) Even though one or more terms are left open a contract for sale does not fail for indefiniteness if the parties have intended to make a contract and there is a reasonably certain basis for giving an appropriate remedy.

The Code, in some instances treats all buyers and sellers alike yet in others it recognizes a merchant as one who is experienced in his field and has a specialized knowledge. Note the wording in Section 2-104:

Merchant means a person who deals in goods of the kind or otherwise by his occupation holds himself out as having knowledge or skill peculiar to the practices or goods involved in the transaction or to whom such knowledge or skill may be attributed by his employment of an agent or broker or other intermediary who by his occupation holds himself out as having such knowledge or skill.

At this point, it will be of interest to the student to note the effect of the Code upon two aspects of contract law—*offer* and *acceptance.*

Offers

Contract law relative to offers is applicable to sales except as limited by Section 2-205 of the Code which provides that

An offer by a merchant to buy or sell goods in a signed writing which by its terms gives assurance that it will be held open is not revocable, for lack of consideration, during the time stated or if no time is stated for a reasonable time, but in no event may such a period of irrevocability exceed three months; but any such term of assurance on a form supplied by the offeree must be separately signed by the offeror.

Acceptance

The general principle of contract law that an offer may be accepted in any manner and by any medium which is reasonable under the circumstances, unless a specifically prescribed medium is indicated, is clearly emphasized by the Code in Section 2-206(a):

(1) Unless otherwise unambiguously indicated by the language or circumstances.

(a) an offer to make a contract shall be construed as inviting acceptance in any manner and by any medium reasonable in the circumstances.

With respect to the modification of a contract, the Code deviates from the principles of contract law as provided by Section 2-209:

(1) An agreement modifying a contract within this Article needs *no consideration* to be binding. (*Italics supplied*).

Transfer of Title and Risk of Loss

In a simple sales transaction, the buyer receives the goods, pays for them and thus completes the transaction. Unfortunately, our commercial system allows for sales to be made whereby the goods are shipped to distant ports and payments are made conditional upon delivery, inspection and acceptance. During the time of this transaction, creditors of the seller may seize the goods; creditors of the buyer may seize the goods; the merchandise may become damaged; the buyer and the seller may want to insure themselves against the loss of "their property." Clearly then, rules must apply for the purpose of ascertaining when title to property passes in a sales transaction. Thus, in discussing the applicable rules of law, the student should bear in mind that they apply only in the absence of contrary agreements by the parties concerned.

Nature of Goods

Goods may be identified in three ways:
1. Existing goods.
2. Identified goods.
3. Future goods.

Existing goods are those that are physically in existence and owned by the seller.

Identified goods are those that have been picked out by the seller for purposes of selling them or have been chosen by the buyer for purchase.

Future goods are those that are neither existing nor identifiable.

Terms of Transaction

Whenever goods are purchased, contractual terms often designate the manner of delivery. For example, the seller may be obligated to deliver the goods at a particular destination or the contract may only require that the goods be shipped to the buyer. Note here that under the latter contract, the seller's part is performed when he turns over the goods to a carrier for delivery; contrasted with a delivery at a destination provision, under which the seller's part of the contract is not completed until the merchandise is brought to the destination point and there tendered to the buyer.

In other situations, the transaction may relate to a transfer of a document of title representing the goods. This usually happens when the goods are stored in a warehouse and the buyer wants to leave them there.

Transfer of Title

a. Existing Goods Identified at Time of Contracting

If the goods that are subject to a sales agreement are existing and identified at the time of the sale, the title to such goods passes to the buyer at the time and place of contracting. Thus the buyer is now the owner and creditors of the seller cannot seize the goods. Also, the buyer, as owner, has an insurable interest in the goods and therefore he can protect himself against loss via the purchase of appropriate insurance.

On the other hand, if the seller is a merchant, the risk of loss passes to the buyer when he receives the goods from the merchant. If the seller is not a merchant, the risk of loss passes when the seller tenders or makes available the goods to the buyer. It should be clear from the above that the risk of loss remains longer on the merchant seller than on the non-merchant seller. The philosophy behind this reasoning being that the merchant seller, being in business, can more readily protect himself against such losses or risks.

b. Negotiable Documents Representing Existing Goods Identified at Time of Contracting

In this situation, the buyer has a property interest, but not title, and an insurable interest in the goods at the time and place of contracting; but he does not ordinarily acquire the title nor become subject to the risk of loss until he receives delivery of the documents [Section 2-509(2)(c)].

c. Contract for Shipment of Future Goods

Here, the buyer has placed an order for goods that will be shipped to him at a future date. Thus, the contract is performed by the seller when he delivers the goods for shipment to the buyer. Under this arrangement, the title and risk of loss pass to the buyer when the goods are delivered to the carrier at the time and place of shipment.

In this situation, the presence of a bill of lading issued by the carrier will not bring the transaction within the realm of that described under (b) previously.

Damage or Destruction of Goods

In the absence of a contrary agreement, damage to or destruction of the goods affects the transaction as follows:

a. Damage to Identified Goods Before Risk of Loss Passes

If the goods are damaged or destroyed without the fault of either party before the risk of loss has passed, the contract is avoided if the loss is total. On the other hand, if the loss is partial or if the goods have been damaged, the buyer has the option, after inspection, to (a) avoid the contract, or (b) accept the goods subject to an allowance or deduction from the original contract price. Clearly in this situation the buyer cannot sue the seller for breach of contract [Section 2-303].

b. Damage to Identified Goods After Risk of Loss Passes

If goods are damaged or destroyed after the risk of loss has passed, it is the buyer's loss. In some instances, he may be able to recover the amount of the damages from a third person causing the loss.

c. Damage to Unidentified Goods

Whenever the goods are unidentified, no risk of loss passes to the buyer. Therefore if they are damaged or destroyed during this period, it is the loss of the seller. The buyer is still entitled to receive the goods for which he contracted. If the seller fails to deliver, he is liable to the buyer for breach of contract. Generally, contracts for the sale of unidentified goods provide that destruction of the seller's supply shall be deemed a release of the seller's liability.

Liability Arising from Drug Sales

Legal actions, arising from the use of drugs that have been purchased, have been pursued along such standard lines as misrepresentation, deceit, fraud and warranty.

Misrepresentation may include (a) an intent to deceive, (b) negligence (negligent misrepresentation) and (c) statements made under circumstances which give rise to a policy of strict liability, as for example through warranty.

Although deceit is available as a basis for legal action in drug cases, it is not commonly used because there are two elements essential to the action that are extremely difficult to prove: (a) *scienter*, or a knowledge or belief on the part of the defendant that the representation was false; and (b) the *intent* to induce the plaintiff to do or refrain from doing some act in reliance upon the misrepresentation. In many drug liability cases, the representation is innocently made and therefore the case cannot rest upon deceit.

Although negligent misrepresentation is rarely used today, it deserves some explanation. Cases using it require no proof of an *intentional* misstatement. Instead, the plaintiff need only show that the representation from which the product-caused injury is alleged to have flowed was one that an ordinarily careful man would not have made under the circumstances.[23]

The representation may be negligent because of the manner of expression, or because of the type of business involved.[24,25] In other words, if the person who makes the representation does so in the course of a business or profession of supplying services which require special competence, he should have the ability and skill thus professed. The basis of this liability is the reliance of the consumer upon the qualifications of one who has a particular profession, talent, skill or knowledge.

Strict Liability

Strict liability is defined as liability without fault. It can be imposed by statute, by warranty or in tort. At the present time, warranty is a species of strict liability in that wrongful intent or negligence on the part of the defendant need not be shown. Lest the student receive the impression that an action for recovery in product liability cases is limited to the above mentioned grounds he should readily realize that the following are suitable if the appropriate proof is available: negligence;[26] warranty;[27] deceit;[28] strict liability in tort[29] and statutory liability under the pure food laws.[30]

Plaintiffs who seek to recover damages for their injuries will, if warranty is the basis for their law suit, have difficulty in proving that a sale took place. Some courts have denied any implication of warranty by insisting on proof of a technical sale. There are three ways whereby a sale problem may develop:

1. Administration of a drug by a doctor.
2. Administration of the drug during experimental testing.
3. Public distribution of vaccines.

Some of the rationales employed to justify strict liability are the following:

1. One who undertakes to supply products which may endanger person or property has a special responsibility imposed upon him to protect those who are forced to rely on his products.
2. The manufacturer is in the best position to discover defects and should therefore be motivated to improve his product and use all possible care.
3. Strict liability generally places the loss on the one best able to handle and distribute it.

One writer[31] has criticized strict liability "as an expression of radical jurisprudence, of dubious morality, as well as a novel social theory and bad economics." Nonetheless, it is here to stay.

Insofar as drugs are concerned, strict liability simply means that the manufacturer will be liable without fault for an injury caused by his product if there is proof that the drug caused the injury.

Warranty

Reference to the Uniform Commercial Code indicates the basis upon which recovery may be had in warranty. Section 2-313 speaks of "seller", "buyer" and "bargain." The definitions section of the U.C.C., 2-106, purports to cover the entire sales article when it defines a sale as the passing of title from *seller* to *buyer* for a *price*.

Privity

With respect to the requirement that privity exists between the parties, modern trends seem to be that no privity need be proved and the award is made on the basis of warranty. A good example of this trend was the case involving Cutter Laboratories.[32] The case involved the sale of polio vaccine which was later shown to have caused poliomyelitis in some of the recipients. Here privity was dispensed with the holding that "the policy favoring drug companies and freedom for them" is not warranted where the drug actively caused the disease it was designed to prevent. The privity requirement should not however rest on a policy of protecting the producer. Thus, the court in the Cutter case abrogated it by demonstrating the seriousness of the injury caused.

Further reference to U.C.C. Section 2-313 indicates that there can be an *express* warranty between seller and buyer. An express warranty results from negotiations between the two principals whereas *implied* warranty rests on the surrounding facts of the sale.

Merchantability

Section 2-314 deals with the implied warranty of merchantability. The section provides as follows:

(1) Unless excluded or modified. . . . a warranty that the goods shall be merchantable is implied in a contract for their sale if the seller is a merchant with respect to goods of that kind. Under this section the serving for value of food or drink to be consumed either on the premises or elsewhere is a sale.

(2) Goods to be merchantable must be at least such as

   (a) pass without objection in the trade under the contract description;

   (b) in the case of fungible goods, are of fair average quality with the description;

   (c) are fit for the ordinary purposes for which such goods are used;

   (d) run, within the variations permitted by the agreement, of even kind, quality and quantity within each unit and among all units involved;

   (e) are adequately contained, packaged, and labeled as the agreement may require; and

   (f) conform to the promises or affirmations of fact made on the container or label if any.

(3) Unless otherwise excluded (Sect. 2-316) other implied warranties may arise from course of dealing or usage of trade.

Although drugs are not specifically mentioned in the above section, it is clear that a drug which is not compatible with the purpose for which it is intended is unmerchantable under this section.

Fitness

Section 2-315 entitled "Implied Warranty: Fitness for Particular Purpose" provides that

> Where the seller at the time of contracting has reason to know any particular purpose for which the goods are required and that the buyer is relying on the seller's skill or judgment to select or furnish suitable goods, there is unless excluded or modified—an implied warranty that the goods shall be fit for such purpose.

Under the above, the buyer must actually rely on the seller but need not affirmatively indicate his reliance to the seller so long as the circumstances are such that the seller should know of it. Clearly, this would be a factual as opposed to a legal question in any litigation.

TAXATION

The sixteenth Amendment of the Constitution of the United States provides that

> The Congress shall have power to lay and collect taxes on incomes, from whatever source derived, without apportionment among the several States, and without regard to any census or enumeration.

and, as such, provides the basis for the levying of income taxes upon the citizenry.

Other constitutional provisions pertaining to taxation are the following:

> Article I, Section 7, Clause 1
> All bills for raising revenue shall originate in the house of representatives; but the senate may propose to concur with amendments as on other bills.

Article I, Section 8, Clause 1

The Congress shall have power to lay and collect taxes, duties, imposts, and excises, to pay the debts and provide for the common defence and general welfare of the United States; but all duties, imposts and excises shall be uniform throughout the United States.

Because of the limited scope of this text, it will not be possible to provide the student with a comprehensive presentation of the tax laws. However, an endeavor has been made to present, briefly, materials on the income tax law which are of interest to the pharmacist. In addition, the subject of an income tax return audit is presented in detail because it appears to be a segment of the law with which the taxpayer is least familiar despite the fact that it is in existence only to protect his rights.

Income Tax

Every citizen or resident of the United States, whether an adult or minor, must file a tax return under the following circumstances:

1. The individual is single, an unmarried head of a household, or surviving widow(er) with a dependent child; and the individual's income was $1700 or more ($2300 if 65 or over).
2. The individual is a married person entitled to file jointly and the combined (husband's and wife's) income is $2300 or more ($2900 if either is 65 or over), provided
   a. The individual and spouse had the same household as their home at the close of the taxable year.
   b. No other person is entitled to claim an exemption for the individual and spouse, and
   c. The individual's spouse does not file a separate return.
3. The individual is not covered under (1) or (2) above yet had income of $600 or more. Those having net earnings from self-employment of $400 or more must also file.

Income

All income in whatever form received which is not specifically exempt must be included in the tax return, even though it may be offset by adjustments or deductions. The following are examples of income which must be reported:

Wages, salaries, bonuses, commissions, fees, tips and gratuities.

Dividends.

Earnings (interest) from savings and loan associations, mutual savings banks, credit unions, etc.

Interest on tax refunds.

Interest on bank deposits, bonds, notes.

Interest on U.S. Savings Bonds.

Profits from business or profession.

Your share of partnership profits.

Pensions, annuities, endowments.

Supplemental annuities under Railroad Retirement Act (but not regular Railroad Retirement Act Benefits).

Profits from sales or exchanges of real estate, securities, or other property.

Rents and royalties.

Your share of estate or trust income.

Employer unemployment benefits.

Alimony, separate maintenance or support payments received from (and deductible by) your husband (or wife).

Prizes and awards (contests, raffles, etc.).

Refunds of state and local taxes (principal amounts) if deducted in a prior year and resulted in tax benefits.

The following are examples of personal income which should not be reported:

Disability retirement payments and other benefits paid by the Veterans Administration.

Dividends on Veterans' Insurance.

Life insurance proceeds upon death.

Workmen's compensation, insurance, damages, etc., for injury or sickness.

Interest on certain state and municipal bonds.

Federal social security benefits.

Gifts, inheritances, bequests.

Deductions

The income tax regulations also provide for deductions which may be taken either personally or as business deductions subject to certain limitations. Some allowable personal deductions are:

Accountant's fees connected with income tax and investments.
Alimony payments.
Amusement taxes, state and local.
Attorney's fees connected with income tax and investments.
Automobile taxes.
Bad debts (personal).
Burglary losses.
Capital loss carry-over.
Capital losses.
Casualty losses.
Consumers' taxes, state and local.
Contributions.

Cooperative apartment, share of interest and taxes.
Custodian fees for securities.
Dental expense.
Eyeglasses.
Fire losses.
Flood losses.
Gambling losses to extent of gains.
Gasoline and oil taxes, state and local.
Gifts to government or charity.
Health insurance premiums.
Holdup losses.
Hospital bills.
Hospitalization insurance premiums.
Hurricane losses.
Income-producing expenses.
Income taxes, state and local.
Interest payments.
Investment expenses.
Medical expense.
Partnership, share of deductions.
Property taxes.
Safe deposit rental, for investments.
Sales taxes, state and local.
Separate maintenance payments.
Storm losses.
Taxes.
Theft losses.
Travel expense for medical care.

Business Deductions

The normal current costs incurred in the operation of one's trade or business are classified as *business expenses*. To be deductible, they must qualify as being both ordinary and necessary expenses directly connected with or related to the operation of the trade, profession or business. Again these may be subject to limitations. The following are examples of business deductions:

Accountant's fees.
Advertising expense.
Attorney's fees.
Automobile expense:
    Collision damage.
    Depreciation.
    Driver's salary.
    Garage expense.
    Gas and oil.
    Insurance.
    Interest on installment payments.
    License fees.
    Repairs.
    Tolls and parking fees.
Bad debts.
Bonus for lease.
Book purchases and magazine subscriptions.
Bottles, cost of.
Burglary insurance premiums.

Burglary losses.
Burglary protection service.
Casualty losses.
Chamber of Commerce dues.
Contributions, promotional.
Convention costs.
Cost of goods sold.
Delivery service fees.
Depreciation.
Discounts to customers.
Doctors, gifts to.
Dues in connection with business (national, state, and local retail druggists'
    associations, Rotary, Kiwanis, Lions, etc.).
Electric bills.
Equipment rental.
Express charges.
Fire insurance premiums.
Fire losses.
Flood losses.
Floor polishing expense.
Freight charges.
Gas bills.
Gifts, promotional
Glass breakage.
Holdup insurance premiums.
Holdup losses.
Hotel bills, business trips.
Insurance premiums.
Interest.
Labels.
Legal expense.
Liability insurance premiums.
License fees.
Lodging furnished employees.
Losses.
Losses on sales of assets.
Losses on taxable exchanges.
Meals furnished employees.
Meals on business trips.
Narcotics license stamp.
Net operating loss.
Obsolescence of equipment.
Parking facilities for customers.
Payroll.
Payroll taxes.
Pilfering by clerks.
Plate glass breakage.
Plate glass insurance.
Postage.
Prescription blanks.
Promotional expense.
Property taxes.
Purchases of merchandise.
Rent.
Repairs.
Residence, charges allocable to business.
Rubbish removal.
Scrapped equipment.
Snow removal.

Social Security taxes.
State taxes.
Stationery.
Store jackets and cleaning.
Storm losses.
Supplies.
Telephone.
Telephone answering service.
Telephone at home for emergencies.
Trade association dues.
Trade periodicals.
Transportation charges.
Traveling expenses.
Unemployment insurance taxes.
Uniforms and cleaning.
Wages.
Water rates.
Window washing.
Workmen's compensation premiums.

Educational Expenses

In certain instances, the ordinary and necessary expenses incurred as an employee for education are deductible. The education must:

1. Meet the express requirements of the employer, or requirements of law or regulations, for keeping one's salary, status or employment, if the requirements imposed serve a bona fide business purpose; or

2. Maintain or improve skills required in performing the duties of one's present employment, or trade or business.

If the new education is solely for the purpose of qualifying the individual for a new trade or business, its cost is not deductible. Further, educational expense is not deductible if it is incurred for education needed to meet the minimum educational requirements for qualification in one's present employment.

Educational expenses include amounts spent for tuition, books, supplies, laboratory fees and similar items. Travel expenses associated with the education sought are deductible if limited solely to obtaining the education and not of a personal nature. An important factor in determining whether a trip is primarily personal or mainly to obtain an education is the amount of time devoted to personal, as compared with educational activities.

Examination of the Tax Return

A taxpayer's return may be examined for a number of reasons among which are included (a) apparent failure to pay all of the required tax, (b) the presence of mathematical errors or (c) irregularities in the reporting of income and deductions.

There are three levels within the Internal Revenue Service at which agreement to the results of an examination may be reached. The first level is the audit by an examing officer, the second is a conference with a member of the District Conference Staff, and the third is the Service's Appellate Division. All three levels generally are available to the taxpayer whether the Internal Revenue Service instituted the proceedings or, instead, is verifying a claim which was submitted.

Audit

Examination of the tax return form may take place in the taxpayer's home, place of business or at the office of the Internal Revenue Service. Occasionally, the examination may be conducted by correspondence.

When the tax return has been prepared by an individual who is not enrolled to practice before the Internal Revenue Service, a special procedure permits him to represent his client during the examination of any returns that he completed and personally signed. However, this representation is limited to practice before a revenue agent or an examining officer in the Audit Division and may concern itself only with matters relating to the tax liability for the tax year covered by the return that he prepared. He may not represent the taxpayer at the *District Conference* or before the *Appellate Division*. If the taxpayer chooses to have such an individual represent him, Form 2848-D must be completed and, as such, serves as the taxpayer's authorization for the unenrolled preparer to represent him.

When the examining officer has completed his review of the return, he will explain any adjustment he proposes to make. If these adjustments are satisfactory to the taxpayer, a waiver form, showing the amount of increase or decrease in tax liability, should be signed. Since interest at the rate of six percent per year is charged on any assessed additional tax resulting from the examination, the signing of the waiver stops the interest from running 30 days after the filing of the waiver. No further interest is charged unless, after receipt of the notice of additional tax and interest, the taxpayer fails to pay the amount due within 10 days after the date of the notice. If payment is made when the waiver is signed, interest stops running on the date of payment.

If the examination results in a refund, the taxpayer will, ordinarily, receive interest at the rate of six percent a year on the amount of the refund.

If at the conclusion of a field audit the taxpayer disagrees with the proposed adjustments, a copy of the examining officer's report is forwarded to him with a letter of transmittal. This letter, commonly called a "30-day letter" explains the appeal procedures available and requests the selection of one within 30 days.

The first appeal step is a District Audit Division conference. If the total amount of proposed additional tax, proposed overassessment, or claimed refund exceeds $2500 for any year, a written "protest" must be filed setting forth the facts, law and agreement relied upon.

If upon the conclusion of this portion of the appeal, the taxpayer is still of contrary opinion, the second step of the appellate procedure is the District Conference.

The District Conference

At the District Conference, the taxpayer or his representative is accorded the opportunity of establishing the case and citing the law upon which the case relies.

If an agreement is reached at the District Conference, a waiver is proffered for signature. The effect of signing this document is the same as described above.

If no agreement is reached, the taxpayer may request that the case be considered by the Appellate Division of the Office of the Regional Commissioner; this appeal must be made in writing.

If, after a District Conference has been held, an increase in tax is proposed, the taxpayer may secure a statutory notice of deficiency (called a 90-day letter) either by requesting it or by failing to request an Appellate hearing. Under these circumstances, if an appeal is still desirable, it must be filed with the Tax Court of the United States within 90 days from the date of notice.

On proper occasion, the taxpayer has the option of not appealing to the Tax Court but to pay the additional tax and subsequently file a claim for a refund. If the claim is disallowed, then a suit for its recovery is filed in a United States District Court or in a United States Court of Claims.

The statute of limitations in these matters is two years; that is, a suit must be filed within two years from the date of mailing, by certified or registered mail, of a notice of disallowance of the claim or, if a waiver has been signed, within two years of the said signing.

The Appellate Division

The Appellate Division is the third level within the Internal Revenue Service at which an agreement may be reached. At this hearing, the discussions involve questions of tax law rather than questions of fact. A settlement reached within the Appellate Division reflects a binding agreement by both parties. If no agreements are reached at this level, the taxpayer might file suit in a United States District Court or the United States Court of Claims.

Other Taxes

Although the income tax is the most widely known tax measure, it is of importance that the student recognize that there are in existence many other federal tax measures. These include the following:

a. Stamp Taxes

These taxes apply to bond and stock issues and transfers, deeds, playing cards, casualty and indemnity bonds and life, sickness, accident, annuities and reinsurance policies.

b. Admissions

These cover admission tickets and cabarets.

c. Manufacturers' Excise Taxes

These are applied to such items as air conditioners, automobiles, appliances, cameras, tires and tubes, pencils, pens, etc.

d. Retailers' Excise Taxes

Retailers must collect a tax on the sale of cosmetics and toilet preparations, furs, jewelry, luggage, handbags, wallets, etc.

e. Taxes on Communications, Amusements, Services

These taxes are levied on bowling alleys; amusement machines; safe deposit boxes; telephone, telegraph, radio and cable facilities; transportation of persons.

f. Liquor Taxes

Distilled spirits and imported perfumes containing distilled spirits are subject to this tax.

g. Tobacco Taxes

Tobacco, snuff, cigars and cigarettes are taxed.

h. Occupational Taxes

Certain occupations are subjected to annual taxes. These include cheese manufacturer wholesaler and retailer; firearms importer or manufacturer; manufacturers of stills and condensers and importers, manufacturers, producers, wholesalers, retailers of narcotics.

The pharmacist is most frequently involved with the retailers' excise tax in view of the fact that he retails taxable items and must therefore collect the Federal tax on them. In this regard, Section 7501 of the *Internal Revenue Code* of 1954 entitled "Liability For Taxes Withheld or Collected" is of importance:

> Whenever any person is required to collect or withhold any internal revenue tax from any other person and to pay over such tax to the United States, the amount of tax so collected or withheld shall be held to be a special fund in trust for the United States. The amount of such fund shall be assessed, collected and paid in the same manner and subject to the same provisions and limitations (including penalties) as are applicable with respect to the taxes from which such funds arose.

Federal Gift Tax

Any citizen or resident who within the calendar year makes gifts in excess of $3000 to any one individual, or any gift of a future interest, regardless of value, must file a gift tax return on or before April 15th of the following year. In addition to the annual $3000 exclusion for each person to whom gifts are made, each donor also has a specific lifetime exemption of $30,000. This latter exemption may be taken all at one time or spread out over the years.

Whenever a husband or wife transfers, by gift, an interest in property to the other spouse a deduction in computing the gift tax will be allowed to the extent of one-half of the value of the gift. Also gifts to a third party by either spouse may be treated as made one-half by each.

ESTATE PLANNING

The words "estate planning" have different meanings to different people. To the naive, they conjure thoughts of rich men manipulating huge fortunes for the purpose of evading or avoiding inheritance taxes. To the reasonably intelligent person, they mean a long-range plan for conserving one's assets in a manner that is advantageous to his or her family. This is accomplished by the use of wills and simple trusts.

Black's Law Dictionary (4th Ed.) cites the following definitions of the word "estate:"

> The degree, quantity, nature and extent of interest which a person has in real property is usually referred to as an estate, and it varies from absolute ownership down to naked possession.

* * * * *

> In another sense, 'estate' designates the property (real or personal) in which one has a right or interest; the subject matter of ownership; the corpus of property. Thus, we speak of a 'valuable estate', 'all my estate', 'separate estate', 'trust estate', etc.

Frequently, people die without having left a will. Legally, they are said to have died intestate. As such, the various states apply to their estates laws known as "the laws of intestate succession." Generally, these laws provide that a percentage of the assets (usually one-third to one half) goes to the surviving spouse, if any, and the balance is divided among the children, with additional provisions to govern when there is no surviving spouse or children. In the broadest sense possible, the above might be said to be an estate plan of sorts.

Often, one hears the question asked, "Who needs an estate plan? I don't have sufficient assets to warrant one!" Most people, however, particularly the head of a household, do need such a plan. Even a young family can generate a modest estate. Consider the following sources of assets:

1. Equity in a home.
2. Bank accounts.
3. Life insurance.
4. Vested interest in a retirement plan.
5. Ownership in a pharmacy or other business.
6. Inheritance from parents' estate.
7. Ownership of securities or bonds.

Where the total estate is under $60,000, the main concern is generally to conserve as much of the estate for the use of the surviving spouse for family maintenance and care. This is accomplished through the creation of reciprocal wills and a simple trust.

If the estate is in excess of $60,000, the concern switches towards the minimization of estate taxes. Federal estate tax laws provide for a $60,000 exemption for each estate and further permit a marital deduction of up to one-half of the value of the entire estate for property passing to a surviving spouse.

In very large estates, those in excess of $120,000, the tax considerations will be significant if not decisive factors in any estate plan.

Estate taxes on a taxable estate of $10,000 may approximate $500, however, for a taxable estate of $50,000 the tax is nearly $5000 and for $100,000 the tax is approximately $20,000.

Much has been written on the subject of estate planning, much of it in great technical detail. It is best interpreted when applied to the facts surrounding a particular estate plan. Pharmacists should be aware of the need for estate planning early in their careers as well as for the need for periodic review of existing plans for updating in light of current fiscal status.

Finally, pharmacists must realize that there is no substitute for competent counsel in this area.

INSURANCE

The subject of insurance is most complex and is probably the one area that is least understood by the practitioner. Very simply defined, insurance is a contract whereby, for a stipulated consideration, one party agrees to compensate the other for a loss on a specified subject by specific perils. The party agreeing to pay for the loss is called the "insurer" or "underwriter," the other, the "insured" or "assured." The consideration in this contract is the "premium" and the contract itself is the "policy."

Classification

In today's modern world of business, it is prudent to insure against losses due to the risks or perils of conducting the business, trade or profession. Thus, the insurance industry has blossomed into a major factor in the country's economy. The following are but a sampling of the various types of insurance contracts that can be underwritten:

a. Accident Insurance

Indemnifies the insured against expense and loss resulting from accidents which cause injury to him.

b. Automobile Insurance

Protects the insured vehicle against loss of or damage caused by fire, windstorm, theft, collision or other insurable hazards. In addition, these policies may also cover the insured against legal liability for personal injuries or damage to another person's property resulting from the operation of the vehicle.

c. Burglary Insurance

Insures against losses of property to thieves.

d. Casualty Insurance

Similar to accident insurance.

e. Employer's Liability Insurance

Generally referred to as workmen's compensation, it protects the employer against suits for damage resulting from an accident, injury or death of an employee.

f. Fidelity Insurance

Also known as guaranty insurance, this policy protects the employer against losses due to the dishonesty or infidelity of his employees.

g. Fire Insurance

A policy that undertakes to indemnify the assured against losses due to accidental fire happening within a specified period of time.

h. Liability Insurance

Provides indemnity against liability resulting from injuries to the person or property of another. Professional people refer to this type of insurance as "malpractice insurance."

i. Life Insurance

This policy insures the risk of death of a particular person within a specified period of time. There are three basic forms of life insurance protection—whole life, term life and endowment life.

Whole life insurance protects the insured indefinitely. Whole life coverage is available under two types of policies (1) straight life and (2) limited payment. The former policies carry the lowest premium rate and must be carried for life whereas the latter become "paid-up" with no further premiums due after a certain number of years.

Term life insurance, sometimes described as "Temporary protection" is issued for a specific number of years and is designed to meet special needs. It is particularly suited for young families with limited incomes and heavy financial responsibilities.

Endowment life insurance is basically a guaranteed savings fund with life insurance protection. It guarantees that a specific dollar goal will be achieved, i.e., the cash value at maturity will be the full face value of the policy.

j. Marine Insurance

Insures a ship, boat, freight or cargo, subject to the risks of marine navigation.

k. Plate-glass Insurance

Protects against loss from the accidental breaking of plate-glass windows, doors etc.

l. Steam-boiler Insurance

Insures against the destruction of steam boilers by their explosion. Often the insured includes in this coverage indemnity against injuries to other property resulting from the explosion.

m. Title Insurance

This form of insurance is taken out by the purchaser of property for the purpose of protecting against loss or damage resulting from defects or failure of title to a particular parcel of realty or from the enforcement of liens existing against it at the time of the insurance.

n. Business Interruption Insurance

This is a worthwhile policy for the business man in view of the fact that it protects against loss of earnings due to a temporary interruption of business while the premises are being repaired after damage.

o. Other

There are many other important coverages such as water damage, sprinkler leakage, accounts receivable, health and accident, and owner, landlord and tenants liability insurance. Modern insurance practice has now eliminated the separate policy concept and has developed a "package" which combines many lines of coverage. Thus, under the umbrella of one policy the pharmacist can secure basic and optional coverages to meet specific requirements.

Special Provisions

Nearly all available insurance policies allow for the addition of "riders" or special provisions to permit additional protection at relatively small additional cost. For example, the following provisions are available with nearly all life insurance policies:

a. Waiver of Premium

If the insured becomes totally and permanently disabled, the premiums will be waived, however the policy will continue in full force.

b. Disability Income

This "rider" provides for a lifelong income in case of total and permanent disability in addition to the basic life insurance protection.

c. Accidental Death

Should the insured be accidentally killed, a policy carrying an "A.D. rider" (accidental death rider) would pay the stated beneficiary an extra amount of money. The total death payment is usually two or three times the face amount of the policy. This additional protection is referred to as "double or triple indemnity."

Dividends

In the strict sense, a dividend is a share allotted to each of several persons who are entitled to share in the division of profits or property. Thus, the so-called "dividend" paid by a life insurance company is not a true dividend but represents the refund of an excess payment of premiums over actual cost.

Mutual companies generally issue participating policies for which premium rates are intentionally set higher than the company's obligations are known to be. The extra premium is considered as a safety margin to protect against the possibility of an unusual increase in mortality or an unusual decline in investment income. If no such declines or losses occur, the company refunds part of the premium in the form of policy "dividends."

Stock companies generally issue non-participating policies on which premiums are calculated much closer to anticipated costs and therefore no dividends are paid. In this instance the stockholders bear the risk of unusual losses.

Policy dividends can never be guaranteed in advance and there is no assurance that any dividend would be paid if a company's mortality experience and investment earnings are not satisfactory. However, if a policy dividend is issued, the insured may use it to reduce premium payments, purchase small amounts of "paid-up" insurance, allow it to accumulate at interest or may collect it in cash.

Beneficiaries

A beneficiary is the individual(s) for whose benefit or protection the insurance is purchased. The insured has the right to name the beneficiary, however it behooves him to exercise due care both in the designation of the beneficiary and the choice of language in so designating him. This is of great importance in the handling of the estate of the deceased.

Husbands frequently name their wives, but there may be compelling reasons for naming another party. For example, if the estate is large enough to involve estate taxes, naming the spouse might result in double taxation of the proceeds—once at the husband's death and again at her death.

References

1. Uniform Partnership Act, Sec. 6 (1).

2. Massachusetts General Laws ch. 108A, Sec. 6.

3. Cardullo v. Landau, 105 N.E. 2nd 843.

4. Rosenblum v. Springfield Produce Brokerage Co., 137 N.E. 357.

5. Massachusetts General Laws ch. 108A, Sec. 7.

6. Massachusetts General Laws ch. 108A, Sec. 8.

7. Massachusetts General Laws ch. 108A, Sec. 9.

8. Massachusetts General Laws ch. 108A, Sec. 18.

9. Massachusetts General Laws ch. 108A, Sec. 29.

10. Massachusetts General Laws ch. 108A, Sec. 31.

11. Massachusetts General Laws ch. 108A, Sec. 32.

12. BLACK'S LAW DICTIONARY, 4th Ed., West Publishing Co., St. Paul, Minn.

13. G. HAROLD: CORPORATION FINANCE, 3rd Ed. Rev., Barnes & Noble, N.Y., 1956, p. 19.

14. *Supra,* p. 22.

15. F. BURTCHETT: CORPORATION FINANCE, Harper & Bros., N.Y., 1934, p. 905.

16. Massachusetts General Laws ch. 155, Sec. 51.

17. Samia v. Central Oil Co. of Worcester 339 Mass. 101.

18. Massachusetts General Laws ch. 15, Sec. 19, 20.

19. Massachusetts General Laws ch. 155, Sec. 56.

20. J. Smith and H. Ault: *The Corporate Professional—United States v. Empey,* MASS. LAW QUARTERLY, 54: 2: 14.

21. H. Ault: *Professional Corporations—Recent Developments,* MASS. LAW QUARTERLY, 54: 2L152.

22. T.I.R. 1019, 697 CCH 6807.

23. Cunningham v. C.R. Pease House Finishing Co., 74 N.H. 435, 69 A. 120.

24. Nash v. Minnesota Title Insurance & Trust Co., 163 Mass. 574, 40 N.E. 1039.

25. Toth v. Vazquez, 3 N.J. Super 379, 65 A 2nd 778.

26. Carter v. Yardley & Co. Ltd., 319 Mass. 92.

27. Boston Woven Hose & Rubber Co. v. Kendall, 178 Mass. 232.

28. Cooper v. R. J. Reynolds Co., 234 F. 2nd 170.

29. Greenman v. Yuba Power Products, Inc., 59 Cal. 2nd 67.

30. Flynn v. Growers Outlet, 307 Mass. 373.

31. The Deep Pocket Rule and the Jumping Warranty: Strict Product Liability of Manufacturers, 18 Food Drug Cosmetic, L. J. 654 (1963).

32. Gottsdanker v. Cutter Laboratories, 182 Cal. App. 2nd. 602.

CHAPTER 7

Administrative Law

Several authors have commented on the difficulty in describing and discussing the administrative process:

> The American administrative process is a figment of the imagination. No political theory has proposed it. No man has created it. It cannot be described, because it does not exist.
>
> . . . .
>
> The fact is, of course, that public administration exists in abundance. What does not exist is any integrated, coherent, unwavering element of government that can be identified as *the* administrative process. There are innumerable processes rather than one.
>
> . . . .
>
> The widespread tendency to discuss the administrative process in the singular, much as one discusses *the* legislature or *the* judiciary, has created the too easy assumption that all administrative agencies share the same vices, virtues and problems, and may therefore be lumped together for purposes of analysis, organization, and reform. Nothing could be less realistic.[1]

From the foregoing, it should now be clear to the reader that executive legislation is a complex, often unpublished, more frequently sought unsuccessfully by lawyers and citizens alike, body of law. Executive legislation consists primarily of those rules and regulations promulgated by agencies within the Executive Department, and represents that department's interpretation and interstitial extension of statutory law.[2] These regulations, when properly adopted, have the force and effect of law. In fact, they are every bit as binding on the citizenry as if they were enacted by the legislative branch of government. Many of these carry penal sanctions e.g., the alcoholic beverage laws and the public health laws. Other regulations carry penal sanctions insofar as they interpret statutes the violation of which carries a penalty. Examples here would include those regulations made by the Internal Revenue Service or State Tax Commission. Still another group of regulations—those of the Commissioner of Public Welfare—can substantially affect a person's access to the necessities of life.

Finally, those regulations that govern our daily activities should be considered. If one wishes to pursue certain professions or trades, he must qualify and be licensed to practice the same within certain rigid regulations. Anyone who operates a business, no matter how large or small must know of and comply with the regulations promulgated by the Department of Labor and Industries.

Administrative rules and regulations may be obtained from the agency involved; in most instances, however, the lack of funds prohibits their publication and dissemination. Although this situation is quite common at the state level, it is vastly different at the federal echelon. Here, the adoption of the Federal Register Act of 1934 resolved the problem by requiring each agency to publish its regulations in the *Federal Register*.*

The regulatory material appearing therein is keyed to the *Code of Federal Regulations,* which is published under fifty titles pursuant to Section 11 of the *Federal Register Act*, as amended (44 U.S.C. 1510). The *Code of Federal Regulations* is also sold by the Superintendent of Documents. There are no restrictions on the republication of material appearing in either of these two publications.

The following agencies generally appear in each issue of the *Federal Register*:

The President
Civil Aeronatics Board
Civil Service Commission
Commerce Department
Commodity Credit Corporation
Consumer and Marketing Service
Education Office
Engineers Corps
Federal Aviation Administration
Federal Crop Insurance Corporation
Federal Home Loan Bank Board
Federal Power Commission
Federal Trade Commission
Food and Drug Administration
Foreign Assets Control Office
General Services Administration
Geological Survey
Hazardous Materials Regulations Board
Internal Revenue Service
International Commerce Bureau
Interstate Commerce Commission
Maritime Administration
Public Health Service

*At present, this document is published daily, Tuesday through Saturday (no publication on Sundays, Mondays or on the day after an official federal holiday), by the Office of the Federal Register, National Archives and Records Service, General Services Administration whose offices are located in Washington, D.C. Distribution is made only by the Superintendent of Documents, U.S. Government Printing Office in Washington.

The *Federal Register* is furnished by mail to subscribers, free of postage, for $2.50 per month or $25.00 per year, payable in advance.

Small Business Administration
Smithsonian Institution
State Department

Because pharmacists, in the practice of their profession, will be subjected to the administrative regulations of federal and state agencies it is necessary for them to be familiar with the Federal Administrative Procedure Act and their respective State Administrative Procedure Act. Since it is not possible to devote all of the space necessary for the publication of the administrative procedure acts of the 50 states, the presentation of Model State Administrative Procedure Act (see page 98) will familiarize the student with the typical contents and thereby help him better to understand not only the rule making process but his rights to appeal and contest the regulations, decisions or orders.

FEDERAL ADMINISTRATIVE PROCEDURE ACT
(June 11, 1946.   60 Stat. 237, 5 U.S.C. §§ 1001–1011)

TITLE

Section 1.   This Act may be cited as the "Administrative Procedure Act".

DEFINITIONS

Sec. 2.   As used in this Act—

(a) **Agency.**—"Agency" means each authority (whether or not within or subject to review by another agency) of the Government of the United States other than Congress, the courts, or the governments of the possessions, Territories, or the District of Columbia. Nothing in this Act shall be construed to repeal delegations of authority as provided by law.   Except as to the requirements of section 3, there shall be excluded from the operation of this Act (1) agencies composed of representatives of the parties or of representatives of organizations of the parties to the disputes determined by them, (2) courts martial and military commissions, (3) military or naval authority exercised in the field in time of war or in occupied territory, or (4) functions which by law expire on the termination of present hostilities, within any fixed period thereafter, or before July 1, 1947, and the functions conferred by the following statutes: Selective Training and Service Act of 1940; Contract Settlement Act of 1944; Surplus Property Act of 1944; [Housing and Rent Act of 1947; Sugar Control Extension Act of 1947; Veterans' Emergency Housing Act of 1946].[1]

(b) **Person and party.**—"Person" includes individuals, partnerships, corporations, associations, or public or private organizations of any character other than agencies.   "Party" includes any person or agency named or admitted as a party, or properly seeking and entitled as of right to be admitted as a party, in any agency proceeding;

---

[1] The statutes listed in the brackets have been added to the APA by amendment. See also Commission on Organization of the Executive Branch of the Government, Task Force Report on Legal Services and Procedure 142–143 (1955).

but nothing herein shall be construed to prevent an agency from admitting any person or agency as a party for limited purposes.

(c) **Rule and rule making.**—"Rule" means the whole or any part of any agency statement of general or particular applicability and future effect designed to implement, interpret, or prescribe law or policy or to describe the organization, procedure, or practice requirements of any agency and includes the approval or prescription for the future of rates, wages, corporate or financial structures or reorganizations thereof, prices, facilities, appliances, services or allowances therefor, or of valuations, costs, or accounting, or practices bearing upon any of the foregoing. "Rule making" means agency process for the formulation, amendment, or repeal of a rule.

(d) **Order and adjudication.**—"Order" means the whole or any part of the final disposition (whether affirmative, negative, injunctive, or declaratory in form) of any agency in any matter other than rule making but including licensing. "Adjudication" means agency process for the formulation of an order.

(e) **License and licensing.**—"License" includes the whole or part of any agency permit, certificate, approval, registration, charter, membership, statutory exemption, or other form of permission. "Licensing" includes agency process respecting the grant, renewal, denial, revocation, suspension, annulment, withdrawal, limitation, amendment, modification, or conditioning of a license.

(f) **Sanction and relief.**—"Sanction" includes the whole or part of any agency (1) prohibition, requirement, limitation, or other condition affecting the freedom of any person; (2) withholding of relief; (3) imposition of any form of penalty or fine; (4) destruction, taking, seizure, or withholding of property; (5) assessment of damages, reimbursement, restitution, compensation, costs, charges, or fees; (6) requirement, revocation, or suspension of a license; or (7) taking of other compulsory or restrictive action. "Relief" includes the whole or part of any agency (1) grant of money, assistance, license, authority, exemption, exception, privilege, or remedy; (2) recognition of any claim, right, immunity, privilege, exemption, or exception; or (3) taking of any other action upon the application or petition of, and beneficial to, any person.

(g) **Agency proceeding and action.**—"Agency proceeding" means any agency process as defined in subsections (c), (d), and (e) of this section. "Agency action" includes the whole or part of every agency rule, order, license, sanction, relief, or the equivalent or denial thereof, or failure to act.

PUBLIC INFORMATION

Sec. 3. Except to the extent that there is involved (1) any function of the United States requiring secrecy in the public interest or (2) any matter relating solely to the internal management of an agency—

(a) **Rules.**—Every agency shall separately state and currently publish in the Federal Register (1) descriptions of its central and field organization including delegations by the agency of final authority and the established places at which, and methods whereby, the public may secure information or make submittals or requests; (2) statements of the general course and method by which its functions are channeled and determined, including the nature and requirements of all formal or informal procedures available as well as forms and instructions as to the scope and contents of all papers, reports, or examinations; and (3) substantive rules adopted as authorized by law and statements of general policy or interpretations formulated and adopted by the agency for the guidance of the public, but not rules addressed to and served upon named persons in accordance with law. No person shall in any manner be required to resort to organization or procedure not so published.

(b) **Opinions and orders.**—Every agency shall publish, or, in accordance with published rule, make available to public inspection all final opinions or orders in the adjudication of cases (except those required for good cause to be held confidential and not cited as precedents) and all rules.

(c) **Public records.**—Save as otherwise required by statute, matters of official record shall in accordance with published rule be made available to persons properly and directly concerned except information held confidential for good cause found.

RULE MAKING

Sec. 4. Except to the extent that there is involved (1) any military, naval, or foreign affairs function of the United States or (2) any matter relating to agency management or personnel or to public property, loans, grants, benefits, or contracts—

(a) **Notice.**—General notice of proposed rule making shall be published in the Federal Register (unless all persons subject thereto are named and either personally served or otherwise have actual notice thereof in accordance with law) and shall include (1) a statement of the time, place, and nature of public rule-making proceedings; (2) reference to the authority under which the rule is proposed; and (3) either the terms or substance of the proposed rule or a description of the subjects and issues involved. Except where notice or hearing is required by statute, this subsection shall not apply to interpretative rules, general statements of policy, rules of agency organization, procedure, or practice, or in any situation in which the agency for good cause finds (and incorporates the finding and a brief statement of the reasons therefor in the rules issued) that notice and public procedure thereon are impracticable, unnecessary, or contrary to the public interest.

(b) **Procedures.**—After notice required by this section, the agency shall afford interested persons an opportunity to participate in the rule making through submission of written data, views, or arguments with or without opportunity to present the same orally in any manner; and, after consideration of all relevant matter presented, the agency shall incorporate in any rules adopted a concise general statement of their basis and purpose. Where rules are required by statute to be made on the record after opportunity for an agency hearing, the requirements of sections 7 and 8 shall apply in place of the provisions of this subsection.

(c) **Effective dates.**—The required publication or service of any substantive rule (other than one granting or recognizing exemption or relieving restriction or interpretative rules and statements of policy) shall be made not less than thirty days prior to the effective date thereof except as otherwise provided by the agency upon good cause found and published with the rule.

(d) **Petitions.**—Every agency shall accord any interested person the right to petition for the issuance, amendment, or repeal of a rule.

ADJUDICATION

Sec. 5. In every case of adjudication required by statute to be determined on the record after opportunity for an agency hearing, except to the extent that there is involved (1) any matter subject to a subsequent trial of the law and the facts de novo in any court; (2) the selection or tenure of an officer or employee of the United States other than examiners appointed pursuant to section 11; (3) proceedings in which decisions rest solely on inspections, tests, or elections; (4) the conduct of military, naval, or foreign affairs functions; (5) cases in which an agency is acting as an agent for a court; and (6) the certification of employee representatives—

(a) **Notice.**—Persons entitled to notice of an agency hearing shall be timely informed of (1) the time, place, and nature thereof; (2) the legal authority and jurisdiction under which the hearing is to be held; and (3) the matters of fact and law asserted. In instances in which private persons are the moving parties, other parties to the proceeding shall give prompt notice of issues controverted in fact or law; and in other instances agencies may by rule require responsive pleading. In fixing the times and places for hearings, due regard shall be had for the convenience and necessity of the parties or their representatives.

(b) **Procedure.**—The agency shall afford all interested parties opportunity for (1) the submission and consideration of facts, arguments, offers of settlement, or proposals of adjustment where time, the nature of the proceeding, and the public interest permit, and (2) to the extent that the parties are unable so to determine any controversy by consent, hearing, and decision upon notice and in conformity with sections 7 and 8.

(c) **Separation of functions.**—The same officers who preside at the reception of evidence pursuant to section 7 shall make the recommended decision or initial decision required by section 8 except where such officers become unavailable to the agency. Save to the extent required for the disposition of ex parte matters as authorized by law, no such officer shall consult any person or party on any fact in issue unless upon notice and opportunity for all parties to participate; nor shall such officer be responsible to or subject to the supervision or direction of any officer, employee, or agent engaged in the performance of investigative or prosecuting functions for any agency. No officer, employee, or agent engaged in the performance of investigative or prosecuting functions for any agency in any case shall, in that or a factually related case, participate or advise in the decision, recommended decision, or agency review pursuant to section 8 except as witness or counsel in public proceedings. This subsection shall not apply in determining applications for initial licenses or to proceedings involving the validity or application of rates, facilities, or practices of public utilities or carriers; nor shall it be applicable in any manner to the agency or any member or members of the body comprising the agency.

(d) **Declaratory orders.**—The agency is authorized in its sound discretion, with like effect as in the case of other orders, to issue a declaratory order to terminate a controversy or remove uncertainty.

ANCILLARY MATTERS

Sec. 6. Except as otherwise provided in this Act—

(a) **Appearance.**—Any person compelled to appear in person before any agency or representative thereof shall be accorded the right to be accompanied, represented, and advised by counsel or, if permitted by the agency, by other qualified representative. Every party shall be accorded the right to appear in person or by or with counsel or other duly qualified representative in any agency proceeding. So far as the orderly conduct of public business permits, any interested person may appear before any agency or its responsible officers or employees for the presentation, adjustment, or determination of any issue, request, or controversy in any proceeding (interlocutory, summary, or otherwise) or in connection with any agency function. Every agency shall proceed with reasonable dispatch to conclude any matter presented to it except that due regard shall be had for the convenience and necessity of the parties or their representatives. Nothing herein shall be construed either to grant or to deny to any person who is not a lawyer the right to appear for or represent others before any agency or in any agency proceeding.

(b) **Investigations.**—No process, requirement of a report, inspection, or other investigative act or demand shall be issued, made, or enforced in any manner or for any purpose except as authorized by law. Every person compelled to submit data or evidence shall be entitled to retain or, on payment of lawfully prescribed costs, procure a copy or transcript thereof, except that in a nonpublic investigatory proceeding the witness may for good cause be limited to inspection of the official transcript of his testimony.

(c) **Subpenas.**—Agency subpenas authorized by law shall be issued to any party upon request and as may be required by rules of procedure, upon a statement or showing of general relevance and reasonable scope of the evidence sought. Upon contest the court shall sustain any such subpena or similar process or demand to the extent that it is found to be in accordance with law and, in any proceeding for enforcement, shall issue an order requiring the appearance of the witness or the production of the evidence or data within a reasonable time under penalty of punishment for contempt in case of contumacious failure to comply.

(d) **Denials.**—Prompt notice shall be given of the denial in whole or in part of any written application, petition, or other request of any interested person made in connection with any agency proceeding. Except in affirming a prior denial or where the denial is self-explanatory, such notice shall be accompanied by a simple statement of procedural or other grounds.

HEARINGS

Sec. 7. In hearings which section 4 or 5 requires to be conducted pursuant to this section—

(a) **Presiding officers.**—There shall preside at the taking of evidence (1) the agency, (2) one or more members of the body which comprises the agency, or (3) one or more examiners appointed as provided in this Act; but nothing in this Act shall be deemed to supersede the conduct of specified classes of proceedings in whole or part by or before boards or other officers specially provided for by or designated pursuant to statute. The functions of all presiding officers and of officers participating in decisions in conformity with section 8 shall be conducted in an impartial manner. Any such officer may at any time withdraw if he deems himself disqualified; and, upon the filing in good faith of a timely and sufficient affidavit of personal bias or disqualification of any such officer, the agency shall determine the matter as a part of the record and decision in the case.

(b) **Hearing powers.**—Officers presiding at hearings shall have authority, subject to the published rules of the agency and within its powers, to (1) administer oaths and affirmations, (2) issue subpenas authorized by law, (3) rule upon offers of proof and receive relevant evidence, (4) take or cause depositions to be taken whenever the ends of justice would be served thereby, (5) regulate the course of the hearing, (6) hold conferences for the settlement or simplification of the issues by consent of the parties, (7) dispose of procedural requests or similar matters, (8) make decisions or recommend decisions in conformity with section 8, and (9) take any other action authorized by agency rule consistent with this Act.

(c) **Evidence.**—Except as statutes otherwise provide, the proponent of a rule or order shall have the burden of proof. Any oral or documentary evidence may be received, but every agency shall as a matter of policy provide for the exclusion of irrelevant, immaterial, or unduly repetitious evidence and no sanction shall be imposed or rule or order be issued except upon consideration of the whole record or such portions thereof as may be cited by any party and as supported by and in accordance with the reliable, probative, and substantial evidence. Every party shall have the right to present his case or defense by oral or documentary evidence, to submit rebuttal evidence, and to conduct such cross-examination as may be required for a full and true disclosure of the facts. In rule making or determining claims for money or benefits or applications for initial licenses any agency may, where the interest of any party will not be prejudiced thereby, adopt procedures for the submission of all or part of the evidence in written form.

(d) **Record.**—The transcript of testimony and exhibits, together with all papers and requests filed in the proceeding, shall constitute the exclusive record for decision in accordance with section 8 and, upon payment of lawfully prescribed costs, shall be made available to the parties. Where any agency decision rests on official notice of a material fact not appearing in the evidence in the record, any party shall on timely request be afforded an opportunity to show the contrary.

DECISIONS

Sec. 8. In cases in which a hearing is required to be conducted in conformity with section 7—

(a) **Action by subcrdinates.**—In cases in which the agency has not presided at the reception of the evidence, the officer who presided (or, in cases not subject to subsection (c) of section 5, any other officer or officers qualified to preside at hearings pursuant to section 7) shall initially decide the case or the agency shall require (in specific cases or by general rule) the entire record to be certified to it for initial decision. Whenever such officers make the initial decision and in the absence of either an appeal to the agency or review upon motion of the agency within time provided by rule, such decision shall without further proceedings then become the decision of the agency. On appeal from or review of the initial decisions of such officers the agency shall, except as it may limit the issues upon notice or by rule, have all the powers which it would have in making the initial decision. Whenever the agency makes the initial decision without having presided at the reception of the evidence, such officers shall first recommend a decision except that in rule making or determining applications for initial licenses (1) in lieu thereof the agency may issue a tentative decision or any of its responsible officers may recommend a decision or (2) any such procedure may be omitted in any case in which the agency finds upon the record that due and timely execution of its function imperatively and unavoidably so requires.

(b) **Submittals and decisions.**—Prior to each recommended, initial, or tentative decision, or decision upon agency review of the decision of subordinate officers the parties shall be afforded a reasonable opportunity to submit for the consideration of the officers participating in such decisions (1) proposed findings and conclusions, or (2) exceptions to the decisions or recommended decisions of subordinate officers or to tentative agency decisions, and (3) supporting reasons for such exceptions or proposed findings or conclusions. The record shall show the ruling upon each such finding, conclusion, or exception presented. All decisions (including initial, recommended, or tentative decisions) shall become a part of the record and include a statement of (1) findings and conclusions, as well as the reasons or basis therefor, upon all the material issues of fact, law, or discretion presented on the record; and (2) the appropriate rule, order, sanction, relief, or denial thereof.

SANCTIONS AND POWERS

Sec. 9. In the exercise of any power or authority—

(a) **In general.**—No sanction shall be imposed or substantive rule or order be issued except within jurisdiction delegated to the agency and as authorized by law.

(b) **Licenses.**—In any case in which application is made for a license required by law the agency, with due regard to the rights or privileges of all the interested parties or adversely affected persons and with reasonable dispatch, shall set and complete any proceedings required to be conducted pursuant to sections 7 and 8 of this Act or other proceedings required by law and shall make its decision. Except in cases of willfulness or those in which public health, interest, or safety requires otherwise, no withdrawal, suspension, revocation, or annulment of any license shall be lawful unless, prior to the institution of agency proceedings therefor, facts or conduct which may warrant such action shall have been called to the attention of the licensee by the agency in writing and the licensee shall have been accorded opportunity to demonstrate or achieve compliance with all lawful requirements. In any case in which the licensee has, in accordance with agency rules, made timely and sufficient application for a renewal or a new license, no license with reference to any activity of a continuing nature shall expire until such application shall have been finally determined by the agency.

JUDICIAL REVIEW

Sec. 10. Except so far as (1) statutes preclude judicial review or (2) agency action is by law committed to agency discretion—

(a) **Right of review.**—Any person suffering legal wrong because of any agency action, or adversely affected or aggrieved by such action within the meaning of any relevant statute, shall be entitled to judicial review thereof.

(b) **Form and venue of action.**—The form of proceeding for judicial review shall be any special statutory review proceeding relevant to the subject matter in any court specified by statute or, in the absence or inadequacy thereof, any applicable form of legal action (including actions for declaratory judgments or writs of prohibitory or mandatory injunction or habeas corpus) in any court of competent jurisdiction. Agency action shall be subject to judicial review in civil or criminal proceedings for judicial enforcement except to the extent that prior, adequate, and exclusive opportunity for such review is provided by law.

(c) **Reviewable acts.**—Every agency action made reviewable by statute and every final agency action for which there is no other adequate remedy in any court shall be subject to judicial review. Any preliminary, procedural, or intermediate agency action or ruling not directly reviewable shall be subject to review upon the review of the final agency action. Except as otherwise expressly required by statute, agency action otherwise final shall be final for the purposes of this subsection whether or not there has been presented or determined any application for a declaratory order, for any form of reconsideration, or (unless the agency otherwise requires by rule and provides that the action meanwhile shall be inoperative) for an appeal to superior agency authority.

(d) **Interim relief.**—Pending judicial review any agency is authorized, where it finds that justice so requires, to postpone the effective date of any action taken by it. Upon such conditions as may be required and to the extent necessary to prevent irreparable injury, every reviewing court (including every court to which a case may be taken on appeal from or upon application for certiorari or other writ to a reviewing court) is authorized to issue all necessary and appropriate process to postpone the effective date of any agency action or to preserve status or rights pending conclusion of the review proceedings.

(e) **Scope of review.**—So far as necessary to decision and where presented the reviewing court shall decide all relevant questions of law, interpret constitutional and statutory provisions, and determine the meaning or applicability of the terms of any agency action. It shall (A) compel agency action unlawfully withheld or unreasonably delayed; and (B) hold unlawful and set aside agency action, findings, and conclusions found to be (1) arbitrary, capricious, an abuse of discretion, or otherwise not in accordance with law; (2) contrary to constitutional right, power, privilege, or immunity; (3) in excess of statutory jurisdiction, authority, or limitations, or short of statutory right; (4) without observance of procedure required by law; (5) unsupported by substantial evidence in any case subject to the requirements of sections 7 and 8 or otherwise reviewed on the record of an agency hearing provided by statute; or (6) unwarranted by the facts to the extent that the facts are subject to trial de novo by the reviewing court. In making the foregoing determinations the court shall review the whole record or such portions thereof as may be cited by any party, and due account shall be taken of the rule of prejudicial error.

EXAMINERS

Sec. 11. Subject to the civil-service and other laws to the extent not inconsistent with this Act, there shall be appointed by and for each agency as many qualified and competent examiners as may be necessary for proceedings pursuant to sections 7 and 8, who shall be assigned to cases in rotation so far as practicable and shall perform no duties inconsistent with their duties and responsibilities as examiners. Examiners shall be removable by the agency in which they are employed only for good cause established and determined by the Civil Service Commission (hereinafter called the Commission) after opportunity for hearing and upon the record thereof. Examiners shall receive compensation prescribed by the Commission independently of agency recommendations or ratings and in accordance with the Classification Act of 1923, as amended, except that the provisions of paragraphs (2) and (3) of subsection (b) of section 7 of said Act, as amended, and the provisions of section 9 of said Act, as amended, shall not be applicable. Agencies occasionally or temporarily insufficiently staffed may utilize examiners selected by the Commission from and with the consent of other agencies. For the purposes of this section, the Commission is authorized to make investigations, require reports by agencies, issue reports, including an annual report to the Congress, promulgate rules, appoint such advisory committees as may be deemed necessary, recommend legislation, subpena witnesses or records, and pay witness fees as established for the United States courts.

CONSTRUCTION AND EFFECT

Sec. 12. Nothing in this Act shall be held to diminish the constitutional rights of any person or to limit or repeal additional requirements imposed by statute or otherwise recognized by law. Except as otherwise required by law, all requirements or privileges relating to evidence or procedure shall apply equally to agencies and persons. If any provision of this Act or the application thereof is held invalid, the remainder of this Act or other applications of such provision shall not be affected. Every agency is granted all authority necessary to comply with the requirements of this Act through the issuance of rules or otherwise. No subsequent legislation shall be held to supersede or modify the provisions of this Act except to the extent that such legislation shall do so expressly. This Act shall take effect three months after its approval except that sections 7 and 8 shall take effect six months after such approval, the requirement of the selection of examiners pursuant to section 11 shall not become effective until one year after such approval, and no procedural requirement shall be mandatory as to any agency proceeding initiated prior to the effective date of such requirement.

State Act

Nearly thirty years ago the American Bar Association and the National Conference of Commissioners on Uniform State Laws began drafting legislation relating to state administrative rule making, adjudication and judicial review. The result was the Model State Administrative Procedure Act reprinted below.

Not all of the states have adopted the Model Act, however, it has probably exerted due influence upon those states which have drafted their own administrative procedure acts.

MODEL STATE ADMINISTRATIVE PROCEDURE ACT

An Act Concerning Procedure of State Administrative Agencies and Review of Their Determinations

Section 1. (Definitions.)

For the purpose of this Act:

(1) "Agency" means any state [board, commission, department, or officer], authorized by law to make rules or to adjudicate contested cases, except those in the legislative or judicial branches, and except . . . [here insert the names of any agencies such as the parole boards of certain states, which, though authorized to hold hearings, exercise purely discretionary functions].

(2) "Rule" includes every regulation, standard, or statement of policy or interpretation of general application and future effect, including the amendment or repeal thereof, adopted by an agency, whether with or without prior hearing, to implement or make specific the law enforced or administered by it or to govern its organization or procedure, but does not include regulations concerning only the internal management of the agency and not directly affecting the rights of or procedures available to the public.

(3) "Contested case" means a proceeding before an agency in which the legal rights, duties, or privileges of specific parties are required by law or constitutional right to be determined after an agency hearing.

Section 2. (Adoption of Rules.)

In addition to other rule-making requirements imposed by law:

(1) Each agency shall adopt rules governing the formal and informal procedures prescribed or authorized by this act. Such rules shall include rules of practice before the agency, together with forms and instructions.

(2) To assist interested persons dealing with it, each agency shall so far as deemed practicable supplement its rules with descriptive statements of its procedures.

(3) Prior to the adoption of any rule authorized by law, or the amendment or repeal thereof, the adopting agency shall so far as practicable, publish or otherwise circulate notice of its intended action and afford interested persons opportunity to submit data or views orally or in writing.

Section 3. (Filing and Taking Effect of Rules.)

(1) Each agency shall file forthwith in the office of the [Secretary of State] a certified copy of each rule adopted by it, including all rules now in effect. The [Secretary of State] shall keep a permanent register of such rules open to public inspection.

(2) Each rule hereafter adopted shall become effective upon filing, unless a later date is required by statute or specified in the rule.

Section 4. (Publication of Rules.)

(1) The [Secretary of State] shall, as soon as practicable after the effective date of this act, compile, index, and publish all rules adopted by each agency and remaining in effect. Compilations shall be supplemented or revised as often as necessary [and at least once every two years].

(2) The [Secretary of State] shall publish a [monthly] bulletin in which he shall set forth the text of all rules filed during the preceding [month], excluding rules in effect upon the adoption of this act.

(3) The [Secretary] may in his discretion omit from the bulletin or the compilation rules the publication of which would be unduly cumbersome, expensive or otherwise inexpedient, if such rules are made available in printed or processed form on application to the adopting agency, and if the bulletin or compilation contains a notice stating the general subject matter of the rules so omitted and stating how copies thereof may be obtained.

(4) Bulletins and compilations shall be made available upon request to [officials of this state] free of charge, and to other persons at a price fixed by the [Secretary of State] to cover publication and mailing costs.

Section 5. (Petition for Adoption of Rules.)

Any interested person may petition an agency requesting the promulgation, amendment, or repeal of any rule. Each agency shall prescribe by rule the form for such petitions and the procedure for their submission, consideration, and disposition.

Section 6. (Declaratory Judgment on Validity of Rules.)

(1) The validity of any rule may be determined upon petition for a declaratory judgment thereon addressed to the [District Court] of . . . County, when it appears that the rule, or its threatened application, interferes with or impairs, or threatens to interfere with or impair, the legal rights or privileges of the petitioner. The agency shall be made a party to the proceeding. The declaratory judgment may be rendered whether or not the petitioner has first requested the agency to pass upon the validity of the rule in question.

(2) The court shall declare the rule invalid if it finds that it violates constitutional provisions or exceeds the statutory authority of the agency or was adopted without compliance with statutory rule-making procedures.

Section 7. (Petition for Declaratory Rulings by Agencies.)

On petition of any interested person, any agency may issue a declaratory ruling with respect to the applicability to any person, property, or state of facts of any rule or statute enforceable by it. A declaratory ruling, if issued after argument and stated to be binding, is binding between the agency and the petitioner on the state of facts alleged, unless it is altered or set aside by a court. Such a ruling is subject to review in the [District Court] in the manner hereinafter provided for the review of decisions in contested cases. Each agency shall prescribe by rule the form for such petitions and the procedure for their submission, consideration, and disposition.

Section 8. (Contested Cases; Notice, Hearing, Records.)

In any contested case all parties shall be afforded an opportunity for hearing after reasonable notice. The notice shall state the time, place, and issues involved, but if, by reason of the nature of the proceeding, the issues cannot be fully stated in advance of the hearing, or if subsequent amendment of the issues is necessary, they shall be fully stated as soon as practicable, and opportunity shall be afforded all parties to present evidence and argument with respect thereto. The agency shall prepare an official record, which shall include testimony and exhibits, in each contested case, but it shall not be necessary to transcribe shorthand notes unless requested for purposes of rehearing or court review. Informal disposition may also be made of any contested case by stipulation, agreed settlement, consent order, or default. Each agency shall adopt appropriate rules of procedure for notice and hearing in contested cases.

Section 9. (Rules of Evidence: Official Notice.)

In contested cases:

(1) Agencies may admit and give probative effect to evidence which possesses probative value commonly accepted by reasonably prudent men in the conduct of their affairs. They shall give effect to the rules of privilege recognized by law. They may exclude incompetent, irrelevant, immaterial, and unduly repetitious evidence.

(2) All evidence, including records and documents in the possession of the agency of which it desires to avail itself, shall be offered and made a part of the record in the case, and no other factual information or evidence shall be considered in the determination of the case. Documentary evidence may be received in the form of copies or excerpts, or by incorporation by reference.

(3) Every party shall have the right of cross-examination of witnesses who testify, and shall have the right to submit rebuttal evidence.

(4) Agencies may take notice of judicially cognizable facts and in addition may take notice of general, technical, or scientific facts within their specialized knowledge. Parties shall be notified either before or during hearing, or by reference in preliminary reports or otherwise, of the material so noticed, and they shall be afforded an

opportunity to contest the facts so noticed. Agencies may utilize their experience, technical competence, and specialized knowledge in the evaluation of the evidence presented to them.

Section 10. (Examination of Evidence by Agency.)

Whenever in a contested case a majority of the officials of the agency who are to render the final decision have not heard or read the evidence, the decision, if adverse to a party to the proceeding other than the agency itself, shall not be made until a proposal for decision, including findings of fact and conclusions of law, has been served upon the parties, and an opportunity has been afforded to each party adversely affected to file exceptions and present argument to a majority of the officials who are to render the decision, who shall personally consider the whole record or such portions thereof as may be cited by the parties. [This section shall not apply to the following agencies . . .].

Section 11. (Decisions and Orders.)

Every decision and order adverse to a party to the proceeding, rendered by an agency in a contested case, shall be in writing or stated in the record and shall be accompanied by findings of fact and conclusions of law. The findings of fact shall consist of a concise statement of the conclusions upon each contested issue of fact. Parties to the proceeding shall be notified of the decision and order in person or by mail. A copy of the decision and order and accompanying findings and conclusions shall be delivered or mailed upon request to each party or to his attorney of record.

Section 12. (Judicial Review of Contested Cases.)

(1) Any person aggrieved by a final decision in a contested case, whether such decision is affirmative or negative in form, is entitled to judicial review thereof under this act [but nothing in this section shall be deemed to prevent resort to other means of review, redress, relief or trial de novo, provided by law].

(2) Proceedings for review shall be instituted by filing a petition in the [District Court] within [thirty] days after the service of the final decision of the agency. Copies of the petition shall be served upon the agency and all other parties of record. [In the manner provided by . . .]. The court, in its discretion, may permit other interested persons to intervene.

(3) The filing of the petition shall not stay enforcement of the agency decision; but the agency may do so, or the reviewing court may order a stay upon such terms as it deems proper.

(4) Within [thirty] days after service of the petition, or within such further time as the court may allow, the agency shall transmit to the reviewing court the original or a certified copy of the entire

record of the proceeding under review; but, by stipulation of all parties to the review proceeding, the record may be shortened. Any party unreasonably refusing to stipulate to limit the record may be taxed by the court for the additional costs. The court may require or permit subsequent corrections or additions to the record when deemed desirable.

(5) If, before the date set for hearing, application is made to the court for leave to present additional evidence on the issues in the case, and it is shown to the satisfaction of the court that the additional evidence is material and that there were good reasons for failure to present it in the proceeding before the agency, the court may order that the additional evidence be taken before the agency upon such conditions as the court deems proper. The agency may modify its findings and decision by reason of the additional evidence and shall file with the reviewing court, to become a part of the record, the additional evidence, together with any modifications or new findings or decision.

(6) The review shall be conducted by the court without a jury and shall be confined to the record, except that in cases of alleged irregularities in procedure before the agency, not shown in the record, testimony thereon may be taken in the court. The court shall, upon request, hear oral argument and receive written briefs.

(7) The court may affirm the decision of the agency or remand the case for further proceedings; or it may reverse or modify the decision if the substantial rights of the petitioners may have been prejudiced because the administrative findings, inferences, conclusions, or decisions are:

(a) in violation of constitutional provisions; or

(b) in excess of the statutory authority or jurisdiction of the agency; or

(c) made upon unlawful procedure; or

(d) affected by other error of law; or

(e) unsupported by competent, material, and substantial evidence in view of the entire record as submitted; or

(f) arbitrary or capricious.

[Section 13. (Appeals.)

An aggrieved party may secure a review of any final judgment of the [District Court] under this act by appeal to the [Supreme Court]. Such appeal shall be taken in the manner provided by law for appeals from the [District Court] in other civil cases.]

[Section 14. (Constitutionality.)

If any provision of this act or the application thereof to any person or circumstance is held invalid, such invalidity shall not affect other provisions or applications of the act which can be given effect without the invalid provision or application, and to this end the provisions of this act are declared to be severable.]

Section 15.   (Repeal.)

All acts or parts of acts which are inconsistent with the provisions of this act are hereby repealed, but such repeal shall not affect pending proceedings.

Section 16.   (Time of Taking Effect.)

This act shall take effect . . .

Application of the Model Act Principles

In an earlier chapter, it was noted that American law is divided into two forms—case law and legislation. In this instance, our main interest lies in the application of legislation towards the creation of a board with authority to issue its own rules and regulations. For example, the legislatures of the various states have enacted legislation which manifests control over the profession of pharmacy. The power to control the profession is vested in a Board of Registration in Pharmacy. Subsequently, the Board in carrying out its mission finds it necessary to write various rules and regulations which govern the conduct of the practice of profession as well as the practitioner.

This sequence is best demonstrated by referring to typical existing legislation followed by the rules and regulations. Accordingly, the following legislation is excerpted from Massachusetts General Laws Chapter 112; the rules and regulations represent a small segment of the regulatory mandates of the Massachusetts Board of Registration in Pharmacy which are not atypical of those enacted in other states.

AN ENACTMENT OF A LEGISLATIVE BODY
REGISTRATION OF PHARMACISTS

§ **24.** **Registration of pharmacists; examination; fees.** A person who desires to do business as a pharmacist shall, upon payment of ten dollars to the board of registration in pharmacy, herein and in sections twenty-five to forty-two, inclusive, called the board, be entitled to examination; provided, that he shall have been graduated from a school or college of pharmacy approved by the board. If any such person is found qualified on examination, he shall be registered as a pharmacist, and shall receive a certificate signed by the president and secretary of the board. Any person failing to pass such examination shall upon request be re-examined, after the expiration of three months, at any regular meeting of the board, upon payment of ten dollars. The board may grant certificates of registration as assistants after examination upon the terms above named, and such certificates shall entitle the holder thereof to all the privileges of a registered pharmacist during the temporary absence of the latter, which absence shall be not more than six hours in any one period of twenty-four consecutive hours; provided, that, upon application to the board, such an assistant may be permitted to exercise the privileges of a registered pharmacist for such further period as the board shall determine. No such certificate as assistant shall allow the holder thereof to engage in the drug business on his own account or as a manager to conduct a pharmacy or drug store. The board may grant certificates of registration to such persons as shall furnish with their applications satisfactory proof that they have been registered by examination in some other state; provided, that such other state shall require a degree of competency equal to that required of applicants in this commonwealth. Every such applicant for registration as a registered pharmacist shall pay to the secretary of the board twenty-five dollars at the time of filing his application. No such certificate shall be granted until the person applying therefor shall have signified his intention of acting under the same in this commonwealth. No certificate shall be granted under this section unless the applicant shall have submitted evidence satisfactory to the board that he is a citizen of the United States; provided, however, that an alien may be examined by the board if he first offers evidence which is satisfactory to said board that he has filed his declaration of intention to become a citizen of the United States, and a certificate may be granted if he passes such examination. In case such applicant is subsequently registered, his certificate of registration shall be revoked and his registration cancelled, unless he shall present to the board, within five years following the issuance of said certificate, his naturalization papers showing that he is a citizen of the United States. As amended St.1932, c. 227; St.1933, c. 126; St.1937, c. 343, § 1; St.1941, c. 52, § 1; St.1945, c. 502, § 1; St.1952, c. 585, § 23; St.1957, c. 463.

§ **24A.** **Records; expiration of registrations; renewals; reinstatement; fees.** The board shall keep an official record of the names of all registered pharmacists and registered assistant pharmacists. All registrations of registered pharmacists and registered assistant pharmacists shall expire on December thirty-first of each even-numbered year. Any holder of a certificate of registration as a pharmacist or assistant pharmacist issued under section twenty-four and remaining uncancelled shall be entitled to have such certificate biennially renewed by registration by the board, upon the payment of a biennial renewal fee of five dollars. On the first day of November of each even-numbered year the board shall send written notice to this effect to every registered pharmacist and every registered assistant pharmacist, and shall enclose with each notice a proper blank for such registration. If said blank properly filled out, together with said fee of five dollars, shall not on or before the thirty-first day of December of such even-numbered year be received by said board from any pharmacist or assistant pharmacist so notified, said board shall strike from the register the name of such pharmacist or assistant pharmacist; provided, that at any time thereafter, any pharmacist or assistant pharmacist whose name shall have been so removed from the register may, upon submission to the board of proof satisfactory to it of his moral and physical fitness, have his name restored by it upon the payment to it of all accrued biennial renewal fees, together with a reinstatement fee of five dollars. Added St.1945, c. 502, § 3, as amended St.1955, c. 429; St.1956, c. 575.

§ **24B.** **Standards for schools of pharmacy; certificates of approval; courses.** The board and the commissioner of education shall forthwith establish standards to be met by schools or colleges of pharmacy and when, in the opinion of the board and the commissioner, such standards have been met by any school or college of pharmacy, a certificate of approval shall be awarded to such approved school or college of pharmacy; provided, that if at any time such approved school or college of pharmacy has, in the opinion of the board and said commissioner, lowered its standards below that established by the board and said commissioner, such certificate, after notice and hearing, may be revoked by the board and said commissioner. No person, school or college of pharmacy or other institution of learning shall establish, conduct or offer any course in pharmacy for residents or non-residents of the commonwealth unless and until such course meets the standards established by the board and said commissioner under authority of this section. Whoever violates any provision of this section shall be punished by a fine of not less than one hundred nor more than one thousand dollars, or by imprisonment for not more than one year, or both. Added St.1946, c. 194, as amended St.1947, c. 503.

§ **25.** **Records; annual reports.** The board shall keep a record of the names of all persons examined and registered by it, of all persons to whom permits are issued under section thirty-nine, and of all money received and disbursed by it, and a duplicate thereof shall be open to public inspection in the office of the state secretary. The board shall make an annual report of the condition of pharmacy in the commonwealth.

§ **26.** **Display of certificate.** Every person receiving a certificate of registration from the board shall conspicuously display the same in his place of business.

§ **27.** **Complaint; notice; hearing.** The board shall hear all complaints made to it against any person registered as a pharmacist charging him in his business as a pharmacist with violating any of the rules or regulations of the board or any laws of the commonwealth, and especially the laws relating to the sale of alcoholic beverages, as defined in section one of chapter one hundred and thirty-eight, and alcohol; or with engaging with, or aiding or abetting, another in the violation of said rules, regulations or laws; or, if he himself is not the owner and actively engaged in such business, with suffering or permitting the use of his name or certificate of registration by others in the conduct of the business of pharmacy. Such complaint shall set out the offence alleged and be made within fifteen days after the date of the act complained of, or within thirty days after a conviction by a court of competent jurisdiction. The board shall notify the person complained against of the charge against him and of the time and place of the hearing at which he may appear with his witnesses and be heard by counsel. It may summon witnesses and compel their attendance at said hearings. Witnesses shall testify on oath and may be sworn by a member of the board. Three members of the board shall be a quorum for any such hearing. As amended St.1934, c. 328, § 2; St.1937, c. 343, § 2.

§ **28.** **Decision of board of registration in pharmacy; effect.** If the full board sitting at such hearing finds the person guilty, the board may suspend the effect of his certificate of registration as a pharmacist for such term as it fixes. The board may at any time reconsider its action in cases where it has suspended or revoked the license or certificate of registration of a pharmacist, and may change its determination as justice shall require.

§ **29.** **Suspension of certificate of registration.** It may, by a majority vote of all its members, after hearing, suspend the certificate of registration of a registered pharmacist, who, in its judgment, is a menace to the public by reason of the improper use of intoxicating liquor or drugs.

§ **30.** **Unlawful sale of drugs, medicines, chemicals or poisons.** Except as provided in section sixty-five, whoever, not being registered under section twenty-four or corresponding provisions of earlier laws, sells or offers for sale at retail, compounds for sale or dispenses for medicinal purposes drugs, medicines, chemicals or poisons, except as provided in sections thirty-five and thirty-six, shall be punished by a fine of not more than fifty dollars. This section shall not prohibit the employment of apprentices or assistants and the sale by them of any drugs, medicines, chemicals or poisons, provided a registered pharmacist is in charge of the store and present therein or an assistant is in charge thereof during the temporary absence of the registered pharmacist, or as otherwise permitted by the board, as provided for in section twenty-four; nor shall it apply to any unregistered co-partner or unregistered stockholder in a corporation doing a retail drug business who was actively engaged in the drug business on May twenty-eighth, nineteen hundred and thirteen. As amended St.1937, c. 343, § 3.

§ **31.** **Marking of signs advertising place of business and labels for medicinal preparations.** Every registered pharmacist carrying on the drug business as proprietor or manager shall cause his name to appear on every sign indicating or advertising his place of business and on every label used for medicinal preparations compounded in his place of business.

§ **32.** **Investigation of complaints.** The board shall investigate all complaints of the violation of any provision of sections twenty-four to forty-two, inclusive, or of section sixty-five, so far as it relates to pharmacy, and report the same to the proper prosecuting officers, and especially investigate and cause to be prosecuted all violations of sections twenty-nine to thirty G, inclusive, of chapter one hundred and thirty-eight. As amended St.1934, c. 328, § 3.

§ **33.** **Access to documents.** A registered pharmacist against whom a complaint or charge is pending before the board, or his counsel, shall have the same right of access to documents in the possession of said board as a person charged with crime in the courts of the commonwealth would have to documents in the possession of the clerk of the court or the prosecuting officer.

§ **34.** **Certificate of conviction of pharmacist; notification of board.** The court or magistrate before whom a person is convicted of a violation of section thirty of this chapter, or of any provision of sections twenty-nine to thirty F, inclusive, of chapter one hundred and thirty-eight relating to the retention, filing or inspection of prescriptions, or of section two of chapter two hundred and seventy shall send to the board a certificate under seal showing the time, cause and place of conviction. As amended St.1934 c. 328, § 4.

§ 35. **Application of laws to physicians who dispense medicines to their patients.** Sections thirty and thirty-six A to forty-one, inclusive, of this chapter, sections twenty-nine to thirty G, inclusive, of chapter one hundred and thirty-eight and section two of chapter two hundred and seventy shall not apply to physicians who put up their own prescriptions or dispense medicines to their patients; nor to the manufacture of patent and proprietary medicines, nor to the sale of such medicines other than the sale of those intended for internal use which are hypnotics or which contain barbituric acid or its derivatives and other than the sale of such medicines which are exclusively prepared for hypodermic use in the human system; nor to the manufacture or sale of the following drugs and chemicals used in the arts, or as household remedies: alum, ammonia, bicarbonate of soda, borax, camphor, castor oil, chlorinated lime, citric acid, cod liver oil, copperas, cotton seed oil, cream of tartar, dyestuffs, Epsom salt, flaxseed, flaxseed meal, gelatine, ginger, Glauber's salt, glycerine, gum arabic, gum tragacanth, hops, hyposulphite of soda, licorice, lime water, linseed oil, litharge, magnesia, olive oil, peroxide of hydrogen, petrolatum, phosphate of soda, rhubarb, Rochelle salt, rosin, sal ammoniac, salt-peter, senna, slippery elm bark, spices for seasoning, sugar of milk, sulphate of copper, sulphur, tartaric acid, turpentine, extract of witch hazel and zinc oxide; nor to the sale in the original packages of the following, if put up by registered pharmacists, manufacturers or wholesale dealers in conformity with law: flavoring essences or extracts, essence of Jamaica ginger, insecticides, rat exterminators, aromatic spirits of ammonia, spirits of camphor, sweet spirits of niter, syrup of rhubarb, tincture of arnica and tincture of rhubarb; nor to the sale of the following poisons used in the arts, if properly labelled and recorded as provided by section two of chapter two hundred and seventy: muriatic acid, oxalic acid, nitric acid, sulphuric acid, arsenic, cyanide of potassium, mercury, phosphorus and sulphate of zinc. As amended St.1934, c. 328, § 5; St.1935, c. 306; St.1937, c. 343, § 4; St.1948, c. 539, § 1.

§ 36. **Continuance of business of deceased or incapacitated registered pharmacists.** The widow, executor or administrator of a registered pharmacist who has died or the wife of one who has become incapacitated may continue his business under a registered pharmacist, who may also be considered qualified to receive a certificate of fitness under section thirty of chapter one hundred and thirty-eight authorizing him to exercise upon the premises of said deceased or incapacitated pharmacist the rights conferred by section twenty-nine of said chapter upon holders of said certificates; provided, that the registered pharmacist under whom the business is continued is in charge of the premises and present therein. As amended St.1934, c. 328, § 6.

§ 36A. **Licensing of sale, distribution and delivery of drugs or medicines.** Except as otherwise provided in section thirty-five, no person shall engage in the sale, distribution or delivery, at wholesale, of drugs or medicines within the commonwealth without a license so to do.   Added St.1948, c. 539, § 2.

§ **36B.**   **Licenses; fees; renewals.** The board shall upon application and the payment of an annual license fee of ten dollars issue licenses required by section thirty-six A; provided, that no such license shall be issued to any applicant unless the board is satisfied that he or it is actually engaged in and is carrying on such wholesale business. Such license shall be renewed on or before December first of each year upon the payment of a license fee of ten dollars. Added St.1948, c. 539, § 2.

§ **36C.**   **Use of words "wholesale druggist"; inspection and investigation of wholesale dealers; reports of violations; complaints.** No person shall use the words "wholesale druggist" or any other words of similar import, holding himself or itself out to be engaged in the sale, distribution or delivery of drugs or medicines, at wholesale, without first having been licensed as provided in sections thirty-six A and thirty-six B. The agents of the board shall have authority. during business hours, to inspect and investigate all wholesale dealers in drugs or medicines, and shall report all violations of sections thirty-six A to thirty-six D, inclusive, to the board, upon the direction of which such agents shall apply for criminal complaints against persons guilty of any such violations. Added St.1948, c. 539, § 2.

§ **36D.**   **Penalties.** Whoever, not being licensed as provided in sections thirty-six A and thirty-six B, engages in the sale, distribution or delivery, at wholesale, of drugs or medicines, or uses the words "wholesale druggist" or any other words of similar import in connection with his business to indicate the sale, distribution or delivery of such commodities, at wholesale, or whoever sells, distributes or delivers such commodities at retail, and holds himself out to be a wholesale druggist by using the words, "wholesale druggist" or words of similar import in connection with his business, or in advertising the same, shall be punished by a fine of not more than one thousand dollars or by imprisonment in a jail or house of correction for not less than thirty days nor more than one year, or both. Added St.1948, c. 539, § 2.

§ **37.**   **Drug business; definition.** "Drug business", as used in the two following sections, shall mean the sale, or the keeping or exposing for sale of drugs, medicines, chemicals or poisons, except as otherwise provided in section thirty-five, also the sale or the keeping or exposing for sale of opium, morphine, heroin, codeine or other narcotics, or any salt or compound thereof, or any preparation containing the same. or cocaine, alpha or beta eucaine, or any synthetic substitute therefor, or any salt or compound thereof, or any preparation containing the same, and the said term shall also mean the compounding and dispensing of physicians' prescriptions.

§ **38.** **Transaction of retail drug business; registration; permit; display of permit.** No store shall be kept open for the transaction of the retail drug business, or be advertised or represented as transacting such business, by means of any sign or advertisement containing the words "drug store", "pharmacy", "apothecary", "drug", "drugs", "medicine shop", or any combination of such words, or otherwise, unless it is registered with, and a permit therefor has been issued by, the board, as provided in the following section; provided, that said words, or any of them, may, with the written permission of the board, be used with respect to a store not registered with, and not having a permit issued by, the board as aforesaid, if in the town, or voting precinct thereof, where such store is located there is no store so registered and having such a permit. The permit shall be displayed in a conspicuous place in the store for which it is issued. The word "town", as used in this section, shall not include city. As amended St.1934, c. 236.

§ **39.** **Registration; permits; fees.** The board may, upon application made in such manner and form as it shall determine, register a store for the transaction of the retail drug business and issue to such person as it deems qualified to conduct such store, a permit to keep it open; but no such registration shall be made or permit issued in the case of a corporation unless it shall appear to the satisfaction of the board that the management of the drug business in such store is in the hands of a registered pharmacist. Such permit shall expire on January first following the date of its issue, and the fee therefor shall be ten dollars. As amended St.1939, c. 138; St.1951, c. 410; St.1953, c. 281.

§ **40.** **Suspension or revocation of registration and permit; notice; hearing.** The board may suspend or revoke any registration made under the preceding section and any permit issued thereunder for any violation of the law pertaining to the drug business or the sale of alcoholic beverages, as defined in section one of chapter one hundred and thirty-eight, or for any violation of the rules and regulations established by the board, or for aiding or abetting in a violation of any such law, rules or regulations; but before such suspension or revocation the board shall give a hearing to the holder of the permit, after due notice to him of the charges against him and of the time and place of the hearing. Such holder may appear at the hearing with witnesses and be heard by counsel. Witnesses shall testify on oath and any member of the board may administer oaths to them. The board may require the attendance of persons and compel the production of books and documents. Three members of the board shall be a quorum for such a hearing, but no registration or permit shall be suspended or revoked unless upon the affirmative vote of three or more members thereof. As amended St.1934, c. 328, § 6A; St.1937, c. 343 § 5.

§ **41.** **Penalty.** Whoever violates any provision of section thirty-eight shall be punished by a fine of not less than five nor more than one hundred dollars or by imprisonment for not more than one month, or both.

§ **42.** **Authorization of expenditures.** For the purpose of carrying out the five preceding sections, the board may expend annually a sum not exceeding one thousand dollars.

§ **42A.** **Rules and regulations of board.** The board may make such rules and regulations as it deems necessary to enable it to properly enforce the provisions of law relating to the retail drug business and pharmacy, and regarding any other matter within its jurisdiction; provided, that nothing herein shall authorize the board to make a rule or regulation requiring, as a prerequisite to the examination of an applicant under section twenty-four, or to his qualification, that he be the holder of a degree. Added St.1937, c. 343, § 6.

RULES AND REGULATIONS OF AN ADMINISTRATIVE BODY

Rule 49. CODE OF PROFESSIONAL CONDUCT OF PHARMACY (Adopted September 29, 1961) The following rules and regulations of professional conduct are adopted by the Massachusetts Board of Registration in Pharmacy, as authorized by Section 42A, of Chapter 112 of the General Laws of the Commonwealth, as amended by Chapter 634 of the Acts of 1960, in order to insure that the public receive the best possible pharmaceutical services and the public health be protected:

Item 1. The registered pharmacist shall at all times conduct his profession in conformity with Federal, State, and Municipal laws, ordinances and regulations, and the rules and regulations of the State Board of Registration in Pharmacy.

Item 2. A registered pharmacist must be on duty at all times when the pharmacy is open for business.

Item 3. The registered pharmacist shall uphold the legal standards of the U.S.P. and N.F.

Item 4. The registered pharmacist shall not substitute any other product in place of brand-named drugs prescribed, unless approval is obtained from the prescriber at the time of dispensing.

Item 5. The registered pharmacist or pharmacy, shall not accept for return any medication already dispensed in good faith, since the medication may have been exposed to possible and uncontrolled contamination or adulteration.

Item 6. A registered pharmacist or pharmacy shall refrain from advertising in any form or in any media, the dispensing or promoting of the sale of narcotics or exempt narcotic preparations in any form.

Item 7. The registered pharmacist charged with the management of the pharmacy shall keep his pharmacy clean, orderly and sanitary.

Item 8. The registered pharmacist charged with the management of the pharmacy shall be responsible for the proper storage and preservation of all drugs in his pharmacy, including proper refrigeration of all drugs requiring the same.

Item 9. A registered pharmacist or a pharmacy shall not advertise nor make claim to, in any way, professional superiority in the filling of prescriptions or in the sale of drug or medicinal preparations, nor shall such pharmacist or pharmacy advertise, in any way, his or its professional services in a manner which may undermine public confidence in the ability, character and integrity of other practitioners of pharmacy or claim a superior capacity to supply all the drug needs of their individual communities.

Item 10. A registered pharmacist or a pharmacy shall not supply or divert drugs, biologicals, medicines, substances or devices, legally sold in licensed pharmacies, by which unqualified persons can circumvent the statutes or rules and regulations pertaining to the legal sale of such articles.

Item 11. A registered pharmacist or a pharmacy shall not make publication or circulation of any statement of a character tending to deceive, misrepresent or mislead the public.

Item 12. A registered pharmacist or a pharmacy shall not enter into an agreement or arrangement with a physician, dentist, podiatrist, veterinarian, administrator or owner of a convalescent home or hospital, for the compounding or dispensing of secret formula or coded prescriptions.

Item 13. A registered pharmacist or a pharmacy shall not split fees for professional services with any physician, dentist, podiatrist, veterinarian, administrator, owner of a convalescent home or hospital, or employees thereof.

Item 14. A registered pharmacist shall not aid or abet a person not licensed or authorized to practice pharmacy in this state, to so practice.

Item 15. A registered pharmacist shall not perform, be a party to, or an accessory to any fraudulent or deceitful practice or transaction in pharmacy or the retail drug business.

Item 16. The registered pharmacist or a pharmacy shall not advertise or promote in any way, or through any media, either by trade-name or by generic name, articles or medical preparations for sale or for the compounding, filling or refilling of prescriptions which contain harmful, dangerous or so-called legend drugs or preparations and thereby create the unsafe and possible harmful and dangerous effect upon the public and by such advertising and promotion encourage the sale or unnecessary or unneeded use of such articles or medical preparations by the public. Such advertising or promotion is considered a fraud upon and deceit of the public and is therefore, unethical and an act of malpractice, because a practitioner's prescription is required before such drugs may be acquired by the public.

Item 17. The registered pharmacist or pharmacy shall not enter into any plan, agreement or arrangement with a prescriber, whereby gifts, merchandise, rebates or any other articles are given to the prescriber in order to induce directly or indirectly the prescriber to advise, suggest, advertise or counsel the use or patronage of such pharmacy and thereby to discourage the right of free choice by the prescriber's patients.

Item 18. The registered pharmacist or pharmacy shall not buy, sell, use or distribute substandard or counterfeit drugs or drugs acquired in any way, from a manufacturer or wholesaler unlicensed by law to do or transact business within or without the Commonwealth.

Item 19. The registered pharmacist or pharmacy shall not sell drugs or medical preparations for the purpose of resale to persons who are not licensed to sell such drugs or preparations.

Item 20. The registered pharmacist or pharmacy shall not advertise by any means, in any form or through or by any media, harmful or dangerous drugs, medicines, or prescription items, normally compounded, sold or dispensed by a registered pharmacist in his professional capacity, by the use of terms "cut-rate" or "discount" or any similar phrase or word which would tend to degrade the professional nature of pharmaceutical services, provided that nothing in this regulation shall prevent the furnishing of professional information to qualified practitioners.

Item 21. The registered pharmacist or pharmacy shall not participate in any plan, arrangement, or agreement which eliminates or affects detrimentally the patient-pharmacist-prescriber relationship, such as mail order prescription business, since such a plan, arrangement or agreement is detrimental to the public health, public welfare and safety of the public and is therefore unethical.

Item 22. A registered pharmacist connected with and employed by a hospital or clinic shall only dispense medicines or drugs to in-patients, and to out-patients who are under the immediate treatment of the hospital or clinic.

Item 23. No pharmacy or pharmacist, shall have, participate in, or permit an arrangement, branch, connection or affilation whereby prescriptions are advertised, solicited, accepted, collected, or picked up from or at any location other than a pharmacy for which a drug store permit in good standing has been issued by the board.

Item 24. A pharmacy being established, remodelled or moving to a new location shall not, after the effective date of these rules and regulations, maintain a prescription department in the pharmacy which is less than 20% of the total floor area of the pharmacy or retail drug store and in no case shall be less than 300 square feet in area; and such prescription department shall contain proper and sufficient pharmaceutical equipment, apparatus and supplies in order that such prescription department shall be carried on and maintained to provide and allow for efficient, safe and proper service to the public and for the public welfare in the dispensing and filling of prescriptions.

Item 25. The registered pharmacist shall refrain from attempting in any manner to diagnose illness and prescribe therefor, except in case of emergency and then only until a physician can be called or arrives nor shall the registered pharmacist advise a patient as to the therapeutic value or effect of a medical preparation or device prescribed, nor indicate the nature of the illness for which the medication or device may have been prescribed for or disclose the details or composition of such medical preparation which the prescriber has withheld.

Item 26. No registered pharmacist or pharmacy shall solicit professional practice by means of providing physicians or other practitioners with prescription blanks imprinted with any material referring to a pharmacy or pharmacist in any manner whatsoever.

Item 27. No registered pharmacist or pharmacy shall disseminate, directly or indirectly any false, misleading or fraudulent advertisement in connection with, or with a view toward the sale or distribution of drugs, devices, medicines, cosmetics or any other items generally sold in a pharmacy.

Item 28. A pharmacy shall not engage in a restricted, limited partial or closed-door service or operation to the public or to any group of persons, but must hold out a full pharmaceutical service to the entire public and thereby service the well-being and the public health of the entire public. The denial of a full and complete pharmaceutical service to the entire public shall not be deemed a bona fide offering of pharmaceutical service but shall be considered a closed-door, limited, partial or restricted service and shall therefore, be considered unethical, malpractice and against the best interests of the public health and public well-being.

Item 29. No new application for a pharmacy will be approved by the Board and a pharmacy now licensed by the Board will be denied a renewal thereof, if an assurance is not received by and given to the Board by the applicant, that the pharmacy does not and will not engage in the practice of customarily refusing to compound or dispense prescriptions which may reasonably be expected to be compounded or dispensed for the general public in a pharmacy by pharmacists. Such an assurance shall be considered essential to prevent the restricted practice or closed-door operation of the pharmacy and such practice shall be deemed as a practice or operation against the best interests of the public health and public well-being.

Item 30. A registered pharmacist or pharmacy shall not purchase manufacturers' samples of dangerous or harmful drugs from representatives of manufacturers or from manufacturers, from physicians or anyone else for purposes of using said samples in the compounding or dispensing of prescriptions or the sale of said drugs in any manner. If a registered pharmacist or pharmacy has received samples gratuitously from the manufacturer or its representatives or from a physician for use in connection with compounding or dispensing prescriptions, such samples shall be kept in containers suitably labelled to conform to and in accordance with the Federal Food and Drug Act and the State Food and Drug Laws.

NARCOTIC DRUG REGULATIONS

Pursuant to the authority granted by Section 2 of Chapter 345 of the Acts of 1961, the following regulations are hereby jointly adopted by the Commissioner of Public Health, acting jointly with the Board of Registration in Pharmacy: —

1.   The Commissioner of Public Health, acting jointly with the Board of Registration in Pharmacy, hereby declares the following to be exempt narcotics:

(a)   Opium Preparations: containing not more than two grains of opium per fluid or avoirdupois ounce along with therapeutically active non-narcotic ingredients.

(b)   Morphine Preparations: containing not more than one-fourth grain morphine, or any of its salts, per fluid or avoirdupois ounce.

(c)   Codeine Preparations: containing not more than one grain codeine, or any of its salts, per fluid or avoirdupois ounce.

(d)   Dihydrocodeine Preparations: containing not more than one-half grain dihydrocodeine, or any of its salts, per fluid or avoirdupois ounce.

(e)   Ethylmorphine Preparations: containing not more than one-fourth grain ethylmorphine, or any of its salts, per fluid or avoirdupois ounce.

(f)   Diphenoxylate Preparations: Pharmaceutical preparations in solid forms containing not more than 2.5 mg. diphenoxylate and not less than 25 micrograms of atropine sulfate per dosage unit.

(g)   Noscapine Preparations: any pharmaceutical preparation containing noscapine, without limit in quantity, along with either active or inactive non-narcotic ingredients of the type used in medicinal preparations.

(h)   Papaverine Preparations: any pharmaceutical preparation containing papaverine, without limit in quantity, along with either active or inactive non-narcotic ingredients of the type used in medicinal preparations.

(i)   Narceine Preparations: any pharmaceutical preparation containing narceine, without limit in quantity, along with either active or inactive non-narcotic ingredients of the type used in medicinal preparations.

(j)   Cotarnine Preparations: any pharmaceutical preparation containing cotarnine, without limit in quantity, along with either active or inactive non-narcotic ingredients of the type used in medicinal preparations.

(k)   Nalorphine Preparations: any pharmaceutical preparation containing nalorphine, without limit in quantity, along with either active or inactive non-narcotic ingredients of the type used in medicinal preparations. (Nalline, etc.)

2.   The above preparations shall be classified as exempt narcotics, provided that not more than four ounces of the same are administered, dispensed or sold to a person during any twenty-four hour period, excepting in the case of paregoric, wherein the quantity shall be limited to one fluid ounce.

3.   If the purchaser of an exempt narcotic is not personally known to the pharmacist, said pharmacist shall require identification of the purchaser and the purchaser to sign the record book.

Approved: August 30, 1961

The variety of the regulatory matter that can emanate from the state boards of pharmacy is further demonstrated by the fact that the following have been the subject of rules and regulations by a state board of pharmacy:

1. Prescription refills.
2. Prescription label content.
3. Licensed practical pharmacists.
4. Poison sales.
5. Reciprocity.
6. Length of time to keep prescription files.
7. Sales restriction of certain classes of drugs.
8. Pertaining to "copy" of a prescription.
9. Drug substitution.
10. Hospital pharmacies.
11. Inspection of pharmacy files.
12. Narcotic handling.
13. Mechanical dispensing devices.
14. Professional conduct.
15. Alcohol sales.

References

1. W. GELLHORN and C. BYSE: ADMINISTRATIVE LAW-CASES AND COMMENTS, 4th Ed., The Foundation Press, Brooklyn, New York, 1960, p. ix.
2. J. O'Leary: *The Right to be Informed*, MASS. LAW QUARTERLY, 54:1:63 (1969).

CHAPTER 8

The Federal
Food, Drug, and
Cosmetic Act

The Federal Food, Drug, and Cosmetic Act was signed into law by President Franklin D. Roosevelt on June 25, 1938. In an article describing the evolution of the law, Franklin M. Depew stated that the Act

> holds vital significance for our people and a fundamental place in our jurisprudence. Its provisions impose an unusual responsibility on those who handle the Nation's life-sustaining foods and drugs. The Act may be ranked as the commercial law of greatest social and economic importance in the land because it regulates food and drugs, our two most vital consumer products.[1]

Since the passage of the Act, Congress has seen fit to enact strengthening amendments which have had the effect of keeping the Act current with new developments in the science and technology of food and drug production and marketing. In brief, the current FDC Act is one of the best in the world and serves the purpose of assuring the American public that its food, drugs and cosmetics are safe for human use.

One of the Congressional committees studying the proposed Act reported that

> This bill has been prepared with three basic principles in mind: first, it must not weaken the existing laws; second, it must strengthen and extend the law's protection of the consumer; and third, it must impose on honest industrial enterprise no hardship which is unnecessary or unjustified in the public interest.[1]

The courts have given great support to the purposes of the Act. The Supreme Court in a far-reaching decision[2] stated:

> The prosecution . . . is based on a now familiar type of legislation whereby penalties serve as effective means of regulation. Such legislation dispenses with

the conventional requirement for criminal conduct—awareness of some wrong-doing. In the interest of the larger good it puts the burden of acting at hazard upon a person otherwise innocent but standing in responsible relation to a public danger (*United States* v. *Balint*, 258 U.S. 250). And so it is clear that shipments like those now in issue are punished by the Statute if the article is misbranded (or adulterated), and that the article may be misbranded (or adulterated) without any conscious fraud at all. It was natural enough to throw this risk on shippers with regard to the identity of their wares . . . (*United States* v. *Johnson*. 221 U.S. 488, 497-98).

The following quotation from the same case further emphasizes the Court's empathy:

The purposes of this legislation thus touch phases of the lives and health of people which, in the circumstances of modern industrialism, are largely beyond self-protection. Regard for these purposes should infuse construction of the legislation if it is to be treated as a working instrument of government and not merely as a collection of English words.

The major concern of the 1938 Act is the prohibition of the introduction or delivery for introduction into interstate commerce of any food, drug, device, or cosmetic which is adulterated or misbranded as defined within the Act. Numerous administrative regulations were introduced, including standards of identity for food, and the labeling of dietetic foods to inform the purchaser of its vitamin and mineral content. The law required preclearance of new drugs to show safety of use when taken as indicated and for the stated conditions.

The enforcement provisions of the 1938 Act included criminal, seizure and injunction sanctions in the federal courts. The law authorized regulations covering enforcement, inspection and sample collections. In addition, the agency was authorized to issue releases relative to its investigations and activities.

Some of the principal amendments to the 1938 Act are the Insulin and Antibiotic Certification Amendments, the Prescription Drug Amendment, the Pesticide Chemicals Amendment, the Food Additives Amendment, the Color Additive Amendments, the Drug Amendments of 1962 and the Drug Abuse Control Amendments of 1965 and 1970.

The Insulin and Antibiotic Certification Amendments provide for the certification of batches of these categories of drugs by the federal government.

The Prescription Drug Amendment deals with drugs and devices—their production, control and distribution.

The Pesticide Chemicals Amendment provides that pesticide chemicals registered with the Department of Agriculture and certified as useful in food production by the Secretary of Agriculture be proven safe for use in the food supply.

The Food Additives Amendment authorized beneficial progress in food technology by permitting the use of valuable food additives at safe levels.

The Color Additive Amendments authorized the use of colors in safe amounts.

The Drug Amendments of 1962 were intended to add new controls to assure the quality of all drugs, old and new; to simplify drug nomenclature; to improve inspections; to regulate investigational drug use; to require that drugs be shown effective as well as safe before they are marketed; to improve the new drug and antibiotic clearance procedure; to increase surveillance over chemical and other agents and to regulate prescription-drug advertising.

The Drug Abuse Control Amendments, enacted in 1965, were intended to eliminate illicit traffic in depressant or stimulant drugs. They prescribe that a system of record keeping be maintained to permit government agents to trace the movement of such drugs from producer to consumer. They further provide for inspections and the vesting of a power of arrest in the agent.

Contents of the Act

Because it will not be possible to publish the Federal Food, Drug, and Cosmetic Act in its entirety in this textbook, the table of contents of the Act is being presented in order to acquaint the student with its format and scope:

*References in brackets [] are to Title 21 U.S. Code.

Federal Food, Drug, and Cosmetic Act, Chapters I, II and V–Drugs and Devices

To provide the pharmacy student with the original language of the Act, Chapters I, II, III and V of the Federal Food, Drug, and Cosmetic Act are reproduced in the Appendix. (Those sections dealing with food and cosmetics are not of principal interest to the pharmacy student.) The original text is important because all too often the student does not grasp the detailed comprehensiveness of the legislation because the instructor has overly simplified its presentation.

The Federal Food, Drug, and Cosmetic Act, as amended and as it appears in the Appendix, includes the provisions of the Comprehensive Drug Abuse Prevention and Control Act of 1970. The Act appears in the United States Code under Title 21. Corresponding section numbers of the Code appear in brackets after the section number of the Act.

Footnote references are made to regulations promulgated under the Federal Food, Drug, and Cosmetic Act, by parts numbered according to the Code of Federal Regulations, Title 21.

Comments on the Act

Article 1, Section 8 of the Constitution of the United States provides that

The Congress shall have power to lay and collect taxes, duties, imposts and excises, to pay the debts and provide for the common defense and general welfare of the United States; but all duties, imposts and excises shall be uniform throughout the United States.

From the above, it should be clear that power is vested in the federal government to regulate interstate commerce. Thus, since the Federal Food, Drug, and Cosmetic Act is an act to prohibit the movement in interstate commerce of adulterated and misbranded food, drugs, devices and cosmetics, it derives its power from the Federal Constitution.

The Federal Food, Drug, and Cosmetic Act is of importance to the practicing pharmacist in that it contains provisions which require that:

1. Legend drugs must be limited to prescriptions only.
2. Refills may be had only after due authorization.
3. Accurate drug records must be kept.
4. Labeling of both legend and over-the-counter drugs must be in accord with the requirements.
5. Violation of the labeling requirement shall be deemed to be "misbranding."
6. Violation of the Act, irrespective of malintent, shall be deemed to be either a misdemeanor or a felony. In this regard, the Court has observed that "[s]pecific criminal intent was not an essential element of offense for violation of the Federal Food, Drug, and Cosmetic Act."*
7. Agents of the FDA may search for and seize adulterated or misbranded drugs, if done within the parameters of the law.
8. Violators both agent and principal may be prosecuted, if guilty.

Accordingly, the student is urged to study each section of the Act in conjunction with the following condensation of the Act.

As in any piece of legislation, it is important to define the more important terms used within the text of the law. Generally, terms relating to the persons involved, agencies involved and items are defined. Thus Chapter II, Section 201, defines the terms *State, Territory, interstate commerce, Department* (as it relates to H.E.W.), *Secretary* (as it relates to H.E.W.), *person, food, drug, counterfeit drug, device, cosmetic, official compendium, label, immediate container, labeling, new drug, color additive, depressant* or *stimulant drug*, and *new animal drug.*

Chapter III, Section 301, of the Act provides for the prohibitions under the law and the penalties for any violations. The law most clearly prohibits the following:

1. Introduction into interstate commerce of any adulterated food, drug, device or cosmetic.
2. The adulteration or misbranding of any food, drug, device or cosmetic.
3. Receipt and delivery thereof for pay or otherwise.
4. Refusal to grant entry of agents for lawful inspection purposes.
5. The manufacture of any adulterated or misbranded food, drug, device or cosmetic.
6. Illegal use of identification devices which imply conformity to regulations.
7. Possession of equipment which prints the counterfeit identification devices.

*U.S. v. Vitamin Industry Inc., 130 F. Supp. 755.

8. Alteration, mutilation, destruction, obliteration or removal, in whole or in part, of the labeling affixed to a food, drug, device or cosmetic while such article is held for sale.

9. Failure of the manufacturer to provide clinical and other information, particularly of a prescription drug offered for sale in interstate commerce, to a licensed practitioner who requests same.

Section 303 of the Act provides for the penalties for violation and these range from imprisonment for not more than one year, or a fine of not more than $1000, or both such imprisonment and fine to imprisonment for not more than six years, or a fine of not more than $15,000, or both such imprisonment and fine.

Of major importance to the practitioner of pharmacy is the following exclusion:

> (c) No person shall be subject to the penalties of subsection (a) of this section, (1) for having received in interstate commerce any article and delivered it or proffered delivery of it, if such delivery or proffer was made in good faith, unless he refuses to furnish on request of an officer or employee duly designated by the Secretary the name and address of the person from whom he purchased or received such article and copies of all documents, if any there be, pertaining to the delivery of the article to him.

Chapter V of the Act deals specifically with the matter of adulterated drugs and devices. Section 501 provides the definition of an adulterated drug or device and Section 502 gives insight as to the interpretation of misbranding of drugs and devices.

With respect to adulterated drugs, Section 501 states it to be adulterated if

> the methods used in, or the facilities or controls used for, its manufacture, processing, packing, or holding do not conform to or are not operated or administered in conformity with current good manufacturing practice.

In addition to false or misleading labeling, the Act states, in Section 502, that a drug is misbranded unless

> (A) its label bears, to the exclusion of any other nonproprietary name . . . (i) the established name . . . (ii) in case it is fabricated from two or more ingredients, the established name and quantity of each active ingredient, including the quantity, kind, and proportion of any alcohol, and also including whether active or not, the established name and quantity or proportion of any bromides, ether, chloroform, acetanilid, acetophenetidin, amidopyrine, antipyrine, atropine, hyoscine, hyoscyamine, arsenic digitalis, digitalis glucosides, mercury, ouabain, strophanthin, strychnine, thyroid, or any derivative or preparation of any such substances, contained therein: *Provided*, that the requirement for stating the quantity of the active ingredients, other than the quantity of those specifically named in this paragraph, shall apply only to prescription drugs.

Administrative Hearings in FDA

After having studied the contents of the Federal Food, Drug, and Cosmetic Act and certain notices published by the Agency in the *Federal Register,* the student will note that the accused party has a right to be heard prior to the confiscation of his property. This "hearing," although a part of the administrative process of law, is probably the least understood by the private citizen.

The procedure for carrying out the hearing is not left to the whims of an administrative bureaucrat but is clearly defined in the Administrative Procedure Act signed by President Truman in 1946. Senator McCarran, then a member of the Senate Committee on the Judiciary, wrote the *Foreword* to Senate Document No. 248. It is quoted here because it succinctly describes this Act:

> Although it is brief, it is a comprehensive charter of private liberty and a solemn undertaking of official fairness. It is intended as a guide to him who seeks fair play and equal rights under law, as well as to those invested with executive authority. It upholds law and yet lightens the burden of those on whom the law may impinge. It enunciates and emphasizes the tripartite form of our democracy and brings into relief the ever essential declaration that this is a government of law rather than of men.

Administrative hearings held under the Federal Food, Drug, and Cosmetic Act, as amended (21 U.S.C. 321, et seq.), are conducted pursuant to particular statutory provisions set out in this Act under sections which will be mentioned later. These hearings are also subject to the Administrative Procedure Act. Thus, both the provisions of the Administrative Procedure Act and the applicable provisions of the Federal Food, Drug, and Cosmetic Act govern the administrative hearings held by the Administration.

The purpose of the Administrative Procedure Act is stated in its preamble: "An Act to improve the administration of justice by prescribing fair administrative procedure."

This law prescribes what steps must be taken by administrative agencies to accomplish this improvement of the administration of justice. It provides for two basic types of administrative hearings, two different conduits through which justice is to reach the governed. One type is called "rule-making," the other "adjudication." "Rule-making" is defined in this law as the "agency process for the formulation, amendment, or repeal of a rule" [Sec. 2 (c), 5 U.S.C. 551 (4)]. A "rule" is defined in this law as "the whole or any part of any agercy statement of general or particular applicability and future effect designed to implement, interpret, or prescribe law or policy or to describe the organization, procedure, or practice requirements of any agency." "Rule-making" and the resultant "rule" are therefore legislative in nature. It is the means by which agencies announce their policy decisions, their interpretations of laws under which they operate, and it is the means by which they carry out those duties and responsibilities assigned to them by Congress.

The second type of administrative hearing provided for in the Administrative Procedure Act is the "adjudicatory" type. The definition of the term "adjudication" in this law is the "agency process for the formulation of an Order" [Sec. 2 (d), 5 U.S.C. 551 (7)]. The term "order" is defined as "the whole, or any part of the final disposition . . . of any agency in any matter other than rule-making but including licensing" [Sec. 2 (d), 5 U.S.C. 551 (6)]. The ambiguity and lack of precision obvious in this definition has been the subject of considerable evaluation by the courts. Fortunately, the courts have clarified this definition so that it is now universally accepted that an agency "order" resulting from agency "adjudication" means the administrative pronouncement to an individual or limited number of individuals of their rights and privileges based upon their past conduct.

The "adjudicatory" type of proceeding is accusatory in nature as opposed to the legislative aspect of "rule-making." Where an agency rule is prospective in effect, where it usually affects a large number or groups of individuals, and is bottomed upon policy considerations in large measure, it is classified as "rule-making." On the other hand, "adjudications" and orders resulting therefrom are based upon someone's past conduct, resulting in an agency determination of that person's rights or privileges based upon established laws, rules or regulations.

Under the Federal Food, Drug, and Cosmetic Act, both types of administrative hearings are held; that is, the "rule-making" type, which is conducted pursuant to Section 701 of the Act (21 U.S.C. 321), and the "adjudicatory" type which is conducted under the New Drug provisions of the Act, Section 505 (21 U.S.C. 355).

One more historical reference appears appropriate to show accurately the intent of Congress in relation to the administrative processes of government. For its first 20 years of life, the Administrative Procedure Act went unamended. Then on July 4, 1966, President Johnson signed Public Law 89-487, which became effective on July 4, 1967. This law, known popularly as the "Freedom of Information Act," and technically as the "Public Information Act," amended Section 3 of the Administrative Procedure Act. This amendment voices "a general philosophy of full agency disclosure" of information in the agency files affecting citizens, with some clearly defined exceptions. Former Attorney General Ramsey Clark summarizes this philosophy in his Foreword to the Attorney General's Memorandum on the Public Information Section of the Administrative Procedure Act, where he states:

> If government is to be truly of, by, and for the people, the people must know in detail the activities of government. Nothing so diminishes democracy as secrecy. Self-government, the maximum participation of the citizenry in affairs of state, is meaningful only with an informed public. How can we govern ourselves if we know not how we govern? Never was it more important than in our times of mass society, when government affects each individual in so many ways, that the right of the people to know the actions of their government be secure.

Brennan, a hearing examiner for the FDA, has concisely summed up the process in the following:

> Those matters which can be made the subject of a rule-making type of hearing under the Food and Drug Act are governed by Section 701 of the Act. Among other matters, the following types of subjects may become the subject for this type of hearing: whether any drug is a habit-forming drug or has a potential for abuse (Sec. 201 (v) (2) (c) and (3)); the establishment of definitions and

standards of identity for foods (Sec. 401); the labeling of foods for special dietary uses (Sec. 403 (j)); tolerances for poisonous ingredients in foods (Sec. 406); the listing and certification of color additives (Sec. 706); matters dealing with the labeling of hazardous substances (Sec. 3 (a) (2)) of the Federal Hazardous Substances Act; and matters dealing with the labeling of foods, drugs, and devices under the Fair Packaging and Labeling Act.

The detailed procedures followed in this type of hearing are set forth in the relatively new, revised regulations appearing in Part 2 of the Code of Federal Regulations, entitled "Rules of Practice and Procedure For Filing Proposals, Petitions, Objections, and Holding Public Hearings Under Section 701 of the Federal Food, Drug, and Cosmetic Act." Under these procedures, which amplify the statutory provisions of Section 701 of the Act, future Rules and Regulations of the Food and Drug Administration, whether initiated by the Commissioner of Food and Drugs or by private parties, first appear in the form of a Proposal published in the *Federal Register*. Under the law, "all interested persons" must have an opportunity to present their views regarding the Proposal either orally or in writing (21 U.S.C. 371 (e) (1)). After the receipt and consideration of the comments which are filed on any Proposal, the next document published is a Proposed Order which also appears in the *Federal Register*. Under the law, "any person who will be adversely affected" by such Order if placed in effect may file objections thereto with the Agency, specifying with particularity the provisions of the Order deemed objectionable, stating the grounds therefor, and requesting a public hearing upon such objection (21 U.S.C. 371 (e) (2)). The law also provides that "the filing of such objections shall operate to stay the effectiveness of those provisions of the order to which objections are made" (21 U.S.C. 371 (e) (3)).

The next step commanded by the law is for the Agency to publish in the *Federal Register* a notice " . . . specifying those parts of the order which have been stayed by the filing of objections and, if no objections have been filed, stating that fact (21 U.S.C. 371 (e) (3)). After the receipt of objections and a request for a public hearing for the purpose of receiving evidence relevant and material to the issues raised by such objections have been made, the proceedings are conducted in accord with [21 U.S.C. 371 (3)]."

The last step, taken before the hearing actually begins, is the publication in the Federal Register of a Notice of Time and Place for the hearing. Under the rules governing this type of proceeding, prehearing conferences may be called to simplify issues, to exchange documents, to identify witnesses, to explore the possibility of stipulations, and to deal with any other preliminary matter which may expedite the hearing-in-chief. These conferences are normally attended by the lawyers who will be representing the parties at the hearing.

Once the hearing-in-chief commences it resembles in practice a trial in a court of law. Witnesses are presented, are sworn or give affirmation, and are then questioned by their own attorneys on direct examination. The witnesses are then subject to cross-examination by the other parties to the hearing. All the proceedings which take place in the hearing are transcribed by court stenographers and a printed transcript is compiled which reflects the testimony, argument, and rulings made during the course of the hearing. Documentary evidence is also introduced into evidence and becomes a part of the record for decision. After all parties have presented all of their evidence which is relevant and material to the issues, the hearing is then closed, terminating this phase of the administrative process. An opportunity is then given to participants to submit proposed written findings of fact and conclusions based upon the evidence to the Hearing Examiner who has conducted the hearing. The

Examiner then takes this record for decision, consisting of the transcript of testimony, the exhibits, and any written arguments that have been filed, and drafts his report. This report together with the record for decision is then certified to the Commissioner of Food and Drugs, who prepares a Tentative Order and publishes this Order in the *Federal Register*. Any party to the hearing may take exception to any provision of this Tentative Order and may file these exceptions together with written arguments and a request for oral argument with the Commissioner. After all exceptions and arguments have been received and considered, the Commissioner then issues the final Agency Order and publishes this Order in the *Federal Register*. This ends the Agency proceeding, terminating in a Final Order.

This Final Order may be appealed to the appropriate Circuit Court of Appeals of the United States by any person who is adversely affected by it (21 U.S.C. 371 (f) (1)). The judgment of the Circuit Court of Appeals is thereafter subject to review by the Supreme Court of the United States (21 U.S.C. 371 (4)).

We are able to see, then, through this administrative process, the means provided by the law by which the governed may meaningfully participate in the formulation of the Rules and Regulations which will goven them in the future. The governed may meaningfully participate in the governing processes by filing comments to published Proposals; they may file objections and request hearings; they may participate in hearings and present evidence in support of their position and arguments; they may be heard by the Commissioner upon exceptions to his Tentative Order, and finally they may ask the courts to review the Agency actions.

The other type of administrative hearing provided for in the Administrative Procedure Act, the "adjudicatory" type, is held by the Food and Drug Administration under Section 505 of the Federal Food, Drug, and Cosmetic Act.

To carry out the overall purpose of the Food and Drug Act, namely, protection of consumers, Congress in Section 505 of the Act has prohibited the interstate movement of any new drug unless an approval of a New Drug Application has been secured from FDA. The procedures to be followed by an applicant in obtaining this approval are set forth in this Section of the Act and in Part 130 of the Code of Federal Regulations, called popularly the "new drug regulations." After the submission of a New Drug Application, which most frequently is a multivolume submission, the Commissioner of Food and Drugs acts on the responsibility delegated from the Secretary of the Department either to approve the application or to give the applicant an opportunity for a hearing on the question of whether it is approvable (21 U.S.C. 355 (c)).

If the Food and Drug Administration has previously approved a New Drug Application but evidence subsequent to this approval indicates that the approval should be withdrawn, the Commissioner, again by law, may withdraw approval of the application subject to offering the applicant an opportunity for a hearing, during which evidence and arguments may be submitted as to why the prior approval should not be withdrawn. The grounds upon which the Commissioner may refuse to approve or withdraw a prior approval of a New Drug Application are set forth in Section 505 of the Act as amplified in more specificity in the "new drug regulations" (21 C.F.R. 130, et seq.).

Under these provisions of law and regulations, the Commissioner serves upon the new drug applicant a notice of his intention to either refuse approval or withdraw prior approval of a New Drug Application. He must afford the applicant an opportunity to elect a hearing in the matter. These notices are also published in the *Federal Register*.

When an applicant elects to avail himself of his right to a hearing, a Hearing Examiner is designated and a hearing is held. This type of hearing is governed by both the provisions of the Administrative Procedure Act and the regulations set forth in Part 130 of the Food and Drug Regulations. In substantial and practical effect, this type of hearing pretty much coincides with the type of hearing held under Section 701 of the Act; that is, witnesses are sworn or make affirmation, give direct testimony, are subject to cross-examination, and documentary exhibits where relevant and material are admitted into evidence. At the conclusion of the hearing, parties are afforded an opportunity to file written arguments and briefs.

The next step is the preparation by the Examiner of a Tentative Order supported by tentative findings of fact, which are served upon both the applicant and the Food and Drug Administration. Exceptions to the Tentative Order may be filed by either party and either may request oral argument before the Commissioner. After consideration of exceptions and any arguments, the Commissioner then issues the Final Order in the proceedings. Just as with the Final Order issued under Section 701 of the Act, the Final Order issued under Section 505 of the Act may be appealed to the appropriate U.S. Court of Appeals and the judgment of the Circuit Court is appealable to the Supreme Court of the United States (21 U.S.C. 355 (h)).[3]

DURHAM-HUMPHREY AMENDMENT

Section 503 [353 b] of the Act is a part of the Durham-Humphrey Amendment which became a part of the Federal Food, Drug, and Cosmetic Act in 1951. Contained within the Durham-Humphrey Amendment is the legal definition of the kinds of drugs intended for human consumption that may be dispensed by the pharmacist on the prescription of "practitioner licensed by law to administer such drugs." The student should note here that the federal law leaves to the state medical practice laws and administrative agencies the right to determine who is qualified to act in such capacity.

The Durham-Humphrey law makes it illegal for a pharmacist to dispense any prescription legend drug without a prescription or to refill a prescription for same without the authorization of a duly qualified and licensed prescriber. This authorization for prescription drugs (except for certain narcotics) may be transmitted by telephone with the proviso that such prescriptions and authorizations promptly be reduced to writing and filed by the pharmacist.

The three categories of legend drugs (those bearing the words: CAUTION: Federal Law Prohibits Dispensing Without Prescription) defined in the Durham-Humphrey Amendment are:

1. Hypnotic or habit-forming drugs that are specifically named in the law [Section 502 (d)], and their derivatives, unless specifically exempted.
2. A drug deemed to be not safe for self-medication "because of its toxicity or other potentiality for harmful effect, or the method of its use, or the collateral measures necessary to its use."
3. A new drug not yet proven to be safe for use in self-medication, and which, under the terms of an effective new-drug application, is limited to prescription dispensing.

The above discussion should not be misinterpreted by the student to mean that the statutory provisions apply only to toxic or habit-forming drugs. On the contrary, they apply to all drugs that require adequate medical supervision while in use. This is one of the reasons for the difference in labeling requirements between OTC (over-the-counter) drugs and legend drugs—namely, a layman would know how to use certain agents if given adequate instructions whereas with others he would not. In this regard, drugs that may be sold over-the-counter must bear what has come to be described as a "7-point label," which must contain the following seven items of information:

1. The name of the product.
2. The name and address of the manufacturer, packer or distributor.
3. The net contents of the package.
4. The established name of all active ingredients, and the quantity of certain other ingredients, whether active or not.
5. The name of any habit-forming drug contained therein.
6. Cautions and warnings.
7. Adequate directions for safe use.

The Act also provides for special treatment for new drugs [Section 505], certification of drugs containing insulin [Section 506] and certification of antibiotics [Section 507].

The authority to designate official names for any drug is vested in the Secretary by Section 508. The Secretary first determines that

> such action is necessary or desirable in the interest of usefulness and simplicity. Any official name designated under this section for any drug shall be the only official name of that drug used in any official compendium published after such name has been prescribed or for any other purpose of this Act. In no event, however, shall the Secretary establish an official name so as to infringe a valid trademark.

Refill Records

The Food and Drug Administration has not issued any formal guidelines for keeping a refill record. The record should be kept, however, in such a manner that the pharmacist on duty can readily ascertain a prescription's status when it is presented for refilling. Since every prescription must be looked up by the pharmacist, it may be best to maintain the record of refills either on the back side or the front side of the original prescription.

The P.R.N. Refill

Any designation that does not limit the frequency of refilling, or the length of time that a prescription may be refilled is not a valid authorization for refilling a prescription. Examples of these illegal designations are "Refill P.R.N." and "Refill ad lib."

A pharmacist who receives a prescription with such a designation must use care and professional judgment in handling it. He should refill it only with a frequency consistent with the directions for use and he should consult the physician about further refills. Unfortunately, his dilemma will be markedly increased if the signa is also marked "P.R.N."

Change of Drug Status

On occasion, a drug's status may change from that of a prescription legend drug to an OTC product. When this happens, the drug is technically misbranded and is illegal as an article of commerce. In order to correct this situation, the pharmacist must relabel the product in accord with the law or he should affix to the package the sticker label which is generally provided by the manufacturer. Generally, most pharmacists either return the package to the manufacturer or retain it for the purpose of filling prescriptions.

Identifying Prescription Contents

Although the law requires that a package containing a drug carry certain information (such as name and address of dispenser, name of prescriber, serial number, date and directions), nevertheless placing the name of the prescription contents on the label is not prohibited. This practice has been recommended by many as an aid to identifying the package contents in an emergency situation.

Copies of Prescriptions

There is no prohibition against giving the patient a copy of his prescription provided that it is clearly marked as a copy. The pharmacist must bear in mind that a copy of a prescription in not a legal prescription and therefore he must exercise professional judgment and due care when presented with a copy for refill purposes.

Status of Out-of-State Prescribers

Pharmacists generally raise the question of whether it is illegal to fill a prescription written by an out-of-state physician. Unless prohibited by state law, the pharmacist must exercise professional judgment and ascertain that there exists a bona fide physician-patient-pharmacist relationship. If this does exist, he may dispense the medication and usually no issue is made of the technical legality of the prescriber's competence to prescribe within the state.

Statute of Limitations

Under the statute of limitations in the Durham-Humphrey amendment, the minimal number of years that prescription records may be kept to show compliance with the law is five years.

Drug Abuse Control Amendments of 1965

The Drug Abuse Control Amendments of 1965 (DACA) amended the Federal Food, Drug, and Cosmetic Act; it placed additional controls over stimulant and depressant drugs through increased record keeping and inspection requirements providing control over interstate traffic in these drugs, and made possession of them illegal under certain specified conditions.

For the convenience of the pharmacist, the law required manufacturers to identify all DACA drugs with one of the following symbols:

FIG. 7. Symbols Used to Identify Controlled Drugs
Under the Drug Abuse Control Amendments of 1965.

On October 27, 1970, President Nixon signed into law the Comprehensive Drug Abuse Prevention and Control Act of 1970; this act brought new control measures into play and voided the Drug Abuse Control Amendments of 1965.

COMPREHENSIVE DRUG ABUSE PREVENTION AND CONTROL ACT OF 1970

The above Act, also known as Public Law 91-513, and as the Controlled Substances Act, has as its purpose "to amend the Public Health Service Act and other laws to provide increased research into, and prevention of, drug abuse and drug dependence; to provide for treatment and rehabilitation of drug abusers and drug dependent persons; and to strengthen existing law enforcement authority in the field of drug abuse."[10]

The Act is divided into four "titles" dealing with the following subjects:

Title I   — Rehabilitation Programs Relating to Drug Abuse
Title II   — Control and Enforcement
Title III   — Importation and Exportation; Amendments and Repeals of Revenue Laws
Title IV   — Report on Advisory Councils

Title I, Rehabilitation Programs Relating to Drug Abuse, amends Part D of the *Community Mental Health Centers Act* to include under its provisions persons with drug abuse and drug dependence problems. In addition, it provides for increased budgetary allocations for drug abuse education programs; funding for special projects for narcotic addicts and drug dependent persons; broader treatment authority in public health service hospitals; and research under the Public Health Service Act in drug use, abuse and addiction.

Of interest to all is the definition of the term *drug dependent person* provided in paragraph (q) of Part E which states:

> The term "drug dependent person" means a person who is using a controlled substance (as defined in section 102 of the Controlled Substances Act) and who is in a state of psychic or physical dependence, or both, arising from the use of that substance on a continuous basis. Drug dependence is characterized by behavioral and other responses which include a strong compulsion to take the substance on a continuous basis in order to experience its psychic effects or to avoid the discomfort caused by its absence.

Title II, dealing with control and enforcement is also known as the Controlled Substances Act. In passing this Act, the Congress made the following findings and declarations:

1. Drugs included under this title have a legitimate and useful medical purpose and are necessary to maintain the health and general welfare of the American people.
2. Illegal importation, manufacture, distribution, possession and improper use of controlled substances have a detrimental effect on the health and welfare of the American people.
3. The manufacture, local distribution, and possession of controlled substances have a direct effect upon interstate commerce.
4. Local distribution and possession of controlled substances contribute to the interstate traffic in such substances.
5. It is not a practical matter to attempt to differentiate between controlled substances manufactured and distributed interstate and controlled substances manufactured and distributed intrastate.
6. Federal control of both types of traffic is essential.
7. The United States must establish effective control over domestic and international traffic in controlled substances to be in compliance with the Single Convention on Narcotic Drugs of 1961—to which it was a party.

In order to understand the contents of Title II completely, it is necessary first to be familiar with the definitions contained within its text:

Addict: any individual who habitually uses any narcotic drug so as to endanger the public morals, health, safety or welfare, or who is so far addicted to the use of narcotic drugs as to have lost the power of self-control with reference to his addiction.

Administer: the direct application of a controlled substance to the body of a patient or research subject by a practitioner or his agent or by the patient or research subject at the direction and in the presence of the practitioner.

Agent: an authorized person who acts on behalf of or at the direction of a manufacturer, distributor or dispenser; exceptions being common contract carriers and warehouse men.

Control: the addition of a drug or other substance, or immediate precursor, to a schedule under Part B of this title, whether by transfer from another schedule or otherwise.

Controlled Substances: a drug or other substance, or immediate precursor, included in Schedule I, II, III, IV or V of Part B of this title. The term does not include distilled spirits, wine, malt beverages or tobacco, as those terms are defined or used in subtitle E of the Internal Revenue Code of 1954.

Counterfeit Substance: a controlled substance whose container or label has, without authorization, the identification of a producer other than the actual producer.

Deliver or Delivery: the actual, constructive, or attempted transfer of a controlled substance, whether or not there exists an agency relationship.

Depressant or Stimulant Substance:

(A)   a drug which contains any quantity of (1) barbituric acid or any of the salts of barbituric acid; or (2) any derivative of barbituric acid which has been designated by the Secretary as habit-forming under section 502 (d) of the Federal Food, Drug, and Cosmetic Act [21 U.S.C. 352 (d)] ; or

(B)   a drug which contains any quantity of (1) amphetamine or any of its optical isomers; (2) any salt of amphetamine or any salt of an optical isomer of amphetamine; or (3) any substance which the Attorney General, after investigation, has found to be, and by regulation designated as, habit-forming because of its stimulant effect on the central nervous system; or

(C)   lysergic acid diethylamide; or

(D)   any drug which contains any quantity of a substance which the Attorney General, after investigation, has found to have, and by regulation designated as having, a potential for abuse because of its depressant or stimulant effect on the central nervous system or its hallucinogenic effect.

Dispense: to deliver a controlled substance to an ultimate user or research subject by, or pursuant to the legal order of a practitioner, including the prescribing and administering of a controlled substance and the packaging, labeling, or compounding necessary to prepare the substance for such delivery.

Dispenser: a practitioner who so delivers a controlled substance to an ultimate user or research subject.

Distribute: to deliver (other than by administering or dispensing) a controlled substance.

Distributor: a person who so delivers a controlled substance.

Drug: the same as that provided by section 201 (g) (1) of the Federal Food, Drug, and Cosmetic Act.

Immediate Precursor: a substance which

(A)   the Attorney General has found to be and by regulation designated as being the principal compound used, or produced primarily for use, in the manufacture of a controlled substance;

(B) which is an immediate chemical intermediary used or likely to be used in the manufacture of such controlled substances; and

(C) the control of which is necessary to prevent, curtail, or limit the manufacture of such controlled substances.

Manufacture: the production, preparation, propagation, compounding, or processing of a drug or other substance, either directly or by extraction from substances of natural origin, or independently by means of chemical synthesis or by a combination of extraction and chemical synthesis, and includes any packaging or repackaging of such substance or labeling or relabeling of its container; except that such term does not include the preparation, compounding, packaging, or labeling of a drug or other substance in conformity with applicable state or local law by a practitioner as an incident to his administration or dispensing of such drug or substance in the course of his professional practice. The term "manufacturer" means a person who manufactures a drug or other substance.

Manufacturer: a person who manufactures a drug or other substance.

"Marihuana": all parts of the plant *Cannabis sativa L.*, whether growing or not; the seeds thereof; the resin extracted from any part of such plant; and every compound, manufacture, salt, derivative, mixture, or preparation of such plant, its seeds or resin. Such term does not include the mature stalks of such plant, fiber produced from such stalks, oil or cake made from the seeds of such plant, any other compound, manufacture, salt, derivative, mixture, or preparation of such mature stalks (except the resin extracted therefrom), fiber, oil, or cake, or the sterilized seed of such plant which is incapable of germination.

Narcotic Drug: means any of the following, whether produced directly or indirectly by extraction from substances of vegetable origin, or independently by means of chemical synthesis, or by a combination of extraction and chemical synthesis:

(A) opium, coca leaves and opiates.

(B) a compound, manufacture, salt, derivative, or preparation of opium, coca leaves or opiates.

(C) a substance (any compound, manufacture, salt, derivative, or preparation thereof) which is chemically identical with any substance referred to in (A) or (B) above. Excluded are decocainized coca leaves or extracts of coca leaves which do not contain cocaine or ecognine.

Opiate: any drug or other substance possessing an addiction-forming or addiction-sustaining liability similar to morphine or being converted into a drug having such capabilities.

Opium Poppy: the plant (excluding the seeds of the species *Papaver somniferum L.*

Practitioner: a physician, dentist, veterinarian, scientific investigator, pharmacy, hospital, or other person licensed, registered, or otherwise permitted, by the United States or the jurisdiction in which he practices or does research, to distribute, dispense, conduct research with respect to, administer, or use in teaching or chemical analysis, a controlled substance in the course of professional practice or research.

Production: includes the manufacture, planting, cultivation, growing or harvesting of a controlled substance.

Ultimate User: a person who has lawfully obtained, and who possesses, a controlled substance for his own use or for the use of a member of his household or for an animal owned by him or a member of his household.

Authority to Control

Part B of Title II authorizes the Attorney General to apply the provisions of this title to the controlled substances listed within Section 202 of this title and (a) add to such a schedule or transfer between such schedules any drug or other substance if he finds that such material has a potential for abuse, and (b) remove any drug or other substance from the schedules if he finds that the drug or other substance does not meet the requirements for inclusion in any schedule. In making these decisions, the Attorney General is required to give consideration to the following factors:

1. The drug's or other substances' actual or relative potential for abuse.
2. Scientific evidence of its pharmacological effect, if known.
3. The state of current scientific knowledge regarding the drug or other substance.
4. Its history and current pattern of abuse.
5. The scope, duration and significance of abuse.
6. What, if any, risk there is to the public health.
7. Its psychic or physiological dependence liability.
8. Whether the substance is an immediate precursor of a substance already controlled under this title.

The Attorney General may disregard the requirements of this title and control any drug or substance if control of such is required by United States obligations under international treaties, conventions or protocols. He may also, without regard to the findings required by this title, place an immediate precursor in the same schedule in which the controlled substance of which it is an immediate precursor is placed or in any other schedule with a higher numerical designation. Excepted is the drug dextromethorphan although the exclusionary wording allows for its control at some future time if such becomes necessary.

Schedules of Controlled Substances

The key section of Public Law 91-513 is Section 202 (a) for within it are created the five schedules of controlled substances, known as Schedules I, II, II,

IV and V. The listings within each schedule must be updated and republished one year after the date of enactment and annually thereafter.

Except where control is required by a United States obligation, a drug or other substance may not be placed in any schedule unless the findings required for each schedule are made with respect to such drug or other substance. The findings required for each of the schedules are as follows:

> (1) SCHEDULE I
>> (A) The drug or other substance has a high potential for abuse.
>> (B) The drug or other substance has no currently accepted medical use in treatment in the United States.
>> (C) There is a lack of accepted safety for use of the drug or other substance under medical supervision.
>
> (2) SCHEDULE II
>> (A) The drug or other substance has a high potential for abuse.
>> (B) The drug or other substance has a currently accepted medical use in treatment in the United States or a currently accepted medical use with severe restrictions.
>> (C) Abuse of the drug or other substances may lead to severe psychological or physical dependence.
>
> (3) SCHEDULE III
>> (A) The drug or other substance has a potential for abuse less than the drugs or other substances in schedules I and II.
>> (B) The drug or other substance has a currently accepted medical use in treatment in the United States.
>> (C) Abuse of the drug or other substance may lead to moderate or low physical dependence or high psychological dependence.
>
> (4) SCHEDULE IV
>> (A) The drug or other substance has a low potential for abuse relative to the drugs or other substances in schedule III.
>> (B) The drug or other substance has a currently accepted medical use in treatment in the United States.
>> (C) Abuse of the drug or other substance may lead to limited physical dependence or psychological dependence relative to the drugs or other substances in schedule III.
>
> (5) SCHEDULE V
>> (A) The drug or other substance has a low potential for abuse relative to the drugs or other substances in schedule IV.
>> (B) The drug or other substance has a currently accepted medical use in treatment in the United States.
>> (C) Abuse of the drug or other substance may lead to limited physical dependence or psychological dependence relative to the drugs or other substances in schedule IV.

(c) Schedules I, II, III, IV, and V shall, unless and until amended pursuant to section 201, consist of the following drugs or other substances, by whatever official name, common or usual name, chemical name, or brand name designated.

Accordingly, the following are listings of the controlled drugs within their respective schedules:

> SCHEDULE I
> (a) Unless specifically excepted or unless listed in another schedule, any of the following opiates, including their isomers, esters, ethers, salts, and salts of isomers, esters, and ethers, whenever the existence of such isomers, esters, ethers, and salts is possible within the specific chemical designation:
>> (1) Acetylmethadol.

    (2)   Allylprodine.
    (3)   Alphacetylmethadol.
    (4)   Alphameprodine.
    (5)   Alphamethadol.
    (6)   Benzethidine.
    (7)   Betacetylmethadol.
    (8)   Betameprodine.
    (9)   Betamethadol.
  (10)   Betaprodine.
  (11)   Clonitazene.
  (12)   Dextromoramide.
  (13)   Dextrorphan.
  (14)   Diampromide.
  (15)   Diethylthiambutene.
  (16)   Dimenoxadol.
  (17)   Dimepheptanol.
  (18)   Dimethylthiambutene.
  (19)   Dioxaphetyl butyrate.
  (20)   Dipipanone.
  (21)   Ethylmethylthiambutene.
  (22)   Etonitazene.
  (23)   Etoxeridine.
  (24)   Furethidine.
  (25)   Hydroxypethidine.
  (26)   Ketobemidone.
  (27)   Levomoramide.
  (28)   Levophenacylmorphan.
  (29)   Morpheridine.
  (30)   Noracymethadol.
  (31)   Norlevorphanol.
  (32)   Normethadone.
  (33)   Norpipanone.
  (34)   Phenadoxone.
  (35)   Phenampromide.
  (36)   Phenomorphan.
  (37)   Phenoperidine.
  (38)   Piritramide.
  (39)   Proheptazine.
  (40)   Properidine.
  (41)   Racemoramide.
  (42)   Trimeperidine.

    (b) Unless specifically excepted or unless listed in another schedule, any of the following opium derivatives, their salts, isomers, and salts of isomers whenever the existence of such salts, isomers, and salts of isomers is possible within the specific chemical designation:

    (1)   Acetorphine.
    (2)   Acetyldihydrocodeine.
    (3)   Benzylmorphine.
    (4)   Codeine methylbromide.
    (5)   Codeine-N-Oxide.
    (6)   Cyprenorphine.
    (7)   Desomorphine.
    (8)   Dihydromorphine.
    (9)   Etorphine.
  (10)   Heroin.
  (11)   Hydromorphinol.
  (12)   Methyldesorphine.
  (13)   Methylhydromorphine.
  (14)   Morphine methylbromide.

   (15)   Morphine methylsulfonate.
   (16)   Morphine-N-Oxide.
   (17)   Myrophine.
   (18)   Nicocodeine.
   (19)   Nicomorphine.
   (20)   Normorphine.
   (21)   Phoclodine.
   (22)   Thebacon.

(c) Unless specifically excepted or unless listed in another schedule, any material, compound, mixture, or preparation, which contains any quantity of the following hallucinogenic substances, or which contains any of their salts, isomers, and salts of isomers whenever the existence of such salts, isomers, and salts of isomers is possible within the specific chemical designation:

   (1)   3,4-methylenedioxy amphetamine.
   (2)   5-methoxy-3,4-methylenedioxy amphetamine.
   (3)   3,4,5-trimethoxy amphetamine.
   (4)   Bufotenine.
   (5)   Diethyltryptamine.
   (6)   Dimethyltryptamine.
   (7)   4-methyl-2,5-dimethoxylamphetamine.
   (8)   Ibogaine.
   (9)   Lysergic acid diethylamide.
  (10)   Marihuana.
  (11)   Mescaline.
  (12)   Peyote.
  (13)   N-ethyl-3-piperidyl benzilate.
  (14)   N-methyl-3-piperidyl benzilate.
  (15)   Psilocybin.
  (16)   Psilocyn.
  (17)   Tetrahydrocannabinols.

SCHEDULE II

(a) Unless specifically excepted or unless listed in another schedule, any of the following substances whether produced directly or indirectly by extraction from substances of vegetable origin, or independently by means of chemical synthesis, or by a combination of extraction and chemical synthesis:

   (1) Opium and opiate, and any salt, compound, derivative, or preparation of opium or opiate.

   (2) Any salt, compound, derivative, or preparation thereof which is chemically equivalent or identical with any of the substances referred to in clause (1), except that these substances shall not include the isoquinoline alkaloids of opium.

   (3) Opium poppy and poppy straw.

   (4) Coca leaves and any salt, compound, derivative, or preparation of coca leaves, and any salt, compound, derivative, or preparation thereof which is chemically equivalent or identical with any of these substances, except that the substances shall not include decocainized coca leaves or extraction of coca leaves, which extractions do not contain cocaine or ecgonine.

(b) Unless specifically excepted or unless listed in another schedule, any of the following opiates, including their isomers, esters, ethers, salts, and salts of isomers, esters and ethers, whenever the existence of such isomers, esters, ethers, and salts is possible within the specific chemical designation:

   (1)   Alphaprodine.
   (2)   Anileridine.
   (3)   Bezitramide.
   (4)   Dihydrocodeine.
   (5)   Diphenoxylate.

(6) Fentanyl.

(7) Isomethadone.

(8) Levomethorphan.

(9) Levorphanol.

(10) Metazocine.

(11) Methadone.

(12) Methadone-Intermediate, 4-cyano-2-dimethylamino-4, 4-diphenyl butane.

(13) Moramide-Intermediate, 2-methyl-3-morpholino-1, 1-diphenyl-propane-carboxylic acid.

(14) Pethidine.

(15) Pethidine-Intermediate-A, 4-cyano-1-methyl-4-phenylpiperidine.

(16) Pethidine-Intermediate-B, ethyl-4-phenylpiperidine-4-carboxylate.

(17) Pethidine-Intermediate-C, 1-methyl-4-phenylpiperidine-4-carboxylic acid.

(18) Phenazocine.

(19) Piminodine.

(20) Racemethorphan.

(21) Racemorphan.

(c) Unless specifically excepted or unless listed in another schedule, any injectable liquid which contains any quantity of methamphetamine, including its salts, isomers, and salts of isomers.

SCHEDULE III

(a) Unless specifically excepted or unless listed in another schedule, any material, compound, mixture, or preparation which contains any quantity of the following substances having a stimulant effect on the central nervous system:

(1) Amphetamine, its salts, optical isomers, and salts of its optical isomers.

(2) Phenmetrazine and its salts.

(3) Any substance (except an injectable liquid) which contains any quantity of methamphetamine, including its salts, isomers, and salts of isomers.

(4) Methylphenidate.

(b) Unless specifically excepted or unless listed in another schedule, any material, compound, mixture, or preparation which contains any quantity of the following substances having a depressant effect on the central nervous system:

(1) Any substance which contains any quantity of a derivative of barbituric acid, or any salt of a derivative of barbituric acid.

(2) Chlorhexadol.

(3) Glutethimide.

(4) Lysergic acid.

(5) Lysergic acid amide.

(6) Methyprylon.

(7) Phencyclidine.

(8) Sulfondiethylmethane.

(9) Sulfonethylmethane.

(10) Sulfonmethane.

(c) Nalorphine.

(d) Unless specifically excepted or unless listed in another schedule, any material, compound, mixture, or preparation containing limited quantities of any of the following narcotic drugs, or any salts thereof:

(1) Not more than 1.8 grams of codeine per 100 milliliters or not more than 90 milligrams per dosage unit, with an equal or greater quantity of an isoquinoline alkaloid of opium.

(2) Not more than 1.8 grams of codeine per 100 milliliters or not more than 90 milligrams per dosage unit, with one or more active, nonnarcotic ingredients in recognized therapeutic amounts.

(3) Not more than 300 milligrams of dihydrocodeinone per 100 milliliters or not more than 15 milligrams per dosage unit, with a fourfold or greater quantity of an isoquinoline alkaloid of opium.

(4) Not more than 300 milligrams of dihydrocodeinone per 100 milliliters or not more than 15 milligrams per dosage unit, with one or more active, nonnarcotic ingredients in recognized therapeutic amounts.

(5) Not more than 1.8 grams of dihydrocodeine per 100 milliliters or not more than 90 milligrams per dosage unit, with one or more active, nonnarcotic ingredients in recognized therapeutic amounts.

(6) Not more than 300 milligrams of ethylmorphine per 100 milliliters or not more than 15 milligrams per dosage unit, with one or more active, nonnarcotic ingredients in recognized therapeutic amounts.

(7) Not more than 500 milligrams of opium per 100 milliliters or per 100 grams, or not more than 25 milligrams per dosage unit, with one or more active, nonnarcotic ingredients in recognized therapeutic amounts.

(8) Not more than 50 milligrams of morphine per 100 milliliters or per 100 grams with one or more active, nonnarcotic ingredients in recognized therapeutic amounts.

SCHEDULE IV

(1) Barbital.
(2) Chloral betaine.
(3) Chloral hydrate.
(4) Ethchlorvynol.
(5) Ethinamate.
(6) Methohexital.
(7) Meprobamate.
(8) Methylphenobarbital.
(9) Paraldehyde.
(10) Petrichloral.
(11) Phenobarbital.

SCHEDULE V

Any compound, mixture, or preparation containing any of the following limited quantities of narcotic drugs, which shall include one or more non-narcotic active medicinal ingredients in sufficient proportion to confer upon the compound, mixture, or preparation valuable medicinal qualities other than those possessed by the narcotic drug alone:

(1) Not more than 200 milligrams of codeine per 100 milliliters or per 100 grams.

(2) Not more than 100 milligrams of dihydrocodeine per 100 milliliters or per 100 grams.

(3) Not more than 100 milligrams of ethylmorphine per 100 milliliters or per 100 grams.

(4) Not more than 2.5 milligrams of diphenoxylate and not less than 25 micrograms of atropine sulfate per dosage unit.

(5) Not more than 100 milligrams of opium per 100 milliliters or per 100 grams.

(d) The Attorney General may by regulation except any compound, mixture, or preparation containing any depressant or stimulant substance in paragraph (a) or (b) of Schedule III or in schedule IV or V from the application of all or any part of this title if (1) the compound, mixture, or preparation contains one or more active medicinal ingredients not having a depressant or stimulant effect on the central nervous system, and (2) such ingredients are included therein in such combinations, quantity, proportion, or concentration as to vitiate the potential for abuse of the substances which do have a depressant or stimulant effect on the central nervous system.

Registration Requirements

Part C of this title describes the registration of manufacturers, distributors and dispensers of controlled substances. Generally, it authorizes the Attorney General to promulgate rules and regulations and to charge reasonable fees relating to the registration and control of the manufacture, distribution and dispensation of controlled substances.

Every person falling into one or more of the above cited areas must obtain annually a registration issued by the Attorney General. Exempted from registering are the following:

1. An agent or employee of any registered manufacturer, distributor, or dispenser of any controlled substance if he is acting within the usual scope of the business or employment.
2. A common or contract carrier or warehouseman, or an employee thereof, whose possession of the controlled substance is in the usual scope of his business or employment.
3. An ultimate user who possesses such substance for his own use or for the use of a member of his household or for an animal owned by him or a member of his household.

A separate registration is required at each principal place of business or professional practice where the applicant manufactures, distributes, or dispenses controlled substances.

Since the new law went into effect, the Internal Revenue Service and the Food and Drug Administration are no longer issuing a registration authorizing a person or firm to handle controlled substances. Registration with the Bureau of Narcotics and Dangerous Drugs (BNDD) became effective with the new law. Registration is accomplished by completing Form BND 224A (Ed. 1/71) or Form 225B, Application for Registration, and returning it to the BNDD with the appropriate fee.

The registration fees are as follows:

Manufacturer (includes repackers and relabelers)	$50
Distributor (wholesalers)	25
Importer or Import Broker/Forwarder	25
Exporter or Export Broker/Forwarder	25
Foreign Firm (manufacturing for importation into the U.S.A.)	25
Retail Pharmacy	5
Hospital and Clinic	5
Practitioner	5
Researcher	5
Analytical Laboratory	5
Teaching Institution	5

The Attorney General may, in accord with the rules and regulations promulgated by him, inspect the establishment of a registrant or applicant for registration.

Registration may be granted to the applicant if the Attorney General determines that such registration is in the public interest. The following are some of the factors that are considered in determining the public interest:

1. Maintenance of effective control against diversion of the controlled substances into other than legal channels;
2. Compliance with applicable state and municipal law;
3. Prior conviction record of the applicant;
4. Past experience in the distribution of controlled substances;
5. Such other factors as may be relevant to and consistent with the public health and safety.

Labeling and Packaging Requirements

Labeling and packaging requirements under this law are cited in Section 305 (a), (b), (c) and (d). Generally, they require that containers of controlled substances must meet the labeling requirements of the Federal Food, Drug, and Cosmetic Act or the regulations to be promulgated by the Attorney General.

Each controlled substance manufactured after December 1, 1971 must have on its label a symbol designating to which schedule it belongs. The symbol will be a letter C with the Roman numeral I, II, III, IV or V. This symbol will appear in the upper right hand portion of the label. Manufacturers and other registrants will be given adequate time, to be specified by regulations, in order to comply with the symbol requirements.

Records and Reports

Records and reports of registrants are important factors under this law. These are described in Section 307 (a) through (3) and provide for the following:

1. An inventory of all of the controlled substances must be taken on the effective date of the law (May 1, 1971) and every second year thereafter.
2. After inventory, every registrant shall maintain, on a current basis, a complete and accurate record of each substance manufactured, received, sold, delivered or otherwise disposed of by him. A perpetual inventory is not required.
3. Records to be kept must be in conformity with the regulations of the Attorney General.
4. Records of the controlled substances must be maintained separately from all other records of the registrant.
5. Records of the non-narcotic controlled substances must be in such form that information required by the Attorney General is readily retrievable from the ordinary business records of the registrant.

6. All records shall be kept available for at least two years.

The foregoing provisions do not apply in the following instances:

1. With respect to narcotic controlled substances in Schedule II, III, IV or V, to the prescribing or administering of such substances by a practitioner in the lawful course of his professional practice; or
2. With respect to non-narcotic controlled substances in Schedule II, III, IV or V, to any practitioner who dispenses such substances to his patients, unless the practitioner is regularly engaged in charging his patients, either separately or together with charges for other professional services, for substances so dispensed.
3. To the use of controlled substances, at institutions registered under this title which keep records with respect to such substances, in research conducted in conformity with an exemption granted under Section 505 (i) or 512 (j) of the Federal Food, Drug, and Cosmetic Act.
4. To the use of controlled substances at establishments registered under this title which keep records with respect to such substances, in preclinical research or in teaching.

Records pertaining to substances in Schedule II and narcotic substances in Schedules III, IV and V must be kept separate. All records pertaining to controlled substances shall be made available for inspection and copying by officers of the United States authorized by the Attorney General.

Inventory Requirements

On Saturday, May 1, 1971 every registrant was required to make a complete and accurate record of all stocks of controlled substances on hand. The inventory record must:

1. Have indicated whether it was taken at the opening or close of business on May 1.
2. Have been signed by the person responsible for taking the inventory.
3. Be maintained at the location appearing on the registration for at least two years.

Order Forms

As under the present narcotic law, it is unlawful for any person to distribute a controlled substance in Schedule I or II except in pursuance of a written order from the person to whom such substance is distributed, made on a form to be issued by the Attorney General to persons validly registered under Sections 302 (d) or 303. A reasonable charge may be made for the issuance of such forms.

As of the effective date of the new law, the Internal Revenue Service ceased the distribution of order forms and the BNDD commenced the issuance of new forms.

Pharmacists who choose to obtain and use the BNDD Order Forms and still possess the IRS Forms must not discard the IRS Forms. A line should be drawn across the face of each unused form and the word VOID written along the line. These cancelled forms must then be kept for at least two years from May 1, 1971.

Several basic changes from the previous order form procedure became effective as of May 1, 1971. They are as follows:

1. After a registrant has issued an order form for Schedule I or II controlled substances and when he receives the items ordered, he must record, on his retained copy in his book, the number of packages and the date such packages were received. A space on the new BNDD Order Forms has been provided for this entry. If the IRS Forms are used, the entry will be made in the "Number and Date Filled" section of the retained copy.
2. As of May 1, 1971, former Class B Narcotics are classified as Schedule III controlled substances and *are not* subject to official order form requirement.
3. An order form containing an item which is not a Schedule I or II controlled substance is deemed to be improperly prepared and the order form *must* be returned to the purchaser without filling *any* item on the form.

Prescriptions

In studying the contents of Section 309 which follows, the reader is urged to make constant reference to the Federal Food, Drug, and Cosmetic Act Section 503 (b).

Section 309 provides the following requirements:

1. Except when dispensed directly by a practitioner, other than a pharmacist, to an ultimate user, no controlled substance in Schedule II, which is a prescription drug as determined under the Federal Food, Drug, and Cosmetic Act, may be dispensed without a written prescription of a practitioner.
2. Drugs may be dispensed on an oral prescription in an emergency situation.
3. Prescriptions shall be retained in conformity with the requirements of this law.
4. No prescription for a controlled substance in Schedule II may be refilled.
5. Controlled substances in Schedule III or IV may not be dispensed without a written or oral prescription in conformity with Section 503 (b) of the Federal Food, Drug, and Cosmetic Act.
6. Such prescriptions may not be filled or refilled more than six months after the date thereof or be refilled more than five times after the the date of the prescription unless renewed by the practitioner.

7. No controlled substance in Schedule V which is a drug may be distributed or dispensed other than for a medical purpose.

Prescriptions filled with controlled substances in Schedule II must be written in ink or indelible pencil and must be signed by the practitioner issuing them.

Although no prescriptions for a controlled substance in Schedule II may be refilled, such prescriptions, as well as prescriptions for narcotic substances in Schedules III, IV, and V, must be kept in a separate file.

Prescriptions for controlled substances in Schedule III or IV may be issued either orally or in writing and may be refilled if so authorized. These prescriptions may not be filled or refilled more than six months after the date issued, or be refilled more than five times after the date issued. After five refills or after six months the practitioner may renew any such prescription. A renewal should be recorded on a new prescription blank and a new prescription number should be assigned to that prescription.

It should be noted that one of the major changes in the law pertaining to prescriptions permits the refilling of prescriptions for drugs that were formerly known as Class B Narcotics, if so authorized by the practitioner.

Offenses and Penalties

Part D concerns itself with a listing of prohibited acts, most of which are familiar to the pharmacist. Examples include:

1. Dispensing controlled drugs without first becoming registered.
2. Removing, altering or obliterating a symbol or label required by this title.
3. Refusing or failing to make, keep or furnish any record, report, notification, declaration, order or order forms, statement, invoice or information required under this title.
4. Refusing an entry into any premises or inspection authorized by this title.

Finally, the section provides for various penalties to be assessed for the various violations and range from fines, imprisonment or both depending upon the seriousness of the violation.

Irrespective of the passage of the DACA 1965 legislation, illicit drug traffic continued to increase. As a result thereof, tighter and more stringent controls were deemed essential for the public welfare. Therefore, the Comprehensive Drug Abuse Prevention and Control Act of 1970 was passed.

INVESTIGATIONAL USE DRUGS IN HUMANS

Since the beginning of recorded medical history, physicians and other researchers in the basic sciences have found it necessary to conduct human experimentation in order to further medical knowledge. Most members of our society accept this as indispensable to the progress of medical science yet firmly believe that it must be controlled to some extent.

Consequently, numerous codes and statements have been developed in the hope that they would serve as guidelines for human experimentation. Although most of these codes, statements, oaths and regulations limit the sphere of medical human experimentation, this text will concern itself only with three in the belief that these will be adequate to demonstrate to the student the basic principles of each—namely, the satisfaction of moral, ethical and legal concepts.

First, the *Declaration of Helsinki* provides recommendations for guiding doctors in clinical research. Contained with the Declaration are the following sections:

I. Basic Principles
1. Clinical research must conform to the moral and scientific principles that justify medical research and should be based on scientifically established facts.
2. Clinical research should be conducted only by scientifically qualified persons and under the supervision of a qualified medical man.
3. Clinical research cannot legitimately be carried out unless the importance of the objective is in proportion to the inherent risk to the subject.
4. Every clinical research project should be preceded by careful assessment of inherent risks in comparison to foreseeable benefits to the subject or to others.
5. Special caution should be exercised by the doctor in performing clinical research in which the personality of the subject is liable to be altered by drugs or experimental procedure.

II. Clinical Research Combined with Professional Care
1. In the treatment of the sick person, the doctor must be free to use a new therapeutic measure, if in his judgment it offers hope of saving life, reestablishing health, or alleviating suffering.

   If at all possible, consistent with patient psychology, the doctor should obtain the patient's freely given consent after the patient has been given a full explanation. In case of legal incapacity, consent should also be procured from the legal guardian; in case of physical incapacity the permission of the legal guardian replaces that of the patient.
2. The doctor can combine clinical research with professional care, the objective being the acquisition of new medical knowledge, only to the extent that clinical research is justified by its therapeutic value for the patient.

III. Non-Therapeutic Clinical Research
1. In the purely scientific application of clinical research carried out on a human being, it is the duty of the doctor to remain the protector of the life and health of that person on whom clinical research is being carried out.
2. The nature, the purpose and the risk of clinical research must be explained to the subject by the doctor.
3a. Clinical research on a human being cannot be undertaken without his free consent after he has been informed; if he is legally incompetent, the consent of the legal guardian should be procured.
3b. The subject of clinical research should be in such a mental, physical and legal state as to be able to exercise fully his power of choice.
3c. Consent should, as a rule, be obtained in writing. However, the responsibility for clinical research always remains with the research worker; it never falls on the subject even after consent is obtained.
4. The investigator must respect the right of each individual to safeguard his personal integrity, especially if the subject is in a dependent relationship to the investigator.

The *Nuremberg Code*, generated by the Nuremberg Military Tribunals in which was vested the authority to conduct the War Crimes Trials after World War II, provides the following:

1. The voluntary consent of the human subject is absolutely essential. This means that the person involved should have legal capacity to give consent; should be so situated as to be able to exercise free power of choice, without the intervention of any element of force, fraud, deceit, duress, over-reaching, or other ulterior form of constraint or coercion; and should have sufficient knowledge and comprehension of the elements of the subject matter involved as to enable him to make an understanding and enlightened decision.

   This latter element requires that before the acceptance of an affirmative decision by the experimental subject there should be made known to him the nature, duration, and purpose of the experiment; the method and means by which it is to be conducted; all inconveniences and hazards reasonably to be expected; and the effects upon his health or person which may possibly come from his participation in the experiment.

   The duty and responsibility for ascertaining the quality of the consent rests upon each individual who initiates, directs, or engages in the experiment. It is a personal duty and responsibility which may not be delegated to another with impunity.

2. The experiment should be such as to yield fruitful results for the good of society, unprocurable by other methods or means of study, and not random and unnecessary in nature.

3. The experiment should be so designed and based on the results of animal experimentation and a knowledge of the natural history of the disease or other problem under study that the anticipated results will justify the performance of the experiment.

4. The experiment should be so conducted as to avoid all unnecessary physical and mental suffering and injury.

5. No experiment should be conducted where there is a priori reason to believe that death or disabling injury will occur, except, perhaps, in those experiments where the experimental physicians also serve as subjects.

6. The degree of risk to be taken should never exceed that determined by the humanitarian importance of the problem to be solved by the experiment.

7. Proper preparations should be made and adequate facilities provided to protect the experimental subject against even remote possibilities of injury, disability, or death.

8. The experiment should be conducted only by scientifically qualified persons. The highest degree of skill and care should be required, through all states of the experiment, of those who conduct or engage in the experiment.

9. During the course of the experiment the human subject should be at liberty to bring the experiment to an end if he has reached the physical or mental state where continuation of the experiment seems to him to be impossible.

10. During the course of the experiment the scientist in charge must be prepared to terminate the experiment at any stage, if he has probable cause to believe, in the exercise of good faith, superior skill, and careful judgment required of him that a continuation of the experiment is likely to result in injury, disability, or death to the experimental subject.

With respect to medical human experimentation in the United States, the FDA has developed rather specific guidelines. For example, a physician desirous of conducting studies on a new drug must comply with a set procedure that requires the following:

A. The pharmaceutical manufacturer sponsoring the investigation must submit to the FDA a *Notice of Claimed Investigational Exemption for a New Drug* (Form 1571). This notice is submitted in accord with the requirements of Section 505 (i) of the Federal Food, Drug, and Cosmetic Act and Section 130.3 of Title 21 of the Code of Federal Regulations. Attachments to Form 1571 must include those required by the following:[4]

1. The best available descriptive name of the drug, including to the extent known the chemical name and structure of any new-drug substance, and a statement of how it is to be administered. (If the drug has only a code name, enough information should be supplied to identify the drug.)

2. Complete list of components of the drug, including any reasonable alternates for inactive components.

3. Complete statement of quantitative composition of drug, including reasonable variations that may be expected during the investigational stage.

4. Description of source and preparation of any new-drug substances used as components, including the name and address of each supplier or processor, other than the sponsor, of each new-drug substance.

5. A statement of the methods, facilities, and controls used for the manufacturing, processing, and packing of the new drug to establish and maintain appropriate standards of identity, strength, quality, and purity as needed for safety and to give significance to clinical investigations made with the drug.

6. A statement covering all information available to the sponsor derived from preclinical investigations and any clinical studies and experience with the drug as follows:

   (a) Adequate information about the preclinical investigations, including studies made on laboratory animals, on the basis of which the sponsor has concluded that it is reasonably safe to initiate clinical investigations with the drug: Such information should include identification of the person who conducted each investigation; identification and qualifications of the individuals who evaluated the results and concluded that it is reasonably safe to initiate clinical investigations with the drug and a statement of where the investigations were conducted and where the records are available for inspection; and enough details about the investigations to permit scientific review. The preclinical investigations shall not be considered adequate to justify clinical testing unless they give proper attention to the conditions of the proposed clinical testing. When this information, the outline of the plan of clinical pharmacology, or any progress report on the clinical pharmacology, indicates a need for full review of the preclinical data before a clinical trial is undertaken, the Department will notify the sponsor to submit the complete preclinical data and to withhold clinical trials until the review is completed and the sponsor notified. The Food and Drug Administration will be prepared to confer with the sponsor concerning this action.

   (b) If the drug has been marketed commercially or investigated (e.g. outside the United States), complete information about such distribution or investigation shall be submitted, along with a complete bibliography of any publications about the drug.

(c) If the drug is a combination of previously investigated or marketed drugs, an adequate summary of pre-existing information from preclinical and clinical investigations and experience with its components, including all reports available to the sponsor suggesting side-effects, contraindications, and ineffectiveness in use of such components: Such summary should include an adequate bibliography of publications about the components and may incorporate by reference any information concerning such components previously submitted by the sponsor to the Food and Drug Administration. Include a statement of the expected pharmacological effects of the combination.

7. A total of five copies of all informational material, including label and labeling, which is to be supplied to each investigator: This shall include an accurate description of the prior investigations and experience and their results pertinent to the safety and possible usefulness of the drug under the conditions of the investigation. It shall not represent that the safety or usefulness of the drug has been established for the purpose to be investigated. It shall describe all relevant hazards, contraindications, side-effects, and precautions suggested by prior investigations and experience with the drug or chemically or pharmacologically related drugs for the information of clinical investigators.

8. The scientific training and experience considered appropriate by the sponsor to qualify the investigators as suitable experts to investigate the safety of the drug, bearing in mind what is known about the pharmacological action of the drug and the phase of the investigational program that is to be undertaken.

9. The names and a summary of the training and experience of each investigator and of the individual charges with monitoring the progress of the investigation and evaluating the evidence of safety and effectiveness of the drug as it is received from the investigators, together with a statement that the sponsor has obtained from each investigator a completed and signed form, as provided in subparagraph (12) or (13) of this paragraph, and that the investigator is qualified by scientific training and experience as an appropriate expert to undertake the phase of the investigation outlined in section 10 of the "Notice of claimed investigational exemption for a new drug." (In crucial situations, phase 3 investigators may be added and this form supplemented by rapid communication methods, and the signed form FD 1573 shall be obtained promptly thereafter).

10. An outline of any phase or phases of the planned investigations, as follows:

(a) Clinical pharmacology. This is ordinarily divided into two phases: phase 1 starts when the new drug is first introduced into man—only animal and in vitro data are available—with the purpose of determining human toxicity, metabolism, absorption, elimination, and other pharmacological action, preferred route of administration, and safe dosage range; phase 2 covers the initial trials on a limited number of patients for specific disease control or prophylaxis purposes. A general outline of these phases shall be submitted, identifying the investigator or investigators, the hospitals or research facilities where the clinical pharmacology will be undertaken, any expert committees or panels to be utilized, the maximum number of subjects to be involved, and the estimated duration of these early phases of investigation. Modification of the experimental design on the basis of the experience gained need be reported only in the progress reports on these early phases, or in the development of the plan for the clinical trial, phase 3. The first two phases may overlap and, when indicated, may require additional animal data before these phases can be completed or phase 3 can be undertaken. Such animal tests shall be designed to take into account the expected duration of administration of the drug to human beings, the age groups and physical status, as for example, infants, pregnant women, pre-menopausal women, of those human beings to whom the drug may be administered, unless this has already been done in the original animal studies.

(b) Clinical trial. This phase 3 provides the assessment of the drug's safety and effectiveness and optimum dosage schedules in the diagnosis, treatment, or prophylaxis of groups of subjects involving a given disease or condition. A reasonable protocol is developed on the basis of the facts accumulated in the earlier phases, including completed and submitted animal studies. This phase is conducted by separate groups following the same protocol (with reasonable variations and alternatives permitted by the plan) to produce well-controlled clinical data. For this phase, the following data shall be submitted:

(i) The names and addresses of the investigators. (Additional investigators may be added.)

(ii) The specific nature of the investigations to be conducted, together with information or case report forms to show the scope and detail of the planned clinical laboratory tests to be made and reported.

(iii) The approximate number of subjects (a reasonable range of subjects is permissible and additions may be made), and criteria proposed for subject selection by age, sex, and condition.

(iv) The estimated duration of the clinical trial and the intervals, not exceeding 1 year, at which progress reports showing the results of the investigations will be submitted to the Food and Drug Administration.

(The notice of claimed investigational exemption may be limited to any one or more phases, provided the outline of the additional phase or phases is submitted before such additional phases begin. This does not preclude continuing a subject on the drug from phase 2 to phase 3 without interruption while the plan for phase 3 is being developed.)

Ordinarily, a plan for clinical trial will not be regarded as reasonable unless, among other things, it provides for more than one independent competent investigator to maintain adequate case histories of an adequate number of subjects, designed to record observations and permit evaluation of any and all discernible effects attributable to the drug in each individual treated, and comparable records on any individuals employed as controls.

These records shall be individual records for each subject maintained to include adequate information pertaining to each, including age, sex, conditions treated, dosage, frequency of administration of the drug, results of all relevant clinical observations and laboratory examinations made, adequate information concerning any other treatment given and a full statement of any adverse effects and useful results observed, together with an opinion as to whether such effects or results are attributable to the drug under investigation.

11. A statement that the sponsor will notify the Food and Drug Administration if the investigation is discontinued, and the reason therefor.

12. A statement that the sponsor will notify each investigator if a new-drug application is approved, or if the investigation is discontinued.

13. If the drug is to be sold, a full explanation why sale is required and should not be regarded as the commercialization of a new drug for which an application is not approved.

B. The manufacturer must submit to the FDA an *Investigational New Drug Application* (INDA).

C. The clinical investigator must demonstrate his competence to conduct the study via FDA forms 1572 (for clinical pharmacology) and 1573 (for clinical trials).

D. The drug label must state that it is restricted to investigational use.

E. The investigator and sponsor must keep the FDA fully informed as to the progress of the study via adequate records and periodic reports on all clinical observations.

In addition, the FDA has published the following regulations governing the conduct of the clinical investigator[5]:

Sec. 130.3 New drugs for investigational use in human beings; exemptions from section 505(a).

(1) Whenever the Food and Drug Administration has information indicating that an investigator has repeatedly or deliberately failed to comply with the conditions of these exempting regulations outlined in Form FD-1572 or FD-1573 (set forth in paragraph (a) (12) and (13) of this section), or has submitted to the sponsor of the investigation false information in his Form FD-1572 or FD-1573 or in any required report, the Director of the Bureau of Medicine will furnish the investigator written notice of the matter complained of in general terms and offer him an opportunity to explain the matter in an informal conference and/or in writing. If an explanation is offered but not accepted by the Bureau of Medicine, the Commissioner will provide the investigator an opportunity for an informal hearing on the question of whether the investigator is entitled to receive investigational-use drugs, if the hearing is requested within 10 days after receipt of notification that the explanation is not acceptable.

(2) After evaluating all available information, including any explanation and assurance presented by the investigator, if the Commissioner determines that the investigator has repeatedly or deliberately failed to comply with the conditions of the exempting regulations in this section or has repeatedly or deliberately submitted false information to the sponsor of an investigation and has failed to furnish adequate assurance that the conditions of the exemption will be met, the Commissioner will notify the investigator and the sponsor of any investigation in which he has been named as participant that the investigator is not entitled to receive investigational-use drugs with a statement of the basis for such determination.

(3) Each "Notice of Claimed Investigational Exemption for a New Drug" (Form FD-1571 set forth in paragraph (a) (2) of this section) and each approved new-drug application containing data reported by an investigator who has been determined to be ineligible to receive investigational-use drugs will be examined to determine whether he has submitted unreliable data that are essential to the continuation of the investigation or essential to the approval of any new-drug application.

(4) If the Commissioner determines after the unreliable data submitted by the investigator are eliminated from consideration that the data remaining are inadequate to support a conclusion that it is reasonably safe to continue the investigation, he will notify the sponsor and provide him with an opportunity for a conference and an informal hearing in accordance with paragraph (d) of this section. If an imminent hazard to the public health exists, however, he shall terminate the exemption forthwith and notify the sponsor of the termination. In such event the Commissioner, on request,

will afford the sponsor an opportunity for an informal hearing on the question of whether the exemption should be reinstated.

(5) If the Commissioner determines after the unreliable data submitted by the investigator are eliminated from consideration that the data remaining are such that a new-drug application would not have been approved, he will proceed to withdraw approval of the application in accordance with section 505(e) of the act.

(6) An investigator who has been determined to be ineligible may be reinstated as eligible to receive investigational-use drugs when the Commissioner determines that he has presented adequate assurance that he will employ such drugs solely in compliance with the exempting regulations in this section for investigational-use drugs.

In addition he shall notify the sponsor and invite his immediate correction or explanation. A conference will be arranged with the Bureau of Medicine if requested. If the Bureau of Medicine does not accept the explanation and/or the correction submitted by the sponsor, the Commissioner will provide the sponsor an opportunity for an informal hearing on the question of whether his exemption should be terminated, if the hearing is requested within 10 days after receipt of notification that the explanation or correction is not acceptable. After evaluating all the available information including any explanation and/or correction submitted by the sponsor, if the Commissioner determines that the exemption should be terminated he shall notify the sponsor of the termination of the exemption and the sponsor shall recall unused supplies of the drug. If at any time the Commissioner concludes that continuation of the investigation presents an imminent hazard to the public health, he shall terminate the exemption forthwith and notify the sponsor of the termination. The Commissioner will inform the sponsor that the exemption is subject to reinstatement on the basis of additional submissions that eliminate such hazard(s) and will afford the sponsor an opportunity for an informal hearing, on request, on the question of whether the exemption should be reinstated. The sponsor shall recall the unused supplies of the drug upon notification of the termination.

FDA Amendments of 1966

The Federal Food, Drug, and Cosmetic Act was amended in 1966 by a new statement of policy dealing with consent for the use of investigational new drugs which provides as follows:

(a) Section 505(i) of the act provides that regulations on use of investigational new drugs on human beings shall impose the condition that investigators "obtain the consent of such human beings or their representatives, except where they deem it not feasible or, in their professional judgment, contrary to the best interest of such human beings."

(b) This means that the consent of such human beings (or the consent of their representatives) to whom investigational drugs are administered primarily for the accumulation of scientific knowledge, for such purposes as studying drug behavior, body processes, or the course of a disease, must be obtained in all cases and, in all but exceptional cases, the consent of patients under treatment with investigational drugs must be obtained.

(c) *"Under treatment"* applies when the administration of the investigational drug for either diagnostic or therapeutic purposes constitutes responsible medical judgment, taking into account the availability of other remedies or drugs and the individual circumstances pertaining to the person to whom the investigational drug is to be administered.

(d) *"Exceptional cases,"* as used in paragraph (b) of this section, which exceptions are to be strictly applied, are cases where it is not feasible to obtain the patient's consent or the consent of his representative, or where, as a matter of professional judgment exercised in the best interest of a particular patient under the investigator's care, it would be contrary to that patient's welfare to obtain his consent.

(e) *"Patient"* means a person under treatment.

(f) *"Not feasible"* is limited to cases where the investigator is not capable of obtaining consent because of inability to communicate with the patient or his representative; for example, where the patient is in a coma or is otherwise incapable of giving informed consent, his representative cannot be reached, and it is imperative to administer the drug without delay.

(g) *"Contrary to the best interest of such human beings"* applies when the communication of information to obtain consent would seriously affect the patient's disease status and the physician has exercised a professional judgment that under the particular circumstances of this patient's case, the patient's best interest would suffer if consent were sought.

(h) *"Consent" or "informed consent"* means that the person involved has legal capacity to give consent, is so situated as to be able to exercise free power of choice, and is provided with a fair explanation of all material information concerning the administration of the investigational drug, or his possible use as a control, as to enable him to make an understanding decision as to his willingness to receive said investigational drug. This latter element requires that before the acceptance of an affirmative decision by such person the investigator should make known to him the nature, duration, and purpose of the administration of said investigation drug; the method and means by which it is to be administered; all inconveniences and hazards reasonably to be expected, including the fact, where applicable, that the person may be used as a control; the existence of alternative forms of therapy, if any; and the effects upon his health or person that may possibly come from the administration of the investigational drug. Said patient's consent shall be obtained in writing by the investigator.

Minchew and Gallogly[6] have interpreted these regulations in a manner which categorizes a clinical investigation into three phases. *Phase I* studies are stated to be those when a drug is first tried in humans and as a result thereof data on such areas as toxicity, metabolism, absorption, elimination and posology are gathered. *Phase II* covers the initial trials on a very limited number of patients for specific disease control or prophylactic purposes. *Phase III* is the actual general clinical trial designed to assess the drug's efficacy and safety.

Under the above cited regulations, clinical investigators are required to obtain the written informed consent of the patient being used in the experiment. The only exception is under "unusual circumstances" such as when a patient is in a coma, his representative cannot be reached and it is imperative to administer the drug or perform the operative procedure.

Between August 1966 and March 1967 a number of problems were created by the rigidity of the August 1966 Amendments, therefore on June 20, 1967 the FDA modified the guidelines defining procedures for carrying out the patient-consent requirements. Thus, the written informed consent of the patient is required throughout Phases I and II of the study, however in Phase III,

> . . . it is the responsibility of the investigators, taking into consideration the physical and mental state of the patient, to decide when it is necessary or preferable to obtain consent in other than the written form. When such written consent is not obtained, the investigator must obtain oral consent and

record the fact in the medical record of the person. . . . The investigator,
however, is required in all phases of clinical trials to give the patient "pertinent
information" on the investigational drug.

It is a well-documented principle that one may not legally experiment upon
another person to his detriment. This was amply brought out in a now famous
New York research project in which live cancer cells were being injected into
hospitalized patients without their knowledge or consent. The patients used in
the experiment were chronically ill, debilitated patients. The purpose of the
project was to study cancer immunology. The only information given to the
patients to obtain their consent was that an injection would be administered for
the purpose of testing his or her resistance or immunity to disease. They were
further told that a lump would develop but that within a few weeks it would
completely disappear. The patients were not even informed that this procedure
was a research project that was unrelated to their condition or its treatment.

Despite the fact that none of the patients were injured, a large scale investigation was touched off. The following is excerpted from the findings of the
Regents of the University of the State of New York, acting under responsibility
for licensing the medical profession in that state:

> We are of the opinion that there are certain basic ethical standards concerning
> consent to human experimentation which were involved in this experiment
> and which were violated by the respondants. When a patient engages a phys-
> ician or enters a hospital he may reasonably be deemed to have consented to
> such treatment as his physician or hospital staff, in the exercise of their
> professional judgment, deems proper. Consent to normal diagnostic test might
> similarly be presumed. Even so, doctors and hospitals as a matter of routine
> obtain formal written consent for surgery, and in a number of other instances,
> and whether or not a specific consent is required for a specific act must be
> decided on the facts of the particular case.

> No one contends that these 22 patients, by merely being in the hospital, have
> volunteered their bodies for any purpose other than treatment of their condi-
> tion. These injections were made as a part of a cancer research project. The
> incidental and remote possibility . . . that the research might have been bene-
> ficial to a patient is clearly insufficient to bring these injections within the area
> of procedures for which a consent could be implied. Actual consent was
> required.

> What form such an actual consent must take is a matter of applying common
> sense to the particular facts of the case. No consent is valid unless it is made
> by a person with legal and mental capacity to make it, and is based on the
> disclosure of all material facts. Any fact which might influence the giving or
> withholding of consent is material. A patient has the right to know he is being
> asked to volunteer and to refuse to participate in an experiment for any
> reason, intelligent or otherwise, well informed or prejudiced. A physician has
> no right to withhold from a prospective volunteer any fact which he knows
> may influence the decision. It is the volunteer's decision to make, and the
> physician may not take it away from him by the manner in which he asks the
> question or explains or fails to explain the circumstances. There is evidenced
> in the record in this proceeding an attitude on the part of some physicians that
> they can go ahead and do anything which they conclude is good for the
> patient, or which is of benefit experimentally, or educationally, and is not
> harmful to the patient, and the patient's consent is an empty formality. With

this we cannot agree. In his testimony, . . . Dr. . . . took the position that he regards these experiments as beneficial to the patients, both because the experiment might result in a diagnosis of advanced cancer which had not been discovered by the hospital, and also because the participation in the experiment would result in extra-medical attention to the patients involved and possibly other patients in the hospital.

The record indicates that the only additional medical care any of these patients received as a result of this experiment was the injections were made and they were occasionally checked thereafter as to the progress in growth or disappearance of the nodule. The inference that participation in the experiment benefited the patients because of such additional medical care is without foundation in the record. Since the purpose of the experiment was to obtain verification of . . . the hypothesis that diseased patients would reject the implant in the same manner as healthy patients and that their rejection would not be delayed as was that of patients suffering from advanced cancer, it is somewhat inconsistent for Dr. . . . to say before the experiment was completed that he authorized it as a diagnostic measure. In any event, it was clearly not treatment, not experimental therapy, and not a diagnostic test which would reasonably be given to these particular patients. Nevertheless, from the manner in which they were asked for their consent and from the statement made to them that this was a test to determine their immunity or their resistance to disease, the patients could naturally assume that it was being given to help in the diagnosis or treatment of their condition. They were not clearly and unequivocally asked if they wanted to volunteer to participate in an extraneous research project.

There is one point which is undisputed, namely that the patients were not told that the cells to be injected were live cancer cells. From the respondants' standpoint this was not considered to be an important fact. They regarded the experiment as medically harmless. There was not appreciable danger in any harmful effects to the patients as a result of the injections of these cancer cells. It is not uncommon for a doctor to refrain from telling his patient he had cancer where the physician in his professional judgment concludes that such a disclosure would be harmful to the patients. The respondants testified that they felt that telling these patients that the material did consist of live cancer cells would upset them and was immaterial to their concerns. They overlooked the key fact that so far as this particular experiment was concerned, there was not the usual doctor-patient relationship and, therefore, no basis for the exercise of their usual professional judgment applicable to the patient's care. No person can be said to have volunteered for an experiment unless he has first understood what he was volunteering for. Any matter which might influence him in giving or withholding his consent is material. Deliberate nondisclosure of the material fact is misrepresentation of such a fact. The respondants maintained that they did not withhold the fact that these were live cancer cells because some of the patients might have refused to consent to the injection of live cancer cells into their bodies. This was, however, a possibility and a decision that had to be made by the patients and not for them. Accordingly the alleged oral consents that they obtained after deliberately withholding this information were not informed consents and were, for this reason, fraudulently obtained.

Although there is conflicting testimony in evidence in this point, it is our opinion that some of these patients were in such a physical and mental condition that they were incapable of understanding the nature of this experiment or of giving an informed consent thereto. . . . We note that in no case were any relatives of these patients told about this experiment nor were any of these patients asked if they wished to think the matter over or discuss it with their relatives. It is noteworthy that one of these patients was operated on two days after the injections and that prior to making the operation, which was a part of the patient's treatment, the hospital obtained two separate written consents, each signed by both the patient and a relative. If there was any doubt at all concerning te patient's ability to fully comprehend the consent to this experiment, it was the duty of the physicians involved to resolve that doubt before proceeding further. . . . We do not say that it is necessary in all cases of human experimentation to obtain consents from the relatives or to obtain written consents, but certainly upon the fact of this case and in view of the fact that the patients were debilitated, the performance of this experiment on the basis of alleged oral consents from these particular patients falls short of the ethical standards of the medical profession.[7]

Another case dealing with drug experimentation and considered by some to be a landmark case involved a surgeon who at the time was also a professor of surgery on the medical school faculty. The defendant was sued in malpractice because of poor results after an injection of sodium acetrizoate (Urokon) in the performance of an aortogram. In handing down its decision, the court said:

Plaintiff, his wife and son testified that the plaintiff was not informed that anything in the nature of an aortography was to be performed. Dr. . . . and Dr. . . . contradicted this, although admitting that the details of the procedure and the possible dangers therefrom were not explained. The court gave a rather broad instruction upon the duty of the physician to disclose to the patient "all the facts which mutually affect his rights and interests, and of the surgical risk, hazard and danger, if any. . . ." A physician violates his duty to his patient and subjects himself to liability if he withholds any facts which are necessary to form the basis of an intelligent consent by the patient to the proposed treatment. Likewise the physician may not minimize the dangers of the procedure or operation in order to induce his patient to consent. At the same time, the physician must place the welfare of his patient above all else and this very fact places him in a position in which he sometimes must choose between two alternative courses of action. One is to explain to the patient every risk attendant upon any surgical procedure or operation, no matter how remote; this may result in alarming the patient who is already unduly apprehensive and who may as a result refuse to undertake surgery even if there is, in fact, only minimal risk; it may also result in actually increasing the risks by reason of the physiological result of the apprehension itself. The other is to recognize that each patient presents a separate problem, that the patient's mental and emotional condition is important and in certain cases may be crucial, and that in discussing the element of risk a certain amount of discretion must be employed consistent with the full disclosure of facts necessary to an informed consent.[8]

To this point, the student may have reached the opinion that physicians may not legally experiment with drugs in human beings without jeopardizing the experimental technique. Nothing could be further from the truth. All that is asked is that the physician protect the rights of the individual concerned. The fact that a human being becomes ill and requires the services of a physician, thus creating the patient-physician relationship, is not justification to deprive him of his right to be informed of the treatment or the experiment as the case might be.

In the *Salgo* v. *Leland Stanford University* case[8], the California court in reference to the variance of the injected dose of sodium acetriozate with the package insert of a dose of the drug stated:

The mere fact that the physician had departed from the drug manufacturer's recommendation does not make such departure an experiment. The fact that the physician had departed from the customary use followed by the physicians of standing in the locality does not in and of itself cause it to be an experimentation and therefore the permission of the patient is not necessarily required.[8]

Concerning the package insert issued by the drug's manufacturer, another court stated,

> . . . it is not conclusive evidence of standard or accepted practice in the use of the drugs by physicians or surgeons, nor that a departure from such directions is negligent. But it is prima facie proof of a proper method of use, given by the maker, which must be presumed qualified to give directions for its use and warnings of any danger inherent therein. [Citations deleted.]

> Thus, while admissible, it [the package insert] cannot establish as a matter of law the standard of care required of a physician in the use of a drug. It may be considered by the jury along with other evidence in the case to determine whether the particular physician met the standard of care required by him. The court's instructions on the subject should have been limited to this effect.

> The mere fact that a departure from the manufacturer's recommendation where such departure is customarily followed by physicians of standing in the locality does not make the departure an experiment.

> There was in this case no evidence of an experiment and the instructions concerning "experiments" should not have been given. Instructions without support in evidence should not be given.[9]

References

1. F. Depew: *Evolution of a Law,* FDA PAPERS, June 1968, p. 10.
2. United States v. Dotterweich, 320 U.S. 277 (1943).
3. W. Brennan: *Administrative Hearings in FDA*, FDA PAPERS, July-August 1968, p. 16, 25.
4. E. MARTIN, S. ALEXANDER, W. HASSAN, and B. SHERMAN: TECHNIQUES OF MEDICATION, J.B. Lippincott Co., Philadelphia, Pa., 1969, p. 218.
5. FEDERAL REGISTER, Vol. 33. No. 109, June 5, 1968.
6. H. Minchew and C. Gallogy: *Informed Consent*, FDA PAPERS, October 1967, p. 8.
7. Anon.: *New York Verdict Affirms Patient's Rights*, SCIENCE, 151:664-665, 1966.
8. Salgo v. Leland Stanford, Jr., University Board of Trustees, 317 P 2nd 170 California, 1967.
9. Julien v. Barker, 75 Idaho 413, 272 P 2nd 718, 1954.
10. Preamble, Public Law 91-513, 91st Congress, H.R. 18583 October 27, 1970.

CHAPTER 9

Federal Laws
Governing Alcohol

For the purpose of this section, the federal laws governing alcohol will be discussed on the basis of alcohol that is tax-free and alcohol that is subject to taxation.

Alcohol Subject to Taxation

Generally, community pharmacies that are engaged in the retail sale of alcoholic beverages are subject to the payment of a special tax. This tax is payable annually by filing the proper form and $54.00 with the District Director of the Internal Revenue District having jurisdiction over the area where the pharmacy is located. This tax is in addition to any state or local tax that may be levied. It must be remembered that this is a *tax* and should not be confused with a *license* to sell liquor which is obtained from a state or municipal agency.

Pharmacies not engaged in the retail sale of alcoholic beverages are not subject to the special tax even though 190-proof tax-paid alcohol is used in prescription compounding.[1]

With regard to the furnishing of alcoholic beverages to hospitalized patients through the hospital pharmacy, the following is pertinent and controlling in view of the fact that it was promulgated by the Internal Revenue Service division of Alcohol and Tobacco Tax:

> Internal Revenue laws impose special taxes on persons engaging or carrying on the business or occupation of selling, or offering for sale, any alcoholic liquors for use as a beverage whether or not such liquors are fit for such use.

> Regulations issued pursuant to Internal Revenue law provide that hospitals and similar institutions furnishing liquor to patients are not required to pay special tax, provided that no specific or additional charge is made for the liquor so furnished. This regulation is found at Section 194.187 of the Federal Liquor Dealer regulations. The words "no specific or additional charge" are interpreted as applying, for example, to those cases where a hospital or institu-

tion makes a fixed charge for treatment, subsistence, medicine, etc. and the over-all fee or charge remains the same regardless of whether alcoholic liquors are furnished to the patient.

A hospital or similar institution incurs liability for special tax as a retail liquor dealer whenever it furnishes an alcoholic liquor to a patient, whether pursuant to a prescription or otherwise, under conditions constituting a sale. These conditions would include any manner of accounting for a specific or additional charge made to a patient for alcoholic liquor furnished him. Totaling of charges for various items under a general heading, such as "Drugs and Dressings," would not give relief from special tax liability, if a charge for alcoholic liquors is one of the items included in the total.

Any hospital or similar institution which dispenses alcoholic liquors under conditions constituting a sale will be required to pay special tax as a retail liquor dealer. Special tax is paid by filing a tax return on Form 11 with the District Director of Revenue in the district in which the hospital is located. The special tax rate for a retail liquor dealer is $54.00 for each fiscal year beginning July 1.[2]

Alcohol Not Subject to Taxation

Federal law governing tax-free alcohol can be found in Part 213 of Title 26 (1954) Code of Federal Regulations. In addition, the applicability of these regulations to the practice of hospital pharmacy is described in textbooks on the subject.[3]

For the purpose of demonstrating to the student the comprehensive nature of Part 213 of Title 26, the following is a tabulation of the various sections and titles of Chapter 1 Subsection E dealing with the distribution and use of tax-free alcohol. Thereafter, those sections dealing with the practice of pharmacy are reproduced or cited. See page 159.

Subpart A—Scope
Sec.*
213.1   General.
213.2   Territorial extent.
213.3   Related regulations.

Subpart B—Definitions
213.11   Meaning of terms.

Subpart C—Administrative Provisions
AUTHORITIES
Sec.
213.21   Forms prescribed.
213.22   Alternate methods or procedures; and emergency variations from requirements.
213.23   Allowance of claims.
213.24   Permits.
213.25   Bonds and consents of surety.
213.26   Right of entry and examination.
213.27   Detention of containers.

LIABILITY FOR TAX
213.28   Persons liable for tax.

213.29   Responsibility and liability of carriers.

DESTRUCTION OF MARKS AND BRANDS
Sec.
213.30   Time of destruction of marks and brands.

DOCUMENT REQUIREMENTS
213.31   Execution under penalties of perjury.
213.32   Filing of qualifying documents.

Subpart D—Qualification
APPLICATION FOR INDUSTRIAL USE PERMIT
213.41   Application for industrial use permit.

INDUSTRIAL USE PERMIT, FORM 1447
213.44   Conditions of permits.
213.45   Duration of permits.

*AUTHORITY: § § 213.1 to 213.176 issued under sec. 7805, 68A Stat. 917; 26 U.S.C. 7805.

158 . . . LAW FOR THE PHARMACY STUDENT

Federal Laws Governing Alcohol

Subpart A—Scope

§ **213.1 General.**

The regulations in this part relate to tax-free alcohol and cover the procurement, storage, use, and recovery of such alcohol.

§ **213.2 Territorial extent.**

This part applies to the several States of the United States and the District of Columbia.

§ **213.3 Related regulations.**

Regulations related to this part are listed below:

26 CFR Part 186— Gauging Manual.
26 CFR Part 196— Stills.

26 CFR Part 200— Rules of Practices in Permit Proceedings.
26 CFR Part 201— Distilled Spirits Plants.
26 CFR Part 250— Liquors and Articles From Puerto Rico and the Virgin Islands.
26 CFR Part 251— Importation of Distilled Spirits, Wines, and Beer.
31 CFR Part 225— Acceptance of Bonds, Notes, or Other Obligations Issued or Guaranteed by the United States as Security in Lieu of Surety or Sureties on Penal Bonds.

Section 213.11 defines alcohol as "spirits having a proof of 190 degrees or more when withdrawn from bond, including all subsequent dilutions and mixtures thereof, from whatever source or by whatever process produced."

In addition it defines such words and terms as assistant regional commissioner, commissioner, director, fiduciary, gallon or wine gallon, industrial use permit, permittee, person, proof, proof gallon, spirits or distilled spirits and withdrawal permit.

Subpart C, Section 213.21 provides that the Director (Alcohol and Tobacco Tax Division, Internal Revenue Service) shall prescribe all forms necessary to obtain a permit to use and obtain tax-free alcohol.

Method of Applying for Permit

The steps to be taken for obtaining a permit to use and withdraw tax-free alcohol include:

1. Preparation of Form 2600—Application for a Permit to Use Alcohol Tax-Free (Section 213.41) (Figure 8)
2. Preparation of Form 1450—Withdrawal Permit (Section 213.109) (Figure 9)
3. Preparation of Form 1534—Power of Attorney (Section 213.53) (Figure 10)
4. Preparation of Form 1448—Bond (Section 213.71) (Figure 11)
5. Preparation of Form 1447—Permit to use Alcohol Tax-Free (Figure 12)

All forms are executed in duplicate, except Form 1534 (prepared in triplicate) and Form 1447, and filed with the Assistant Regional Commissioner. Alcohol and Tobacco Tax Division. The duplicate copy of Form 2600 (Application for a Permit to Use Tax-Free Alcohol) and Form 1448 (Bond) are returned to the applicant. Form 1447 (Permit) is prepared by the Alcohol and Tobacco Tax regional office and sent to the applicant for posting on the premises. Form 1450 (Withdrawal permit) is returned to the applicant as authorization for the purchase of tax-free alcohol.

FORM **2600** (REV. 7-60)	U. S. TREASURY DEPARTMENT - INTERNAL REVENUE SERVICE **APPLICATION FOR PERMIT TO** **USE ALCOHOL FREE OF TAX**	1. INDUSTRIAL USE PERMIT *(If amendment of industrial use permit)* TF –

This form shall be executed in duplicate and filed with the assistant regional commissioner of the region in which the premises are situated.

Applications on this form which are not executed in accordance with instructions and regulations or which do not contain all the information required by the regulations will be returned to the applicant or permittee for correction.

TO	**ASSISTANT REGIONAL COMMISSIONER (ALCOHOL AND TOBACCO TAX)** *(City and State)*	2. DATE OF APPLICATION

Application is hereby made for an industrial use permit to use alcohol free of tax, as described herein.

3. APPLICATION MADE BY *(If individual owner, give full name and address; if partnership, give full name and address of each person interested in enterprise; if corporation, give name of corporation, State under laws of which incorporated and address of principal office)*

4. TRADE NAME AND OFFICE WHERE REGISTERED	5. MAXIMUM NO. PROOF GALLONS WHICH WILL BE ON HAND, IN TRANSIT, AND UNACCOUNTED FOR AT ANY ONE TIME1/
6. SERIAL NUMBER	7. PURPOSE FOR WHICH FILED *("For original industrial use permit," "For amendment of industrial use permit to authorize (state privilege desired)," etc.)*
8. PERMIT IS FOR ☐ USE OF ALCOHOL FREE OF TAX ☐ RECOVERY OF TAX-FREE ALCOHOL	9. *(If application is made by central authority, as a State, municipality, university, etc., for use of alcohol by an agency, institution, department, etc., thereof, the name of such agency, etc., shall be stated)*

10. PREMISES ON WHICH ALCOHOL WILL BE USED *(Number, street, city or town, zone, State)*

11. ALCOHOL TO BE USED IN THE FOLLOWING MANNER *(The specific use which will be made of the alcohol and resulting products (if any), that is, the purpose or purposes for which the alcohol will be used, shall be stated explicitly, and not in general terms. For example, when the alcohol is to be used at a hospital, the specific purposes for which the alcohol will be used shall be stated, such as clinical use, treatment of patients, compounding medicines for use of patients in the hospital, preserving specimens of anatomy, etc. If alcohol so used is recovered, state that fact)2/*

12. SIZE AND COMPLETE DESCRIPTION OF THE ALCOHOL STORAGE FACILITIES

CONDITIONS

The applicant fully understands that any permit that may be issued pursuant to this application will be subject to the following conditions:

1. That this application contains no misrepresentation of fact; that he and all persons employed by him in any connection with such permit privileges, and all persons employed by him while on the permit premises, will in good faith observe and conform to all the terms and conditions of said permit, the laws of the United States relating to the manufacture, taxation, and control of and traffic in, intoxicating liquors, and all regulations issued pursuant to such laws which are now, or may hereafter be, in force; and he

will pay the tax, together with penalties and interest, on all alcohol diverted while being transported to him, and on all alcohol withdrawn, transported, used, or disposed of by him in violation of laws and regulations now or hereafter in force; and that he and all persons interested in the business to be conducted under said permit are duly qualified, under the law and regulations pertaining thereto, to receive the permit privileges herein applied for.

2. That all data, written statements, evidence, affidavits, and other documents, submitted in support of this application, or upon hearing thereon, shall be deemed to be included in the provisions and conditions of this application and any permit, issued pursuant thereto the same as if set out at length therein.

I declare under the penalties of perjury that this application has been examined by me and to the best of my knowledge and belief is a true, correct, and complete application.

13. SIGNATURE OF APPLICANT 3/	14. BY *(Name and capacity)*

Fig. 8. Application for Permit to Use Alcohol Free of Tax.

FORM 1450 (REV. MARCH 1967)	U. S. TREASURY DEPARTMENT - INTERNAL REVENUE SERVICE **APPLICATION AND WITHDRAWAL PERMIT TO PROCURE SPIRITS FREE OF TAX**	1. INDUSTRIAL USE PERMIT TF-

INSTRUCTIONS - Complete the application (Part I) in duplicate, and send both copies of the form to the Assistant Regional Commissioner (Alcohol and Tobacco Tax) for the region in which your permit premises are located. If the application is approved, one copy will be returned to you. You must submit the approved copy to your supplier before you can obtain spirits free of tax.

PART I - APPLICATION

2. **TO**	**Assistant Regional Commissioner** (Alcohol and Tobacco Tax)	CITY AND STATE	3. DATE
4. **FROM**	4A. NAME AND ADDRESS OF APPLICANT *(Number, Street, City, State, ZIP Code)*	4B. ADDRESS OF PERMIT PREMISES *(If different from 4A)*	

As holder of the industrial use permit identified above, I hereby apply for a withdrawal permit to procure from any qualified distilled spirits plant, during the period specified below, spirits, free of tax, to be used in the manner stated in the application for the permit identified above.

5. PERIOD OF WITHDRAWAL From: To:	6. ESTIMATED AVERAGE MONTHLY REQUIREMENT, IN PROOF GALLONS *(The quantity specified shall be in accordance with the applicant's bona fide needs)*

Under the penalties of perjury, I declare that this application has been examined by me and to the best of my knowledge and belief it is true, correct, and complete.

7. APPLICANT	8. BY *(Signature and title)*

PART II - PERMIT (Applicant will make no entry in this part)

9. OFFICE OF ASSISTANT REGIONAL COMMISSIONER *(City and State)*	10. DATE

11. Permit is hereby granted the applicant to procure spirits free of tax in the quantities and for the period specified in Part I of this form, except as may be specified below:

CONDITIONS AND EXCEPTIONS:

1. THE QUANTITY OF SPIRITS WHICH MAY BE ON HAND, IN TRANSIT, AND UNACCOUNTED FOR AT ANY ONE TIME SHALL NOT
   EXCEED_____PROOF GALLONS, INCLUDING ANY RECOVERED ALCOHOL ON HAND.

2. WITHDRAWALS OF SPIRITS DURING ANY ONE CALENDAR MONTH SHALL NOT EXCEED: *(Check one)*
   ☐ _____PROOF GALLONS;   ☐ 55 WINE GALLONS (110 PROOF GALLONS).

3. THE TOTAL QUANTITY OF SPIRITS TO BE WITHDRAWN UNDER THIS PERMIT SHALL NOT EXCEED_____
   PROOF GALLONS.

12. SIGNATURE, ASSISTANT REGIONAL COMMISSIONER (ALCOHOL AND TOBACCO TAX)

Fig. 9. Withdrawal Permit.

PART III - RECORD OF SHIPMENTS - *(To be filled in by shipper)*				
DATE OF SHIPMENT (a)	QUANTITY *(Proof Gallons)* (b)		SIGNATURE OF SHIPPER (c)	PLANT NO. (d)

FORM 1450 (REV. 3-67)

Fig. 9. *cont'd.*

	U. S. TREASURY DEPARTMENT – INTERNAL REVENUE SERVICE
FORM 1534 (REV. MAY 1960)	**POWER OF ATTORNEY** (Pursuant to Internal Revenue Code and Federal Alcohol Administration Act) *(Prepare in triplicate. See instructions on reverse)*

PRINCIPAL | ADDRESS *(Number, street, city, zone, State)*

BUSINESS IN WHICH ENGAGED

NAME OF ATTORNEY | ADDRESS *(Number, street, city, zone, State)*

KNOW ALL MEN BY THESE PRESENTS: That the above-named principal, engaged in the business shown, has made, constituted, and appointed the above-named person the true and lawful attorney of the principal, for and in the name of the principal to:

(If this power of attorney is to be restricted to particular powers, paragraph (a) should be deleted and the authority conferred specifically enumerated in paragraph (b))

(a) Execute all applications, notices, bonds, tax returns, and other instruments, claims, offers in compromise, letters, writings, and papers, and to do all acts for the principal in dealings with the Internal Revenue Service in connection with matters relating to the laws and regulations issued pursuant thereto, administered by the Alcohol and Tobacco Tax Division of the Internal Revenue Service; and the principal hereby authorizes the said attorney to receive on behalf of the principal any and all notices, papers, and letters from said Internal Revenue Service in connection with all such matters, hereby giving and granting to said attorney full power and authority to do and perform all and every act and thing whatsoever requisite and necessary to be done in and about the premises, as fully and to all intents and purposes as the principal might or could do if personally present, with full power of substitution and revocation, hereby ratifying and confirming all that said attorney shall lawfully do or cause to be done by virtue hereof.

(b)

This power is to apply to the following (If authority is restricted to a particular factory, plant, premises, etc., give name (as "Distilled Spirits Plant," "Tobacco Factory," "Cigar Factory," "Cigarette Factory," establishment of "Dealer in Tobacco Materials" or "Tobacco Export Warehouse," etc.) and address and number thereof, or if a "Wholesale Liquor Dealer" give permit number thereof):

The following is the true signature of the attorney herein appointed:

WITNESS THE HAND AND SEAL of the said principal this _____ day of _____ , 19 ____

Signed, sealed, and delivered in the presence of:

WITNESS	PRINCIPAL
ADDRESS	PRINCIPAL
WITNESS	PRINCIPAL
ADDRESS	PRINCIPAL

BY *(Signature and capacity)*

Fig. 10. Power of Attorney.

| FORM 1448
(REV. JULY 1960) | U.S. TREASURY DEPARTMENT – INTERNAL REVENUE SERVICE
TAX-FREE ALCOHOL USER'S BOND
(File in duplicate. See instructions on reverse) | IND. USE PERMIT NO.

TF– |

| PRINCIPAL | ADDRESS *(Number, street, city or town, zone, State)* |

| SURETY(IES) | AMOUNT OF BOND | EFFECTIVE DATE |

NAME OR STYLE

| NAME OF SCIENTIFIC INSTITUTION, LABORATORY, HOSPITAL, ETC. | ADDRESS *(Number, street, city or town, zone, State)* |

KNOW ALL MEN BY THESE PRESENTS, That the above-named principal and surety (or sureties) are held and firmly bound unto the United States of America in the above-named amount, lawful money of the United States, for the payment of which we bind ourselves, our heirs, executors, administrators, successors, and assigns, jointly and severally, firmly by these presents.

This bond shall not in any case be effective before the above-named date, but if accepted by the United States it shall be effective according to its terms on and after that date without notice to the obligors: *Provided,* That if no date is inserted in the space above provided therefor, the date of execution shall be the effective date of the bond.

WHEREAS, the principal has filed application for a permit or now holds a permit under Chapter 51, Internal Revenue Code, and regulations issued pursuant thereto, under the name or style shown above for the use of alcohol, free of tax, by the above-named institution at the location shown; and

WHEREAS, it is intended by this bond —

(a) To insure the payment of the tax on all alcohol used by the principal for any purpose other than that specified in his application for permit, and on all alcohol withdrawn, removed, transported, used, or sold by him in violation of law or regulations now or hereafter in force;

(b) To secure compliance with any permit, which has been or hereafter may be issued to the principal, pursuant to law and regulations now or hereafter in force, and all extension, amendments, and supplements thereto, authorizing the use of alcohol free of tax; and

(c) To insure compliance with all requirements of the laws of the United States and regulations issued thereunder now or hereafter in force, respecting the use of alcohol free of tax.

NOW, THEREFORE, the conditions of this bond are such that if the principal —

(1) Shall pay, or cause to be paid, the tax on all alcohol used by him for any purpose other than that specified in his application for permit, and on all alcohol withdrawn, removed, transported, used, or sold by him in violation of law or regulations now or hereafter in force;

(2) Shall fully and faithfully comply with the terms of such permit and all extensions, amendments, and supplements thereto, and all the requirements of the laws of the United States and regulations issued thereunder now or hereafter in force respecting the withdrawal, removal, transportation, use, storage, and recovery of tax-free alcohol; and

(3) Shall not engage in any attempt, by himself, or in collusion with others, to defraud the United States of any taxes through the use of tax-free alcohol for other than lawful tax-free purposes;

Then this obligation is to be null and void, but otherwise to remain in full force and effect.

We, the obligors, for ourselves, our heirs, executors, administrators, successors, and assigns, also agree that all stipulations, covenants, and agreements of this bond shall extend to and apply equally to any change in the business address of the premises, the extension or curtailment of such premises, including the buildings thereon, or any part thereof, or in equipment, or any other change which requires the principal to file a new or amended application or notice, except where the change constitutes a change in the proprietorship of the business or in the location of the premises.

And we, the obligors, for ourselves, our heirs, executors, administrators, successors, and assigns, do further covenant and agree that upon the breach of any of the covenants of this bond, the United States may pursue its remedies against the principal or surety independently, or against both jointly, and the said surety hereby waives any right or privilege it may have of requiring, upon notice, or otherwise, that the United States shall first commence action, intervene in any action of any nature whatsoever already commenced, or otherwise exhaust its remedies against the principal.

WITNESS our hands and seals this _____ day of _____ , 19____ .

Signed, sealed, and delivered in the presence of —

_____   _____ (SEAL)

_____   _____ (SEAL)

_____   _____ (SEAL)

| TYPE OF BOND *(Check applicable box)* | ☐ ORIGINAL | ☐ STRENGTHENING | ☐ SUPERSEDING |

Fig. 11. Tax-Free Alcohol User's Bond.

	U. S. TREASURY DEPARTMENT · INTERNAL REVENUE SERVICE	1. PERMIT NO.
FORM **1447** (REV. JUNE 1959)	**PERMIT TO USE ALCOHOL FREE OF TAX** **Under section 5271, Internal Revenue Code**	2. EFFECTIVE DATE
		3. DATE OF APPLICATION

4. NAME OF PERMITTEE AND ADDRESS OF PERMIT PREMISES

Pursuant to application, you are hereby permitted to use, at the above address, alcohol withdrawn free of tax under section 5214(a)(2) or (3), Internal Revenue Code, for the following purposes and for no other purpose:

subject to applicable law and regulations and to the conditions set forth on the reverse side of this permit.

This permit is continuing, and will remain in force until suspended, revoked, voluntarily surrendered, or automatically terminated.

This permit is not transferable. In the event of any lease, sale, or other transfer of the operations authorized, or of any other change in the proprietor of such operations this permit shall automatically terminate (if permittee is a corporation, see reverse side).

5. SIGNATURE. ASSISTANT REGIONAL COMMISSIONER *(Alcohol and Tobacco Tax)*

FORM **1447** (REV. 6-59)

Fig. 12. Permit to Use Alcohol Free of Tax.

Code of Federal Regulations—Part 213 of Title 26

In view of the fact that these regulations all fall into the "do" or "don't do" classification, they are easily comprehended by the student and are therefore hereinafter reproduced.[4]

Subpart B—Definitions

§ 213.11 Meaning of terms.

When used in this part and in forms prescribed under this part, where not otherwise distinctly expressed or manifestly incompatible with the intent thereof, terms shall have the meaning ascribed in this section. Words in the plural form shall include the singular, and vice versa, and words importing the masculine gender shall include the feminine. The terms "includes" and "including" do not exclude things not enumerated which are in the same general class.

Alcohol. Spirits having a proof of 190 degrees or more when withdrawn from bond, including all subsequent dilutions and mixtures thereof, from whatever source or by whatever process produced.

Assistant regional commissioner. An assistant regional commissioner (alcohol and tobacco tax) who is responsible to and functions under the direction and supervision of, a regional commissioner.

CFR. The Code of Federal Regulations.

Commmissioner. The Commissioner of Internal Revenue.

Director. The Director, Alcohol and Tobacco Tax Division, Internal Revenue Service, Washington, D.C.

Executed under penalties of perjury. Signed with the prescribed declaration under the penalties of perjury as provided on or with respect to the claim, form, or other document or, where no form of declaration is prescribed, with the declaration "I declare under the penalties of perjury that this _____ (insert type of document, such as statement, report, certificate, application, claim, or other document), including the documents submitted in support thereof, has been examined by me and, to the best of my knowledge and belief, is true, correct, and complete."

Fiduciary. A guardian, trustee, executor, administrator, receiver, conservator, or any person acting in any fiduciary capacity for any person.

Gallon or wine gallon. The liquid measure equivalent to the volume of 231 cubic inches.

Industrial use permit. The document issued pursuant to section 5271(a), I.R.C., authorizing the person named therein to use tax-free alcohol, as described therein.

I.R.C. The Internal Revenue Code of 1954, as amended.

Internal revenue officer. An officer or employee of the Internal Revenue Service duly authorized to perform any function relating to the administration or enforcement of this part.

Permittee. Any person holding an industrial use permit on Form 1447.

Person. An individual, trust, estate, partnership, association, company, or corporation.

Proof. The ethyl alcohol content of a liquid at 60 degrees Fahrenheit, stated as twice the percent of ethyl alcohol by volume.

Proof gallon. A gallon at 60 degrees Fahrenheit which contains 50 percent by volume of ethyl alcohol having a specific gravity of 0.7939 at 60 degrees Fahrenheit referred to water at 60 degrees Fahrenheit as unity, or the alcoholic equivalent thereof.

Region. An internal revenue region.

Regional Commissioner. A regional commissioner of internal revenue.

Restoration. Restoring to the original state of recovered tax-free alcohol, including redistillation of the recovered alcohol to 190 degrees or more of proof and the removal of foreign materials by redistillation, filtration, or other suitable means.

Secretary. The Secretary of the Treasury.

Spirits or distilled spirits. The substance known as ethyl alcohol, ethanol, or spirits of wine, having a proof of 190 degrees or more when withdrawn from bond, including all subsequent dilutions and mixtures thereof, from whatever source or by whatever process produced.

This chapter. Chapter I, Title 26, Code of Federal Regulations.

U.S.C. The United States Code.

Withdrawal permit. The document issued pursuant to section 5271(a), I.R.C., authorizing the person named therein to withdraw tax-free alcohol, as specified therein, from the premises of a distilled spirits plant.

Subpart C—Administrative Provisions

AUTHORITIES

§ 213.21 Forms prescribed.

The Director is authorized to prescribe all forms required by this part. All of the information called for in each form shall be furnished, as indicated by the headings on the form and the instructions thereon or issued in respect thereto, and as required by this part.

§ 213.22 Alternate methods or procedures;

and emergency variations from requirements.

(a) *Alternate methods or procedures.* The permittee, on specific approval by the Director as provided in this paragraph, may use an alternate method or procedure in lieu of a method or procedure specifically prescribed in this part. The Director may approve an alternate method of procedure, subject to stated conditions, when he finds that –

(1) Good cause has been shown for the use of the alternate method or procedure;

(2) The alternate method or procedure is within the purpose of, and consistent with the effect intended by the specifically prescribed method or procedure, and affords equivalent security to the revenue; and

(3) The alternate method or procedure will not be contrary to any provision of law, and will not result in an increase in cost to the Government or hinder the effective administration of this part.

No alternate method or procedure relating to applications for permits or amendment or renewal of permits, or to the giving of any bond shall be authorized under this paragraph. Where the permittee desires to employ an alternate method or procedure, he shall submit a written application so to do, in triplicate, to the assistant regional commissioner, for transmittal to the Director. The application shall specifically describe the proposed alternate method or procedure, and shall set forth the reasons therefor. Alternate methods or procedures shall not be employed until the application has been approved by the Director. The permittee shall, during the period of authorization of an alternate method or procedure, comply with the terms of the approved application. Authorization for any alternate method or procedure may be withdrawn whenever in the judgment of the Director the revenue is jeopardized or the effective administration of this part is hindered by the continuation of such authorization. As used in this paragraph, alternate methods or procedures shall include alternate construction or equipment.

(b) *Emergency variations from requirements.* The Director may approve construction, equipment, and methods of operation other than as specified in this part, where he finds that an emergency exists and the proposed variations from the specified requirements are necessary, and the proposed variations:

(1) Will afford the security and protection to the revenue intended by the prescribed specifications;

(2) Will not hinder the effective administration of this part; and

(3) Will not be contrary to any provision of law.

Variations from requirements granted under this paragraph are conditioned on compliance with the procedures, conditions, and limitations with respect thereto set forth in the approval of the application. Failure to comply in good faith with such procedures, conditions, and limitations shall automatically terminate the authority for such variations and the permittee thereupon shall fully comply with the prescribed requirements of regulations from which the variations were authorized. Authority for any variation may be withdrawn whenever in the judgment of the Director the revenue is jeopardized or the effective administration of this part is hindered by the continuation of such variation. Where the permittee desires to employ such variation, he shall submit a written application so to do, in triplicate, to the assistant regional commissioner for transmittal to the Director. The application shall describe the proposed variations and set forth the reasons therefor. Variations shall not be employed until the application has been approved.

(72 Stat. 1395; 26 U.S.C. 5552)

§ 213.23 **Allowance of claims.**

The assistant regional commissioner is authorized to allow claims for losses of tax-free alcohol.

§ 213.24 **Permits.**

The Director shall issue permits covering the use of tax-free spirits by the United States or a Governmental agency thereof. The assistant regional commission is authorized to issue all other industrial use permits and withdrawal permits required under this part.

§ 213.25 **Bonds and consents of surety.**

The assistant regional commissioner is authorized to approve all bonds and consents of surety required by this part.

§ 213.26 **Right of entry and examination.**

An internal revenue officer may enter during regular business hours any premises qualified under this part for the purpose of inspecting records and reports required to be maintained on such premises. Such officer may also inspect and take samples of tax-free alcohol to which such records and reports relate.

(72 Stat. 1373; 26 U.S.C. 5275)

§ 213.27 Detention of containers.

Any internal revenue officer may detain any container containing, or supposed to contain, alcohol when he has reason to believe that such alcohol was withdrawn, sold, transported, or used in violation of law or this part; and every such container shall be held by him at a safe place until it shall be determined whether the property so detained is liable by law to be proceeded against for forfeiture; but such summary detention shall not continue in any case longer than 72 hours without process of law or intervention of the assistant regional commissioner, unless the person in possession of the container immediately prior to its detention, in consideration of the container being kept on his premises during detention, executes a waiver of the 72-hours limitation on detention of the container.

(72 Stat. 1375; 26 U.S.C. 5311)

LIABILITY FOR TAX

§ 213.28 Persons liable for tax.

Any person who removes, sells, transports, or uses alcohol, withdrawn free of tax, in violation of laws or regulations pertaining thereto, and all such alcohol shall be subject to all provisions of law pertaining to distilled spirits subject to tax, including those requiring payment of the tax thereon; and the person so removing, selling, transporting, or using the alcohol shall be required to pay such tax.

(72 Stat. 1314; 26 U.S.C. 5001)

§ 213.29 Responsibility and liability of carriers.

For the responsibilities and liabilities of carriers, see sections 5001(a)(5), 5214, and 5271, I.R.C.

DESTRUCTION OF MARKS AND BRANDS

§ 213.30 Time of destruction of marks and brands.

The marks and brands required by regulations to be placed on containers of tax-free alcohol shall not be destroyed or altered until all of the alcohol has been removed from the package. When containers of tax-free alcohol have been emptied, the marks and brands shall be effaced or obliterated.

(72 Stat. 1358; 26 U.S.C. 5205)

DOCUMENT REQUIREMENTS

§ 213.31 Execution under penalties of perjury.

Where a form or other document called for under this part is required by this part or in the instructions on or with the form or other document to be executed under penalties of perjury, it shall be so executed, as defined in § 213.11, and shall be signed by the permittee or other duly authorized person.

(68A Stat. 749; 26 U.S.C. 6065)

§ 213.32 Filing of qualifying documents.

All documents returned to a permittee or other person as evidence of compliance with requirements of this part, or as authorizations, shall, except as otherwise provided, be kept readily available for inspection by an internal revenue officer during business hours.

Subpart D--Qualification

APPLICATION FOR INDUSTRIAL USE PERMIT

§ 213.41 Application for industrial use permit.

Every person desiring to use tax-free alcohol shall, before commencing such use, make application for and obtain an industrial use permit, Form 1447. Application, Form 2600, and necessary supporting documents, as required by this subpart, shall be filed with the assistant regional commissioner. All data, written statements, affidavits, and other documents submitted in support of the application shall be deemed to be a part thereof. A State, municipal subdivision thereof, or the District of Columbia may file an application for and receive a single permit on Form 1447 authorizing the use of alcohol free of tax in a number of institutions under its control if the method of storing, distributing, and accounting for the alcohol withdrawn under the permit is satisfactory to the assistant regional commissioner. Such application shall be accompanied by evidence which will establish the authority of the officer or other person who executes the application to execute the same and, where applicable, by the application for a withdrawal permit, Form 1450, required by § 213.109.

(72 Stat. 1370; 26 U.S.C. 5271)

§ 213.42 Data for application.

Each application on Form 2600 shall include the following information:

(a) Serial number and purpose for which filed.

(b) Name and principal business address of applicant.

(c) Location, or locations, where tax-free alcohol is to be used if different from the business address.

(d) Statement as to the type of business organization and of the persons interested in the business, supported by the items of information listed in § 213.52.

(e) Statement showing the specific manner in which, or purposes for which, tax-free alcohol will be used and the estimated maximum quantity, in proof gallons, which will be on hand, in transit, and unaccounted for at any one time.

(f) Listing of the size, description, and location of each storeroom or compartment where tax-free alcohol will be stored and of principal equipment for the recovery and restoration of alcohol (including the serial number, kind, capacity, name and address of owner, and intended use of distilling apparatus).

(g) Trade names (see § 213.51).

(h) List of the offices, the incumbents of which are authorized by the articles of incorporation, the bylaws, or the board of directors to act on behalf of the applicant or to sign his name.

(i) On specific request of the assistant regional commissioner, furnish a statement showing whether any of the persons whose names and addresses are required to be furnished under the provisions of §§ 213.52(a)(2) and (c) have (1) ever been convicted of a felony or misdemeanor under Federal or State law relating to intoxicating liquors, (2) ever been arrested or charged with any violation of State or Federal law relating to intoxicating liquors, or (3) ever applied for, held, or been connected with a permit, issued under Federal law, to manufacture, distribute, sell, or use spirits or products containing spirits, whether or not for beverage use, or held any financial interest in any business covered by any such permit, and, if so, give the number and classification of such permit, the period of operation thereunder, and state in detail whether

such permit was ever suspended, revoked, annulled, or otherwise terminated.

Where any of the information required by paragraphs (d) through (h) of this section is on file with the assistant regional commissioner, the applicant may, by incorporation by reference thereto, state that such information is made a part of the application for an industrial use permit. The applicant shall, when so required by the assistant regional commissioner, furnish as a part of his application for an industrial use permit such additional information as may be necessary for the assistant regional commissioner to determine whether the applicant is entitled to the permit.

(72 Stat. 1318, 1370; 26 U.S.C. 5005, 5271)

§ 213.43 Exceptions to application requirements.

The assistant regional commissioner may, in his discretion, waive detailed application and supporting data requirements in the case of applications, Form 2600, filed by States, political subdivisions thereof, the District of Columbia, and other applicants where the amount of tax-free alcohol to be obtained does not exceed 120 proof gallons per year: *Provided*, That such waiver shall not include information required under paragraphs (a), (b), (c), and (e), and insofar as it relates to recovery, paragraph (f), of § 213.42.

(72 Stat. 1370; 26 U.S.C. 5271)

INDUSTRIAL USE PERMIT, FORM 1447

§ 213.44 Conditions of permits.

Industrial use permits shall designate the acts which are permitted, and shall include any limitations imposed on the performance of such acts. All of the provisions of this part relating to the use or recovery of tax-free alcohol shall be deemed to be included in the provisions and conditions of the permit, the same as if set out therein.

(72 Stat. 1370; 26 U.S.C. 5271)

§ 213.45 Duration of permits.

Industrial use permits are continuing unless automatically terminated by the terms thereof, suspended or revoked as provided in § 213.49, or voluntarily surrendered. The provisions of § 213.55 shall be deemed to be a part of the terms and conditions of all industrial use permits.

(72 Stat. 1370; 26 U.S.C. 5271)

§ 213.46 Posting of permits.

Industrial use permits shall be kept posted available for inspection on the premises covered by the permit.

(72 Stat. 1370; 26 U.S.C. 5271)

§ 213.47 Disapproval of application.

If, on examination of an application, Form 2600, for an industrial use permit (or on basis of an inquiry or investigation with respect thereto), the assistant regional commissioner has reason to believe that:

(a) The applicant is not authorized by law and regulations issued pursuant thereto to withdraw or use alcohol free of tax; or

(b) The applicant (including, in the case of a corporation, any officer, director, or principal stockholder, and, in the case of a partnership, a partner) is, by reason of his business experience, financial standing, or trade connections, not likely to maintain operations in compliance with Chapter 51, I.R.C., or regulations issued thereunder; or

(c) The applicant has failed to disclose any material information required, or has made any false statement as to any material fact, in connection with his application; or

(d) The premises on which the applicant proposes to conduct the business are not adequate to protect the revenue;

The assistant regional commissioner may institute proceedings for the disapproval of the application in accordance with the procedures set forth in Part 200 of this chapter.

(72 Stat. 1370; 26 U.S.C. 5271)

§ 213.48 Correction of permits.

Where an error in an industrial use permit is discovered, the permittee shall, on demand of the assistant regional commissioner, immediately return the permit for correction.

(72 Stat. 1370; 26 U.S.C. 5271)

§ 213.49 Suspension or revocation of permits.

Whenever the assistant regional commissioner has reason to believe that any person holding an industrial use permit:

(a) Has not in good faith complied with the provisions of chapter 51, I.R.C., or regulations issued thereunder; or

(b) Has violated the conditions of such permit; or

(c) Has made any false statements as to any material fact in his application therefor; or

(d) Has failed to disclose any material

information required to be furnished; or

(e) Has violated or conspired to violate any law of the United States relating to intoxicating liquor or has been convicted of an offense under Title 26, U.S.C., punishable as a felony or of any conspiracy to commit such offense; or

(f) Is, by reason of his operations, no longer warranted in procuring or using the tax-free alcohol authorized by his permit; or

(g) Has not engaged in any of the operations authorized by the permit for a period of more than 2 years;

The assistant regional commissioner may institute proceedings for the revocation or suspension of such permit in accordance with the procedures set forth in Part 200 of this chapter.

(72 Stat. 1370; 26 U.S.C. 5271)

§ 213.50 Rules of practice in permit proceedings.

The regulations in Part 200 of this chapter are made applicable to the procedure and practice in connection with the disapproval of any application for an industrial use permit and in connection with the suspension and revocation of such permit.

§ 213.51 Trade names.

Where a trade name is to be used by an applicant or permittee, he shall list such trade name on Form 2600 and the offices where such name is registered, supported by copies of any certificate or other document filed or issued in respect of such name. Operations shall not be conducted under a trade name until the permittee is in possession of an industrial use permit, Form 1447, covering the use of such name.

§ 213.52 Organizational documents.

The supporting information required by paragraph (d) of § 213.42 includes, as applicable:

(a) *Corporate documents.* (1) Certified true copy of the certificate of incorporation, or certified true copy of certificate authorizing the corporation to operate in the State where the premises are located (if other than that in which incorporated).

(2) Certified list of names and addresses of officers and directors.

(3) Statement showing the number of shares of each class of stock or other evidence of ownership, authorized and outstanding, the par value thereof, and the voting rights of the respective owners or holders.

(b) *Articles of partnership.* True copy of the articles of partnership or association, if any, or certificate of partnership or association where required to be filed by any State, county, or municipality.

(c) *Statement of interest.* (1) Names and addresses of the 10 persons having the largest ownership or other interest in each of the classes of stock in the corporation, or legal entity, and the nature and amount of the stockholding or other interest of each, whether such interest appears in the name of the interested party or in the name of another for him. If a corporation is wholly owned or controlled by another corporation, those persons of the parent corporation who meet the above standards are considered to be the persons interested in the business of the subsidiary, and the names and addresses of such persons shall be submitted to the assistant regional commissioner on his specific request.

(2) In the case of an individual owner or partnership, name and address of every person interested in the business, whether such interest appears in the name of the interest party or in the name of another for him.

§ 213.53 Powers of attorney.

An applicant or permittee shall execute and file with the assistant regional commissioner a Form 1534, in accordance with the instructions on the form, for every person authorized to sign or to act on his behalf. (Not required for persons whose authority is furnished in accordance with § 213.42(h)).

CHANGES AFTER ORIGINAL QUALIFICATION

§ 213.54 Changes affecting applications and permits.

Where there is a change relating to any of the information contained in or considered as a part of the application on Form 2600 for an industrial use permit, the permittee shall within 10 days (except as otherwise provided in this subpart) file with the assistant regional commissioner a written notice, in duplicate, of the details of such change. In case of a change in officers or directors, the notice shall be supported by a certified list, in duplicate, of such changes. Such notice is not required where there is a change in respect of information waived by the assistant regional commissioner in the original application for an industrial use permit in accordance with the provisions of § 213.43, unless, in the case of a permittee

other than a State, political subdivision thereof, or the District of Columbia, the quantity of tax-free alcohol to be obtained will exceed 120 proof gallons per year. Where the change affects the terms of an industrial use permit, the permittee shall file an application on Form 2600 for an amended industrial use permit. Items which remain unchanged may be marked "No change since Form 2600 Serial No. _____."

(72 Stat. 1370; 26 U.S.C. 5271)

§ 213.55 Automatic termination of permits.

(a) *Permits not transferable.* Industrial use permits shall not be transferred. In the event of the lease, sale, or other transfer of such a permit, or of the operations authorized thereby, the permit shall thereupon automatically terminate.

(b) *Corporations.* In the case of a corporation holding an industrial use permit, if actual or legal control of the permittee corporation changes, directly or indirectly, whether by reason of change in stock ownership or control (in the permittee corporation or in any other corporation), by operation of law, or in any other manner, the permittee shall, within 10 days of such change, give written notice thereof, executed under the penalties of perjury, to the assistant regional commissioner; such permit may remain in effect with respect to the operation covered thereby until the expiration of 30 days after such change, whereupon such permit shall automatically terminate: *Provided,* That if within such 30-day period an application for a new permit covering such operation is made, then the outstanding permit may remain in effect with respect to the continuation of the operation covered thereby until final action is taken on such application. When such final action is taken, such outstanding permit shall thereupon automatically terminate.

§ 213.56 Adoption of documents by a fiduciary.

If the business is to be operated by a fiduciary, such fiduciary may, in lieu of qualifying as a new proprietor, file an application on Form 2600 to amend his predecessor's industrial use permit and furnish a consent of surety on Form 1533 extending the terms of the predecessor's bond, if any. The effective date of the qualifying documents filed by a fiduciary shall coincide with the effective date of the court order or the date specified therein for him to assume control. If the fiduciary was not appointed by the court, the date of his assuming control shall coincide with the effective date of the qualifying documents filed by him.

§ 213.57 Continuing partnerships.

Where, under the laws of the particular State, the partnership is not terminated on death or insolvency of a partner, but continues until the winding up of the partnership affairs is completed, and the surviving partner has the exclusive right to the control and possession of the partnership assets for the purpose of liquidation and settlement, such surviving partner may continue to withdraw and use tax-free alcohol under the prior qualification of the partnership: *Provided*, That a consent of surety, wherein the surety and the surviving partner agree to remain liable on any bond given on Form 1448, is filed. If such surviving partner acquires the business on completion of the settlement of the partnership, he shall qualify in his own name from the date of acquisition, as provided in § 213.58. The rule set forth in this section shall also apply where there is more than one surviving partner.

§ 213.58 Change in proprietorship.

An industrial use permit shall not be transferred. In the event of a change in proprietorship of the business of a permittee (as for instance, by reason of incorporation, the withdrawal or the taking in of one or more partners, or succession by any person who is not a fiduciary) the successor shall qualify in the same manner as the proprietor of a new business.

§ 213.59 Change in name of permittee.

Where there is to be a change in the individual, firm, or corporate name, the permittee shall file application on Form 2600 to amend his industrial use permit. Operations may not be conducted under the new name prior to issuance of the amended permit.

§ 213.60 Change in trade name.

Where there is to be a change in, or addition of, a trade name, the permittee shall file application on Form 2600 to amend his industrial use permit. A new bond or consent of surety will not be required. Operations may not be conducted under the trade name prior to issuance of the amended permit.

§ 213.61 Change in location.

When a permittee intends to move to a new location within the same region, he shall file application on Form 2600 for an amended industrial use permit and, if a bond on Form 1448 had been given, furnished a consent of surety, Form 1533, or a new bond to cover the new location. Tax-free alcohol may not be stored or used at the new location prior to issuance of the amended permit.

(72 Stat. 1370; 26 U.S.C. 5271)

REGISTRY OF STILLS

§ 213.62 Registry of stills.

The provisions of Part 196 of this chapter are applicable to stills located on the premises of a permittee. The listing of the stills on Form 2600 and the issuance of the industrial use permit shall constitute registration of the stills. The alternate use of a registered still or distilling apparatus for the distillation of a byproduct or chemical for which registry is not required will not require the filing of Form 26.

PERMANENT DISCONTINUANCE OF USE OF TAX-FREE ALCOHOL

§ 213.63 Notice of permanent discontinuance.

Where a permittee permanently discontinues the use of tax-free alcohol, he shall file with the assistant regional commissioner a letterhead notice, in duplicate, to cover such discontinuance. Such notice shall be accompanied by the industrial use permit, any withdrawal permits issued to the permittee, and by a report on Form 1451 covering the discontinuance and marked "Final Report." The notice shall contain (a) a request that such permits be canceled, (b) a statement of the disposition made, as provided in § 213.164, of all tax-free alcohol, including recovered alcohol, if any, and (c) the date of discontinuance. The bond of a permittee shall not be canceled until all tax-free alcohol, including recovered alcohol, has been properly disposed of in accordance with the provisions of this part.

(72 Stat. 1370; 26 U.S.C. 5271)

Subpart E—Bonds and Consents of Surety

§ 213.71 Bond, Form 1448.

Every person filing an application, Form 2600, shall, before issuance of the industrial use permit, file bond, Form 1448, with the assistant regional commissioner, except that no bond will be required where the application is filed by a State, any political subdivision thereof, or the District of Columbia, or where the quantity of tax-free alcohol authorized to be withdrawn does not exceed 120 proof gallons per annum and the quantity which may be on hand, in transit, or unaccounted for at any one time will not exceed 10 proof gallons. The penal sum of the bond on Form 1448 shall be computed on each proof gallon of tax-free alcohol, including recovered and restored tax-free alcohol, authorized to be on hand, in transit to the permittee, and unaccounted for at any one time, at the rate prescribed by law as the internal revenue tax on distilled spirits: *Provided*, That the penal sum of any bond (or the total of the penal sums where original and strengthening bonds are filed) shall not exceed $100,000 nor be less than $500.

(72 Stat. 1314, 1372; 26 U.S.C. 5001, 5272)

§ 213.72 Corporate surety.

Surety bonds required by this part may be given only with corporate sureties holding certificates of authority from, and subject to the limitations prescribed by, the Secretary as set forth in the current revision of Treasury Department Circular 570. Powers of attorney and other evidence of appointment of agents and officers to execute bonds or to consent to changes in the terms of bonds on behalf of corporate sureties are required to be filed with, and passed on by, the Commissioner of Accounts, Surety Bonds Branch, Treasury Department.

(61 Stat. 648; 6 U.S.C. 6, 7)

§ 213.73 Deposit of securities in lieu of corporate surety.

In lieu of corporate surety, the principal may pledge and deposit, as surety for his bond, securities which are transferable and are guaranteed as to both interest and principal by the United States, in accordance with the provisions of 31 CFR Part 225.

(61 Stat. 650; 6 U.S.C. 15)

§ 213.74 Consents of surety.

Consents of surety to changes in the terms of bonds shall be executed on Form 1533 by the principal and by the surety with the same formality and proof of authority as is required for the execution of bonds.

§ 213.75 Strengthening bonds.

In all cases where the penal sum of any bond becomes insufficient, the principal shall either give a strengthening bond with the same surety to attain a sufficient penal sum or give a new bond covering the entire liability. Strengthening bonds shall not be approved where any notation is made thereon which is intended or which may be construed to be a release of any former bond or as limiting the amount of any bond to less than its full penal sum. Strengthening bonds shall show the date of execution and the effective date, and be marked "Strengthening Bond".

(72 Stat. 1372; 26 U.S.C. 5272)

§ 213.76 Superseding bonds.

New bonds shall be required in case of insolvency or removal of any surety, and may, at the discretion of the assistant regional commissioner, be required in any other contingency affecting the validity or impairing the efficiency of the bond. Where, under the provisions of § 213.77, the surety on any bond given under this subpart has filed an application to be relieved of liability under said bond and the principal desires or intends to continue the operations to which such bond relates, he shall file a valid superseding bond to be effective on or before the date specified in the surety's notice. Superseding bonds must show the date of execution and the effective date, and be marked "Superseding Bond." If the principal does not file a new bond when required, he shall not conduct any operation under his permit.

(72 Stat. 1372; 26 U.S.C. 5272)

§ 213.77 Notice by surety of termination of bond.

A surety on any bond required by this part may at any time serve notice in writing on the principal and the assistant regional commissioner in whose office the bond is on file, that he desires, after a date named, to be relieved of liability under said bond. Such date shall be not less than 90 days after the date the notice is received by the assistant regional commissioner. This notice may not be given by an agent of the surety unless it is accompanied by a power of attorney, duly executed by the surety, authorizing him to give such notice, or by a statement, executed under the penalties of perjury, that such power of attorney is on file with the Commissioner of Accounts, Surety Bonds Branch, Treasury Department. The surety shall also file with the assistant regional commissioner an acknowledgment or other proof of service of such notice on the principal.

(72 Stat. 1372; 26 U.S.C. 5272)

§ 213.78 **Termination of rights and liability under a bond.**

If the notice of termination given by the surety is not thereafter in writing withdrawn, the rights of the principal as supported by the subject bond shall be terminated on the date named in the notice. The surety shall be relieved from his liability under a bond as to any operations which are wholly subsequent to: (a) The date named in a notice of termination (§ 213.77); (b) the effective date of a superseding bond (§ 213.76); or (c) the date of approval of the discontinuance of operations by the principal. If the principal fails to file a valid superseding bond prior to the date on which the surety desires to be relieved from liability under the bond, the surety, notwithstanding his release from liability as specified in paragraph (a) of this section, shall continue to remain liable under the bond for all tax-free alcohol on hand or in transit to the principal on said date until the same has been lawfully disposed of or a new bond has been filed by the principal covering the same.

(72 Stat. 1372; 26 U.S.C. 5272)

§ 213.79 **Release of pledged securities.**

Securities of the United States, pledged and deposited as provided in § 213.73, shall be released only in accordance with the provisions of 31 CFR Part 225. When the assistant regional commissioner is satisfied that they may be released, he shall fix the date or dates on which a part or all of such securities may be released. At any time prior to the release of such securities, the assistant regional commissioner may extend the date of release for such additional length of time as he deems necessary.

(61 Stat. 650; 6 U.S.C. 15)

Subpart F—Premises and Equipment

§ 213.91 **Premises.**

A tax-free alcohol user qualified under this part shall have premises suitable for the business being conducted and adequate for the protection of the revenue. Storage facilities shall be provided on the premises for tax-free alcohol received or recovered thereon. These storage facilities shall consist of a storeroom or compartment, or stationary storage tanks, or a combination thereof.

§ 213.92 **Storerooms.**

Storerooms or compartments shall be so constructed and secured as to prevent unauthorized access to the tax-free alcohol. Such storage facilities shall be of sufficient capacity to hold the maximum quantity of tax-free alcohol which will be on hand at any one time and shall be equipped for locking.

§ 213.93 **Storage tanks.**

Each stationary tank used for the storage of tax-free alcohol shall be equipped for locking in such manner as to control access to the spirits. Means shall be provided whereby the contents can be accurately measured.

§ 213.94 **Equipment for recovery of tax-free alcohol.**

If tax-free alcohol is to be recovered for reuse, all equipment to be used shall be located on the permit premises. Distilling apparatus or other equipment, including pipelines, for such recovery shall be constructed and secured in such a manner as to prevent unauthorized access to the tax-free alcohol and so arranged as to be readily inspected.

§ 213.95 **Storage tanks for recovered and restored alcohol.**

If tax-free alcohol is to be recovered, suitable storage tanks shall be provided. Each such tank shall be durably marked to indicate its use and capacity, shall be equipped with a measuring device whereby the actual contents will be indicated, and shall be equipped for locking to prevent access to the contents.

Subpart G—Withdrawal and Use of Tax-Free Alcohol

§ 213.101 **Authorized uses.**

Alcohol may be withdrawn from the bonded premises of a distilled spirits plant, free of tax, by and for the use of any State, any political subdivision thereof, or the District of Columbia, for nonbeverage purposes. Alcohol may also be so withdrawn by persons eligible to use tax-free alcohol, for nonbeverage purposes and not for resale or use in the manufacture of any product for sale, as follows:

(a) For the use of any educational organization described in section 503(b) (2), I.R.C., which is exempt from income tax under section 501(a), I.R.C., or for the use of any scientific university or college of learning;

(b) For any laboratory for use exclusively in scientific research;

(c) For use at any hospital, blood bank, or sanitarium (including use in making any analysis or test at such hospital, blood bank, or sanitarium), or at any pathological laboratory exclusively engaged in making analyses, or tests, for hospitals or sanitariums; or

(d) For the use of any clinic operated for charity and not for profit (including use in the compounding of bona fide medicines for treatment outside of such clinics of patients thereof).

Tax-free alcohol shall be withdrawn and used only as provided by law and this part.

(72 Stat. 1362, 1370; 26 U.S.C. 5214, 5271)

§ 213.102 States and the District of Columbia.

Except as otherwise provided in this section, tax-free alcohol withdrawn by a State, a political subdivision thereof, or the District of Columbia shall be used solely for mechanical and scientific purposes, and except on approval of the Director, such use or the use of any resulting product shall be confined to the premises under the control of the State, political subdivision thereof, or the District of Columbia. Tax-free alcohol so withdrawn for use at hospitals, clinics, and other establishments specified in §§ 213.103 to 213.107, operated by a State, political subdivision, or the District of Columbia, shall be used in the manner prescribed in the applicable section for such establishments.

(72 Stat. 1362; 26 U.S.C. 5214)

§ 213.103 Educational organizations, scientific universities, and colleges of learning.

Educational organizations authorized to withdraw tax-free alcohol under § 213.101 are those organizations which normally maintain a regular faculty and curriculum and which normally have a regularly enrolled body of students in attendance at the place where their educational activities are regularly carried on and which are exempt

from Federal income tax under section 501(a), I.R.C. Colleges of learning for the purposes of this subpart are such as have a recognized curriculum and confer degrees after specified periods of attendance at classes or research work. Scientific university shall include any university incorporated or organized under any Federal or State law which provides training in the sciences. Tax-free alcohol withdrawn by such educational organizations, scientific universities, and colleges of learning shall be used only for scientific, medicinal, and mechanical purposes. Use of the tax-free alcohol and resulting products shall be limited as provided in § 213.108.

(72 Stat. 1362; 26 U.S.C. 5214)

§ 213.104 Hospitals, blood banks, and sanitariums.

Tax-free alcohol withdrawn by hospitals, blood banks, and sanitariums shall be used only for medicinal, mechanical, and scientific purposes and in the treatment of patients. Such use includes making any analysis or test at such hospital, blood bank, or sanitarium. Medicines made with tax-free alcohol may not be sold, but a separate charge may be made for such medicines compounded on the hospital or sanitarium premises for use of patients on the premises. Where a hospital holding permit to use tax-free alcohol operates a clinic on the hospital premises, tax-free alcohol withdrawn under the permit of the hospital may be used in the clinic to the same extent as it may be used in the hospital: *Provided*, That in the case of a clinic operated for charity and not for profit, medicines compounded with tax-free alcohol may be furnished to patients for use off the premises if such medicine is not sold and no fee or other charge is exacted by reason of the furnishing of the medicine to the patient. Similarly, tax-free alcohol withdrawn by a hospital or sanitarium may be used in a pathological or other laboratory operated in connection with such hospital or sanitarium, on the hospital or sanitarium premises, to the same extent as it may otherwise be used by the hospital or sanitarium. The use of tax-free alcohol and of products resulting from such use shall be confined strictly to the permit premises except as provided herein and in § 213.108.

(72 Stat. 1362; 26 U.S.C. 5214).

§ 213.105 Clinics.

Tax-free alcohol withdrawn by clinics operated for charity and not for profit shall be used only for medicinal, scientific, and mechanical purposes and in the treatment of patients. Medicine compounded with such tax-free alcohol may be furnished to patients for use off the premises if such medicine is not sold and no fee or other charge is exacted by reason of the furnishing of the medicine to the patient. A separate charge may be made for medicine compounded on the clinic premises with tax-free alcohol for use of patients on the premises. Except as provided herein and in § 213.108, the use of tax-free alcohol and of products resulting from such use shall be confined strictly to the premises of the clinic.

(72 Stat. 1362; 26 U.S.C. 5214)

§ 213.106 Pathological laboratories.

Pathological laboratories, other than such laboratories which are a part of a hospital or sanitarium, may withdraw tax-free alcohol under this part only if engaged exclusively in making analyses or tests for hospitals or sanitariums. Such independent pathological laboratories may not obtain tax-free alcohol if tests or analyses are made for doctors, dentists, or for any other purpose than as provided in this section. Except as provided in § 213.108, the use of tax-free alcohol and of products resulting from such use shall be confined strictly to the premises of the pathological laboratory.

(72 Stat. 1362; 26 U.S.C. 5214)

§ 213.107 Other laboratories.

Except in the case of a pathological laboratory, specified in § 213.106, any laboratory withdrawing alcohol free of tax shall use such alcohol exclusively in scientific research. The use of the alcohol and of any product resulting from such use shall be limited to the permit premises except as provided in § 213.108.

(72 Stat. 1362; 26 U.S.C. 5214)

§ 213.108 Prohibited usage of tax-free alcohol.

Under no circumstances may tax-free alcohol withdrawn under this part be used for beverage purposes, or in any food product, or in any preparation used in preparing beverage or food products. Universities, colleges, educational organizations, laboratories, hospitals, clinics, blood banks, and sanitariums are prohibited from (a) selling tax-free alcohol, (b) using tax-free alcohol in the manufacture of any product for sale, or (c) selling any product resulting from the use of tax-free alcohol: *Provided*, That a charge may be made by a hospital, sanitarium, or clinic for medicines dispensed to patients for use on the premises to the extent authorized in § § 213.104 and 213.105. Persons holding permit on Form 1447 may not remove tax-free alcohol or products resulting from the use of such alcohol from premises under their control unless such removals are specifically authorized by the terms of their permit, or permission is obtained from the assistant regional commissioner: *Provided*, That (1) products made through the use of such alcohol which contain no alcohol may be removed to other premises for the sole purpose of further research, and (2) bona fide medicines compounded by a clinic operated for charity and not for profit may be used outside of such clinic for treatment of its patients if the medicine is distributed without charge to the extent authorized in § § 213.104 and 213.105. Hospitals may not furnish tax-free alcohol for use of physicians in their private practice. Tax-free permittees who use tax-free alcohol in any manner prohibited by this section become liable for the tax on such alcohol. A tax-free permittee who sells alcohol also becomes liable for special tax as a liquor dealer.

(72 Stat. 1314, 1343; 26 U.S.C. 5001, 5121)

§ 213.109 Application for withdrawal permit.

Every person, other than as provided for in Subpart I of this part, desiring to procure tax-free alcohol shall file an application on Form 1450 with the assistant regional commissioner for a withdrawal permit. The application shall show the total quantity, in proof gallons, of tax-free alcohol to be withdrawn during the term of the permit, and the total quantity, in proof gallons, to be withdrawn during any one calendar month. The total quantity to be withdrawn shall not be more than is sufficient to meet the bona fide needs of the applicant. Where the applicant desires to withdraw more than one-sixth of his annual requirements during any month, he should state his needs and furnish sufficient information for the assistant regional commissioner to determine whether such withdrawals should be authorized: *Provided*, That where one-sixth of the applicant's annual requirements is less than the equivalent of one drum (55 wine gallons), he may show as his monthly allowance a quantity not to exceed the equivalent of one drum without stating his needs for the additional quantity, if his bond is in a sufficient penal sum, computed in accordance with § 213.71. A permittee may, if he so desires, file applications for more than one withdrawal permit and have his total annual withdrawals divided among such permits.

(72 Stat. 1370; 26 U.S.C. 5271)

§ 213.110 Issuance and duration of withdrawal permit.

If the application submitted in accordance with § 213.109 is approved, the assistant regional commissioner shall issue withdrawal permit on Form 1450 and shall forward the original to the permittee. Withdrawal permits on Form 1450 shall terminate on April 30 of each year: *Provided*, That a permit issued less than six months before April 30 of any year shall remain in effect through April 30 of the following year.

(72 Stat. 1370; 26 U.S.C. 5271)

§ 213.111 Application for renewal of withdrawal permit.

Application on Form 1450 for renewal of a withdrawal permit expiring April 30 of a year shall be submitted by the permittee to the assistant regional commissioner on or before January 10 of such year in order that the renewal permit may be issued and become available for withdrawals by May 1. The user's report on Form 1451 which is required to be submitted on or before January 10 shall be submitted with the renewal application. The provisions of §§ 213.109 and 213.110 with respect to application for, and issuance of, withdrawal permits, respectively, are applicable to the renewal of such permits.

§ 213.112 Denial, correction, and suspension or revocation; changes after original qualification; and automatic termination of withdrawal permits.

All of the provisions of Subpart D of this part with respect to the denial, correction, suspension or revocation, automatic termination, changes after original qualification, and rules of practice in permit proceedings are applicable to withdrawal permits.

(72 Stat. 1370; 26 U.S.C. 5271)

§ 213.113 Cancellation of withdrawal permit.

Should an industrial use permit on Form 1447 be terminated or surrendered, or

should the withdrawal permit on Form 1450 issued to the permittee be revoked, the withdrawal permit shall be returned immediately to the assistant regional commissioner for cancellation.

(72 Stat. 1370; 26 U.S.C. 5271)

§ 213.114 Withdrawals under permit.

When the permittee desires to procure tax-free alcohol, he shall forward the original of the withdrawal permit to the proprietor of the distilled spirits plant from whom he will procure such alcohol. Shipments shall not be made by the proprietor of a distilled spirits plant until he is in possession of a valid withdrawal permit, nor shall shipments exceed the quantity authorized by such permit. On shipment, the consignor shall enter the transaction on the withdrawal permit and return it to the permittee, unless he has been authorized to retain it for the purpose of making future shipments.

(72 Stat. 1370; 26 U.S.C. 5271)

§ 213.115 Regulation of withdrawals.

Withdrawals by a permittee shall not exceed the quantity authorized by his permit on Form 1450 and shall be so regulated by him that he will not have on hand, in transit, and unaccounted for at any one time more than the quantity of tax-free alcohol shown in his application on Form 2600 for an industrial use permit. Recovered alcohol and alcohol received under § 213.117 shall be taken into account in determining the quantity of alcohol on hand. For this purpose, tax-free alcohol and recovered alcohol shall be deemed to be unaccounted for if lost under circumstances where a claim for allowance is required by this part and has not been allowed or if used or disposed of otherwise than as provided in this part.

§ 213.116 Receipt of tax-free alcohol.

As soon as received, tax-free alcohol shall be placed in the storage facilities prescribed by § 213.91 and kept there under lock until withdrawn for use. Unless required by city or State fire code regulations or authorized by the assistant regional commissioner or the terms of the permit, the permittee may not remove tax-free alcohol from the original packages or containers in which received until such alcohol is withdrawn for use. If the tax-free alcohol is transferred to "safety" containers in accordance with such fire code regulations, the container to which they are transferred shall be appropriately marked to show the serial number of the package from which transferred, the quantity transferred, the date of transfer, and the name and address of the vendor. On receipt of tax-free alcohol by the permittee, he shall ascertain and account for any losses in transit in accordance with Subpart J of this part, receipt for the shipment on the original and copy of Form 1473 received from the consignor, noting thereon any loss or deficiency in the shipment, forward the original to the assistant regional commissioner of his region, and file the copy in chronological order, by months.

§ 213.117 Alcohol received from General Services Administration.

Any eleemosynary institution holding an industrial use permit, Form 1447, and receiving alcohol from General Services Administration under the provisions of section 5688(a) (2) (B) of the Internal Revenue Code shall include any quantity of alcohol so received in computing the quantity of tax-free alcohol that may be procured under its withdrawal permit, Form 1450, during the calendar month. Such alcohol shall on receipt, be placed in the storage facilities prescribed in § 213.91 and kept there under lock until withdrawn for use.

§ 213.118 Records and reports.

Tax-free alcohol users shall keep records and render reports as required under Subpart L of this part.

Subpart H—Recovery of Tax-Free Alcohol

§ 213.131 General.

Persons desiring to recover tax-free alcohol for reuse shall first receive approval therefor pursuant to the filing of appropriate qualifying documents, in accordance with the applicable provisions of Subparts D and E of this part. Restoration may be accomplished by the permittee or by the proprietor of a distilled spirits plant.

§ 213.132 Deposit in tanks.

All recovered tax-free alcohol shall be accumulated in tanks equipped for locking and properly marked for identification. Where the recovered alcohol is to be shipped to a distilled spirits plant for redistillation, it may be transferred to appropriately marked packages. All tax-free alcohol recovered shall be measured before being redistilled or reused and shall be kept separate from new tax-free alcohol.

§ 213.133 Shipment for redistillation.

Recovered alcohol requiring redistillation, unless the same is to be done on the permittee's premises, shall be shipped to a distilled spirits plant for restoration. Packages shall be numbered in serial order, beginning with "1" and continuing in regular sequence, and have marked or stenciled thereon the name, address, and permit number of the permittee, the quantity, in gallons, of alchol contained therein, and the words "Recovered tax-free alcohol."

§ 213.134 Notice of shipment.

When recovered tax-free alcohol is shipped as provided for in § 213.133, the consignor shall prepare Form 1473, in quadruplicate (quintuplicate if consignee is located in another region) and, on the day of shipment, forward the original and one copy to the proprietor of the distilled spirits plant to which shipment is made, one copy (two copies if shipment is made to a consignee in another region) to the assistant regional commissioner of his region, and retain the remaining copy for his files.

Subpart I—Use of Tax-Free Spirits by the United States or Governmental Agency

§ 213.141 General.

Tax-free spirits may be withdrawn under this part from a distilled spirits plant for use of the United States or any Governmental agency thereof for non-beverage purposes, as authorized by section 5214(a) (2), I.R.C. No industrial use permit or bond is required. However, a permit to procure spirits, free of tax, for nonbeverage purposes must be obtained in accordance with this subpart before tax-free spirits may be withdrawn for such use. The withdrawal, free of tax, of imported spirits from customs custody for the use of the United States shall be in accordance with the applicable provisions of Part 251 of this chapter.

(72 Stat. 1362; 26 U.S.C. 5214)

§ 213.142 Application and permit, Form 1441.

Application, Form 1444, by the United States or a Governmental agency thereof for a permit to procure tax-free spirits from a distilled spirits plant for nonbeverage purposes shall be executed in duplicate and shall be signed by the head of the department or independent bureau or agency to which such tax-free spirits are to be shipped, or by some person duly authorized by such head of a department or independent bureau or agency. Evidence of authority to sign for the head of a department or independent bureau or agency shall be furnished the Director. The permit may be left with the supplier during the term of its use or retained by the agency and furnished to the supplier with each order for spirits. Every appropriate precaution shall be taken by the agency to insure that the tax-free spirits so procured will be used only for Governmental purposes.

(72 Stat. 1370; 26 U.S.C. 5271)

§ 213.143 Procurement of tax-free spirits.

When tax-free spirits are to be procured by the United States or a Governmental agency thereof, the permit, Form 1444, shall be forwarded to the vendor. A purchase order shall be submitted by the Governmental agency for any tax-free spirits shipped under the permit. At the time of shipment, the vendor shall record the shipment on the permit and return it to the Governmental agency unless he has been authorized by such agency to retain the permit for the purpose of making future shipments.

§ 213.144 Receipt of shipment.

On receipt of a shipment of tax-free spirits, the representative of the Governmental agency receiving the same shall execute the certificate of receipt on the original and copy of Form 1473 received from the proprietor of the distilled spirits plant, after noting thereon any loss or deficiency in the shipment, and shall forward the original to the assistant regional commissioner of the region in which the consignor is located and retain the copy for his files.

§ 213.145 Discontinuance of use.

When no more tax-free spirits will be procured under a permit the Governmental agency shall return the permit to the Director for cancellation.

§ 213.146 Disposition of excess spirits.

Any excess spirits in the possession of a Governmental agency shall be disposed of to another agency of the United States holding a permit, returned to a distilled spirits plant on approval of the assistant regional commissioner of the region in which the plant is located, or disposed of otherwise as may be authorized by the Director. In no case may such spirits be disposed of to the general public.

Subpart J—Losses

§ 213.151 Losses by theft.

The quantity of tax-free alcohol lost by theft shall be determined at the time the loss is discovered. Such losses on the premises of users shall be recorded in the records required by § 213.171 and reported on Form 1451. Those occurring in transit shall be reported on the Form 1473. The permittee shall immediately report such loss to the assistant regional commissioner, explaining the circumstances under which the loss occurred. Claim for allowance for all such losses, regardless of the percentage of loss, shall be made by the permittee.

§ 213.152 Losses in transit.

The quantity of tax-free alcohol lost while in transit to the premises of a permittee shall be determined at the time shipment or report of loss is received and shall be reported on Form 1473. Except as provided in § 213.151, where the quantity lost from wooden packages contained in a shipment exceeds 3 percent of their original aggregate contents or the loss from any other containers in a shipment exceeds 1 percent of their original aggregate contents, and the quantity lost is more than 5 proof gallons, claim for allowance of the entire quantity lost shall be filed by the permittee. Where losses in transit do not exceed the quantities specified in this section and there are no circumstances indicating that any part of the quantity lost was unlawfully used or removed, no claim for allowance will be required.

§ 213.153 Losses at user's premises.

The quantity of tax-free alcohol lost on the premises of a permittee shall, except as provided in § 213.151 and in the case of casualty and unusual losses, be determined and recorded at the end of each month when the inventory of tax-free alcohol required under § 213.172 is taken. Casualty or other unusual losses shall be determined and recorded in the records required by § 213.171 at the time of discovery. All losses on the premises of the permittee shall be reported on Form 1451. If the quantity lost during any one month exceeds 1 percent of the quantity of tax-free alcohol to be accounted for during the month, and is more than 5 proof gallons, claim for allowance of the entire quantity lost shall be made by the permittee. Where losses on the premises do not exceed the quantities specified in this section and there are no circumstances indicating that any part of the loss was unlawfully used or removed, claim for loss will not be required, except in the case of losses under § 213.151.

§ 213.154 Claims.

Claims for allowance of losses of tax-free alcohol shall be filed, on Form 2635, with the assistant regional commissioner within 30 days from the date the loss is ascertained, and shall set forth the following:

(a) Name, address, and permit number of the claimant;

(b) Identification and location of the container or containers from which the tax-free alcohol was lost;

(c) Quantity of tax-free alcohol lost from each container, the total quantity of such alcohol covered by the claim, and the aggregate quantity involved;

(d) Date of the loss (or, if not known, date of discovery), the cause or nature thereof, and all the facts relative thereto, including facts establishing whether the loss occurred as a result of any negligence, connivance, collusion, or fraud on the part of any person participating in, or responsible in any manner for, the transaction, or any employee or agent of such person; and

(e) Name of carrier where a loss in transit is involved.

The assistant regional commissioner may require the submission of additional evidence.

Subpart K—Destruction, Return, or Reconsignment of Tax-Free Alcohol and Disposition of Recovered Alcohol

§ 213.161 Destruction.

Tax-free alcohol in the possession of a permittee may be destroyed by him on approval of the assistant regional commissioner. The permittee shall file application to do so with the assistant regional commissioner, in duplicate, stating fully the reasons therefor. On approval of the application, the assistant regional commissioner shall instruct the permittee whether or not the destruction shall be witnessed by an internal revenue officer. If an internal revenue officer is assigned, he shall certify to the destruction on the original and copy of the approved application, specifying the date and manner of destruction. If no internal revenue officer is assigned, such certification

shall be made by the permittee. The copy of the approved application shall be filed by the permittee and the original returned to the assistant regional commissioner.

§ 213.162 Return.

For any legitimate reason, a permittee may return tax-free alcohol to a distilled spirits plant (whether or not such plant was the original shipper), if the distilled spirits plant proprietor consents to the return and permission for the transfer is in each instance first obtained from the assistant regional commissioner. Application for such permission shall be filed in triplicate (quadruplicate if the distilled spirits plant is in another region). If the application is approved the assistant regional commissioner shall forward a copy to the permittee, a copy to the proprietor of the distilled spirits plant and the additional copy, if any, to the consignee's assistant regional commissioner.

§ 213.163 Reconsignment in transit.

Where, prior to or on arrival at the premises of a consignee, tax-free alcohol is found to be unsuitable for the purpose for which intended, was shipped in error, or, for any other bona fide reason, is not accepted by such consignee, or is not accepted by a carrier, it may be reconsigned to another permittee by the proprietor of the distilled spirits plant making shipment, or returned to the shipping plant, on notification by the consignor to the assistant regional commissioner of the consignor's region of such action. In such case, the bond of the permittee to whom the tax-free alcohol was reconsigned or the bond of the proprietor to whom the alcohol was returned shall cover such spirits while in transit after reconsignment. Notice of cancellation of the Form 1473 covering the shipment to the original consignee shall be made by the consignor to each person receiving a copy of Form 1473. Where reconsignment is to another permittee the consignor shall also prepare a new Form 1473 and place thereon the word "Reconsignment." The entry on the withdrawal permit covering the original shipment shall be voided, and the appropriate entries shall be made by the consignor on the withdrawal permit of the permittee to whom the tax-free alcohol was reconsigned.

§ 213.164 Disposition on permanent discontinuance of use.

When a permittee permanently discontinues the use of tax-free alcohol, any tax-free alcohol remaining on hand at the time of such discontinuance may be returned to a distilled spirits plant in accordance with the procedure prescribed in § 213.162, destroyed in accordance with the procedure prescribed in § 213.161, or, on approval of an application therefor by the assistant regional commissioner, disposed of to another permittee, if consent of surety is filed on the consignee's bond extending the terms thereof to cover the transportation of the alcohol to his premises. The application for disposition to another permittee shall be prepared and disposed of in the manner prescribed in § 213.162.

§ 213.165 Notice of shipment.

When tax-free alcohol is shipped in accordance with § 213.162 or § 213.164, the consignor shall prepare Form 1473, in quadruplicate (quintuplicate if the consignee is located in another region) and, on the day of shipment, forward the original and one copy to the consignee, one copy (two if the consignee is located in another region) to the assistant regional commissioner of his region, and retain the remaining copy for his files.

§ 213.166 Disposition after revocation of permit.

When any industrial use permit, Form 1447, is revoked, all tax-free alcohol in transit to and in the possession of the former permittee, and all recovered alcohol, may continue to be lawfully possessed by him for a period of 60 days after such revocation, but only for the purpose of making lawful disposition thereof, pursuant to proper permit therefor, which the permittee shall do within said period. Unless such stocks are disposed of within the period of 60 days they are subject to seizure and forfeiture.

(68A Stat. 867, 72 Stat. 1370; 26 U.S.C. 7302, 5271)

§ 213.167 Disposition of recovered tax-free alcohol on permanent discontinuance of use.

Recovered tax-free alcohol in possession of a permittee at the time of permanent discontinuance of the use of tax-free alcohol shall be disposed of only as authorized by the assistant regional commissioner after full advice respecting its condition and the disposition it is desired to make of such recovered alcohol has been submitted to him.

Subpart L—Records and Reports

§ 213.171 Records.

Persons holding permit on Form 1447 to use tax-free alcohol, shall keep records in sufficient detail (a) to enable any internal revenue officer to verify all transactions in tax-free alcohol and to ascertain whether there has been compliance with law and regulations, and (b) to enable the permittee to prepare Form 1451. Such records shall identify the tax-free alcohol by proof, shall show the date of each transaction and the actual quantities of alcohol involved, and shall include tax-free alcohol received from General Services Administration and the recovery of alcohol and disposition thereof. Records of receipt and authorized removals of tax-free alcohol shall show the name, address, and registry or permit number (if any) of each consignee or consignor, and the type, number, and serial numbers of containers involved. Records must be kept current at all times.

(72 Stat. 1373; 26 U.S.C. 5275)

§ 213.172 Monthly inventories.

At the end of every calendar month, each permittee shall take and record an actual inventory of all tax-free alcohol in his possession. Recovered tax-free alcohol and alcohol received from General Services Administration, if any, shall be listed separately.

§ 213.173 Reports.

Every person holding industrial use permit, Form 1447, shall prepare an annual report on Form 1451. Spirits received from General Services Administration under § 213.117, if any, and spirits recovered pursuant to Subpart H of this part, if any, shall be reported separately. In the case of a State, municipal subdivision thereof, or the District of Columbia, holding a permit covering the use of tax-free alcohol in a number of institutions under its control, Form 1451, submitted by such permittee shall include alcohol used by its dependent agencies, institutions, or departments. The permittee shall submit the original to the assistant regional commissioner not later than the 10th day of January of each year, together with his renewal application, Form 1450, if any, and retain the duplicate copy for his files.

(72 Stat. 1373; 26 U.S.C. 5275)

§ 213.174 Time for making of entries.

Each transaction required by this subpart to be shown in the records shall be entered therein on the day on which the operations occur, except where supplemental or auxiliary records are prepared of, and concurrent with, the individual transaction or operation from which the records can be posted, the making of entries on the records may be deferred to not later than the close of the business day next succeeding the day on which the operation or transaction occurred.

(72 Stat. 1373; 26 U.S.C. 5275)

§ 213.175 Filing and retention of records and copies of reports.

All records required by this part and copies of all reports submitted to the assistant regional commissioner shall be filed and maintained for a period of not less than three years after the date of the report covering the transaction, in such manner as to facilitate inspection by internal revenue officers: *Provided*, That the assistant regional commissioner may require such records to be kept for an additional period of not exceeding three years in any case where he deems such retention necessary or advisable. Records and reports shall be filed at the premises where such operations are conducted, except that such records may be kept by a State, municipal subdivision thereof, or the District of Columbia qualified to procure tax-free alcohol for the use of dependent agencies, institutions, or departments. The files of records and reports shall be available during regular business hours for examination and taking of abstracts therefrom by internal revenue officers.

§ 213.176 Photographic copies of records.

Persons who desire to record, copy, or reproduce records required to be preserved under § 213.175 by any photographic, photostatic, microfilm, microcard, miniature photographic, or other process which accurately reproduces or forms a durable medium for so reproducing the original of such records, shall make application to the assistant regional commissioner, in triplicate, to do so, describing:

(a) The records to be reproduced.

(b) The reproduction process to be employed.

(c) The manner in which the reproductions are to be preserved.

(d) The provisions to be made for examining, viewing, and using such reproductions.

The assistant regional commissioner shall not approve any application unless (1) the Director has approved that type of record for reproduction and the reproduction process to be employed, and (2) the manner of preservation of the reproductions and the provisions for examining, viewing, and using such reproductions are, in the assistant regional commissioner's opinion, satisfactory. Whenever records are reproduced under this section, the reproduced records shall be preserved in conveniently accessible files, and provisions shall be made for examining, viewing, and using the reproduced record the same as if it were the original record, and it shall be treated and considered for all purposes as though it were the original record; all provisions of law and regulations applicable to the reproduced record. As used in this section "original record" shall mean the record required by this part to be maintained or preserved, even though it may be an executed duplicate or other copy of the document.

(72 Stat. 1395; 26 U.S.C. 5555)

[SEAL]   DANA LATHAM,
Commissioner of Internal Revenue.

Approved: June 23, 1960.

FRED C. SCRIBNER, JR.,
Acting Secretary of the Treasury.

[F.R. Doc. 60-5944; Filed, June 28, 1960;
8:45 a.m.]

Published in the Federal Register, June 29, 1960, effective July 1, 1960.

FORM 1451 (REV. MAY 1961)

U. S. TREASURY DEPARTMENT - INTERNAL REVENUE SERVICE

REPORT OF TAX-FREE ALCOHOL USER

(See instructions on reverse)

1. INDUSTRIAL USE PERMIT No. TF -

2. NAME OF PERMITTEE

3. ADDRESS (Number, street, city, zone, State)

4. REPORT FOR CALENDAR YEAR 19......

5. TOTAL ANNUAL ALLOWANCE (Proof gallons)

MONTH (a)	ON HAND BEGINNING OF MONTH (Proof gallons) (b)	RECEIVED (Proof gallons) (c)	RECOVERED (Proof gallons) (d)	USED (Proof gallons) (e)	ON HAND END OF MONTH* (Proof gallons) (f)	GAINS (Proof gallons) (g)	LOSSES (Proof gallons) (h)	RECAPITULATION (Proof gallons) (i)	
Jan.								ON HAND BEGINNING OF YEAR	
Feb.								TOTAL RECEIVED	
Mar.								TOTAL RECOVERED	
April								GAINS	
May								TO BE ACCOUNTED FOR	
June									
July								TOTAL USED	
Aug.									
Sept.									
Oct.								LOSSES	
Nov.								ON HAND END OF YEAR	
Dec.								ACCOUNTED FOR	
6. Cumulative totals									

IMPORTANT: Regulations require actual physical inventory of tax-free alcohol to be taken at the end of each month (See 26 CFR 213.172)

I declare under the penalties of perjury that this report (including any accompanying explanations, statements, and schedules) has been examined by me and, to the best of my knowledge and belief, is a true, correct, and complete report and includes all transactions required by law or regulations to be reported.

7. DATE

8. SIGNATURE

9. TITLE AND CAPACITY

For use of Assistant Regional Commissioner

AUDITED BY: (Initials)

DATE:

Fig. 13. Report of Tax-Free Alcohol User.

FORM **1473** (REV. JULY 1960)	U. S. TREASURY DEPARTMENT - INTERNAL REVENUE SERVICE **NOTICE OF SHIPMENT OF SPECIALLY DENATURED, TAX-FREE, OR RECOVERED SPIRITS**	1. CONSIGNOR D.S.P. OR PERMIT NO.
2. SHIPPED BY -	3A. SHIPPED TO -	4. CONSIGNEE D.S.P. OR PERMIT NO.
		5. PURCHASE ORDER NO.
	3B. ☐ USER ☐ BONDED DEALER ☐ U.S. GOV'T ☐ D.S. PLANT	
6. SHIPPED VIA .	7. SERIAL NOS. OF SEALS USED	8. DATE SHIPPED

9. DESCRIPTION OF SHIPMENT

KIND OF SPIRITS (a)	PROOF (b)	TYPE AND NUMBER OF CONTAINERS (c)	SERIAL NUMBERS (d)	☐ WINE ☐ PROOF GALLONS (e)

10. REMARKS	**For use of ARC -** Verified with report of ___	☐ CON- SIGNOR Initials ☐ CON- SIGNEE

CONSIGNEE'S CERTIFICATE OF RECEIPT

	11. DATE

I hereby certify that this shipment, except as shown below, was received on →

12. EXCEPTIONS:

13. SIGNATURE AND TITLE

14. DATE OF CERTIFICATION	15. SEND ORIGINAL TO *(Enter city and State)* Assistant Regional Commissioner, A & TT at-

**Fig. 14. Notice of Shipment
of Specially Denatured,
Tax-Free, or Recovered Spirits.**

7

References

1. Treasury Department Ruling 6468, 1960.
2. Internal Revenue Service, Division of Alcohol and Tobacco Tax, Industry Memorandum No. NA-65-7, 1965.
3. W. HASSAN, JR.: "Tax-Free Alcohol - Its Procurement and Control," in HOSPITAL PHARMACY, Lea & Febiger, Philadelphia, Pennsylvania, 1967, p. 210–222.
4. U.S. Treasury Department, Internal Revenue Service Publication No. 444 (9-60).

CHAPTER 10

Public Information Act of 1966

The "Freedom of Information Act," Public Law 89-487, became effective July 4, 1967. It amended Section 3 of the Administrative Procedure Act and is known as the Public Information Act of 1966.

This federal legislation requires administrative agencies to adopt new guidelines for the publication and disclosure of information under their control. Thus, the Federal Food and Drug Administration attempted to accomplish two goals: "an informed public through full agency disclosure and the protection of private and individual interests through proper application of the exemptions contained within the new law."[1]

Mamana states that "to a large extent, the disclosure of industry information and data under FDA's control is restricted by the exemptions in subsection (e)."[1] Of the nine exemptions, two through seven are most pertinent to FDA:

Exemption (2) applies primarily to FDA's internal operations. It exempts from disclosure matters 'related solely to the internal personnel rules and practices of any agency.' The House report of the Committee on Government Operations included in this category 'operating rules, guidelines, and manuals of procedure for Government investigators or examiners . . . .'

Department Regulation 5.72 includes guidelines and instructions relating to tolerances, selection of cases, and quantums of proof. In FDA's situation, this would include internal documents, such as regulatory procedures, program guidelines to District Directors, Bureau guidelines, work plans, and any other internal instructions which cannot be disclosed to the public without prejudicing regulatory functions.

Personnel instructions for an administrative management nature, such as work hours, leave rules, and promotion plans, are being disclosed.

Exemption (3) exempts from disclosure matters which are 'specifically exempted from disclosure by statute.' This exemption includes Sec. 301 (j) of the Federal Food, Drug, and Cosmetic Act. This section prohibits: 'The using by any person to his own advantage, or revealing, other than to the Secretary or officers or employees of the Department, or to the courts when relevant in any judicial proceeding under this Act, any information acquired under authority of sections 404, 409, 505, 506, 507, 704, or 706 concerning any method or process which as a trade secret is entitled to protection.'

The restriction against disclosure of trade secret information to the public or for personal gain under 301 (j) still prevails. Therefore, any method or process which is a trade secret submitted in a New Drug Application under section 505 cannot be disclosed under Public Law 89-487. The same applies to a trade secret obtained during the course of an inspection under section 704.

The House report indicates that exemption (3) was intended to continue such statutory restrictions: 'There are nearly 100 statutes or parts of statutes which restrict public access to specific Government records. These would not be modified by the public records provisions of S. 1160.'

Closely related to exemption (3) is exemption (4). It exempts from disclosure 'trade secrets and commercial or financial information obtained from any person and privileged or confidential.' Exemption (4) would include any trade secrets obtained by FDA through other means and for other purposes than those cited in 301 (j). The House report states: 'This exemption would assure the confidentiality of information obtained by the Government through questionnaires or through material submitted and disclosures made in procedures such as the mediation of labor-management controversies. It exempts such material if it would not customarily be made public by the person from whom it was obtained by the Government.' The House report also includes under exemption (4), 'information customarily subject to the doctor-patient, lawyer-client, or lender-borrower privileges . . . . '

One example of the doctor-patient privilege, which has been honored in the past by FDA, is the nondisclosure of reports of adverse drug reactions received from the medical profession, hospitals, and drug manufacturers. The raw data sometimes include the name of patients, physicians, and personal information about the patient which is not disclosed. However, the analysis and conclusions from such data can be of public health importance and are published by FDA when the need arises.

Department Regulation 5.74 recognizes under exemption (4) that information 'obtained from any person under an explicit or implicit pledge of confidentiality' is also exempt from disclosure. It also recognizes the 'Government-informer' privilege which is an important aspect of investigations by the Bureau of Drug Abuse Control.

Exemption (5) exempts from disclosure matters in 'Inter-agency or intra-agency memorandums or letters which would not be available by law to a private party in litigation with the agency.'

The purpose of this exemption is to permit the internal exchange of ideas and communications within FDA, without fear of criticism before an official position is adopted. Such premature criticism or pressure can have an inhibiting effect on the decision-making processes of the Agency. The House report contains the following comments in reference to this exemption:

'Agency witnesses argued that a full and frank exchange of opinions would be impossible if all internal communications were made public. They contended, and with merit, that advice from staff assistants and the exchange of ideas among agency personnel would not be completely frank if they were forced to operate in a fishbowl.'

This exemption is most important in instances where FDA enforcement officials differ on the course of legal action to be taken in a given case. Other areas of possible internal disagreement are governed by exemption (5), such as the need for a new regulation, or the recommendation that a present enforcement policy be changed because circumstances in industry have changed. Staff papers and recommendations prepared by outside consultants for the purpose of supporting FDA regulatory activities would also come under this exemption.

Exemption (6) exempts from disclosure 'personnel and medical files and similar files the disclosure of which would constitute a clearly unwarranted invasion of personal privacy.'

This exemption includes such data as clinical information submitted by IND investigators, including the details of the patients' personal histories; the training, experience, and qualifications of the IND investigators; and, in the case of prescription drug establishment inspections, the qualifications of technical and professional personnel.

The House report indicates that this exemption provides 'a proper balance between the protection of an individual's right of privacy and the preservation of the public's right to Government information by excluding those kinds of files the disclosure of which might harm the individual.'

Exemption (7) provides for nondisclosure of 'investigatory files compiled for law enforcement purposes except to the extent available by law to a private party.' Most of FDA's enforcement files and records are exempt from public disclosure under this subsection. These include records and files pertaining to factory inspections, sample collections, sample analyses, surveillance reports, warning letters, notices of hearings issued under 21 U.S.C. 335 and the responses thereto, BDAC investigations and audit reports, and all other investigatory records developed prior to termination of actions in court. The Senate report explains exemption (7) as follows:

'These are the files prepared by Government agencies to prosecute law violators. Their disclosure of such files, except to the extent they are available by law to a private party, could harm the Government's case in court.'

It is also reasonable to conclude that the indiscriminate distribution of FDA investigative files to the public would result in carte blanche interpretation of the facts contained in such files. This would not be in keeping with the principles of fair play and justice to those regulated.[1]

Section 1.105 entitled "Prescription-drug advertisements" contains a wealth of material on the subject and is therefore being reproduced in full.

§ **1.105 Prescription-drug advertisements.**

(a) (1) The ingredient information required by section 502(n) of the Federal Food, Drug, and Cosmetic Act shall appear together, without any intervening written, printed, or graphic matter, except the proprietary names of ingredients, which may be included with the listing of established names.

(2) The order of listing of ingredients in the advertisement shall be the same as the order of listing of ingredients on the label of the product, and the information presented in the advertisement concerning the quan-

tity of each such ingredient shall be the same as the corresponding information on the label of the product.

(3) The advertisement shall not employ a fanciful proprietary name for the drug or any ingredient in such a manner as to imply that the drug or ingredient has some unique effectiveness or composition, when, in fact, the drug or ingredient is a common substance, the limitations of which are readily recognized when the drug or ingredient is listed by its established name.

(4) The advertisement shall not feature inert or inactive ingredients in a manner than creates an impression of value greater than their true functional role in the formulation.

(5) The advertisement shall not designate a drug or ingredient by a proprietary name that, because of similarity in spelling or pronunciation, may be confused with the proprietary name or the established name of a different drug or ingredient.

(b) (1) If an advertisement for a prescription drug bears a proprietary name or designation for the drug or any ingredient thereof, the established name, if such there be, corresponding to such proprietary name or designation shall accompany such proprietary name or designation each time it is featured in the advertisement for the drug; but, except as provided below in this subparagraph, the established name need not be used with the proprietary name or designation in the running text of the advertisement. On any page of an advertisement in which the proprietary name or designation is not featured but is used in the running text, the established name shall be used at least once in the running text in association with such proprietary name or designation and in the same type size used in the running text: *Provided, however*, That if the proprietary name or designation is used in the running text in larger size type, the established name shall be used at least once in association with, and in type at least half as large as the type used for, the most prominent presentation of the proprietary name or designation in such running text. If any advertisement includes a column with running text containing detailed information as to composition, prescribing, side effects, or contraindications and the proprietary name or designation is used in such column but is not featured above or below the column, the established name shall be used at least once in such column of running text in asso-

ciation with such proprietary name or designation and in the same type size used in such column of running text: *Provided, however*, That if the proprietary name or designation is used in such column of running text in larger size type, the established name shall be used at least once in association with, and in type at least half as large as the type used for, the most prominent presentation of the proprietary name or designation in such column of running text. Where the established name is required to accompany or to be used in association with the proprietary name or designation, the established name shall be placed in direct conjunction with the proprietary name or designation, and the relationship between the proprietary name or designation and the established name shall be made clear by use of a phrase such as "brand of" preceding the established name by brackets surrounding the established name, or by other suitable means.

(2) The established name shall be printed in letters that are at least half as large as the letters comprising the proprietary name or designation with which it is joined, and the established name shall have a prominence commensurate with the prominence with which such proprietary name or designation appears, taking into account all pertinent factors, including typography, layout, contrast, and other printing features.

(c) In the case of a prescription drug containing two or more active ingredients, if the advertisement bears a proprietary name or designation for such mixture and there is no established name corresponding to such proprietary name or designation, the quantitative ingredient information required in the advertisement by section 502(n) of the act shall be placed in direct conjunction with the most prominent display of the proprietary name or designation. The prominence of the quantitative ingredient information shall bear a reasonable relationship to the prominence of the proprietary name.

(d) (1) If the advertisement employs one proprietary name or designation to refer to a combination of active ingredients present in more than one preparation (the individual preparations differing from each other as to quantities of active ingredients and/or the form of the finished preparation) and there is no established name corresponding to such proprietary name or designation, a listing showing the established names of the active ingredients shall be placed in direct conjunction with the most prominent display of such proprietary name or designation. The prominence of this listing of active ingredients shall bear a reasonable relationship to the prominence of the proprietary name and the relationship between such proprietary name or designation, and the listing of active ingredients shall be made clear by use of such phrase as "brand of," preceding the listing of active ingredients.

(2) The advertisement shall prominently display the name of at least one specific dosage form and shall have the quantitative ingredient information required by section 502(n) of the act in direct conjunction with such display. If other dosage forms are listed in the advertisement, the quantitative ingredient information for such dosage forms shall appear in direct conjunction and in equal prominence with the most prominent listing of the names of such dosage forms.

(e) True statement of information in brief summary relating to side effects, contraindications, and effectiveness:

(1) *When required.* All advertisements for any prescription drug ("prescription drug" as used in this section means drugs defined in section 503(b)(1) of the act and § 1.106(c), applicable to drugs for use by man and veterinary drugs, respectively), except advertisements described in subparagraph (2) of this paragraph, shall present a true statement of information in brief summary relating to side effects, contraindications (when used in this section "side effects, contraindications" include side effects, warnings, precautions, and contraindications and include any such information under such headings as cautions, special considerations, important notes, etc.) and effectiveness.

(2) *Exempt advertisements.* The following advertisements are exempt from the requirements of subparagraph (1) of this paragraph under the conditions specified:

(i) *Reminder advertisements.* Reminder advertisements if they contain only the proprietary or trade name of a drug (which necessitates declaring the established name, if any, and furnishing the formula showing quantitatively each ingredient of the drug to the extent required for labels) and, optionally, information relating to dosage form, quantity of package contents, price, the name and address of the manufacturer, packer, or distributor or other written, printed, or graphic matter containing no

representation or suggestion relating to the advertised drug: *Provided, however,* That if the Commissioner finds that there is evidence of significant incidence of fatalities or serious damage associated with the use of a particular prescription drug, he may notify the manufacturer, packer, or distributor of the drug by mail that this exemption does not apply to such drug by reason of such finding.

(ii) *Advertisements of bulk-sale drugs.* Advertisements of bulk-sale drugs that promote sale of the drug in bulk packages in accordance with the practice of the trade solely to be processed, manufactured, labeled, or repackaged in substantial quantities and that contain no claims for the therapeutic safety or effectiveness of the drug.

(iii) *Advertisements of prescription-compounding drugs.* Advertisements of prescription-compounding drugs that promote sale of a drug for use as a prescription chemical or other compound for use by registered pharmacists in compounding prescriptions if the drug otherwise complies with the conditions for the labeling exemption contained in § 1.106(k) and the advertisement contains no claims for the therapeutic safety or effectiveness of the drug.

(3) *Scope of information to be included; applicability to the entire advertisement.* (i) The requirement of a true statement of information relating to side effects, contraindications, and effectiveness applies to the entire advertisement. Untrue or misleading information in any part of the advertisement will not be corrected by the inclusion in another distinct part of the advertisement of a brief statement containing true information relating to side effects, contraindications, and effectiveness of the drug. Each feature and theme of the advertisement that would be misleading by reason of the omission of appropriate qualification or pertinent information shall include the appropriate qualification or pertinent information, which may be concise if it is supplemented by a prominent reference on each such page to the presence and location elsewhere in the advertisement of a more complete discussion of such qualification or information.

(ii) The information relating to effectiveness is not required to include information relating to all purposes for which the drug is intended but may optionally be limited to a true statement of the effectiveness of the drug for the selected purpose(s) for which the drug is recommended or suggested in the advertisement. The information relating to effectiveness shall include specific indications for use of the drug for purposes claimed in the advertisement; for example, when an advertisement contains a broad claim that a drug is an anti-bacterial agent, the advertisement shall name a type or types of infections and micro-organisms for which the drug is effective clinically as specifically as required, approved, or permitted in the drug package labeling.

(iii) The information relating to side effects and contraindications shall disclose each specific side effect and contraindication (which include side effects, warnings, precautions, and contraindications and include any such information under such headings as cautions, special considerations, important notes, etc., see subparagraph (1) of this paragraph) contained in required, approved, or permitted labeling for the advertised drug dosage form(s); *Provided however;*

(a) The side effects and contraindications disclosed may be limited to those pertinent to the indications for which the drug is recommended or suggested in the advertisement to the extent that such limited disclosure has previously been approved or permitted in drug labeling conforming to the provisions of § 1.106 (b) or (c); and

(b) The use of a single term for a group of side effects and contraindications (for example, "blood dyscrasias" for disclosure of "leukopenia," "agranulocytosis," and "neutropenia") is permitted only to the extent that the use of such a single term in place of disclosure of each specific side effect and contraindication has been previously approved or permitted in drug labeling conforming to the provisions of § 1.106(b) or (c).

(4) *Substance of information to be included in brief summary.* (i)(a) An advertisement for a prescription drug covered by a new-drug application approved pursuant to section 5.5 of the act after October 10, 1962, or any approved supplement thereto, shall not recommend or suggest any use that is not in the labeling accepted in such approved new-drug application or supplement. The advertisement shall present information from labeling required approved, or permitted in a new-drug application relating to each specific side effect and contraindication in such labeling that relates to the uses of the advertised drug dosage form(s) or

shall otherwise conform to the provisions of subparagraph (3)(iii) of this paragraph.

(b) If a prescription drug was covered by a new-drug application or a supplement thereto that became effective prior to October 10, 1962, an advertisement may recommend or suggest:

(1) Uses contained in the labeling accepted in such new-drug application and any effective, approved, or permitted supplement thereto.

(2) Additional uses contained in labeling in commercial use on October 9, 1962, to the extent that such uses did not cause the drug to be an unapproved "new drug" as "new drug" was defined in section 201 (p) of the act as then in force, and to the extent that such uses would be permitted were the drug subject to subdivision (iii) of this subparagraph.

(3) Additional uses contained in labeling in current commercial use to the extent that such uses do not cause the drug to be an unapproved "new drug" as defined in section 201(p) of the act as amended.

The advertisement shall present information from labeling required, approved, or permitted in a new-drug application relating to each specific side effect and contraindication in such labeling that relates to the uses of the advertised drug dosage form(s) or shall otherwise conform to the provisions of subparagraph (3) (iii) of this paragraph.

(ii) An advertisement for a prescription drug subject to certification under section 507 of the act shall not recommend or suggest any use that is not in the labeling covered by the certification or the applicable certification regulations or regulations providing for exemption from certification. The advertisement shall present information from such labeling covered by the certification or the applicable certification regulations or regulations providing for exemption from certification, relating to each specific side effect and contraindication in such labeling and such regulations for the advertised drug dosage form(s) or shall otherwise conform to the provisions of subparagraph (3)(iii) of this paragraph.

(iii) In the case of an advertisement for a prescription drug other than a drug the labeling of which causes it to be an unapproved "new drug" and other than drugs covered by subdivisions (i) and (ii) of this subparagraph, an advertisement may recommend and suggest the drug only for those uses contained in the labeling thereof:

(*a*) For which the drug is generally recognized as safe and effective among experts qualified by scientific training and experience to evaluate the safety and effectiveness of such drugs; or

(*b*) For which there exists substantial evidence of safety and effectiveness, consisting of adequate and well-controlled investigations, including clinical investigations (as used in this section "clinical investigations," "clinical experience," and "clinical significance" mean in the case of drugs intended for administration to man, investigations, experience, or significance in humans, and in the case of drugs intended for administration to other animals, investigations, experience, or significance in the specie or species for which the drug is advertised), by experts qualified by scientific training and experience to evaluate the safety and effectiveness of the drug involved, on the basis of which it can fairly and responsibly be concluded by such experts that the drug is safe and effective for such uses; or

(*c*) For which there exists substantial clinical experience (as used in this section, this means substantial clinical experience adequately documented in medical literature or by other data (to be supplied to the Food and Drug Administration, if requested)), on the basis of which it can fairly and responsibly be concluded by qualified experts that the drug is safe and effective for such uses; or

(*d*) For which safety is supported under any of the preceding clauses in (*a*), (*b*), and (*c*) of this subdivision and effectiveness is supported under any other of such clauses.

The advertisement shall present information relating to each specific side effect and contraindication that is required, approved, or permitted in the package labeling by § 1.106 (b) or (c) for the drug dosage form(s) or shall otherwise conform to the provisions of subparagraph (3) (iii) of this paragraph.

(5) *"True statement" of information.* An advertisement does not satisfy the requirement that it present a "true statement" of information in brief summary relating to side effects, contraindications, and effectiveness if:

(i) It is false or misleading with respect to side effects, contraindications, or effectiveness; or

(ii) It fails to present a fair balance between information relating to side effects and contraindications and information relating to effectiveness of the drug in that the information relating to effectiveness is presented in greater scope, depth, or detail than required and this information is not fairly balanced by the presentation of true information relating to side effects and contraindications of the drug as a "Brief Discussion Summary" comparable in depth and detail with the information required in the labeling by § 1.106 (b) (3) or (c) (3).

(iii) It fails to reveal facts material in the light of its representations or material with respect to consequences that may result from the use of the drug as recommended or suggested in the advertisement.

(6) *Advertisements that are false, lacking in fair balance, or otherwise misleading.* An advertisement for a prescription drug is false, lacking in fair balance, or otherwise misleading, or otherwise violative of section 502(n) of the act, among other reasons, if it:

(i) Contains a representation or suggestion, not approved or permitted for use in the labeling, that a drug is better, more effective, useful in a broader range of conditions or patients (as used in this section "patients" means humans and in the case of veterinary drugs, other animals), safer, has fewer, or less incidence of, or less serious side effects or contraindications than has been demonstrated by substantial evidence or substantial clinical experience as described in subparagraph (4) (iii) (*b*) and (*c*) of this paragraph) whether or not such representations are made by comparison with other drugs or treatments, and whether or not such a representation or suggestion is made directly or through use of published or unpublished literature, quotations, or other references.

(ii) Contains a drug comparison that represents or suggests that a drug is safer or more effective than another drug in some particular when it has not been demonstrated to be safer or more effective in such particular by substantial evidence or substantial clinical experience.

(iii) Contains favorable information or opinions about a drug previously regarded as valid but which have been rendered invalid by contrary and more credible recent information, or contains literature references or quotations that are significantly more favorable to the drug than has been demonstrated by substantial evidence or substantial clinical experience.

(iv) Contains a representation or suggestion that a drug is safer than it has been demonstrated to be by substantial evidence or substantial clinical experience, by selective presentation of information from published articles or other references that report no side effects or minimal side effects with the drug or otherwise selects information from any source in a way that makes a drug appear to be safer than has been demonstrated.

(v) Presents information from a study in a way that implies that the study represents larger or more general experience with the drug than it actually does.

(vi) Contains references to literature or studies that misrepresent the effectiveness of a drug by failure to disclose that claimed results may be due to concomitant therapy, or by failure to disclose the credible information available concerning the extent to which claimed results may be due to placebo effect (information concerning placebo effect is not required unless the advertisement promotes the drug for use by man).

(vii) Contains favorable data or conclusions from nonclinical studies of a drug, such as in laboratory animals or in vitro, in a way that suggests they have clinical significance when in fact no such clinical significance has been demonstrated.

(viii) Contains information from published or unpublished reports or opinions falsely or misleadingly represented or suggested to be authentic or authoritative.

(ix) Uses a statement by a recognized authority that is apparently favorable about a drug but fails to refer to concurrent or more recent unfavorable data or statements from the same authority on the same subject or subjects.

(x) Uses a quote or paraphrase out of context to convey a false or misleading idea.

(xi) Uses literature quotations or references that purport to support an advertising claim but in fact do not support the claim or have relevance to the claim.

(xii) Uses literature, quotations, or references for the purpose of recommending or suggesting conditions of drug use that are not approved or permitted in the drug package labeling.

(xiii) Offers a combination of drugs for the treatment of patients suffering from a condition amenable to treatment by any of the components rather than limiting the indications for use to patients for whom concomitant therapy as provided by the fixed combination drug is indicated, unless such condition is included in the uses permitted under subparagraph (4) of this paragraph.

(xiv) Uses a study on a small number of patients or on normal subjects without disclosing the small number of patients or the fact that the subjects were normal.

(xv) Uses "statistics" on numbers of patients, or counts of favorable results or side effects, derived from pooling data from various insignificant or dissimilar studies in a way that suggests either that such "statistics" are valid if they are not or that they are derived from large or significant studies supporting favorable conclusions when such is not the case.

(xvi) Uses erroneously a statistical finding of "no significant difference" to claim clinical equivalence or to deny or conceal the potential existence of a real clinical difference.

(xvii) Uses statements or representations that a drug differs from or does not contain a named drug or category of drugs, or that it has a greater potency per unit of weight, in a way that suggests falsely or misleadingly or without substantial evidence or substantial clinical experience that the advertised drug is safer or more effective than such other drug or drugs.

(xviii) Uses data favorable to a drug derived from patients treated with dosages different from those recommended in approved or permitted labeling if the drug advertised is subject to section 505 or 507 of the act, or, in the case of other drugs, if the dosages employed were different from those recommended in the labeling and generally recognized as safe and effective. This provision is not intended to prevent citation of reports of studies that include some patients treated with dosages different from those authorized, if the results in such patients are not used.

(xix) Uses headline, subheadline, or pictorial or other graphic material in a way that is misleading.

(xx) Represents or suggests that drug dosages properly recommended for use in the treatment of certain classes of patients or disease conditions are safe and effective for the treatment of other classes of patients or disease conditions when such is not the case.

(xxi) Fails to present information concerning side effects and contraindications in depth and detail (not exceeding that required in the labeling by § 1.106 (b) (3) or (c) (3)) comparable to that used for claims for effectiveness or safety of the drug, taking into account the length of the advertisement and the nature of its message. This means that there may be two permissible levels of summarization:

(*a*) If the claims for effectiveness or safety are presented briefly without dosage information and the advertisement as a whole appears on three pages or less, the side effects and contraindications may be presented concisely provided that each specific side effect and contraindication contained in the approved or permitted labeling, to the extent required by subparagraph (4) of this paragraph, is presented in a "Brief Summary" or its equivalent elsewhere in the advertisement;

(*b*) If the claims for effectiveness or safety are presented in detail or in discussion form, or dosage information is presented, or parts of the advertisement appear on more than three pages of a periodical of page size larger than 50 square inches, or more than four pages of a periodical of 50 square inches or smaller page size, side effect and contraindication information shall be presented as a "Brief Discussion Summary" comparable in depth and detail with the information required in the drug labeling under § 1.106 (b) (3) or (c) (3).

(xxii) Presents required information relating to side effects or contraindications by means of a general term for a group in place of disclosing each specific side effect and contraindication (for example employs the term "blood dyscrasias" instead of "leukopenia," "agranulocytosis," "neutropenia," etc.) unless the use of such general term conforms to the provisions of subparagraph (3) (iii) of this paragraph.

(7) *Advertisements that may be false, lacking in fair balance, or otherwise misleading.* An advertisement may be false, lacking in fair balance, or otherwise misleading or otherwise violative of section 502(n) of the act if it:

(i) Contains favorable information or conclusions from a study that is inadequate in design, scope, or conduct to furnish significant support for such information or conclusions.

(ii) Uses the concept of "statistical significance" to support a claim that has not been demonstrated to have clinical significance or validity, or fails to reveal the range of variations around the quoted average results.

(iii) Uses statistical analyses and techniques on a retrospective basis to discover and cite findings not soundly supported by the study, or to suggest scientific validity and rigor for data from studies the design or protocol of which are not amenable to formal statistical evaluations.

(iv) Uses tables or graphs to distort or misrepresent the relationships, trends, differences, or changes among the variables or products studied; for example, by failing to label abscissa and ordinate so that the graph creates a misleading impression.

(v) Uses reports or statements represented to be statistical analyses, interpretations, or evaluations that are inconsistent with or violate the established principles of statistical theory, methodology, applied practice, and inference, or that are derived from clinical studies the design, data, or conduct of which substantially invalidate the application of statistical analyses, interpretations, or evaluations.

(vi) Contains claims concerning the mechanism or site of drug action that are not generally regarded as established by scientific evidence by experts qualified by scientific training and experience without disclosing that the claims are not established and the limitations of the supporting evidence.

(vii) Fails to provide sufficient emphasis for the information relating to side effects and contraindications, when such information is contained in a distinct part of an advertisement, because of repetition or other emphasis in that part of the advertisement of claims for effectiveness or safety of the drug.

(viii) Fails to present information relating to side effects and contraindications with a prominence and readability reasonably comparable with the presentation of information relating to effectiveness of the drug, taking into account all implementing factors such as typography, layout, contrast, headlines, paragraphing, white space, and any other techniques apt to achieve emphasis.

(ix) Fails to provide adequate emphasis (for example, by the use of color scheme, borders, headlines, or copy that extends across the gutter) for the fact that two facing pages are part of the same advertisement when one page contains information relating to side effects and contraindications.

(x) In an advertisement promoting use of the drug in a selected class of patients (for example, geriatric patients or depressed patients), fails to present with adequate emphasis the significant side effects and contraindications or the significant dosage considerations, when dosage recommendations are included in an advertisement, especially applicable to that selected class of patients.

(xi) Fails to present on a page facing another page (or on another full page) of an advertisement on more than one page, information relating to side effects and contraindications when such information is in a distinct part of the advertisement.

(xii) Fails to include on each page or spread of an advertisement the information relating to side effects and contraindications or a prominent reference to its presence and location when it is presented as a distinct part of an advertisement.

(f) through (i) [Revoked]

(j)(1) No advertisement concerning a particular prescription drug may be disseminated without prior approval by the Food and Drug Administration if:

(i) The sponsor or the Food and Drug Administration has received information that has not been widely publicized in medical literature that the use of drug may cause fatalities or serious damage;

(ii) The Commissioner (or in his absence the officer acting as Commissioner), after evaluating the reliability of such information, has notified the sponsor that the information must be a part of the advertisements for the drug; and

(iii) The sponsor has failed within a reasonable time as specified in such notification to present to the Food and Drug Administration a program, adequate in light of the nature of the information, for assuring that such information will be publicized promptly and adequately to the medical profession in subsequent advertisements.

If the Commissioner finds that the program presented is not being followed, he will notify the sponsor that prior approval of all advertisements for the particular drug will be required. Nothing in this paragraph is to be construed as limiting the Commissioner's or the Secretary's rights, as authorized by law, to issue publicity, to suspend any new-drug application, to decertify any antibiotic, or to recommend any regulatory action.

(2) Within a reasonable time after information concerning the possibility that a drug may cause fatalities or serious damage

has been widely publicized in medical literature, the Food and Drug Administration shall notify the sponsor of the drug by mail that prior approval of advertisements for the drug is no longer necessary.

(3) Dissemination of an advertisement not in compliance with this paragraph shall be deemed to be an act that causes the drug to be misbranded under section 502(n) of the act.

(4) Any advertisement may be submitted to the Food and Drug Administration prior to publication for comment. If the advertiser is notified that the submitted advertisement is not in violation and, at some subsequent time, the Food and Drug Administration changes its opinion, the advertiser will be so notified and will be given a reasonable time for correction before any regulatory action is taken under this section. Notification to the advertiser that a proposed advertisement is or is not considered to be in violation shall be in written form.

(k) An advertisement issued or caused to be issued by the manufacturer, packer, or distributor of the drug promoted by the advertisement and which is not in compliance with section 502(n) of the act and the applicable regulations thereunder shall cause stocks of such drug in possession of the person responsible for issuing or causing the issuance of the advertisement, and stocks of the drug distributed by such person and still in the channels of commerce, to be misbranded under section 502(n) of the act.

(1) (1) Advertisements subject to section 502(n) of the act include advertisements in published journals, magazines, other periodicals, and newspapers, and advertisements broadcast through media such as radio, television, and telephone communication systems.

(2) Brochures, booklets, mailing pieces, detailing pieces, file cards, bulletins, calendars, price lists, catalogs, house organs, letters, motion picture films, film strips, lantern slides, sound recordings, exhibits, literature, and reprints and similar pieces of printed, audio, or visual matter descriptive of a drug and references published (for example, the "Physicians' Desk Reference") for use by medical practitioners, pharmacists, or nurses, containing drug information supplied by the manufacturer, packer, or distributor of the drug and which are disseminated by or on behalf of its manufacturer, packer, or distributor are hereby determined to be labeling as defined in section 201(m) of the act.

The Package Insert

The basic purpose of labeling a drug is to provide the physician and pharmacist with adequate information about the product. The package insert, a prime example of labeling, is concerned with a *drug*. It is not intended to instruct the physician in the diagnoses of disease, or in recognition of pathological conditions; nor is it intended to replace the physician's basic medical education in pharmacology or drug therapy.

Generally, package inserts consist of a single sheet of paper and contain the following information, in an order of headings recommended by the FDA. The order is: name of drug, description, actions, indications, contraindications, warnings, precautions, adverse reactions, dosage and administration and references.

Jennings concisely summarizes the contents of each heading as follows:

Name: This must include the established or 'generic' name of the active components. The structural or graphic formula may be given along with the chemical name. Forms other than oral must list inert ingredients as well.

Description: This includes a physical-chemical description of the active components, and of the dosage form when it has some bearing on the product's effectiveness. Data given may include such items as melting point, solubility, and stability.

Actions: This includes the pharmacologic effects in animals and man, including absorption, metabolism, excretion, etc. Such basic animal data as acute LD_{50} may be included here.

Indications: The indications for a drug's use are now listed as specifically as possible. If the drug is not definitive treatment but rather an adjunct, a statement to this effect may be required.

Contraindications: This includes absolute contraindications and perhaps strong relative contraindications. If the drug is contraindicated in pregnancy, this information is given here.

Warnings: This includes extraordinary hazards, dangers of treatment, special conditions, and sometimes important precautions. If there is any question of safety in pregnancy, the information is presented here under the heading 'USE IN PREGNANCY.'

Precautions: This includes cautions to be observed in the use and administration of the drug under routine and special conditions.

Adverse Reactions: This includes all known adverse reactions, including side effects, and those adverse reactions in which a causal relation is strongly probable. Drugs that have essentially the same indications and that pharmacologically belong to a 'class' such as the thiazides, steroids, and phenothiazines, as a rule carry the 'class' adverse reactions unless there is good evidence that they should be exempt.

Dosage and Administration: Here are listed the recommended dosage, routes, frequency and duration of administration for various indications and age groups. If common labeling is used for more than one dosage form or mode of administration (for example, for intramuscular and intravenous), any difference in preparation and administration is to be clearly stated.

The Food and Drug Administration's concern with the package insert does not end with the approval of the New Drug Application. Each time a manufacturer makes a major change in the production of a drug or a change in mode of the drug's presentation to the medical community, he must submit a supplemental application to the original NDA. For example, after FDA's approval, a manufacturer often continues investigational research for indications other than those approved in the package insert. When the manufacturer feels he has sufficient data to support new claims, he submits it as a Supplemental New Drug Application. This material is subjected to the same scrutiny as the original NDA; it requires 'adequate well-controlled studies' for approval of efficacy. If the data meet FDA criteria, the supplemental application is approved, then the package insert is revised.[2]

Because package inserts and other types of FDA-approved labeling have been introduced as evidence when professional liability litigation has involved the use of drugs, the question has been raised as to whether or not an FDA-approved package insert establishes a standard for medical practice.

The AMA Law Division answered the question in the following manner:

Determinations of the FDA do not establish standards for medical practice. Such standards are established by the customary practice of reputable physicians. The information in the approved package insert in effect puts a prescribing physician on notice of possible hazards of the drug and may place a burden on him, in the event of litigation, to explain his reasons for deviation if he has done so.

Approval by the FDA of a recommended usage or dosage as stated in the labeling does not protect a physician from legal responsibility if he follows the approved recommendations and does not impose liability upon him automatically if he departs from its recommendations. To the extent that FDA-approved recommendations generally are considered reasonable and are followed by physicians, however, reasons for the variation may have to be explained. If the usage is, in fact, a variation from accepted practice in the medical profession, the procedure would be 'experimental' in a legal sense.[3]

In a 1957 California case, the question of the evidentiary value of the manufacturer's brochure was stated by the Appellate Court as follows:

Thus, while admissible, it [the brochure] cannot establish as a matter of law the standard of care required of a physician in the use of the drug. It may be considered by the jury along with other evidence in the case to determine whether the particular physician met the standard of care required of him. The mere fact of a departure from the manufacturer's recommendation where such departure is customarily followed by physicians of standing in the locality does not make the departure an 'experiment.' There was in this case no evidence of experiment and the instructions concerning 'experiment' should not have been given."[4]

References

1. J. Mamana: *FDA's Obligation Under the 1966 Public Information Act*, FDA PAPERS, September, 1967, p. 16.
2. J. Jennings: *The R_x Label: Basis for all Prescribing Information*, FDA PAPERS, November, 1967, p. 12.
3. B. Anderson: *Package Inserts as Evidence*, JAMA, 208: 3: 589, April 21, 1969.
4. Salgo v. Leland Stanford Jr. University Board of Trustees, 317 P 2nd 170.

CHAPTER 11

The Truth in Lending Act

The Truth in Lending Act, also known as Public Law 90-321, became effective July 1, 1969. The Act seeks to assure a meaningful disclosure of credit terms so consumers can readily compare various forms of available credit in an informed manner. It deserves the attention of everyone who extends credit.

The Act has four main parts which deal with the various phases of credit activities and provides both criminal and civil prosecution for noncompliance with its provisions. The following is a summary of the contents of the four sections:

Title I is intended to protect the consumer in credit use by requiring full disclosure of the terms and conditions of finance charges in credit transactions or in offers to extend credit. Minimal standards for disclosure of credit terms in face-to-face business dealings and advertising by anyone who regularly engages in credit transactions are established.

Title II is concerned with extortionate credit transactions which are characterized by the express or implicit threat of harm to the debtor, his family, his reputation or his property as a means of enforcing payment.

Title III is intended to protect the average, overextended consumer by limiting the amount of money a creditor may attach from the debtor's wages and prohibiting the debtor's employer from firing him because of the wage attachment.

Title IV created a National Commission on Consumer Finance to study the functioning and structure of the consumer finance industry as well as consumer credit transactions and to report their recommendations to the President and Congress by January 1, 1971.

The answer to the critical question of "when does the Act apply?" is based upon whether or not any credit or service or late payment charge is made on credit accounts. Where credit is extended but no charge of any kind is made for so doing, the transaction is exempt.

Where a pharmacist has a revolving credit plan and includes a financing charge of any nature or levies a "slow payment" charge, all the provisions and requirements of the credit disclosure and advertising portion of the act become applicable.

Although many pharmacists do not generally offer their patrons the option to charge their purchases, it appears that the national trend in the direction of charge sales is on the increase. Some pharmacists have chosen to extend credit via the use of one or more of the popular credit card plans. Other pharmacists offer the customer 30-day credit but make no interest or service charge, while still others charge either interest, a service charge or, in certain situations, both.

Because the consumer was never fully informed as to the total effect of the rate of interest being charged, the federal government enacted The Truth in Lending Act. Regulation Z which implements the Act became effective on July 1, 1969. From the viewpoint of the pharmacy practitioner, the Act is of double importance in that it affects him as a private consumer and as a businessman extending credit to other private consumers.

The Federal Trade Commission is responsible for the enforcement of the Act and of Regulation Z.

The purpose of this legislation is stated to be the assurance that every customer who has need for consumer credit is given meaningful information with respect to the cost of that credit which, in most cases, must be expressed in the *dollar amount of the finance charge, and as an annual percentage rate computed on the unpaid balance* of the amount financed. Neither the Act nor Regulation Z is intended to control charges for consumer credit, or to interfere with trade practices except to the extent that such practices may be inconsistent with the purpose of the Act [Section 226.1].

Generally, pharmacies, drug wholesalers, and other suppliers will be affected under the following circumstances:

1. Where the vendor charges interest and/or a finance or service charge on his accounts receivable.

2. Where the vendor extends credit wherein the balance is, or may be, payable in five or more installments, irrespective of whether or not a finance or interest charge is made.

3. Where the vendor, as a convenience to his customers, arranges financing from an outside source such as a bank, finance company or other commercial lender, and processes the loan application, note and/or other papers connected with the transaction.

In those instances where the vendor makes an interest or finance charge, the note evidencing the indebtedness must clearly disclose the following information:

1. Amount financed.
2. Finance charged.
3. Annual percentage rate.
4. Number, amount and due dates of payments.
5. Identification of the creditor.

The above information must be disclosed on the appropriate form even though the vendor makes arrangements for the financing of the customer's account through a bank, finance company or other commercial lender.

The Act further provides that the terminology specified in it must be used in making disclosures required by the Regulation [Sections 226.6 (a); 226.7 (b), (c); 226.8 (b), (d); 226.9 (b); 226.11 (c)].

Unlike many other records of the retail pharmacy that must be retained for indefinite periods of time, records of compliance with this statute must be retained for two years. Regulation Z [Section 226.6 (i)] provides for the inspection of these records by agents of the proper agency.

Finance Charge

Section 226.4 defines a finance charge as the total of all costs which the consumer must pay, directly or indirectly, for obtaining credit. Some of the more common items that must be included in the finance charge are:

1. Interest.
2. Loan fee.
3. Finder's fee or similar charge.
4. Time-price differential.
5. Amount paid as a discount.
6. Service, transaction or carrying charge.
7. Points.
8. Appraisal fee (except in real estate transactions).
9. Premium for credit life or other insurance if this is a condition for advancing credit.
10. Investigation or credit report fee (except in real estate transaction).

Costs which are not a part of the finance charge include taxes, license fees, registration fees, certain title fees and some legal real estate closing fees.

Because the customer is entitled to be shown the finance charge, it must be clearly typed or written, stating the total dollars and cents, and the annual percentage rate which is defined as "the relative cost of credit in percentage terms."

Prior to January 1, 1971, the annual percentage rate was permitted to be expressed in dollars e.g., $12 finance charge per year per $100 of unpaid balance. However, as of January 1, 1971 the rate must be stated as a percentage [Section 226.6 (j)], and must be accurate to the nearest one quarter of one percent (Section 226.6). (See Figure 14.)

CARD HOLDER AGREEMENT

The undersigned, herein referred to as the Holder, having applied to _____ the Bank, for credit card privileges under the Bank's Charge Account service, hereby agrees to the following terms and conditions.

1. The Holder authorizes the Bank to pay and charge to his account all items reflecting purchases or cash advances made or obtained through the use of any credit card issued to him or at his request by the Bank.

2. Determination of the amount of credit to be extended shall be solely by the Bank, and the Bank shall not be obligated to the Holder to honor any draft or voucher which will increase the outstanding amount of the Holder's credit beyond the maximum fixed by the Bank.

3. If the Bank shall at any time advise the Holder of its determination as to the maximum amount of credit available to the Holder, the Holder shall not thereafter make any purchases or draw any cash advances which would cause such maximum amount to be exceeded. If the total amount of purchases and cash advances outstanding at any time is in excess of the maximum credit, the Holder shall pay the amount of such excess to the Bank within ten days after demand.

4. Any credit card issued to another at the request and for the account of the Holder shall be subject to the provisions hereof and the Holder shall be fully liable with respect thereto.

5. The Bank will send to the Holder a monthly statement on a billing date selected by the Bank, which will show the total amount charges for the purchase of merchandise and services, and for cash advanced through use of credit cards issued hereunder. The Holder may pay the Bank for such charges and advances by any payment plan offered him in his monthly statement. The minimum payment which the Holder shall be required to make each month under the deferred payment plan shall be one-tenth of the sum of all amounts then due from the Holder to the Bank, or $10., whichever is greater, provided however, that the Bank may if it so elects offer the Holder the privilege of making a smaller payment.

6. The Holder agrees to pay to the Bank a finance charge on any unpaid balances resulting from (a) purchases of merchandise or services not fully paid for within 25 days of the first billing date after such purchase; (b) cash advances; and (c) purchases under special written agreements between the Holder and the seller requiring payment of a finance charge. **The finance charge shall be 1½% per month on the first $500. of total obligations outstanding hereunder which is an ANNUAL PERCENTAGE RATE of 18%, but if at any time the unpaid balance shall be greater than $500. the finance charge on the excess over $500. shall be 1% per month which is an ANNUAL PERCENTAGE RATE of 12%.** Payments and credits received during the current billing cycle are deducted from the previous balance before the finance charge under (a) hereinabove is computed. The finance charge on cash advances under (b) above shall be computed from the date of each advance to the date of final payment. Calculation of the finance charge under (c) above shall be in accordance with the provisions of the special agreements concerned. All payments received in respect to bills rendered by the Bank to the Holder shall be applied first to the finance charges billed, second to amounts billed for purchases of merchandise and services, and finally to other items financed as contemplated under (b) and (c) above.

7. The Bank shall not in any way be liable should any participating merchant member refuse to honor any credit card issued hereunder. The Bank shall have no liability with respect to any merchandise or services purchased through use of a credit card issued hereunder, and any claim or defense of the Holder with respect thereto shall be solely against the participating member involved, and not against the Bank. The Holder shall remain fully liable to pay the Bank the cash sale price of such merchandise or services, together with interest thereon as aforesaid, even though the Holder may have some claim or defense against the participating member.

8. The Holder will notify the Bank of the loss or theft of any credit card promptly in writing and until the Bank receives such notice, the Holder will be liable for all charges incurred or advances made through the use of such credit card, together with the prescribed interest thereon.

9. The Bank may at any time terminate or cancel any credit card or privileges extended to the Holder under this agreement with or without cause or notice to the Holder. The Holder will, at the expiration date of any credit card issued to him, or sooner if requested by the Bank, cease to use such card and promptly surrender the same to the Bank. No termination or cancellation shall affect the Holder's obligation to pay to the Bank all amounts owing hereunder and all charges incurred through the use of his credit card until such card shall have been returned to the Bank.

10. The Bank's commitment hereunder shall terminate and all amounts owing hereunder shall become immediately due and payable at the option of the Bank without demand or notice, which are hereby expressly waived, upon failure of the Holder to make any payment required hereunder or to perform any obligation set forth herein or in any cash advance document, or upon death of the Holder or upon institution of any insolvency, bankruptcy, receivership, or arrangement proceeding by or against the Holder, or upon any attachment or garnishment of his property which shall remain undischarged or unreleased for a period of five days.

11. Any sales drafts or vouchers and any cash advance documents whether or not a carbon copy with carbon signature, or microfilm or other photographic copies of any such slips or documents shall be competent evidence in establishing the amount owing by the Holder hereunder, nor shall the return of any sales draft or other document to the undersigned, whether as a voucher accompanying a statement or in any other manner, terminate the obligation of the Holder to pay all unpaid balances chargeable to him hereunder. The Bank may at all times treat all deposits and other property of the Holder in its possession or control as collateral security for all liabilities of the Holder to the Bank hereunder.

12. The Bank may at any time or times amend this agreement or the terms hereof by written notice to the Holder, such amendment to be effective on the date specified in the notice or sixty days after mailing to Holder, whichever is later. After such notice by the Bank, the use of any credit card issued to or at the request of the Holder shall constitute a full acceptance of the provisions of the amendment by the Holder. This agreement is nonassignable by the Holder and, together with all extensions of credit hereunder, shall be governed by the law of the Commonwealth of Massachusetts.

13. The Holder agrees to pay all costs of collection and a reasonable attorney's fee upon default.

Fig. 14. A Sample Credit Card Holder Agreement.

Open End Credit

Open end credit covers most credit cards and revolving charge accounts where finance charges are made on the unpaid balances each month [Section 226.2 (r); 226.7].

Under this law, an open end credit customer must receive the following information in writing to the extent applicable [Section 226.7 (a)]:

1. The conditions under which the finance charge may be imposed and the period in which payment can be made without incurring a finance charge.
2. The method used in determining the balance on which the finance charge is to be made.

3. How the actual finance charge is calculated.
4. The periodic rates used and the range of balances to which each applies.
5. The conditions under which additional charges may be made along with details of how they are calculated.
6. Descriptions of any lien which may be acquired on a customer's property.
7. The minimum payment that must be made on each billing.

The law [Section 226.7 (b)] further requires that a periodic statement be sent to a customer whose account shows an unpaid balance of over $1.00 or where a finance charge is made. The monthly statement must provide the following information:

1. The unpaid balance at the start of the billing period.
2. The amount and date of each extension of credit and identification of each item purchased.
3. Payments made and other credits.
4. The finance charge shown in dollars and cents.
5. The rates used in calculating the finance charge plus the range of balances to which they apply.
6. The annual percentage rate.
7. The unpaid balance on which the finance charge was calculated.
8. The closing date of the billing cycle and the unpaid balance at that point of time.

Credit Other Than Open End

This type of credit usually involves loans and sales credit. Examples of these are the financing of a new car purchase through the automobile dealer or borrowing money from a loan company.

Because these types of transactions are not common in the retail practice of pharmacy, space will not be devoted to them. However, the student may learn more about the mechanics of the transaction by referring to the appropriate sections of Regulation Z.

Advertising Credit Terms

Section 226.10 provides that no advertisement to aid, promote or assist directly or indirectly any extension of credit may state:

1. That a specific amount of credit or installment amount can be arranged unless the creditor customarily does or is willing to arrange credit for that period and for that amount; or
2. That no down payment ... will be accepted in connection with any extension of credit, unless the creditor customarily does or is willing to accept down payment in that amount.

References

1. Code of Federal Regulations, Title 12, Chapter II, Part 226, cited as 12CRF 226.
2. Publication of the Board of Governors of the Federal Reserve System, "Truth in Lending—Regulation Z," Federal Trade Commission, Washington, D.C. 20580.

CHAPTER 12

Medicare Law

Medicare is a federal health insurance program designed to provide two different kinds of health benefits for people aged 65 and over. The benefits provided by the Medicare Law, which is also known as Title 18 of Public Law 89-97, are categorized under *Part A*—the basic hospital insurance benefits portion which makes payments towards the cost of hospital services and certain other specific post-hospital care services in extended care facilities, nursing homes and the patient's own home, and *Part B*—the voluntary supplementary medical insurance benefits portion.

Participation by Hospitals and Allied Health Agencies

The basic responsibility for administration of the hospital insurance program is vested in the Secretary of HEW. Within this authority, the administrative and operational responsibility will be in the Social Security Administration, with responsibility for certain professional aspects in the Public Health Service.

The Social Security Administration will make use of state agencies and organizations to assist in the administration of the program.

The rules governing the aspects of the Medicare program with which the student must be familiar are known as the *Conditions of Participation for Hospitals*. These were issued by the Social Security Administration after extensive consultation with the Health Insurance Benefits Advisory Council (HIBAC).

Accordingly, it is from this document that the following information governing the participation of hospitals and allied health agencies is obtained.

General Hospitals

Since the Joint Commission on Accreditation of Hospitals has adopted a requirement for utilization review, any hospital accredited by this group would generally be conclusively presumed to meet all of the conditions for participation in the program.

The regulations also provide that accreditation by the American Osteopathic Association, or any other national accrediting body, may also be accepted, if it is reasonable to do so, as evidence that a hospital meets some or all of the conditions of participation.

Further stipulations require the hospital to be licensed, certified or approved by the state (local law equivalents to licensing meet this requirement) and it must substantially comply with regulations pertaining to medical records, medical staff bylaws, pharmacy and therapeutics committees to mention a few.

Further requirements necessary to the health and safety of patients may be imposed by the government, however these health and safety requirements cannot be more strict than the comparable conditions enforced by the Joint Commission on Accreditation of Hospitals.

The regulations also permit the state to establish stricter requirements if such are specified under its federal-state medical assistance programs. These stricter requirements may be enforced by the sovereign state even if they are not used in its own programs.

Psychiatric and Tuberculosis Hospitals

In order to avoid paying for care that is merely custodial in nature, the conditions of participation require that the institution:

1. Be accredited by the Joint Commission on Accreditation of Hospitals.
2. Maintain clinical records which are adequate to ascertain the degree and intensity of treatment furnished to the insured.
3. Meet staffing requirements commensurate with those needed for carrying out an active treatment program.

The regulations also dictate that a distinct part of the institution may participate as a psychiatric or tuberculosis hospital, if it meets the above conditions, even though the institution of which it is a part does not. If the distinct part of the institution meets requirements equivalent to accreditation requirements, it may also qualify under the program even though the institution is not accredited.

Extended Care Facility

An extended care facility (ECF) is liberally defined as a nursing home that provides skilled services, or a distinct part of an institution, such as a ward or wing of a hospital. Such a facility does not include an institution which is primarily for the care and treatment of mental diseases or tuberculosis.

In general, extended care facilities will be required to have an agreement with a hospital for the transfer of patients and interchange of medical records. This requirement can be waived where an extended care facility has attempted, in good faith, to arrange a transfer agreement but failed, and the state agency finds that the facility's participation in the hospital insurance program is in the public's interest and essential to assuring necessary care to the insured inhabitants of the community.

It should be emphasized that the requirements for a transfer agreement do not mean that a patient would have to be transferred from a hospital to an extended care facility which have such an arrangement between them. A transfer agreement with any hospital would qualify the facility so that the patient's extended care would be paid for if he was admitted upon transfer from some other hospital.

Since the extended care facility is expected to render high-quality convalescent and rehabilitative care it must meet the following requirements. They include:

1. Around-the-clock nursing services with at least one registered nurse employed full time.
2. The availability of a physician to handle emergencies.
3. Utilization review.
4. Proper methods for handling drugs.
5. The maintenance of adequate medical policies governing the nursing care and related services.

Home Health Agency

Visiting nurse organizations, hospital-operated home care services and agencies specifically established to provide a broad spectrum of home health services are examples of home health agencies which may qualify under the program. A private organization providing home care on a profit basis may qualify if it is licensed, where state law requires it, and if it meets specified standards.

In general, a home health agency, in order to participate will have to be:

1. Publicly owned.
2. A nonprofit organization exempt from federal taxation.
3. Licensed and meet staffing requirements and other conditions and standards prescribed by regulations.

It must be recognized that not all institutions desiring to participate will be certified for this purpose. Therefore, it will be possible for an insured person to encounter a medical emergency and find that he is admitted to a hospital not participating in the hospital insurance program. In these situations, the law permits the payment of benefits for emergency hospital diagnostic services or inpatient care until it is no longer necessary from a medical point of view to care for the patient in a non-participating institution provided that the hospital agrees not to charge the patient amounts (except the deductibles and coinsurance) in addition to the program's payments for covered services.

Medicare Benefits

In general, all persons aged 65 and over may enroll for *Part A* benefits by contacting their local Social Security Administration office. There is no cost to the individual for this phase of the Medicare program. To obtain coverage for the *Part B* benefits of the Medicare program, the individual must subscribe to it at a cost of $5.60 per month (as of July 1, 1971). At the present time, the law does not provide coverage for ambulatory patient prescription drugs.

Both *Part A* and *B* became effective on July 1, 1966 except for the nursing home benefits which became effective on January 1, 1967.

Part A and Part B Coverage

Part A, the basic hospital insurance benefits program, provides for inpatient hospital care for up to ninety days per spell of illness (inpatient psychiatric services are limited to 190 days per lifetime). The patient must pay the first $60.00 during the first sixty days and $15.00 per day for the 61st to the 90th day. A "spell of illness" is defined as that period beginning with the first day that the insured receives covered benefits as a patient in a hospital and ends after the patient has been discharged from the hospital for sixty consecutive days.

Part A also provides for post-hospital care in an extended care facility for up to one hundred days per spell of illness. The plan will pay in full for the first twenty days and the patient must pay $5.00 per day for the 21st through the 100th day. A patient must have been in a hospital for a minimum of three days before being admitted to an extended care facility in order to qualify.

Part A also provides for post-hospital home health visits by visiting nurses, speech, physical or occupational therapists, and other non-medical health workers provided by qualified home health agencies for up to one hundred visits during the year following the patient's discharge from a hospital stay of at least three days or from an extended care facility.

Part A allows for outpatient hospital diagnostic services with the patient paying the first $20.00 and twenty percent of costs above that for each twenty-day period of diagnostic workup.

Patients should be reminded that *Part A* does not pay for services of physicians, private duty nursing, cosmetic surgery, routine dental care, custodial care, personal comfort items, eye or ear examinations or services rendered outside of the United States.

Medical supplies such as gauze, cotton, bandages, surgical dressings, catheters, surgical gloves, rubbing alcohol, irrigating solutions, intravenous fluids and oxygen, and medical appliances such as bed pans, wheel chairs, crutches, hospital beds, trapeze bars, oxygen tents, intermittent positive pressure machines and air pressure mattresses will all be covered under *Part A* of Medicare when patients are cared for by a Home Health Care Agency.

Part B, the voluntary supplementary medical insurance benefits portion of the program, requires that the patient pay the first $50.00 each calendar year for the cost of services covered under the program after which the government will pay eighty percent of the "reasonable" charges or costs for physicians' and surgeons' services and up to one hundred home health visits per calendar year without a requirement of prior hospitalization. This is in addition to the hundred visits provided under *Part A.*

Part B authorizes, in addition to payment for a physician's services, payment for services and supplies that are incidental to the physician's services including the rental (not sale) of durable medical equipment such as iron lungs, oxygen tents, hospital beds and wheel chairs; surgical dressings, splints and casts; leg, arm, back and neck braces.

Medicaid—Title 19

Title 19 was designed to unify, within certain prescribed federal standards, the various government public assistance medical programs such as Kerr-Mills, and the programs for the blind, the disabled, families with dependent children and individuals who were medically indigent; also included were all children under age 21 whose parents qualified under the state income limitations for the medical aid program even if they had not been receiving cash payments under the aid to dependent children program. In replacing Kerr-Mills, Title 19 thus extended the basic Kerr-Mills principle beyond those persons in the over-65 category to include other public assistance groups.

Careful review of the wording of the Act reveals that one of the major objectives incorporated into Title 19 was the substitution of a flexible income standard for the rigid means test. Other innovations included specific provision for five basic medical care services; reimbursement to hospitals on a "reasonable cost" basis; elimination of relative responsibility and residency requirements; modification of lien provisions and state administrative flexibility.

States implementing Title 19 had to provide five basic medical services by July 1, 1967. These are: (1) inpatient hospital services (other than service in an institution for tuberculosis or mental diseases); (2) outpatient hospital services; (3) x-ray and other laboratory services; (4) physician's services, whether furnished in the office, the patient's home, a hospital, a nursing home that provides skilled services or elsewhere; and (5) skilled nursing home services (other than service in an institution for tuberculosis or mental diseases) for persons 21 years of age or older.

All states must have placed Title 19 into operation by January 1, 1970, or have lost federal assistance for their state-operated medical care programs; by July 1, 1975 the states must have a comprehensive program which provides care and services to virtually all individuals meeting the plan's eligibility standards with respect to income and resources, including social services to enable the individual to attain or maintain independence or self-care.

Under the matching formula established by Title 19, the federal government would reimburse the states for a portion of their expenditures based upon an equalization formula ranging from 50 to 83 percent, depending on the per capita income of a state as it is related to the national per capita income. In addition, the individual states would determine their own income standards, and there would be no limitation on the amount of state expenditures the federal government could match.

From a practical standpoint, pharmacists are basically interested in what is meant by the term "Medical Assistance" as it applies to those individuals who qualify for aid under the Act.

Section 1905 of the Medicare law states that the term "Medical Assistance" means payment of part or all of the cost of the following care and services (if such care and services are provided in or after the third month before the month in which the recipient makes application for assistance) for individuals who qualify:

> Medical care, or any other type of remedial care recognized under State law, furnished by licensed practitioners within the scope of their practice as defined by State law;
>
> home health care services;
>
> private duty nursing services;
>
> clinic services;
>
> dental services;
>
> physical therapy and related sources;
>
> prescribed drugs, dentures, and prosthetic devices; and eyeglasses prescribed by a physician skilled in diseases of the eye or by an optometrist, whichever the individual may select;
>
> other diagnostic, screening, preventive and rehabilitative services;
>
> in-patient hospital services and skilled nursing home services for individuals 65 years of age or over in an institution for tuberculosis or mental diseases; and
>
> any other medical, and any other type of remedial care recognized under State Law, specified by the Secretary; EXCEPT that such term does not include—
>
> A. any such payments with respect to care or services for any individual who is an inmate of a public institution (except as a patient in a medical institution); or
>
> B. any such payments with respect to care or services for any individual who has not attained 65 years of age and who is a patient in an institution for tuberculosis or mental diseases.

Pharmacy Participation

The Medicare law provides for hospital pharmacies to participate in the program provided that certain conditions of participation are complied with. These requirements deal with the following:

1. Competent supervision.
2. Adequate physical facilities.
3. Supervision of floor inventory.
4. Staffing.
5. Emergency service.
6. Record keeping.
7. Pharmacy and therapeutics committee.

The above cited requirements are abstracted from Section 405.1027, "Conditions of Participation—Pharmacy or Drug Room" of the "Conditions of Participation, Hospitals, Federal Health Insurance for the Aged" (Code of Federal Regulations, Title 20, Chapter III, Part 405) which follows:

> The Hospital has a pharmacy directed by a registered pharmacist or a drug room under competent supervision. The pharmacy or drug room is administered in accordance with accepted professional principles.
>
> (a) Standard; Pharmacy Supervision. There is a pharmacy directed by a registered pharmacist or a drug room under competent supervision. The factors explaining the standard are as follows:
>
> (1) The pharmacist is trained in the specialized functions of hospital pharmacy.
>
> (2) The pharmacist is responsible to the administration of the hospital for developing, supervising, and coordinating all the activities of the pharmacy department.
>
> (3) If there is a drug room with no pharmacist, prescription medications are dispensed by a qualified pharmacist elsewhere, and only storing and distributing are done in the hospital. A consulting pharmacist assists in drawing up the correct procedures, rules, and regulations, for the distribution of drugs, and visits the hospital on a regularly scheduled basis in the course of his duties. Wherever possible the pharmacist, in dispensing drugs, works from the prescriber's original order or a direct copy.
>
> (b) Standard; Physical Facilities. Facilities are provided for the storage, safeguarding, preparation, and dispensing of drugs. The factors explaining the standard are as follows:
>
> (1) Drugs are issued to floor units in accordance with approved policies and procedures.
>
> (2) Drug cabinets on the nursing units are routinely checked by the pharmacist. All floor stocks are properly controlled.
>
> (3) There is adequate space for all pharmacy operations and the storage of drugs at a satisfactory location provided with proper lighting, ventilation, and temperature controls.
>
> (4) If there is a pharmacy, equipment is provided for the compounding and dispensing of drugs.
>
> (5) Special locked storage space is provided to meet the legal requirements for storage of narcotics, alcohol, and other prescribed drugs.
>
> (c) Standard; Personnel. Personnel competent in their respective duties are provided in keeping with the size and activity of the department. The factors explaining the standard are as follows:
>
> (1) The pharmacist is assisted by an adequate number of additional registered pharmacists and such other personnel as the activities of the pharmacy may require to insure quality pharmaceutical services.
>
> (2) The pharmacy depending upon the size and scope of its operations, is staffed by the following categories of personnel:
>
>> (i) Chief Pharmacist.
>>
>> (ii) One or more assistant chief pharmacists.
>>
>> (iv) Pharmacy residents (where a program has been activated).
>>
>> (v) Nonprofessionally trained pharmacy helpers.
>>
>> (vi) Clerical help.

(3) Provision is made for emergency pharmaceutical services.

(4) If the hospital does not have a staff pharmacist, a consulting pharmacist has overall responsibility for control and distribution of drugs and a designated individual(s) has responsibility for day-to-day operation of the pharmacy.

(d) Standard; Records. Records are kept of the transaction of the pharmacy (or drug room) and correlated with other hospital records where indicated. Such special records are kept as are required by law. The factors explaining the standard are as follows:

(1) The pharmacy establishes and maintains, in cooperation with the accounting department, a satisfactory system of records and bookkeeping in accordance with the policies of the hospital for:

    (i) Maintaining adequate control over the requisitioning and dispensing of all drugs and pharmaceutical supplies, and

    (ii) Charging patients for drugs and pharmaceutical supplies.

(2) A record of the stock on hand and of the dispensing of all narcotic drugs is maintained in such a manner that the disposition of any particular item may be readily traced.

(3) Records for prescription drugs dispensed to each patient (inpatients and outpatients) are maintained in the pharmacy or drug room containing the full name of the patient and the prescribing physician, the prescription number, the name and strength of the drug, the date of issue, the expiration date for all time-dated medications, the lot and control number of the drug, the name of the manufacturer (or trademark) and (unless the physician directs otherwise) the name of the medication dispensed.

(4) The label of each outpatient's individual prescription medication container bears the lot and control number of the drug, the name of the manufacturer (or trademark) and (unless the physician directs otherwise) the name of the medication dispensed.

(e) Standard; Control of Toxic or Dangerous Drugs. Policies are established to control the administration of toxic or dangerous drugs with specific reference to the duration of the order and the dosage. The factors explaining the standard are as follows:

(1) The medical staff has established a written policy that all toxic or dangerous medications, not specifically prescribed as to time or number of doses, will be automatically stopped after a reasonable time limit set by the staff.

(2) The classifications ordinarily thought of as toxic or dangerous drugs are narcotics, sedatives, anticoagulants, antibiotics, oxytocics, and cortisone products.

(f) Standard; Committee. There is a committee of the medical staff to confer with the pharmacist in the formulation of policies. The factors explaining the standard are as follows:

(1) A pharmacy and therapeutics committee (or equivalent committee), composed of physicians and pharmacists, is established in the hospital. It represents the organizational line of communication and the liaison between the medical staff and the pharmacist.

(2) The committee assists in the formulation of broad professional policies regarding the evaluation, appraisal, selection, procurement, storage, distribution, use, and safety procedures, and all other matters relating to drugs in hospitals.

(3)   The committee performs the following specific functions:

    (i)   Serves as an advisory group to the hospital medical staff and the pharmacist on matters pertaining to the choice of drugs;

    (ii)   Develops and reviews periodically a formulary or drug list for use in the hospital;

    (iii)   Establishes standards concerning the use and control of investigational drugs and research in the use of recognized drugs;

    (iv)   Evaluates clinical data concerning new drugs or preparations requested for use in the hospital;

    (v)   Makes recommendations concerning drugs to be stocked on the nursing unit floors and by other services; and

    (vi)   Prevents unnecessary duplication in stocking drugs and drugs in combination having identical amounts of the same therapeutic ingredients.

(4)   The committee meets at least quarterly and reports to the medical staff.

(g) Standard; Drugs To Be Dispensed. Therapeutic ingredients of medications dispensed are included (or approved for inclusion) in the United States Pharmacopoeia, National Formulary, United States Homeopathic Pharmocopoeia, New Drugs, or Accepted Dental Remedies (except for any drugs unfavorably evaluated therein), or are approved for use by the pharmacy and drug therapeutics committee (or equivalent committee) of the hospital staff. The factors explaining the standard are as follows:

(1)   The pharmacist, with the advice and guidance of the pharmacy and therapeutics committee, is responsible for specifications as to quality, quantity, and source of supply of all drugs.

(2)   There is available a formulary or list of drugs accepted for use in the hospital which is developed and amended at regular intervals by the pharmacy and therapeutics committee (or equivalent committee) with the cooperation of the pharmacist (consulting or otherwise) and the administration.

(3)   The pharmacy or drug room is adequately supplied with preparations so approved.

Civil Liability of Consulting Pharmacist

The following material on the subject was prepared by the Social Security Administration and was released as SSR 69-31. Because of its clarity and objectivity, it is presented in its original form:

A question has been presented regarding the potential for civil liability of pharmacists who undertake to act as consultants to hospitals which are participating in the Medicare program.

Any comment on the issue with regard to the Medicare program necessarily must be prefaced by a reference to the structure of title XVIII and an analysis of the regulations, with special attention to the provisions of Section 405.1027 of Regulation No. 5.

The benefit which the program offers for eligible individuals who have received covered institutional medical care is the right to have payment made on their behalf to the institution furnishing such services, providing that the institution is a "provider of services" participating in the program in accordance with section 1866 of the Act. A provider of services is defined in section 1861(u) of the Act to include, among others, a "hospital," as that term is defined in section 1861(e) of the Act. This definition sets forth certain criteria for determining the eligibility of the institution to participate in the program, and any institution which is not in compliance with such criteria, as implemented by the regulations[1] of the Secretary, is not eligible to participate.

On the other hand, participation by a health care institution, even one which meets the statutory definition, is not mandatory, but follows only as a consequence of the filing by the eligible institutions, voluntarily, of an agreement to participate.

No institution is required to satisfy any of the definitional requirements for any purpose other than that of program participation. The Secretary is granted no authority to compel compliance. The only effect of noncompliance, therefore, concerns the right of the institution to participate.[2]

As for a pharmacist's liability under the common law, review of the precedent cases confirms their holdings, establishing a basis for the liability of a dispensing pharmacist when acting in filling a prescription order, personally or through others over whom he has supervisory authority in this regard.

A druggist who is negligent in the performance of his duties may be held liable in damages to any person injured thereby, when that negligence is the proximate cause of the injury.[3] Further, the measure of negligence, or rather, the degree of care to which a dispensing pharmacist is held is not merely ordinary care, but reasonable care as defined by the terms of his calling:

> . . . the legal measure of the duty of druggists towards the patrons, . . . is properly expressed by the phrase "ordinary care," yet it must not be forgotten that it is "ordinary care" with reference to that special and peculiar business. In determining what degree of prudence, vigilance, and thoughtfulness will fill the requirements of "ordinary care" in compounding medicines and filling prescriptions, it is necessary to consider the poisonous character of so many of the drugs with which the apothecary deals, and the grave and fatal consequence which may follow the want of the due care. In such a case "ordinary care" calls for a degree of vigilance and prudence commensurate with the dangers involved.[4]

A pharmacist also may be held liable for the negligent acts of another person,[5] depending upon the extent to which he exercised control over that party's performance. Thus, failure of a pharmacist to carry out his duties and responsibilities in regard to the compounding and dispensing of drugs in a hospital or his failure to periodically inspect the procedures being followed by the hospital employees under his control might well justify a Court, under the common law, in finding the dispensing pharmacist liable for his omissions and for the omissions and affirmative negligent acts of hospital employees.

However, the transition from a discussion of the liability of a dispensing pharmacist for his negligent acts, to one of the liability of a pharmacist acting as a consultant alters these conclusions, especially in the light of the different nature of the assignments a consultant might be called upon to undertake, as outlined in the regulations.

The regulations at issue establish a two-pronged condition for program participation: the hospital must have either a pharmacy directed by a registered pharmacist who is responsible for the compounding and dispensing of drugs in a drug room, operated in accordance with policies and procedures drawn up with the assistance of a consulting pharmacist for the storage and distribution of drugs, with prescription drugs compounded and dispensed by a qualified pharmacist elsewhere.

The alternatives are clearly stated in the broad condition of Section 405.1027, which reads as follows:

> The hospital has a pharmacy directed by a registered pharmacist or a drug room under competent supervision. The pharmacy or drug room is administered in accordance with accepted professional principles.

The seven standards explanatory of this condition contained in this section of the regulations, and the several factors illustrative of each of the seven standards, further demonstrate the dichotomy recognized in the condition, and differentiate with a degree of precision between the responsibilities of a pharmacist who directs a dispensing pharmacy in a hospital and the consultative activities of a consulting pharmacist with reference to a hospital which maintains only a drug room. For example, the standard of "pharmacy supervision," discussed in Section 405.1017(a), repeats the first sentence of the condition, quoted above, then lists three factors, two of which are applicable to pharmacies and a third pointed exclusively to a hospital drug room:

> (3) If there is a drug room with no pharmacist, prescription medications are dispensed by a qualified pharmacist elsewhere, and only storing and distributing are done in the hospital. A consulting pharmacist assists in drawing up the correct procedures, rules and regulations for the distribution of drugs, and visits the hospital on a regularly scheduled basis in the course of his duties. Wherever possible the pharmacist, in dispensing drugs, works from the prescriber's original order or a direct copy.

By this factor, the regulation makes explicit that the drug room is not the equivalent of a hospital pharmacy, and a supervising pharmacist need not be employed to direct the drug room. The hospital, however, is required to have an arrangement with a consulting pharmacist, i.e., a pharmacist who undertakes to assist in establishing the procedure for the operation of the drug room and to visit the hospital on a regular basis to assure compliance with the procedures thus established.

Reference to subsection (b) of this regulation relates the activities of the consulting pharmacists (who "assist" in the formulation of policy) to the medical staff of the hospital. Here it is manifest that the consulting pharmacist does not have exclusive authority to establish policy, but functions in concert with members of the pharmacy and therapeutic committee (or equivalent committee) of the hospital, which acts as liaison between the drug and medical staffs of the institution:

> The committee assists in the formulation of broad professional policies regarding the evaluation, selection, procurement, storage, distribution, use, and safety procedures and all other matters relating to drugs in hospitals. (Section 405.1027 (f) (2) of Regulation No. 5.)

The standard concerning personnel, contained in subsection (c), further indicates the limited nature of the consulting pharmacist's role, as distinguished from that of a dispensing pharmacist operating a hospital pharmacy. There it is indicated that a consulting pharmacist need not be responsible for the day-to-day operations involved in the control and distribution of drugs, as long as such a professional is assigned the overall review responsibility for compliance with policy he has helped develop. This is a significant variation in duties from those imposed by the requirement of the regulations in regard to hospital pharmacies, where drugs are compounded and dispensed, which are required to be directed, as distinguished from supervised, by a full-time registered pharmacist, and other registered assistants as needed.

Nonetheless, a consulting pharmacist may, of course, be exposed to a certain degree of personal liability by virtue of his position. For example, his failure to fulfill properly the obligations he has assumed conceivably could subject him to accountability for the consequences of his inaction or improper actions within the scope of his contractual undertaking with the hospital. However, on the assumption that the consulting pharmacist performs the consultative and overall review services set forth in the regulations, there seems to be no conceivable circumstance under which he could be found liable for damages suffered by a patient of the hospital attributable to acts for which he would be responsible. The hospital in compliance with the regulations, would have imposed on him no duties of supervision over the dispensing of drugs to patients. He is viewed as a part-time advisor on drug room policy (along with the medical staff) and a part-time reviewer of the efficacy of such policies in practice. He would be expected, perhaps, to inform the staff of the content of the policies and practices established by the drug and therapeutics committee of which he would be a member, but he would not be required to supervise each employee of the hospital in the effectuation of the drug room rules on a routine and continuing basis, as would, for example, the dispensing druggist in a hospital pharmacy. The essential element of liability for negligence—the causal connection between the injury and the responsibility therefor—either by direct or by imputed negligence, seems wholly lacking in the relationship between pharmacist and hospital required for compliance with the regulations.

The other facet of the general question relates to potential liability under a theory of statutory negligence by which the violation of a duty imposed by a statute which is designed to protect a given class of persons, results in the violator's liability to any person in the protected class who sustains injury of a type the statute seeks to prevent.

As with the discussion of common law liability, we do not believe this concept to be properly applicable as a source of potential liability for consulting pharmacists under the Medicare program. We are doubtful of its applicability first of all, because these are not statutes but administrative regulations. Courts have taken differing views as to whether the rule of statutory negligence extends to violations of administrative rules and regulations and many jurisdictions have held that "violation of a rule adopted by an administrative body cannot give rise to statutory liability without regard to negligence."[6] Whether or not administrative regulations may have the weight of statutory law in any jurisdiction, more important, in our view, is the fact that there is no duty created by these regulations, and they do not under any approach impose an affirmative obligation on the pharmacist or the hospital.[7] The regulations are established solely as the criteria by which a hospital can qualify for reimbursement under the Medicare program and failure to adhere to them means only that the institution is eligible to participate in this program.

Finally, however, it must be noted that a person who contracts to perform a function is accountable for injuries caused by his negligent failure to act in accordance with his undertaking. To the extent that there is a practice of a pharmacist lending his professional name to a hospital to give the color of compliance, such a practice can carry with it the risks of liability. Furthermore, the development of drug room standards at variance with the accepted professional standards for drug control might be viewed as negligence. These would be instances of nonfeasance and misfeasance arising from failure to fulfill the consultative functions contemplated by this regulation.

In the light of the foregoing considerations, concerning the meaning and effect of Section 405.1027 of Regulation No. 5, and its application to the potential civil liability of consulting pharmacists under the Medicare program, it would appear that the acceptance and proper fulfillment by a pharmacist of the consultant role contemplated by the regulations would not subject him to liability for negligence.

References

1. Regulation No. 5, Conditions of Participation; Hospitals Sections 405.1001–405.1040.
2. *Supra*, Section 405.1002.
3. 28 C.J.S., "Druggists" Section 8 (Civil Liabilities) and Section 9 (Negligence).
4. Tremblay v. Kimball, 107 Md. 53, 57, 77 Atl. 405, 407 (1910).
5. Cox v. Laws, 244 Miss. 696, 145 So. 2nd 703 (1962).
6. 65 C.J.S., "Negligence," Section 19(9).
7. *Supra*, p.2.

CHAPTER 13

The Trial

The legal action, known as a lawsuit, is a complicated process, however for the purpose of this text it is divided into six major steps: *commencement, pleading, pre-trial, trial, appeal* and *execution.* [1]

Prior to entering into a detailed discussion of legal procedure, it is important for the student to recognize that each controversy involves two decision making processes. For example, in a lawsuit two types of questions may arise—questions of law or questions of fact. The former deal with the application of law and are dealt with by the judge. The latter are concerned with issues and therefore must be determined by a jury during the trial. If a judge is sitting alone—that is, a trial without a jury—he determines the facts and applies the relevant law to those facts.

Commencement of the Action

Once a controversy has arisen or a party has suffered an injury, the disputants have cause to seek redress for the wrong. One way of accomplishing this goal is by means of a lawsuit.

Since the time for bringing suit begins to toll from the time the injury was discovered, the lawsuit must be brought within certain specific time limits set forth by the law of the jurisdiction. This law is known as the Statute of Limitations. Actions not pursued within the time set by this Statute are forever barred.

Having ascertained that there exists a cause for a suit, the lawyer next determines the type of action that must be undertaken, e.g., tort for negligence or breach of contract.

Next, the attorney must select the court that has jurisdiction over such matters. Courts also have geographic jurisdiction. Thus, the suit must be brought in a court having jurisdiction over both the subject matter of the controversy and the geographic district where the defendant resides or where the incident causing the action occurred.

The parties to a legal action such as a lawsuit are known as the *plaintiff* and the *defendant*. The plaintiff is the person who brings the action and makes the complaint. The person against whom the action is brought is the defendant.

All of the steps taken to this point represent preliminary items taken care of by the collaborative efforts of the attorney and his client. Once completed, the lawsuit will be commenced by taking one of two courses depending upon the jurisdiction. In some courts a trial action is begun by filing an order with the Clerk of Courts to issue a *writ* or *summons* to a sheriff. This document orders the sheriff to notify the defendant(s) to appear in court at a specific date and time. The second manner of commencing a lawsuit, which is currently in use by the federal court system, is to have the complaint itself filed and served.

Upon being served with a summons or a complaint, the defendant should immediately notify his attorney or insurance carrier if he is insured against this type of cause of action. Since most insurance policies generally require early notice of a suit, failure to do so may bar any right of the insured under the policy with the company.

Pleading

The first pleading filed in an action is the complaint which sets forth the facts in order to give notice to the other party of the basis of the claim against him. After the complaint is filed, a copy is served upon the defendant, who must ordinarily make some reply within a specified number of days. Should the defendant fail to reply, he may be held in default and a judgment entered in favor of the plaintiff. The reply normally made by the defendant is an *answer,* however he does have the right to file preliminary objections before answering the complaint itself. These include calling attention to errors relating to the case: e.g., the complaint was improperly served; the action is being brought in the wrong jurisdiction; the complaint is technically defective or that the complaint, even if believable, does not set forth a claim or cause of action recognized by law and the plaintiff is therefore not entitled to recover. This latter objection is often referred to as a *motion to dismiss.*

Depending upon the nature of the objection, the court may allow the plaintiff to correct his mistake by filing a new or amended complaint or it may decide that he has no complaint and thereby sustain the motion to dismiss. The plaintiff, of course, may appeal the action of the court.

If the court does not sustain the various preliminary objections or motions, the defendant must then file an answer which generally denies the facts stated by the plaintiff.

It is also possible that the defendant may have a justifiable claim against the plaintiff and therefore wishes to file a *counterclaim*.

Once the defendant has filed his answer, the plaintiff may file preliminary objections to that answer and to the counterclaim if the latter is filed. These various objections are disposed of by the court thereby bringing the pleadings to an end.

Pre-Trial Procedures

Although everything that has taken place is in general pre-trial procedure, there are a number of procedural steps which are specifically classified as pre-trial proceedings.[2]

Upon the conclusion of the pleadings, some jurisdictions permit either party to move for a judgment on the pleadings. When this motion is made, the court will examine the case up to this point and may enter a judgment on its merits.

A common pre-trial procedure is the pre-trial conference the purpose of which is to eliminate matters which are not in dispute, and to agree in advance on witnesses, certification of experts and other similar procedural matters relating to the trial.

Despite the fact that the pre-trial conference is not intended to compel parties to settle their case, it often happens because the lawyers involved recognize that the differences between the conflicting issues are not great and an out-of-court settlement is more practical.

In some state courts and in the federal courts, the parties have the right to conduct examinations before trial. Under this procedure, both parties may question each other and third persons under oath. This procedure is called *discovery*.

Prior to the trial, the parties may send a questionnaire to each other asking questions about the facts of the case. These are called *interrogatories*.

A party to the case may require the opposite party and witnesses to appear before an examiner and under oath tell what they know about the case. These sworn statements are called *depositions*.

The Trial

As has been stated earlier, the trial elicits the facts from the evidence presented and to these are applied the relevant principles of law. Thus a conclusion as to liability is reached.

The process whereby witnesses give answers to questions propounded on direct or cross examination is called *testimony*. The answers are one form of *evidence*. Another type of evidence is *real evidence* which consists of tangible items such as guns, bullets, instruments and devices.

The witnesses are generally persons who witnessed certain events that are of importance to the case. If professional or highly technical matters are involved, an expert in the field may be called. He is referred to as an *expert witness* and is expected to state his opinion in answer to a hypothetical question put to him by the attorney.

The jury panel consists of a number of qualified men and women selected to hear cases during a particular session of the court. At the commencement of the trial, the required number of jurors and alternates will be selected from the panel and sworn to the faithful performance of their duty.

Once the jury is impaneled, the attorneys for both sides usually make their opening statements. These generally indicate what each man intends to prove during the trial.

The next step is for the attorney for the plaintiff to call his first witness and conduct a *direct examination*. When the direct examination is completed, the defendant's lawyer may question the witness. This is called *cross examination*. After cross examination, the plaintiff's attorney may ask the same witness more questions in an effort to counteract the effect of the cross examination. This is called *redirect examination.* The same process is repeated until all of the plaintiff's witnesses have been heard. At this point, the plaintiff's attorney indicates to the court that he "rests" his case.

The next move is the defendant's and his attorney may, at this point, make one or more motions to the court for a directed verdict on the grounds that the plaintiff has failed to prove his case or that the evidence presented does not constitute a legal basis for a verdict in his favor.

If the motion for a directed verdict is overruled, the defendant calls his witnesses and they are subjected to direct and cross examination.

The entire trial procedure is generally recorded stenographically and upon transcription forms the trial record. This record is preserved in case the decision is appealed to a higher court.

Upon the completion of the presentation of the evidence by both sides, either party may request the judge to rule that the claim has not been proved or a defense has been inadequate and that the jury be directed to render a verdict to that effect. If these motions are overruled, the attorneys then summarize their cases to the jury. This process is called the *presentation of oral arguments* and the summary is called a *summation.*

Finally, the judge instructs the jury in the applicable law and the jury then "retires" to deliberate and reach a verdict. When the jury reaches a verdict, they report to the judge and he renders a judgment based upon the verdict.

At this point, the losing party has an opportunity to move for a new trial on the grounds that legal errors or mistakes were made during the trial. If the motion is granted, a new trial is held; if not, the judgment becomes final subject to the review of the trial record by the appellate court.[3]

Appeals

If an appeal is to be made, the appellate court will review the trial record as well as written briefs and short oral arguments by the attorneys. The case is then taken under advisement until the judges have reached a decision. An opinion is then prepared explaining the reasons for the court's decision. This is generally the final judgment unless there is strong basis for appeal to the Supreme Court of the United States. A "strong basis" would be a question involving the Constitution of the United States or a statute enacted by the Congress.

Execution of Judgments

If, after the trial and final appeal, the defendant does not comply with the judgment, the plaintiff may cause the judgment to be *executed*. This means that the defendant must comply with the order of the court or be held in contempt of court for which he may be fined or imprisoned. The plaintiff may also cause a sheriff to sell as much of the defendant's property as is necessary to pay the plaintiff's monetary judgment and court costs.

References

1. E. SPRINGER: NURSING AND THE LAW, Aspen Systems Corporation, Pittsburgh, Pennsylvania, 1970, p. 151.
2. G. MOTTLA: MASSACHUSETTS PRACTICE, Volume 9, 3rd Ed., Boston Law Book Co., Boston, Massachusetts, p. 515–526.
3. *Supra*, pp. 527–696.

The Federal Food, Drug, and Cosmetic Act

FEDERAL FOOD, DRUG, AND COSMETIC ACT, AS AMENDED

CHAPTER I—SHORT TITLE

SECTION 1. This Act may be cited as the Federal Food, Drug, and Cosmetic Act.

CHAPTER II—DEFINITIONS

SEC. 201 [321]. For the purposes of this Act—

(a)(1) The term "State", except as used in the last sentence of section 702(a), means any State or Territory of the United States, the District of Columbia, and the Commonwealth of Puerto Rico.

(2) The term "Territory" means any Territory or possession of the United States, including the District of Columbia, and excluding the Commonwealth of Puerto Rico and the Canal Zone.

(b) The term "interstate commerce" means (1) commerce between any State or Territory and any place outside thereof, and (2) commerce within the District of Columbia or within any other Territory not organized with a legislative body.

(c) The term "Department" means the U.S. Department of Health, Education, and Welfare.

(d) The term "Secretary" means the Secretary of Health, Education, and Welfare.

(e) The term "person" includes individual, partnership, corporation, and association.

(f) The term "food" means (1) articles used for food or drink for man or other animals, (2) chewing gum, and (3) articles used for components of any such article.

(g)(1) The term "drug" means (A) articles recognized in the official United States Pharmacopeia, official Homeopathic Pharmacopeia of the United States, or official National Formulary, or any supplement to any of them; and (B) articles intended for use in the diagnosis, cure, mitigation, treatment, or prevention of disease in man or other animals; and (C) articles (other than food) intended to affect the structure or any function of the body of man or other animals; and (D) articles intended for use as a component of any articles specified in clause (A), (B), or (C); but does not include devices or their components, parts, or accessories.

(2) The term "counterfeit drug" means a drug which, or the container or labeling of which, without authorization, bears the trademark, trade name, or other identifying mark, imprint, or device, or any likeness thereof, of a drug manufacturer, processor, packer, or distributor other than the person or persons who in fact manufactured, processed, packed, or distributed such drug and which thereby falsely purports or is represented to be the product of, or to have been packed or distributed by, such other drug manufacturer, processor, packer, or distributor.

(h) The term "device" (except when used in paragraph (n) of this section and in sections 301(i), 403(f), 502(c), and 602(c)) means instruments, apparatus, and contrivances, including their components, parts, and accessories, intended (1) for use in the diagnosis, cure, mitigation, treatment, or prevention of disease in man or other animals; or (2) to affect the structure or any function of the body of man or other animals.

(i) The term "cosmetic" means (1) articles intended to be rubbed, poured, sprinkled, or sprayed on, introduced into, or otherwise applied to the human body or any part thereof for cleansing, beautifying, promoting attractiveness, or altering the appearance, and (2) articles intended for use as a component of any such articles; except that such term shall not include soap.

(j) The term "official compendium" means the official United States Pharmacopeia, official Homeopathic Pharmacopeia of the United States, official National Formulary, or any supplement to any of them.

(k) The term "label" means a display of written, printed, or graphic matter upon the immediate container of any article; and a requirement made by or under authority of this Act that any word, statement, or other information appear on the label shall not be considered to be complied with unless such word, statement, or other information also appears on the outside container or wrapper, if any there be, of the retail package of such article, or is easily legible through the outside container or wrapper.

(l) The term "immediate container" does not include package liners.

(m) The term "labeling" means all labels and other written, printed, or graphic matter (1) upon any article or any of its containers or wrappers, or (2) accompanying such article.

(n) If an article is alleged to be misbranded because the labeling is misleading, then in determining whether the labeling is misleading there shall be taken into account (among other things) not only representations made or suggested by statement, word, design, device, or any combination thereof, but also the extent to which the labeling fails to reveal facts material in the light of such representations or material with respect to consequences which may result from the use of the article to which the labeling relates under the conditions of use prescribed in the labeling thereof or under such conditions of use as are customary or usual.

(o) The representation of a drug, in its labeling, as an antiseptic shall be considered to be a representation that it is a germicide, except in the case of a drug purporting to be, or represented as, an antiseptic for inhibitory use as a wet dressing, ointment, dusting powder, or such other use as involves prolonged contact with the body.

(p) The term "new drug" means—

(1) Any drug (except a new animal drug or an animal feed bearing or containing a new animal drug) the composition of which is such that such drug is not generally recognized, among experts qualified by scientific training and experience to evaluate the safety and effectiveness of drugs, as safe and effective for use under the conditions prescribed, recommended, or suggested in the labeling thereof, except that such drug not so recognized shall not be deemed to be a "new drug" if at any time prior to the enact-

ment oi this Act it was subject to the Food and Drugs Act of June 30, 1906, as amended, and if at such time its labeling contained the same representations concerning the conditions of its use; or

(2) Any drug (except a new animal drug or an animal feed bearing or containing a new animal drug) the composition of which is such that such drug, as a result of investigations to determine its safety and effectiveness for use under such conditions, has become so recognized, but which has not, otherwise than in such investigations, been used to a material extent or for a material time under such conditions.

(q) The term "pesticide chemical" means any substance which, alone, in chemical combination or in formulation with one or more other substances, is an "economic poison" within the meaning of the Federal Insecticide, Fungicide, and Rodenticide Act (7 U.S.C., secs. 135–135k) as now in force or as hereafter amended, and which is used in the production, storage, or transportation of raw agricultural commodities.

(r) The term "raw agricultural commodity" means any food in its raw or natural state, including all fruits that are washed, colored, or otherwise treated in their unpeeled natural form prior to marketing.

(s) The term "food additive" means any substance the intended use of which results or may reasonably be expected to result, directly or indirectly, in its becoming a component or otherwise affecting the characteristics of any food (including any substance intended for use in producing, manufacturing, packing, processing, preparing, treating, packaging, transporting, or holding food; and including any source of radiation intended for any such use), if such substance is not generally recognized, among experts qualified by scientific training and experience to evaluate its safety, as having been adequately shown through scientific procedures (or, in the case of a substance used in food prior to January 1, 1958, through either scientific procedures or experience based on common use in food) to be safe under the conditions of its intended use; except that such term does not include—

(1) a pesticide chemical in or on a raw agricultural commodity; or

(2) a pesticide chemical to the extent that it is intended for use or is used in the production, storage, or transportation of any raw agricultural commodity; or

(3) a color additive; or

(4) any substance used in accordance with a sanction or approval granted prior to the enactment of this paragraph pursuant to this Act, the Poultry Products Inspection Act (21 U.S.C. 451 and the following) or the Meat Inspection Act of March 4, 1907 (34 Stat. 1260), as amended and extended (21 U.S.C. 71 and the following) ; or

(5) a new animal drug.

(t) (1) The term "color additive" means a material which—

(A) is a dye, pigment, or other substance made by a process of synthesis or similar artifice, or extracted, isolated, or otherwise derived, with or without intermediate or final change of identity, from a vegetable, animal, mineral, or other source, and

(B) when added or applied to a food, drug, or cosmetic, or to the human body or any part thereof, is capable (alone or through reaction with other substance) of imparting color thereto;

except that such term does not include any material which the Secretary, by regulation, determines is used (or intended to be used) solely for a purpose or purposes other than coloring.

(2) The term "color" includes black, white, and intermediate grays.

(3) Nothing in subparagraph (1) of this paragraph shall be construed to apply to any pesticide chemical, soil or plant nutrient, or other agricultural chemical solely because of its effect in aiding, retarding, or otherwise affecting, directly or indirectly, the growth or other natural physiological processes of produce of the soil and thereby affecting its color, whether before or after harvest.

(u) The term "safe," as used in paragraph (s) of this section and in sections 409, 512, and 706, has reference to the health of man or animal.

(v)[1] The term "depressant or stimulant drug" means—

(1) any drug which contains any quantity of (A) barbituric acid or any of the salts of barbituric acid; or (B) any derivative of barbituric acid which has been designated by the Secretary under section 502(d) as habit forming;

(2) any drug which contains any quantity of (A) amphetamine or any of its optical isomers; (B) any salt of amphetamine or any salt of an optical isomer of amphetamine; or (C) any substance which the Secretary, after investigation, has found to be, and by regulation designated as, habit forming because of its stimulant effect on the central nervous system; or

(3) any drug which contains any quantity of a substance which the Secretary, after investigation, has found to have, and by regulation designates as having, a potential for abuse because of its depressant or stimulant effect on the central nervous system or its hallucinogenic effect; except that the Secretary shall not designate under this paragraph, or under clause (C) of subparagraph (2), any substance that is now included, or is hereafter included, within the classifications stated in section 4731, and marihuana as defined in section 4761, of the Internal Revenue Code of 1954 (26 U.S.C. 4731, 4761).

(w) The term "new animal drug" means any drug intended for use for animals other than man, including any drug intended for use in animal feed but not including such animal feed,—

(1) the composition of which is such that such drug is not generally recognized, among experts qualified by scientific training and experience to evaluate the safety and effectiveness of animal drugs, as safe and effective for use under the conditions prescribed, recommended, or suggested in the labeling thereof; except that such a drug not so recognized shall not be deemed to be a "new animal drug" if at any time prior to June 25, 1938, it was subject to the Food and Drug Act of June 30, 1906, as amended, and if at such time its labeling contained the same representations concerning the conditions of its use; or

(2) the composition of which is such that such drug, as a result of investigations to determine its safety and effectiveness for use under such conditions, has become so recognized but which has not, otherwise than in such investigations, been used to a material extent or for a material time under such conditions; or

---

[1] Section 201(v) effective July 15, 1965.

(3) which drug is composed wholly or partly of any kind of penicillin, streptomycin, chlortetracyline, chloramphenicol, or bacitracin, or any derivative thereof, except when there is in effect a published order of the Secretary declaring such drug not to be a new animal drug on the grounds that (A) the requirement of certification of batches of such drug, as provided for in section 512(n), is not necessary to insure that the objectives specified in paragraph (3) thereof are achieved and (B) that neither subparagraph (1) nor (2) of this paragraph (w) applies to such drug.

(x) The term "animal feed", as used in paragraph (w) of this section, in section 512, and in provisions of this Act referring to such paragraph or section, means an article which is intended for use for food for animals other than man and which is intended for use as a substantial source of nutrients in the diet of the animal, and is not limited to a mixture intended to be the sole ration of the animal.

The provisions of subsections (e), (f), and (g) of section 701 shall apply to and govern proceedings for the issuance, amendment, or repeal of regulations [2] under subparagraph (2)(C) or (3) of this paragraph.*

CHAPTER III—PROHIBITED ACTS AND PENALTIES

PROHIBITED ACTS

SEC. 301 [331]. The following acts and the causing thereof are hereby prohibited:

(a) The introduction or delivery for introduction into interstate commerce of any food, drug, device, or cosmetic that is adulterated or misbranded.

(b) The adulteration or misbranding of any food, drug, device, or cosmetic in interstate commerce.

(c) The receipt in interstate commerce of any food, drug, device, or cosmetic that is adulterated or misbranded, and the delivery or proffered delivery thereof for pay or otherwise.

(d) The introduction or delivery for introduction into interstate commerce of any article in violation of section 404 or 505.

(e) The refusal to permit access to or copying of any record as required by section 703; or the failure to establish or maintain any record, or make any report, required under section 505 (i) or (j), 507 (d) or (g), or 512 (j), (l), or (m), or the refusal to permit access to or verification or copying of any such required record.

(f) The refusal to permit entry or inspection as authorized by section 704.

² F.D.C. Regs., part 166.
*[The following additional definitions for food are provided for in other acts:
SEC. 201a [321a]. Butter. The Act of March 4, 1923 (42 Stat. 1500), defines butter as "For the purposes of this chapter 'butter' shall be understood to mean the food product usually known as butter, and which is made exclusively from milk or cream, or both, with or without common salt, and with or without additional coloring matter, and containing not less than 80 per centum by weight of milk fat, all tolerances having been allowed for."
SEC. 201b [321b]. Package. The Act of July 24, 1919 (41 Stat. 271), delcares "The word 'package' where it occurs in this chapter shall include and shall be construed to include wrapped meats inclosed in papers or other materials as prepared by the manufacturers thereof for sale."
SEC. 201c [321c]. Nonfat Dry Milk. The Act of July 2, 1956 (70 Stat. 486), defines nonfat dry milk as follows: "* * * for the purposes of the Federal Food, Drug, and Cosmetic Act of June 26 sic, 1938 (ch. 675, sec. 1, 52 Stat. 1040), nonfat dry milk is the product resulting from the removal of fat and water from milk, and contains the lactose, milk proteins, and milk minerals in the same relative proportions as in the fresh milk from which made. It contains not over 5 per centum by weight of moisture. The fat content is not over 1¼ per centum by weight unless otherwise indicated.
"The term'milk', when used herein, means sweet milk of cows."
The definition of oleomargarine appears preceding Sec. 407, page 16.]

(g) The manufacture within any Territory of any food, drug, device, or cosmetic that is adulterated or misbranded.

(h) The giving of a guaranty or undertaking referred to in section 303(c)(2), which guaranty or undertaking is false, except by a person who relied upon a guaranty or undertaking to the same effect signed by, and containing the name and address of, the person residing in the United States from whom he received in good faith the food, drug, device, or cosmetic; or the giving of a guaranty or undertaking referred to in section 303(c)(3), which guaranty or undertaking is false.

(i) Forging, counterfeiting, simulating, or falsely representing, or without proper authority using any mark, stamp, tag, label, or other identification device authorized or required by regulations promulgated under the provisions of section 404, 506, 507, or 706.

(2) Making, selling, disposing of, or keeping in possession, control, or custody, or concealing any punch, die, plate, stone, or other thing designed to print, imprint, or reproduce the trademark, trade name, or other identifying mark, imprint, or device of another or any likeness of any of the foregoing upon any drug or container or labeling thereof so as to render such drug a counterfeit drug.

(3) The doing of any act which causes a drug to be a counterfeit drug, or the sale or dispensing, or the holding for sale or dispensing, of a counterfeit drug.

(j) The using by any person to his own advantage, or revealing, other than to the Secretary or officers or employees of the Department, or to the courts when relevant in any judicial proceeding under this Act, any information acquired under authority of section 404, 409, 505, 506, 507, 512, 704, or 706 concerning any method or process which as a trade secret is entitled to protection.

(k) The alteration, mutilation, destruction, obliteration, or removal of the whole or any part of the labeling of, or the doing of any other act with respect to, a food, drug, device, or cosmetic, if such act is done while such article is held for sale (whether or not the first sale) after shipment in interstate commerce and results in such article being adulterated or misbranded.

(1) The using, on the labeling of any drug or in any advertising relating to such drug, of any representation or suggestion that approval of an application with respect to such drug is in effect under section 505, or that such drug complies with the provisions of such section.

(m) The sale or offering for sale of colored oleomargarine or colored margarine, or the possession or serving of colored oleomargarine or colored margarine in violation of section 407(b) or 407(c).

(n) The using, in labeling, advertising or other sales promotion of any reference to any report or analysis furnished in compliance with section 704.

(o) In the case of a prescription drug distributed or offered for sale in interstate commerce, the failure of the manufacturer, packer, or distributor thereof to maintain for transmittal, or to transmit, to any practitioner licensed by applicable State law to administer such drug who makes written request for information as to such drug, true and correct copies of all printed matter which is required to be included in any package in which that drug is distributed or sold, or such other printed matter as is approved by the Secretary. Nothing in this paragraph shall be construed to exempt any person from any labeling requirement imposed by or under other provisions of this Act.

(p) The failure to register as required by section 510.

(q)(1) The manufacture, compounding, or processing of a drug in violation of section 511(a); (2) the sale, delivery, or other disposition of a drug in violation of section 511(b); (3) the possession of a drug in violation of section 511(c); (4) the failure to prepare or obtain, or the failure to keep, a complete and accurate record with respect to any drug as required by section 511(d); (5) the refusal to permit access to or copying of any record as required by section 511(d); (6) the refusal to permit entry or inspection as authorized by section 511(d); or (7) the filling or refilling of any prescription in violation of section 511(e).

INJUNCTION PROCEEDINGS

SEC. 302 [332]. (a) The district courts of the United States and the United States courts of the Territories shall have jurisdiction, for cause shown, and subject to the provisions of section 381 (relating to notice to opposite party) of Title 28, to restrain violations of section 301 of this title, except paragraphs (h), (i), and (j) of said section.

(b) In case of violation of an injunction or restraining order issued under this section, which also constitutes a violation of this Act, trial shall be by the court, or, upon demand of the accused, by a jury. Such trial shall be conducted in accordance with the practice and procedure applicable in the case of proceedings subject to the provisions of section 22 of such Act of October 15, 1914, as amended. [This section, which appeared as U.S.C., title 28, sec. 387, has been repealed. It is now covered by Rule 42(b), Federal Rules of Criminal Prodecure.]

PENALTIES

SEC. 303 [333]. (a) Any person who violates any of the provisions of section 301 shall be guilty of a misdemeanor and shall on conviction thereof be subject to imprisonment for not more than one year, or a fine of not more than $1,000, or both such imprisonment and fine; but if the violation is committed after a conviction of such person under this section has become final such person shall be subject to imprisonment for not more than three years, or a fine of not more than $10,000, or both such imprisonment and fine: *Provided, however,* That any person who, having attained his eighteenth birthday, violates section 301(q)(2) by selling, delivering, or otherwise disposing of any depressant or stimulant drug to a person who has not attained his twenty-first birthday shall, if there be no previous conviction of such person under this section which has become final, be subject to imprisonment for not more than two years, or a fine of not more than $5,000, or both such imprisonment and fine, and for the second or any subsequent conviction for such a violation shall be subject to imprisonment for not more than six years, or a fine of not more than $15,000, or both such imprisonment and fine.

(b) Not withstanding the provisions of subsection (a) of this section, in case of a violation of any of the provisions of section 301, with intent to defraud or mislead, the penalty shall (except in the case of an offense which is subject to the provisions of the proviso to subsection (a) relating to second or subsequent offenses) be imprisonment for not more than three years, or a fine of not more than $10,000, or both such imprisonment and fine.

(c) No person shall be subject to the penalties of subsection (a) of this section, (1) for having received in interstate commerce any article and delivered it or proffered delivery of it, if such delivery. or proffer was made in good faith, unless he refuses to furnish on request of an officer or employee duly designated by the Secretary the name and address of the person from whom he purchased or received such article and copies of all documents, if any there be, pertaining to the delivery of the article to him; or (2) for having violated section 301 (a) or (d), if he establishes a guaranty or undertaking signed by, and containing the name and address of, the person residing in the United States from whom he received in good faith the article, to the effect, in case of an alleged violation of section 301(a), that such article is not adulterated or misbranded, within the meaning of this Act, designating this Act, or to the effect, in case of an alleged violation of section 301(d), that such article is not an article which may not, under the provisions of section 404 or 505, be introduced into interstate commerce; or (3) for having violated section 301(a), where the violation exists because the article is adulterated by reason of containing a color additive not from a batch certified in accordance with regulations promulgated by the Secretary under this Act, if such person establishes a guaranty or undertaking signed by, and containing the name and address of, the manufacturer of the color additive, to the effect that such color additive was from a batch certified in accordance with the applicable regulations promulgated by the Secretary under this Act; or (4) for having violated section 301 (b), (c), or (k) by failure to comply with section 502(f) in respect to an article received in interstate commerce to which neither section 503(a) nor section 503(b)(1) is applicable, if the delivery or proffered delivery was made in good faith and the labeling at the time thereof contained the same directions for use and warning statements as were contained in the labeling at the time of such receipt of such aticle; or (5) for having violated section 301(i)(2) if such person acted in good faith and had no reason to believe that use of the punch, die, plate, stone, or other thing involved would result in a drug being a counterfeit drug, or for having violated section 301(i)(3) if the person doing the act or causing it to be done acted in good faith and had no reason to believe that the drug was a counterfeit drug.

SEIZURE

SEC. 304 [334]. (a)(1) Any article of food, drug, device, or cosmetic that is adulterated or misbranded when introduced into or while in interstate commerce or while held for sale (whether or not the first sale) after shipment in interstate commerce, or which may not, under the provisions of section 404 or 505, be introduced into interstate commerce, shall be liable to be proceeded against while in interstate commerce, or at any time thereafter, or libel of information and condemned in any district court of the United States within the jurisdiction of which the article is found: *Provided, however,* That no libel for condemnation shall be instituted under this Act, for any alleged misbranding if there is pending in any court a libel for condemnation proceeding under this Act based upon the same alleged misbranding, and not more than one such proceeding shall be instituted if no such proceeding is so pending, except that such limitations shall not apply (A) when such misbranding has been the basis of a solidated for trial and tried. Such order of consolidation shall not apply so as to require the removal of any case the date for trial of which has been fixed. The court granting such order shall give prompt notification thereof to the other courts having jurisdiction of the cases covered thereby.

(c) The court at any time after seizure up to a reasonable time before trial shall by order allow any party to a condemnation proceeding, his attorney or agent, to obtain a representative sample of the article seized and a true copy of the analysis, if any, on which the proceeding is based and the identifying marks or numbers, if any, of the packages from which the samples analyzed were obtained.

(d)(1) Any food, drug, device, or cosmetic condemned under this section shall, after entry of the decree, be disposed of by destruction or sale as the court may, in accordance with the provisions of this section, direct and the proceeds thereof, if sold, less the legal costs and changes, shall be paid into the Treasury of the United States; but such article shall not be sold under such decree contrary to the provisions of this Act or the laws of the jurisdiction in which sold: *Provided*, That after entry of the decree and upon the payment of the costs of such proceedings and the execution of a good and sufficient bond conditioned that such article shall not be sold or disposed of contrary to the provisions of this Act or the laws of any State or Territory in which sold, the court may by order direct that such article be delivered to the owner thereof to be destroyed or brought into compliance with the provisions of this Act under the supervision of an officer or employee duly designated by the Secretary, and the expenses of such supervision shall be paid by the person obtaining release of the article under bond. If the article was imported into the United States and the person seeking its release establishes (A) that the adulteration, misbranding, or violation did not occur after the article was imported, and (B) that he had no cause for believing that it was adulterated, misbranded, or in violation before it was released from customs custody, the court may permit the article to be delivered to the owner for exportation in lieu of destruction upon a showing by the owner that all of the conditions of section 801 (d) can and will be met: *Provided, however*, That the provisions of this sentence shall not apply where condemnation is based upon violation of section 402(a) (1), (2), or (6), section 501(a)(3), section 502(j), or section 601(a) or (d); *And provided further*, That where such exportation is made to the original foreign supplier, then clauses (1) and (2) of section 801(d) and the foregoing proviso shall not be applicable; and in all cases of exportation the bond shall be conditioned that the article shall not be sold or disposed of until the applicable conditions of section 801(d) have been met. Any article condemned by reason of its being an article which may not, under section 404 or 505, be introduced into interstate commerce, shall be disposed of by destruction.

(2) The provisions of paragraph (1) of this subsection shall, to the extent deemed appropriate by the court, apply to any equipment or other thing which is not otherwise within the scope of such paragraph and which is referred to in paragraph (2) of subsection (a).

(3) Whenever in any proceeding under this section, involving paragraph (2) of subsection (a), the condemnation of any equipment or thing (other than a drug) is decreed, the court shall allow the claim

prior judgment in favor of the United States, in a criminal, injunction, or libel for condemnation proceeding under this Act, or (B) when the Secretary has probable cause to believe from facts found, without hearing, by him or any officer or employee of the Department that the misbranded article is dangerous to health, or that the labeling of the misbranded article is fraudulent, or would be in a material respect misleading to the injury or damage of the purchaser or consumer. In any case where the number of libel for condemnation proceedings is limited as above provided the proceeding pending or instituted shall, on application of the claimant, seasonably made, be removed for trial to any district agreed upon by stipulations between the parties, or, in case of failure to so stipulate within a reasonable time, the claimant may apply to the court of the district in which the seizure has been made, and such court (after giving the United States attorney for such district reasonable notice and opportunity to be heard) shall by order, unless good cause to the contrary is shown, specify a district of reasonable proximity to the claimant's principal place of business to which the case shall be removed for trial.

(2) The following shall be liable to be proceeded against at any time on libel of information and condemned in any district court of the United States within the jurisdiction of which they are found:

(A) Any depressant or stimulant drug with respect to which a prohibited act within the meaning of section 301 (p) or (q) by any person had occurred,

(B) Any drug that is a counterfeit drug,

(C) Any container of such depressant or stimulant drug or of a counterfeit drug.

(D) Any equipment used in manufacturing, compounding, or processing a depressant or stimulant drug with respect to which drug a prohibited act within the meaning of section 301 (p) or (q), by the manufacturer, compounder, or processor thereof, has occurred, and

(E) Any punch, die plate, stone, labeling, container, or other thing used or designed for use in making a counterfeit drug or drugs.

(b) The article, equipment, or other thing proceeded against shall be liable to seizure by process pursuant to the libel, and the procedure in cases under this section shall conform, as nearly as may be, to the procedure in admiralty; except that on demand of either party any issue of fact joined in any such case shall be tried by jury. When libel for condemnation proceedings under this section, involving the same claimant and the same issues of adulteration or misbranding, and pending in two or more jurisdictions, such pending proceedings, upon application of the claimant seasonably made to the court of one such jurisdiction, shall be consolidated for trial by order of such court, and tried in (1) any district selected by the claimant where one of such proceedings is pending; or (2) a district agreed upon by stipulation between the parties. If no order for consolidation is so made within a reasonable time, the claimant may apply to the court of one such jurisdiction, and such court (after giving the United States attorney for such district reasonable notice and opportunity to be heard) shall by order, unless good cause to the contrary is shown, specify a district of reasonable proximity to the claimant's principal place of business, in which all such pending proceedings shall be conof any claimant, to the extent of such claimant's interest, for remission or mitigation of such forfeiture if such claimant proves to the satisfaction of the court (i) that he has not committed or caused to be committed any prohibited act referred to in such paragraph (2) and has no interest in any drug referred to therein, (ii) that he has an interest in such equipment or other thing as owner or lienor or otherwise, acquired by him in good faith, and (iii) that he at no time had any knowledge or reason to believe that such equipment or other thing was being or would be used in, or to facilitate, the violation of laws of the United States relating to depressant or stimulant drugs or counterfeit drugs.

(e) When a decree of condemnation is entered against the article, court costs and fees, and storage and other proper expenses, shall be awarded against the person, if any, intervening as claimant of the article.

(f) In the case of removal for trial of any case as provided by subsection (a) or (b)—

(1) The clerk of the court from which removal is made shall promptly transmit to the court in which the case is to be tried all records in the case necessary in order that such court may exercise jurisdiction.

(2) The court to which such case was removed shall have the powers and be subject to the duties for purposes of such case, which the court from which removal was made would have had, or to which such court would have been subject, if such case had not been removed.

HEARING BEFORE REPORT OF CRIMINAL VIOLATION

SEC. 305 [335]. Before any violation of this Act is reported by the Secretary to any United States attorney for institution of a criminal proceeding, the person against whom such proceeding is contemplated shall be given appropriate notice and an opportunity to present his views, either orally or in writing, with regard to such contemplated proceeding.

REPORT OF MINOR VIOLATIONS

SEC. 306 [336]. Nothing in this Act shall be construed as requiring the Secretary to report for prosecution, or for the institution of libel or injunction proceedings, minor violations of this Act whenever he believes that the public interest will be adequately served by a suitable written notice or warning.

PROCEEDINGS IN NAME OF UNITED STATES; PROVISION AS TO SUBPOENAS

SEC. 307 [337]. All such proceedings for the enforcement, or to restrain violations, of this Act shall be by and in the name of the United States. Subpoenas for witnesses who are required to attend a court of the United States, in any district, may run into any other district in any such proceeding.

* * * * * * *

CHAPTER V—DRUGS AND DEVICES

ADULTERATED DRUGS AND DEVICES

SEC. 501 [351]. A drug or device shall be deemed to be adulterated—
(a)(1) If it consists in whole or in part of any filthy, putrid, or decomposed substance; or (2)(A) if it has been prepared, packed, or held under insanitary conditions whereby it may have been contaminated with filth, or whereby it may have been rendered injurious to health; or (B) if it is a drug and the methods used in, or the facilities or controls used for, its manufacture, processing, packing, or holding do not conform to or are not operated or administered in conformity with current good manufacturing practice to assure that such drug meets the requirements of this Act as to safety and has the identity and strength, and meets the quality and purity characteristics, which it purports or is represented to possess; or (3) if it is a drug and its container is composed, in whole or in part, of any poisonous or deleterious substance which may render the contents injurious to health; or (4) if (A) it is a drug which bears or contains, for purposes of coloring only, a color additive which is unsafe within the meaning of section 706(a), or (B) it is a color additive the intended use of which in or on drugs is for purposes of coloring only and is unsafe within the meaning of section 706(a) ; or (5) if it is a new animal drug which is unsafe within the meaning of section 512; or (6) if it is an animal feed bearing or containing a new animal drug, and such animal feed is unsafe within the meaning of section 512.

(b) If it purports to be or is represented as a drug the name of which is recognized in an official compendium, and its strength differs from, or its quality or purity falls below, the standard set forth in such compendium. Such determination as to strength, quality, or purity shall be made in accordance with the tests or methods of assay set forth in such compendium, except that whenever tests or methods of assay have not been prescribed in such compendium, or such tests or methods of assay as are prescribed are, in the judgment of the Secretary, insufficient for the making of such determination, the Secretary shall bring such fact to the attention of the appropriate body charged with the revision of such compendium, and if such body fails within a reasonable time to prescribe tests or methods of assay which, in the judgment of the Secretary, are sufficient for purposes of this paragraph, then the Secretary shall promulgate regulations prescribing appropriate tests or methods of assay in accordance with which such determination as to strength, quality, or purity shall be made. No drug defined in an official compendium shall be deemed to be adulterated under this paragraph because it differs from the standard of strength, quality, or purity therefor set forth in such compendium, if its difference in strength, quality, or purity from such standards is plainly stated on its label. Whenever a drug is recognized in both the United States Pharmacopeia and the Homeopathic Pharmacopeia of the United States it shall be subject to the requirements of the United States Pharmacopeia unless it is labeled and offered for sale as a homeopathic drug, in which case it shall be subject to the provisions of the Homeopathic Pharmacopeia of the United States and not to those of the United States Pharmacopeia.

(c) If it is not subject to the provisions of paragraph (b) of this section and its strength differs from, or its purity or quality falls below, that which it purports or is represented to possess.

(d) If it is a drug and any substance has been (1) mixed or packed therewith so as to reduce its quality or strength or (2) substituted wholly or in part therefor.

MISBRANDED DRUGS AND DEVICES

SEC. 502 [352]. A drug or device shall be deemed to be misbranded—

(a) If its labeling is false or misleading in any particular.

(b) If in a package form unless it bears a label containing (1) the name and place of business of the manufacturer, packer, or distributor; and (2) an accurate statement of the quantity of the contents in terms of weight, measure, or numerical count: *Provided,* That under clause (2) of this paragraph reasonable variations shall be permitted, and exemptions as to small packages shall be established, by regulations prescribed by the Secretary.

(c) If any word, statement, or other information required by or under authority of this Act to appear on the label or labeling is not prominently placed thereon with such conspicuousness (as compared with other words, statements, designs, or devices, in the labeling) and in such terms as to render it likely to be read and understood by the ordinary individual under customary conditions of purchase and use.

(d) If it is for use by man and contains any quantity of the narcotic or hypnotic substance alpha-eucaine, barbituric acid, beta-eucaine, bromal, cannabis, carbromal; chloral, coca, cocaine, codeine, heroin, marihuana, morphine, opium, paraldehyde, peyote, or sulfonmethane; or any chemical derivative of such substance, which derivative has been by the Secretary, after investigation, found to be, and by regulations [15] designated as, habit forming; unless its label bears the name, and quantity or proportion of such substance or derivative and in juxtaposition therewith the statement "Warning—May be habit-forming."

(e)(1) If it is a drug, unless (A) its label bears, to the exclusion of any other nonproprietary name (except the applicable systematic chemical name or the chemical formula), (i) the established name (as defined in subparagraph (2)) of the drug, if such there be, and (ii), in case it is fabricated from two or more ingredients, the established name and quantity of each active ingredient, including the quantity,

---

[15] F.D.C. Regs., part 165.

kind, and proportion of any alcohol, and also including whether active or not, the established name and quantity or proportion of any bromides, ether, chloroform, acetanilide, acetophenetidin, amidopyrine, antipyrine, atropine, hyoscine, hyoscyamine, arsenic, digitalis, digitalis glucosides, mercury, ouabain, strophanthin, strychnine, thyroid, or any derivative or preparation of any such substances, contained therein: *Provided*, That the requirement for stating the quantity of the active ingredients, other than the quantity of those specifically named in this paragraph, shall apply only to prescription drugs; and (B) for any prescription drug the established name of such drug or ingredient, as the case may be, on such label (and on any labeling on which a name for such drug or ingredient is used) is printed prominently and in type at least half as large as that used thereon for any proprietary name or designation for such drug or ingredient: and *Provided*, That to the extent that compliance with the requirements of clause (A)(ii) or clause (B) of this subparagraph is impracticable, exemptions shall be estalished by regulations promulgated by the Secretary.

(2) As used in this paragraph (e), the term "established name", with respect to a drug or ingredient thereof, means (A) the applicable official name designated pursuant to section 508, or (B), if there is no such name and such drug, or such ingredient, is an article recognized in an official compendium, then the official title thereof in such compendium, or (C) if neither clause (A) nor clause (B) of this subparagraph applies, then the common or usual name, if any, of such drug or of such ingredient: *Provided further*, That where clause (B) of this subparagraph applies to an article recognized in the United States Pharmacopeia and in the Homeopathic Pharmacopeia under different official titles, the official title used in the United States Pharmacopeia shall apply unless it is labeled and offered for sale as a homeopathic drug, in which case the official title used in the Homeopathic Pharmacopeia shall apply.

(f) Unless its labeling bears (1) adequate directions for use; and (2) such adequate warnings against use in those pathological conditions or by children where its use may be dangerous to health, or against unsafe dosage or methods or duration of administration or application, in such manner and form, as are necessary for the protection of users: *Provided*, That where any requirement of clause (1) of this paragraph, as applied to any drug or device, is not necessary for the protection of the public health, the Secretary shall promulgate regulations exempting such drug or device from such requirement.

(g) If it purports to be a drug the name of which is recognized in an official compendium, unless it is packaged and labeled as prescribed therein: *Provided*, That the method of packing may be modified with the consent of the Secretary. Whenever a drug is recognized in both the United States Pharmacopeia and the Homeopathic Pharmacopeia of the United States Pharmacopeia with respect to packaging and labeling unless it is labeled and offered for sale as a homeopathic drug, in which case it shall be subject to the provisions of the Homeopathic Pharmacopeia of the United States, and not to those of the United States Pharmacopeia: [and] (ed.) *Provided further*, That, in the event of inconsistency between the requirements of this paragraph and those of paragraph (e) as to the name by which the drug or its ingredients shall be designated, the requirements of paragraph (e) shall prevail.

(h) If it has been found by the Secretary to be a drug liable to deterioration, unless it is packaged in such form and manner, and its label bears a statement of such precautions, as the Secretary shall by regulations require as necessary for the protection of the public health. No such regulation shall be established for any drug recognized in an official compendium until the Secretary shall have informed the appropriate body charged with the revision of such compendium of the need for such packaging or labeling requirements and such body shall have failed within a reasonable time to prescribe such requirements.

(i) (1) If it is a drug and its container is so made, formed, or filled as to be misleading; or (2) if it is an imitation of another drug; or (3) if it is offered for sale under the name of another drug.

(j) If it is dangerous to health when used in the dosage, or with the frequency or duration prescribed, recommended, or suggested in the labeling thereof.

(k) If it is, or purports to be, or is represented as a drug composed wholly or partly of insulin, unless (1) it is from a batch with respect to which a certificate or release has been issued pursuant to section 506, and (2) such certificate or release is in effect with respect to such drug.

(l) If it is, or purports to be, or is represented as a drug (except a drug for use in animals other than man) composed wholly or partly of any kind of penicillin, streptomycin, chlortetracycline, chloramphenicol, bacitracin, or any other antibiotic drug, or any derivative thereof, unless (1) it is from a batch with respect to which a certificate or release has been issued pursuant to section 507, and (2) such certificate or release is in effect with respect to such drug: *Provided*, That this paragraph shall not apply to any drug or class of drugs exempted by regulations promulgated under section 507 (c) or (d).

(m) If it is a color additive the intended use of which in or on drugs is for the purpose of coloring only, unless its packaging and labeling are in conformity with such packaging and labeling requirements applicable to such color additive, as may be contained in regulations [16] issued under section 706.

(n) In the case of any prescription drug distributed or offered for sale in any State, unless the manufacturer, packer, or distributor thereof includes in all advertisements and other descriptive printed matter issued or caused to be issued by the manufacturer, packer, or distributor with respect to that drug a true statement of (1) the established name as defined in section 502(e), printed prominently and in type at least half as large as that used for any trade or brand name thereof, (2) the formula showing quantitatively each ingredient of such drug to the extent required for labels under section 502(e), and (3) such other information in brief summary relating to side effects, contraindications, and effectiveness as shall be required in regulations which shall be issued by the Secretary in accordance with the procedure specified in section 701(e) of this Act: *Provided*, That (A) except in extraordinary circumstances, no regulation issued under this paragraph shall require prior approval by the Secretary of the content of any advertisement, and (B) no advertisement of a prescription drug, published after the effective date of regulations issued under this paragraph applicable to advertisements of prescription drugs, shall,

---

[16] F.D.C. Regs., part 8.

with respect to the matters specified in this paragraph or covered by such regulations, be subject to the provisions of sections 12 through 17 of the Federal Trade Commission Act, as amended (15 U.S.C. 52–57). This paragraph (n) shall not be applicable to any printed matter which the Secretary determines to be labeling as defined in section 201(m) of this Act.

(o) If it is a drug and was manufactured, prepared, propagated, compounded, or processed in an establishment in any State not duly registered under section 510.

EXEMPTIONS IN CASE OF DRUGS AND DEVICES

Sec. 503 [353]. (a) The Secretary is hereby directed to promulgate regulations exempting from any labeling or packaging requirement of this Act drugs and devices which are, in accordance with the practice of the trade, to be processed, labeled, or repacked in substantial quantities at establishments other than those where originally processed or packed, on condition that such drugs and devices are not adulterated or misbranded, under the provisions of this Act upon removal from such processing, labeling, or repacking establishment.

(b) (1) A drug intended for use by man which—

(A) is a habit-forming drug to which section 502(d) applies; or

(B) because of its toxicity or other potentiality for harmful effect, or the method of its use, or the collateral measures necessary to its use, is not safe for use except under the supervision of a practitioner licensed by law to administer such drug; or

(C) is limited by an approved application under section 505 to use under the professional supervision of a practitioner licensed by law to administer such drug,

shall be dispensed only (i) upon a written prescription of a practitioner licensed by law to administer such drug, or (ii) upon an oral prescription of such practitioner which is reduced promptly to writing and filed by the pharmacist, or (iii) by refilling any such written or oral prescription if such refilling is authorized by the prescriber either in the original prescription or by oral order which is reduced promptly to writing and filed by the pharmacist. The act of dispensing a drug contrary to the provisions of this paragraph shall be deemed to be an act which results in the drug being misbranded while held for sale.

(2) Any drug dispensed by filling or refilling a written or oral prescription of a practitioner licensed by law to administer such drug shall be exempt from the requirements of section 502, except paragraphs (a), (i) (2) and (3), (k), and (l), and the packaging requirements of paragraphs (g) and (h), if the drug bears a label containing the name and address of the dispenser, the serial number and date of the prescription or of its filling, the name of the prescriber, and, if stated in the prescription, the name of the patient, and the directions for use and cautionary statements, if any, contained in such prescription. This exemption shall not apply to any drug dispensed in the course of the conduct of a business of dispensing drugs pursuant to diagnosis by mail, or to a drug dispensed in violation of paragraph (1) of this subsection.

(3) The Secretary may by regulation [17] remove drugs subject to section 502(d) and section 505 from the requirements of paragraph

---

[17] F.D.C. Regs., part 130.

(1) of this subsection when such requirements are not necessary for the protection of the public health.

(4)[18] A drug which is subject to paragraph (1) of this subsection shall be deemed to be misbranded if at any time prior to dispensing its label fails to bear the statement "Caution: Federal law prohibits dispensing without prescription." A drug to which paragraph (1) of this subsection does not apply shall be deemed to be misbranded if at any time prior to dispensing its label bears the caution statement quoted in the preceding sentence.

(5) Nothing in this subsection shall be construed to relieve any person from any requirement prescribed by or under authority of law with respect to drugs now included or which may hereafter be included within the classifications stated in section 3220 of the Internal Revenue Code (26 U.S.C. 3220), or to marihuana as defined in section 3238(b) of the Internal Revenue Code (26 U.S.C. 3238(b)).

NEW DRUGS

SEC. 505 [355]. (a) No person shall introduce or deliver for introduction into interstate commerce any new drug, unless an approval of an application filed pursuant to subsection (b) is effective with respect to such drug.

(b) Any person may file with the Secretary an application with respect to any drug subject to the provisions of subsection (a). Such persons shall submit to the Secretary as a part of the application (1) full reports of investigations which have been made to show whether or not such drug is safe for use and whether such drug is effective in use; (2) a full list of the articles used as components of such drug; (3) a full statement of the composition of such drug; (4) a full description of the methods used in, and the facilities and controls used for, the manufacture, processing, and packing of such drug; (5) such samples of such drug and of the articles used as components thereof as the Secretary may require; and (6) specimens of the labeling proposed to be used for such drug.

(c) Within one hundred and eighty days after the filing of an application under this subsection, or such additional period as may be agreed upon by the Secretary and the applicant, the Secretary shall either—

(1) approve the application if he then finds that none of the grounds for denying approval specified in subsection (d) applies, or

(2) give the applicant notice of an opportunity for a hearing before the Secretary under subsection (d) on the question whether such application is approvable. If the applicant elects to accept the opportunity for hearing by written request within thirty days after such notice, such hearing shall commence not more than ninety days after the expiration of such thirty days unless the Secretary and the applicant otherwise agree. Any such hearing shall thereafter be conducted on an expedited basis and the Secretary's order thereon shall be issued within ninety days after the date fixed by the Secretary for filing final briefs.

(d) If the Secretary finds, after due notice to the applicant in accordance with subsection (c) and giving him an opportunity for a

[18] See Sec. 1.108, F.D.C. Regs., part 1.

hearing, in accordance with said subsection, that (1) the investigations, reports of which are required to be submitted to the Secretary pursuant to subsection (b), do not include adequate tests by all methods reasonably applicable to show whether or not such drug is safe for use under the conditions prescribed, recommended, or suggested in the proposed labeling thereof; (2) the results of such tests show that such drug is unsafe for use under such conditions or do not show that such drug si safe for use under such conditions; (3) the methods used in, and the facilities and controls used for, the manufacture, processing, and packing of such drug are inadequate to preserve its identity, strength, quality, and purity; (4) upon the basis of the information submitted to him as part of the application, or upon the basis of any other information before him with respect to such drug, he has insufficient information to determine whether such drug is safe for use under such conditions; or (5) evaluated on the basis of the information submitted to him as part of the application and any other information before him with respect to such drug, there is a lack of substantial evidence that the drug will have the effect it purports or is represented to have under the conditions of use prescribed, recommended, or suggested in the proposed labeling thereof; or (6) based on a fair evaluation of all material facts, such labeling is false or misleading in any particular; he shall issue an order refusing to approve the application. If, after such notice and opportunity for hearing, the Secretary finds that clauses (1) through (6) do not apply, he shall issue an order approving the application. As used in this subsection and subsection (e), the term "substantial evidence" means evidence consisting of adequate and well-controlled investigations, including clinical investigations, by experts qualified by scientific training and experience to evaluate the effectiveness of the drug involved, on the basis of which it could fairly and responsibly be concluded by such experts that the drug will have the effect it purports or is represented to have under the conditions of use prescribed, recommended, or suggested in the labeling or proposed labeling thereof.

(e) The Secretary shall, after due notice and opportunity for hearing to the applicant, withdraw approval of an application with respect to any drug under this section if the Secretary finds (1) that clinical or other experience, tests, or other scientific data show that such drug is unsafe for use under the conditions of use upon the basis of which the application was approved; (2) that new evidence of clinical experience, not contained in such application or not available to the Secretary until after such application was approved, or tests by new methods, or tests by methods not deemed reasonably applicable when such application was approved, evaluated together with the evidence available to the Secretary when the application was approved, shows that such drug is not shown to be safe for use under the conditions of use upon the basis of which the application was approved; or (3) on the basis of new information before him with respect to such drug, evaluated together with the evidence available to him when the application was approved, that there is a lack of substantial evidence that the drug will have the effect it purports òr is represented to have under the conditions of use prescribed, recommended, or suggested in the labeling thereof; or (4) that the application contains any untrue statement of a material fact: *Provided*, That if the Secretary (or in his absence the officer acting as Secretary) finds that there is an imminent hazard to the public health, he may suspend the approval of such spplication immediately, and give the applicant prompt notice of his action and afford the applicant the opportunity for an expedited hearing under this subsection; but the authority conferred by this priviso to suspend the approval of an application shall not be delegated. The Secretary may also, after due notice and opportunity for hearing to the applicant, withdraw the approval of an application with respect to any drug under this section if the Secretary finds (1) that the applicant has failed to establish a system for maintaining required records, or has repeatedly or deliberately failed to maintain such records or to make required reports, in accordance with a regulation or order under subsection (j), or the applicant has refused to permit access to, or copying or verification of, such records as required by paragraph (2) of such subsection; or (2) that on the basis of new information before him, evaluated together with the evidence before him when the application was approved, the methods used in, or the facilities and controls used for, the manufacture, processing, and packing of such drug are inadequate to assure and preserve its identity, strength, quality, and purity and were not made adequate within a reasonable time after receipt of written notice from the Secretary specifying the matter complained of; or (3) that on the basis of new information before him, evaluated together with the evidence before him when the application was approved, the labeling of such drug, based on a fair evaluation of all material facts, is false or misleading in any particular and was not corrected within a reasonable time after receipt of written notice from the Secretary specifying the matter complained of. Any order under this subsection shall state the findings upon which it is based.

(f) Whenever the Secretary finds that the facts so require, he shall revoke any previous order under subsection (d) or (e) refusing, withdrawing, or suspending approval of an application and shall approve such application or reinstate such approval, as may be appropriate.

(g) Orders of the Secretary issued under this section shall be served (1) in person by any officer or employee of the Department designated by the Secretary or (2) by mailing the order by registered mail or by certified mail addressed to the applicant or respondent at his last-known address in the records of the Secretary.

(h) [19] An appeal may be taken by the applicant from an order of the Secretary refusing or withdrawing approval of an application under this section. Such appeal shall be taken by filing in the United States court of appeals for the circuit wherein such applicant resides or has his principal place of business, or in the United States Court of Appeals for the District of Columbia Circuit, within sixty days after the entry of such order, a written petition praying that the order of the Secretary be set aside. A copy of such petition shall be forthwith transmitted by the clerk of the court to the Secretary, or any officer designated by him for that purpose, and thereupon the Secretary shall certify and file in the court the record upon which the order complained of was entered, as provided in section 2112 of title 28, United States Code. Upon the filing of such petition such court shall have exclusive jurisdiction to affirm or set aside such order, except that until the filing of the record the Secretary may modify or set aside his order. No objection to the order of the Secretary shall be considered

---

[19] This amendment shall not apply to any appeal taken prior to the date of enactment of the Drug Amendments of 1962, enacted Oct. 10, 1962.

by the court unless such objection shall have been urged before the Secretary or unless there were reasonable grounds for failure so to do. The finding of the Secretary as to the facts, if supported by substantial evidence, shall be conclusive. If any person shall apply to the court for leave to adduce additional evidence, and shall show to the satisfaction of the court that such additional evidence is material and that there were reasonable grounds for failure to adduce such evidence in the proceeding before the Secretary, the court may order such additional evidence to be taken before the Secretary and to be adduced upon the hearing in such manner and upon such terms and conditions as to the court may seem proper. The Secretary may modify his findings as to the facts by reason of the additional evidence so taken, and he shall file with the court such modified findings which, if supported by substantial evidence, shall be conclusive, and his recommendation, if any, for the setting aside of the original order. The judgment of the court affirming or setting aside any such order of the Secretary shall be final, subject to review by the Supreme Court of the United States upon certiorari or certification as provided in section 1254 of title 28 of the United States Code. The commencement of proceedings under this subsection shall not, unless specifically ordered by the court to the contrary, operate as a stay of the Secretary's order.

(i) The Secretary shall promulgate regulations [20] for exempting from the operation of the foregoing subsections of this section drugs intended solely for investigational use by experts qualified by scientific training and experience to investigate the safety and effectiveness of drugs. Such regulations may, within the discretion of the Secretary, among other conditions relating to the protection of the public health, provide for conditioning such exemption upon—

(1) the submission to the Secretary, before any clinical testing of a new drug is undertaken, of reports, by the manufacturer or the sponsor of the investigation of such drug, of preclinical tests (including tests on animals) of such drug adequate to justify the proposed clinical testing;

(2) the manufacturer or the sponsor of the investigation of a new drug proposed to be distributed to investigators for clinical testing obtaining a signed agreement from each of such investigators that patients to whom the drug is administered will be under his personal supervision, or under the supervision of investigators responsible to him, and that he will not supply such drug to any other investigator, or to clinics, for administration to human beings; and

(3) the establishment and maintenance of such records, and the making of such reports to the Secretary, by the manufacturer or the sponsor of the investigation of such drug, of data (including but not limited to analytical reports by investigators) obtained as the result of such investigational use of such drug, as the Secretary finds will enable him to evaluate the safety and effectiveness of such drug in the event of the filing of an application pursuant to subsection (b).

Such regulations shall provide that such exemption shall be conditioned upon the manufacturer, or the sponsor of the investigation, requiring that experts using such drugs for investigational purposes certify to such manufacturer or sponsor that they will inform any

[20] F.D.C. Regs., part 130.3.

human beings to whom such drugs, or any controls used in connection therewith, are being administered, or their representatives, that such drugs are being used for investigational purposes and will obtain the consent of such human beings or their representatives, except where they deem it not feasible or, in their professional judgment, contrary to the best interests of such human beings. Nothing in this subsection shall be construed to require any clinical investigator to submit directly to the Secretary reports on the investigational use of drugs.

(j) (1) In the case of any drug for which an approval of an application filed pursuant to this section is in effect, the applicant shall establish and maintain such records, and make such reports to the Secretary, of data relating to clinical experience and other data or information, received or otherwise obtained by such applicant with respect to such drug, as the Secretary may by general regulation, or by order with respect to such application, prescribe on the basis of a finding that such records and reports are necessary in order to enable the Secretary to determine, or facilitate a determination, whether there is or may be ground for invoking subsection (e) of this section: *Provided, however,* That regulations and orders issued under this subsection and under subsection (i) shall have due regard for the professional ethics of the medical profession and the interests of patients and shall provide, where the Secretary deems it to be appropriate, for the examination, upon request, by the persons to whom such regulations or orders are applicable, of similar information received or otherwise obtained by the Secretary.

(2) Every person required under this section to maintain records, and every person in charge or custody thereof, shall, upon request of an officer or employee designated by the Secretary, permit such officer or employee at all reasonable times to have access to and copy and verify such records.

CERTIFICATION OF DRUGS CONTAINING INSULIN

SEC. 506 [356]. (a) The Secretary of Health, Education, and Welfare, pursuant to regulations[21] promulgated by him, shall provide for the certification of batches of drugs composed wholly or partly of insulin. A batch of any such drug shall be certified if such drug has such characteristics of identity and such batch has such characteristics of strength, quality, and purity, as the Secretary prescribes in such regulations as necessary to adequately insure safety and efficacy of use, but shall not otherwise be certified. Prior to the effective date of such regulations the Secretary, in lieu of certification, shall issue a release for any batch which, in his judgment, may be released without risk as to the safety and efficacy of its use. Such release shall prescribe the date of its expiration and other conditions under which it shall cease to be effective as to such batch and as to portions thereof.

(b) Regulations providing for such certification shall contain such provisions as are necessary to carry out the purposes of this section, including provisions prescribing (1) standards of identity and of strength, quality, and purity; (2) tests and methods of assay to determine compliance with such standards; (3) effective periods for certificates, and other conditions under which they shall cease to be effective as to certified batches and as to portions thereof: (4) administration

²¹ F.D.C. Regs., part 164.

and procedure; and (5) such fees, specified in such regulations, as are necessary to provide, equip, and maintain an adequate certification service. Such regulations shall prescribe no standard of identity or of strength, quality, or purity for any drug different from the standard of identity, strength, quality, or purity set forth for such drug in an official compendium.

(c) Such regulations, insofar as they prescribe tests or methods of assay to determine strength, quality, or purity of any drug, different from the tests or methods of assay set forth for such drug in an official compendium, shall be prescribed, after notice and opportunity for revision of such compendium, in the manner provided in the second sentence of section 501(b). The provisions of subsections (e), (f), and (g) of section 701 shall be applicable to such portion of any regulation as prescribes any such different test or method, but shall not be applicable to any other portion of any such regulation.

CERTIFICATION OF ANTIBIOTICS

SEC. 507 [357]. (a) The Secretary of Health, Education, and Welfare, pursuant to regulations promulgated by him, shall provide for the certification of batches of drugs (except drugs for use in animals other than man) composed wholly or partly of any kind of penicillin, streptomycin, chlortetracycline, chloramphenicol, bacitracin, or any other antibiotic drug, or any derivative thereof. A batch of any such drug shall be certified if such drug has such characteristics of identity and such batch has such characteristics of strength, quality, and purity, as the Secretary prescribes in such regulations as necesary to adequately insure safety and efficacy of use, but shall not otherwise be certified. Prior to the effective date of such regulations the Secretary, in lieu of certification, shall issue a release for any batch which, in his judgment, may be released without risk as to the safety and efficacy of its use. Such release shall prescribe the date of its expiration and other conditions under which it shall cease to be effective as to such batch and as to portions thereof. For purposes of this section and of section 502(1), the term "antibiotic drug" means any drug intended for use by man containing any quantity of any chemical substance which is produced by a micro-organism and which has the capacity to inhibit or destroy micro-organisms in dilute solution (including the chemically synthesized equivalent of any such substance).

(b) Regulations providing for such certifications shall contain such provisions as are necessary to carry out the purposes of this section, including provisions prescribing (1) standards of identity and of strength, quality, and purity; [22] (2) tests and methods of assay to determine compliance with such standards; [23] (3) effective periods for certificates, and other conditions under which they shall cease to be effective as to certified batches and as to portions thereof; [24] (4) administration and procedure; [24] and (5) such fees, specified in such regulations, as are necessary to provide, equip, and maintain an adequate certification service.[24] Such regulations shall prescribe only such tests and methods of assay as will provide for certification or rejection within the shortest time consistent with the purposes of this section.

[22] F.D.C. Regs., parts 146a–146e incl., 147, 148a–148z incl.
[23] F.D.C. Regs., parts 141, 141a–141e incl., 147, 148a–148z incl;
[24] F.D.C. Regs., part 146.

(c) Whenever in the judgment of the Secretary, the requirements of this section and of section 502(l) with respect to any drug or class of drugs are not necessary to insure safety and efficacy of use, the Secretary shall promulgate regulations exempting such drug or class of drugs from such requirements.[25] In deciding whether an antibiotic drug, or class of antibiotic drugs, is to be exempted from the requirement of certification the Secretary shall give consideration, among other relevant factors, to—

(1) whether such drug or class of drugs is manufactured by a person who has, or hereafter shall have, produced fifty consecutive batches of such drug or class of drugs in compliance with the regulations for the certification thereof within a period of not more than eighteen calendar months, upon the application by such person to the Secretary; or

(2) whether such drug or class of drugs is manufactured by any person who has otherwise demonstrated such consistency in the production of such drug or class of drugs, in compliance with the regulations for the certification thereof, as in the judgment of the Secretary is adequate to insure the safety and efficacy of use thereof.

When an antibiotic drug or a drug manufacturer has been exempted from the requirement of certification, the manufacturer may still obtain certification of a batch or batches of that drug if he applies for and meets the requirements for certification. Nothing in this Act shall be deemed to prevent a manufacturer or distributor of an antibiotic drug from making a truthful statement in labeling or advertising of the product as to whether it has been certified or exempted from the requirement of certification.

(d) The Secretary shall promulgate regulations [25] exempting from any requirement of this section and of section 502(l), (1) drugs which are to be stored, processed, labeled, or repacked at establishments other than those where manufactured, on condition that such drugs comply with all such requirements upon removal from such establishments; (2) drugs which conform to applicable standards of identity, strength, quality, and purity prescribed by these regulations and are intended for use in manufacturing other drugs; and (3) drugs which are intended solely for investigational use by experts qualified by scientific training and experience to investigate the safety and efficacy of drugs. Such regulations may, within the discretion of the Secretary, among other conditions relating to the protection of the public health, provide for conditioning the exemption under clause (3) upon—

(1) the submission to the Secretary, before any clinical testing of a new drug is undertaken, of reports, by the manufacturer or the sponsor of the investigation of such drug, of preclinical tests (including tests on animals) of such drug adequate to justify the proposed clinical testing;

(2) the manufacturer or the sponsor of the investigation of a new drug proposed to be distributed to investigators for clinical testing obtaining a signed agreement from each of such investigators that patients to whom the drug is administered will be under his personal supervision, or under the supervision of investigators responsible to him, and that he will not supply such drug to any other investigator, or to clinics, for administration to

[25] F.D.C. Regs., part 144.

human beings; and

    (3) the establishment and maintenance of such records, and the making of such reports to the Secretary, by the manufacturer or the sponsor of the investigation of such drug, of data (including but not limited to analytical reports by investigators) obtained as the result of such investigational use of such drug, as the Secretary finds will enable him to evaluate the safety and effectiveness of such drug in the event of the filing of an application for certification or release pursuant to subsection (a).

Such regulations shall provide that such exemption shall be conditioned upon the manufacturer, or the sponsor of the investigation, requiring that experts using such drugs for investigational purposes certify to such manufacturer or sponsor that they will inform any human beings to whom such drugs, or any controls used in connection therewith, are being administered, or their representatives, that such drugs are being used for investigational purposes and will obtain the consent of such human beings or their representatives, except where they deem it not feasible or, in their professional judgment, contrary to the best interests of such human beings. Nothing in this subsection shall be construed to require any clinical investigator to submit directly to the Secretary reports on the investigational use of drugs.

    (e) No drug which is subject to section 507 shall be deemed to be subject to any provision of section 505 except a new drug exempted from the requirements of this section and of section 502(l) pursuant to regulations promulgated by the Secretary: *Provided*, That, for purposes of section 505, the initial request for certification, as thereafter duly amended, pursuant to section 507, of a new drug so exempted shall be considered a part of the application filed pursuant to section 505(b) with respect to the person filing such request and to such drug as of the date of the exemption. Compliance of any drug subject to section 502(l) or 507 with sections 501(b) and 502(g) shall be determined by the application of the standards of strength, quality, and purity, the tests and methods of assay, and the requirements of packaging, and labeling, respectively, prescribed by regulations promulgated under section 507.

    (f) Any interested person may file with the Secretary a petition proposing the issuance, amendment, or repeal of any regulation contemplated by this section. The petition shall set forth the proposal in general terms and shall state reasonable grounds therefor. The Secretary shall give public notice of the proposal and an opportunity for all interested persons to present their views thereon, orally or in writing, and as soon as practicable thereafter shall make public his action upon such proposal. At any time prior to the thirtieth day after such action is made public any interested person may file objections to such action, specifying with particularity the changes desired, stating reasonable grounds therefor, and requesting a public hearing upon such objections. The Secretary shall thereupon, after due notice, hold such public hearing. As soon as practicable after completion of the hearing, the Secretary shall by order make public his action on such objections. The Secretary shall base his order only on substantial evidence of record at the hearing and shall set forth as part of the order detailed findings of fact on which the order is based. The order shall be subject to the provisions of section 701 (f) and (g).

    (g) (1) Every person engaged in manufacturing, compounding, or processing any drug within the purview of this section with respect to which a certificate or release has been issued pursuant to this section shall establish and maintain such records, and make such reports to the Secretary, of data relating to clinical experience and other data or information, received or otherwise obtained by such person with respect to such drug, as the Secretary may by general regulation, or by order with respect to such certification or release, prescribe on the basis of a finding that such records and reports are necessary in order to enable the Secretary to make, or to facilitate, a determination as to whether such certification or release should be rescinded or whether any regulation issued under this section should be amended or repealed: *Provided, however,* That regulations and orders issued under this subsection and under clause (3) of subsection (d) shall have due regard for the professional ethics of the medical profession and the interests of patients and shall provide, where the Secretary deems it to be appropriate, for the examination, upon request, by the persons to whom such regulations or orders are applicable, of similar information received or otherwise obtained by the Secretary.

(2) Every person required under this section to maintain records, and every person having charge or custody thereof, shall, upon request of an officer or employee designated by the Secretary, permit such officer or employee at all reasonable times to have access to and copy and verify such records.

(h) In the case of a drug for which, on the day immediately preceding the effective date of this subsection, a prior approval of an application under section 505 had not been withdrawn under section 505(e), the initial issuance of regulations providing for certification or exemption of such drug under this section 507 shall, with respect to the conditions of use prescribed, recommended, or suggested in the labeling covered by such application, not be conditioned upon an affirmative finding of the efficacy of such drug. Any subsequent amendment or repeal of such regulations so as no longer to provide for such certification or exemption on the ground of a lack of efficacy of such drug for use under such conditions of use may be effected only on or after that effective date of clause (3) of the first sentence of section 505(e) which would be applicable to such drug under such conditions of use if such drug were subject to section 505(e), and then only if (1) such amendment or repeal is made in accordance with the procedure specified in subsection (f) of this section (except that such amendment or repeal may be initiated either by a proposal of the Secretary or by a petition of any interested person) and (2) the Secretary finds, on the basis of new information with respect to such drug evaluated together with the information before him when the application under section 505 became effective or was approved, that there is a lack of substantial evidence (as defined in section 505 (d)) that the drug has the effect it purports or is represented to have under such conditions of use.

AUTHORITY TO DESIGNATE OFFICIAL NAMES

SEC. 508 [358]. (a) The Secretary may designate an official name for any drug if he determines that such action is necessary or desirable in the interest of usefulness and simplicity. Any official name designated under this section for any drug shall be the only official name of that drug used in any official compendium published after such name has been prescribed or for any other purpose of this Act. In no event, however, shall the Secretary establish an official name so as to infringe a valid trademark.

(b) Within a reasonable time after the effective date of this section, and at such other times as he may deem necessary, the Secretary shall cause a review to be made of the official names by which drugs are identified in the official United States Pharmacopeia, the official Homeopathic Pharmacopeia of the United States, and the official National Formulary, and all supplements thereto, to determine whether revision of any of those names is necessary or desirable in the interest of usefulness and simplicity.

(c) Whenever he determines after any such review that (1) any such official name is unduly complex or is not useful for any other reason, (2) two or more official names have been applied to a single drug, or to two or more drugs which are identical in chemical structure and pharmacological action and which are substantially identical in strength, quality, and purity, or (3) no official name has been applied to a medically useful drug, he shall transmit in writing to the compiler of each official compendium in which that drug or drugs are identfied and recognized his request for the recommendation of a single official name for such drug or drugs which will have usefulness and simplicity. Whenever such a single official name has not been recommended within one hundred and eighty days after such request, or the Secretary determines that any name so recommended is not useful for any reason, he shall designate a single official name for such drug or drugs. Whenever he determines that the name so recommended is useful, he shall designate that name as the official name of such drug or drugs. Such designation shall be made as a regulation upon public notice and in accordance with the procedure set forth in section 4 of the Administrative Procedure Act (5 U.S.C. 1003).

(d) After each such review, and at such other times as the Secretary may determine to be necessary or desirable, the Secretary shall cause to be compiled, published, and publicly distributed a list which shall list all revised official names of drugs designated under this section and shall contain such descriptive and explanatory matter as the Secretary may determine to be required for the effective use of those names.

(e) Upon a request in writing by any compiler of an official compendium that the Secretary exercise the authority granted to him under section 508(a), he shall upon public notice and in accordance with the procedure set forth in section 4 of the Administrative Procedure Act (5 U.S.C. 1003) designate the official name of the drug for which the request is made.

NONAPPLICABILITY TO COSMETICS

SEC. 509 [359]. This chapter, as amended by the Drug Amendments of 1962, shall not apply to any cosmetic unless such cosmetic is also a drug or device or component thereof.

REGISTRATION OF PRODUCERS AND CERTAIN WHOLESALERS
OF DRUGS [26]

SEC. 510 [360]. (a) As used in this section—

(1) the term "manufacture, preparation, propagation, compounding, or processing" shall include repackaging or otherwise changing the container, wrapper, or labeling of any drug package in furtherance of the distribution of the drug from the original place of manufacture to the person who makes final delivery or sale to the ultimate consumer;

(2) the term "wholesaling, jobbing, or distributing of depressant or stimulant drugs" means the selling or distribution of any depressant or stimulant drug to any person who is not the ultimate user or consumer of such drug; and

(3) the term "name" shall include in the case of a partnership the name of each partner and, in the case of a corporation, the name of each corporate officer and director, and the State of incorporation.

(b) On or before December 31 of each year every person who owns or operates any establishment in any State engaged in the manufacture, preparation, propagation, compounding, or processing of a drug or drugs or in the wholesaling, jobbing, or distributing of any depressant or stimulant drug shall register with the Secretary his name, places of business, and all such establishments. If any such establishment is engaged in the manufacture, preparation, propagation, compounding, or processing of any depressant or stimulant drug, such person shall, at the time of such registration, indicate such fact, in such manner as the Secretary may by regulation prescribe.

(c) Every person upon first engaging in the manufacture, preparation, propagation, compounding, or processing of a drug or drugs or in the wholesaling, jobbing, or distributing of any depressant or stimulant drug in any establishment which he owns or operates in any State shall immediately register with the Secretary his name, place of business, and such establishment. If such establishment is engaged in the manufacture, preparation, propagation, compounding, or processing of any depressant or stimulant drug such person shall, at the time of such registration, indicate such fact, in such manner as the Secretary may by regulation prescribe.

(d) (1) Every person duly registered in accordance with the foregoing subsections of this section shall immediately register with the Secretary any additional establishment which he owns or operates in any State and in which he begins the manufacture, preparation, propagation, compounding, or processing of a drug or drugs or the wholesaling, jobbing, or distributing of any depressant or stimulant drug. If any depressant or stimulant drug is manufactured, prepared, propagated, compounded, or processed in such additional establishment, such person shall, at the time of such registration, indicate such fact, in such manner as the Secretary may by regulation prescribe.

(2) Every person who is registered with the Secretary pursuant to the first sentence of subsection (b) or (c) or paragraph (1) of this subsection, but to whom the second sentence of subsection (b) or (c)

[26] The Congress hereby finds and declares that in order to make regulation of interstate commerce in drugs effective, it is necessary to provide for registration and inspection of all establishments in which drugs are manufactured, prepared, propagated, compounded, or processed; that the products of all such establishments are likely to enter the channels of interstate commerce and directly affect such commerce; and that the regulation of interstate commerce in drugs without provision for registration and inspection of establishments that may be engaged only in intrastate commerce in such drugs would discriminate against and depress interstate commerce in such drugs, and adversely burden, obstruct, and affect such interstate commerce.

or of paragraph (1) of this subsection did not apply at the time of such registration, shall, if any depressant or stimulant drug is thereafter manufactured, prepared, propagated, compounded, or processed in any establishment with respect to which he is so registered, immediately file a supplement to such registration with the Secretary indicating such fact, in such manner as the Secretary may by regulation prescribe.

(e) The Secretary may assign a registration number to any person or any establishment registered in accordance with this section.

(f) The Secretary shall make available for inspection, to any person so requesting, any registration filed pursuant to this section.

(g) The foregoing subsections of this section shall not apply to—

(1) pharmacies which maintain establishments in conformance with any applicable local laws regulating the practice of pharmacy and medicine and which are regularly engaged in dispensing prescription drugs, upon prescriptions of practitioners licensed to administer such drugs to patients under the care of such practitioners in the course of their professional practice, and which do not manufacture, prepare, propagate, compound, or process drugs for sale other than in the regular course of their business of dispensing or selling drugs at retail;

(2) practitioners licensed by law to prescribe or administer drugs and who manufacture, prepare, propagate, compound, or process drugs solely for use in the course of their professional practice;

(3) persons who manufacture, prepare, propagate, compound, or process drugs solely for use in research, teaching, or chemical analysis and not for sale;

(4) such other classes of persons as the Secretary may by regulation [27] exempt from the application of this section upon a finding that registration by such classes of persons in accordance with this section is not necessary for the protection of the public health.

(h) Every establishment in any State registered with the Secretary pursuant to this section shall be subject to inspection pursuant to section 704 and shall be so inspected by one or more officers or employees duly designated by the Secretary at least once in the two-year period beginning with the date of registration of such establishment pursuant to this section and at least once in every successive two-year period thereafter.

(i) Any establishment within any foreign country engaged in the manufacture, preparation, propagation, compounding, or processing of a drug or drugs shall be permitted to register under this section pursuant to regulations promulgated by the Secretary. Such regulations shall include provisions for registration of any such establishment upon condition that adequate and effective means are available, by arrangement with the government of such foreign country or otherwise, to enable the Secretary to determine from time to time whether drugs manufactured, prepared, propagated, compounded, or processed in such establishment, if imported or offered for import into the United States, shall be refused admission on any of the grounds set forth in section 801(a) of this Act.

---

[27] F.D.C. Regs., part 132.

DEPRESSANT AND STIMULANT DRUGS

SEC. 511 [360a]. (a) No person shall manufacture, compound, or process any depressant or stimulant drug, except that this prohibition shall not apply to the following persons whose activities in connection with any such drug are solely as specified in this subsection:

(1)(A) Manufacturers, compounders, and processors registered under section 510 who are regularly engaged, and are otherwise qualified, in conformance with local laws, in preparing pharmaceutical chemicals or prescription drugs for distribution through branch outlets, through wholesale druggists, or by direct shipment, (i) to pharmacies or to hospitals, clinics, public health agencies, or physicians, for dispensing by registered pharmacists upon prescriptions, or for use by or under the supervision of practitioners licensed by law to administer such drugs in the course of their professional practice, or (ii) to laboratories or research or educational institutions for their use in research, teaching, or chemical analysis.

(B) Suppliers (otherwise qualified in conformance with local laws) of manufacturers, compounders, and processors referred to in subparagraph (A).

(2) Wholesale druggists registered under section 510 who maintain establishments in conformance with local laws and are regularly engaged in supplying prescription drugs (A) to pharmacies, or to hospitals, clinics, public health agencies, or physicians, for dispensing by registered pharmacists upon prescriptions, or for use by or under the supervision of practitioners licensed by law to administer such drugs in the course of their professional practice, or (B) to laboratories or research or educational institutions for their use in research, teaching, or clinical analysis.

(3) Pharmacies, hospitals, clinics, and public health agencies, which maintain establishments in conformance with any applicable local laws regulating the practice of pharmacy and medicine and which are regularly engaged in dispensing prescription drugs upon prescriptions of practitioners licensed to administer such drugs for patients under the care of such practitioners in the course of their professional practice.

(4) Practitioners licensed by law to prescribe or administer depressant or stimulant drugs, while acting in the course of their professional practice.

(5) Persons who use depressant or stimulant drugs in research, teaching, or chemical analysis and not for sale.

(6) Officers and employees of the United States, a State government, or a political subdivision of a State, while acting in the course of their official duties.

(7) An employee or agent of any person described in paragraph (1) through paragraph (5), and a nurse or other medical technician under the supervision of a practitioner licensed by law to administer depressant or stimulant drugs, while such employee, nurse, or medical technician is acting in the course of his employment or occupation and not on his own account.

(b) No person, other than—

(1) a person described in subsection (a), while such person is acting in the ordinary and authorized course of his business,

profession, occupation, or employment, or

(2) a common or contract carrier or warehouseman, or an employee thereof, whose possession of any depressant or stimulant drug is in the usual course of his business or employment as such, shall sell, deliver, or otherwise dispose of any depressant or stimulant drug to any other person.

(c) No person, other than a person described in subsection (a) or subsection (b)(2), shall possess any depressant or stimulant drug otherwise than (1) for the personal use of himself or of a member of his household, or (2) for administration to an animal owned by him or a member of his household. In any criminal prosecution for possession of a depressant or stimulant drug in violation of this subsection (which is made a prohibited act by section 301(q)(3), the United States shall have the burden of proof that the possession involved does not come within the exceptions contained in clauses (1) and (2) of the preceding sentence.

(d)(1) Every person engaged in manufacturing, compounding, processing, selling, delivering, or otherwise disposing of any depressant or stimulant drug shall, upon the effective date of this section, prepare a complete and accurate record of all stocks of each such drug on hand and shall keep such record for three years. On and after the effective date of this section, every person manufacturing, compounding, or processing any depressant or stimulant drug shall prepare and keep, for not less than three years, a complete and accurate record of the kind and quantity of each such drug manufactured, compounded, or processed and the date of such manufacture, compounding, or processing; and every person selling, delivering, or otherwise disposing of any depressant or stimulant drug shall prepare or obtain, and keep for not less than three years, a complete and accurate record of the kind and quantity of each such drug received, sold, delivered, or otherwise disposed of, the name and address of the person, and the registration number, if any, assigned to such person by the Secretary pursuant to section 510(e), from whom it was received and to whom it was sold, delivered, or otherwise disposed of, and the date of such transaction. No separate records, nor set form or forms for any of the foregoing records, shall be required as long as records containing the required information are available.

(2)(A) Every person required by paragraph (1) of this subsection to prepare or obtain, and keep, records, and any carrier maintaining records with respect to any shipment containing any depressant or stimulant drug, and every person in charge, or having custody, of such records, shall, upon request of an officer or employee designated by the Secretary permit such officer or employee at reasonable times to have access to and copy such records. For the puposes of verification of such records and of enforcement of this section, officers or employees designated by the Secretary are authorized, upon presenting appropriate credentials and a written notice to the owner, operator, or agent in charge, to enter, at reasonable times, any factory, warehouse, establishment, or vehicle in which any depressant or stimulant drug is held, manufactured, compounded, processed, sold, delivered, or otherwise disposed of and to inspect, within reasonable limits and in a reasonable manner, such factory, warehouse, establishment, or vehicle, and all pertinent equipment, finished and unfinished material, containers and labeling therein, and all things therein (including records, files, papers, processes, controls, and facilities) bearing on violation of this section or section 301(q); and to inventory any stock of any such drug therein and obtain samples of any such drug. If a sample is thus obtained, the officer or employee making the inspection shall, upon completion of the inspection and before leaving the premises, give to the owner, operator, or agent in charge a receipt describing the sample obtained.

(B) No inspection authorized by subparagraph (A) shall extend to (i) financial data, (ii) sales data other than shipment data, (iii) pricing data, (iv) personnel data, or (v) research data, which are exempted from inspection under the third sentence of section 704(a) of this Act.

(3) The provisions of paragraphs (1) and (2) of this subsection shall not apply to a licensed practitioner described in subsection (a)(4) with respect to any depressant or stimulant drug received, prepared, processed, administered, or dispensed by him in the course of his professional practice, unless such practitioner regularly engages in dispensing any such drug or drugs to his patients for which they are charged, either separately or together with charges for other professional services.

(e) No prescription (issued before or after the effective date of this section) for any depressant or stimulant drug may be filled or refilled more than six months after the date on which such prescription was issued and no such prescription which is authorized to be refilled may be refilled more than five times, except that any prescription for such a drug after six months after the date of issue or after being refilled five times may be renewed by the practitioner issuing it either in writing, or orally (if promptly reduced to writing and filed by the pharmacist filling it).

(f)(1) The Secretary may by regulation exempt any depressant or stimulant drug from the application of all or part of this section when he finds that regulation of its manufacture, compounding, processing, possession, and disposition, as provided in this section or in such part thereof, is not necessary for the protection of the public health.

(2) The Secretary shall by regulation exempt any depressant or stimulant drug from the application of this section, if—

(A) such drug may, under the provisions of this Act, be sold over the counter without a prescription; or

(B) he finds that such drug includes one or more substances not having a depressant or stimulant effect on the central nervous system or a hallucinogenic effect and such substance or substances are present therein in such combination, quantity, proportion, or concentration as to prevent the substance or substances therein which do have such an effect from being ingested or absorbed in sufficient amounts or concentrations as, within the meaning of section 201(v), to—

(i) be habit-forming because of their stimulant effect on the central nervous system, or

(ii) have a potential for abuse because of their depressant or stimulant effect on the central nervous system or their hallucinogenic effect.

(g)(1) The Secretary may, from time to time, appoint a committee of experts to advise him with regard to any of the following matters involved in determining whether a regulation under subparagraph (2)(C) or (3) of section 201(v) should be proposed, issued, amended, or repealed: (A) whether or not the substance involved has a depressant or stimulant effect on the central nervous system or a hallucinogenic effect, (B) whether the substance involved has a potential for abuse because of its depressant or stimulant effect on the central nervous system, and (C) any other scientific question (as determined by the Secretary) which is pertinent to the determination of whether such substance should be designated by the Secretary pursuant to subparagraph (2)(C) or (3) of section 201(v). The Secretary may establish a time limit for submission of the committee's report. The appointment, compensation, staffing, and procedure of such committees shall be in accordance with subsections (b)(5)(D), and the admissibility of their reports, recommendations, and testimony at any hearing involving such matters shall be determined in accordance with subsection (d)(2), of section 706. The appointment of such a committee after publication of an order acting on a proposal pursuant to section 701(e)(1) shall not suspend the running of the time for filing objections to such order and requesting a hearing unless the Secretary so directs.

(2) Where such a matter is referred to an expert advisory committee upon request of an interested person, the Secretary may, pursuant to regulations, require such person to pay fees to pay the costs, to the Department, arising by reason of such referral. Such fees, including advance deposits to cover such fees, shall be available, until expended, for paying (directly or by way of reimbursement of the applicable appropriations) the expenses of advisory committees under this subsection and other expenses arising by reason of referrals to such committees and for refunds in accordance with such regulations.

(h) As used in this section and in sections 301 and 304, the term "manufacture, compound, or process" shall be deemed to refer to "manufacture, preparation, propagation, compounding, or processing" as defined in section 510(a), and the term "manufacturers, compounders, and processors" shall be deemed to refer to persons engaged in such defined activities.

[Sec. 10 and sec. 11 of Public Law 89–74, the Drug Abuse Control Amendments of 1965, enacted July 15, 1965, follow:

APPLICATION OF STATE LAW

(a) Nothing in this Act shall be construed as authorizing the manufacture, compounding, processing, possession, sale, delivery, or other disposal of any drug in any State in contravention of the laws of such State.

(b) No provision of this Act nor any amendment made by it shall be construed as indicating an intent on the part of the Congress to occupy the field in which such provision or amendment operates to the exclusion of any State law on the same subject matter, unless there is a direct and positive conflict between such provision or amendment and such State law so that the two cannot be reconciled or consistently stand together.

(c) No amendment made by this Act shall be construed to prevent the enforcement in the courts of any State of any statute of such State prescribing any criminal penalty for any act made criminal by any such amendment.

The foregoing provisions of this Act shall take effect on the first day of the seventh calendar month following the month in which this Act is enacted; except that (1) the Secretary shall permit persons, owning or operating any establishment engaged in manufacturing, preparing, propagating, compounding, processing, wholesaling, jobbing, or distributing any depressant or stimulant drug, as referred to in the amendments made by section 4 of this Act to section 510 of the Federal Food, Drug, and Cosmetic Act, to register their names, places of business, and establishments, and other information prescribed by such amendments, with the Secretary prior to such effective date, and (2) sections 201(v) and 511(g) of the Federal Food, Drug, and Cosmetic Act, as added by this Act, and the provisions of sections 8 and 10 shall take effect upon the date of enactment of this Act.

Approved July 15, 1965.]

NEW ANIMAL DRUGS

SEC. 512 [360b]. (a) (1) A new animal drug shall, with respect to any particular use or intended use of such drug, be deemed unsafe for the purposes of section 501(a) (5) and section 402(a) (2) (D) unless—

(A) there is in effect an approval of an application filed pursuant to subsection (b) of this section with respect to such use or intended use of such drug,

(B) such drug, its labeling, and such use conform to such approved application, and

(C) in the case of a new animal drug subject to subection (n) of this section and not exempted therefrom by regulations it is from a batch with respect to which a certificate or release issued pursuant to subsection (n) is in effect with respect to such drug.

A new animal drug shall also be deemed unsafe for such purposes in the event of removal from the establishment of a manufacturer, packer, or distributor of such drug for use in the manufacture of animal feed in any State unless at the time of such removal such manufacturer, packer, or distributor has an unrevoked written statement from the consignee of such drug, or notice from the Secretary, to the effect that, with respect to the use of such drug in animal feed, such consignee—

(i) is the holder of an approved application under subsection (m) of this section; or

(ii) will, if the consignee is not a user of the drug, ship such drug only to a holder of an approved application under subsection (m) of this section.

(2) An animal feed bearing or containing a new animal drug shall, with respect to any particular use or intended use of such animal feed, be deemed unsafe for the purposes of section 501(a) (6) unless—

(A) there is in effect an approval of an application filed pursuant to subsection (b) of this section with respect to such drug, as used in such animal feed,

(B) there is in effect an approval of an application pursuant to subsection (m) (1) of this section with respect to such animal feed, and

(C) such animal feed, its labeling, and such use conform to the conditions and indications of use published to subsection (i) of this section and to the application with respect thereto approved under subsection (m) of this section.

(3) A new animal drug or an animal feed bearing or containing a new animal drug shall not be deemed unsafe for the purposes of section 501(a) (5) or (6) if such article is for investigational use and conforms to the terms of an exemption in effect with respect thereto under section 512(j).

(b) Any person may file with the Secretary an application with respect to any intended use or uses of a new animal drug. Such person shall submit to the Secretary as a part of the application (1) full reports of investigations which have been made to show whether or not such drug is safe and effective for use; (2) a full list of the articles used as components of such drug; (3) a full statement of the composition of such drug; (4) a full description of the methods used in, and the facilities and controls used for, the manufacture, processing, and packing of such drugs; (5) such samples of such drugs and of the articles used as components thereof, of any animal feed for use in or on which such drug is intended, and of the edible portions or products (before or after slaughter) of animals to which such drug (directly or in or on animal feed) is intended to be administered, as the Secretary may require; (6) specimens of the labeling proposed to be used for such drugs, or in case such drug is intended for use in animal feed, proposed labeling appropriate for such use, and specimens of the labeling for the drug to be manufactured, packed, or distributed by the applicant; (7) a description of practicable methods for determining the quantity, if any, of such drug in or on food, and any substance found in or on food, because of its use; and (8) the proposed tolerance or withdrawal period or other use restrictions for such drug if any tolerance or withdrawal period or other use restrictions are required in order to assure that the proposed use of such drug will be safe.

(c) Within one hundred and eighty days after the filing of an application pursuant to subsection (b), or such additional period as may be agreed upon by the Secretary and the applicant, the Secretary shall either (1) issue an order approving the application if he then finds that none of the grounds for denying approval specified in subsection (d) applies, or (2) give the applicant notice of an opportunity for a hearing before the Secretary under subsection (d) on the question whether such application is approvable. If the applicant elects to accept the opportunity for a hearing by written request within thirty days after such notice, such hearing shall commence not more than ninety days after the expiration of such thirty days unless the Secretary and the applicant otherwise agree. Any such hearing shall thereafter be conducted on an expedited basis and the Secretary's order thereon shall be issued within ninety days after the date fixed by the Secretary for filing final briefs.

(d)(1) If the Secretary finds, after due notice to the applicant in accordance with subsection (c) and giving him an opportunity for a hearing, in accordance with said subsection, that—

(A) the investigations, reports of which are required to be submitted to the Secretary pursuant to subsection (b), do not include adequate tests by all methods reasonably applicable to show whether or not such drug is safe for use under the conditions prescribed, recommended, or suggested in the proposed labeling thereof;

(B) the results of such tests show that such drug is unsafe for use under such conditions or do not show that such drug is safe for use under such conditions;

(C) the methods used in, and the facilities and controls used for, the manufacture, processing, and packing of such drug are inadequate to preserve its identity, strength, quality, and purity;

(D) upon the basis of the information submitted to him as part of the application, or upon the basis of any other information before him with respect to such drug, he has insufficient information to determine whether such drug is safe for use under such conditions;

(E) evaluated on the basis of the information submitted to him as part of the application and any other information before him with respect to such drug, there is a lack of substantial evidence that the drug will have the effect it purports or is represented to have under the conditions of use prescribed, recommended, or suggested in the proposed labeling thereof;

(F) upon the basis of the information submitted to him as part of the application or any other information before him with respect to such drug, the tolerance limitation proposed, if any, exceeds that reasonably required to accomplish the physical or other technical effect for which the drug is intended;

(G) based on a fair evaluation of all material facts, such labeling is false or misleading in any particular; or

(H) such drug induces cancer when ingested by man or animal or, after tests which are appropriate for the evaluation of the safety of such drug, induces cancer in man or animal, except that the foregoing provisions of this subparagraph shall not apply with respect to such drug if the Secretary finds that, under the conditions of use specified in proposed labeling and reasonably certain to be followed in practice (i) such drug will not adversely affect the animals for which it is intended, and (ii) no residue of such drug will be found (by methods of examination prescribed or approved by the Secretary by regulations, which regulations shall not be subject to subsections (c), (d), and (h)), in any edible portion of such animals after slaughter or in any food yielded by or derived from the living animal;

he shall issue an order refusing to approve the application. If, after such notice and opportunity for hearing, the Secretary finds that subparagraphs (A) through (H) do not apply, he shall issue an order approving the application.

(2) In determining whether such drug is safe for use under the conditions prescribed, recommended, or suggested in the proposed labeling thereof, the Secretary shall consider, among other relevant factors, (A) the probable consumption of such drug and of any substance formed in or on food because of the use of such drug, (B) the cumulative effect on man or animal of such drug, taking into account any chemically or pharmacologically related substance, (C) safety factors which in the opinion of experts, qualified by scientific training and experience to evaluate the safety of such drugs, are appropriate for the use of animal experimentation data, and (D) whether the conditions of use prescribed, recommended, or suggested in the proposed labeling are reasonably certain to be followed in practice. Any order

issued under this subsection refusing to approve an application shall state the findings upon which it is based.

(3) As used in this subsection and subsection (e), the term "substantial evidence" means evidence consisting of adequate and well-controlled investigations, including field investigation, by experts qualified by scientific training and experience to evaluate the effectiveness of the drug involved, on the basis of which it could fairly and responsibly be concluded by such experts that the drug will have the effect it purports or is represented to have under the conditions of use prescribed, recommended, or suggested in the labeling or proposed labeling thereof.

(e) (1) The Secretary shall, after due notice and opportunity for hearing to the applicant issue an order withdrawing approval of an application filed pursuant to subsection (b) with respect to any new animal drug if the Secretary finds—

(A) that experience or scientific data show that such drug is unsafe for use under the conditions of use upon the basis of which the application was approved;

(B) that new evidence not contained in such application or not available to the Secretary until after such application was approved, or tests by new methods, or tests by methods not deemed reasonably applicable when such application was approved, evaluated together with the evidence available to the Secretary when the application was approved, shows that such drug is not shown to be safe for use under the conditions of use upon the basis of which the application was approved or that subparagraph (H) of paragraph (1) of subsection (d) applies to such drug;

(C) on the basis of new information before him with respect to such drug, evaluated together with the evidence available to him when the application was approved, that there is a lack of substantial evidence that such drug will have the effect it purports or is represented to have under the conditions of use prescribed, recommended, or suggested in the labeling thereof;

(D) that the application contains any untrue statement of a material fact; or

(E) that the applicant has made any changes from the standpoint of safety or effectiveness beyond the variation provided for in the application unless he has supplemented the application by filing with the Secretary adequate information respecting all such changes and unless there is in effect an approval of the supplemental application. The supplemental application shall be treated in the same manner as the original application.

If the Secretary (or in his absence the officer acting as Secretary) finds that there is an imminent hazard to the health of man or of the animals for which such drug is intended, he may suspend the approval of such application immediately, and give the applicant prompt notice of his action and afford the applicant the opportunity for an expedited hearing under this subsection; but the authority conferred by this sentence to suspend the approval of an application shall not be delegated.

(2) The Secretary may also, after due notice and opportunity for hearing to the applicant, issue an order withdrawing the approval of an application with respect to any new animal drug under this section if the Secretary finds—

10

(A) that the applicant has failed to establish a system for maintaining required records, or has repeatedly or deliberately failed to maintain such records or to make required reports in accordance with a regulation or order under subsection (1), or the applicant has refused to permit access to, or copying or verification of, such records as required by paragraph (2) of such subsection;

(B) that on the basis of new information before him, evaluated together with the evidence before him when the application was approved, the methods used in, or the facilities and controls used for, the manufacture, processing, and packing of such drug are inadequate to assure and preserve its identity, strength, quality, and purity and were not made adequate within a reasonable time after receipt of written notice from the Secretary specifying the matter complained of; or

(C) that on the basis of new information before him, evaluated together with the evidence before him when the application was approved, the labeling of such drug, based on a fair evaluation of all material facts, is false or misleading in any particular and was not corrected within a reasonable time after receipt of written notice from the Secretary specifying the matter complained of.

(3) Any order under this subsection shall state the findings upon which it is based.

(f) Whenever the Secretary finds that the facts so require, he shall revoke any previous order under subsection (d), (e), or (m) refusing, withdrawing, or suspending approval of an application and shall approve such application or reinstate such approval, as may be appropriate.

(g) Orders of the Secretary issued under this section (other than orders issuing, amending, or repealing regulations) shall be served (1) in person by any officer or employee of the department designated by the Secretary or (2) by mailing the order by registered mail or by certified mail addressed to the applicant or respondent at his last known address in the records of the Secretary.

(h) An appeal may be taken by the applicant from an order of the Secretary refusing or withdrawing approval of an application filed under subsection (b) or (m) of this section. The provisions of subsection (h) of section 505 of this Act shall govern any such appeal.

(i) When a new animal drug application filed pursuant to subsection (b) is approved, the Secretary shall by notice, which upon publication shall be effective as a regulation, publish in the Federal Register the name and address of the applicant and the conditions and indications of use of the new animal drug covered by such application, including any tolerance and withdrawal period or other use restrictions and, if such new animal drug is intended for use in animal feed, appropriate purposes and conditions of use (including special labeling requirements) applicable to any animal feed for use in which such drug is approved, and such other information, upon the basis of which such application was approved, as the Secretary deems necessary to assure, the safe and effective use of such drug. Upon withdrawal of approval of such new animal drug application or upon its suspension, the Secretary shall forthwith revoke or suspend, as the case may be, the regulation published pursuant to this subsection (i) insofar as it is based on the approval of such application.

(j) To the extent consistent with the public health, the Secretary shall promulgate regulations for exempting from the operation of this section new animal drugs, and animal feeds bearing or containing new animal drugs, intended solely for investigational use by experts qualified by scientific training and experience to investigate the safety and effectiveness of animal drugs. Such regulations may, in the discretion of the Secretary, among other conditions relating to the protection of the public health, provide for conditioning such exemption upon the establishment and maintenance of such records, and the making of such reports to the Secretary, by the manufacturer or the sponsor of the investigation of such article, of data (including but not limited to analytical reports by investigators) obtained as a result of such investigational use of such article, as the Secretary finds will enable him to evaluate the safety and effectiveness of such article in the event of the filing of an application pursuant to this section. Such regulations, among other things, shall set forth the conditions (if any) upon which animals treated with such articles, and any products of such animals (before or after slaughter), may be marketed for food use.

(k) While approval of an application for a new animal drug is effective, a food shall not, by reason of bearing or containing such drug or any substance formed in or on the food because of its use in accordance with such application (including the conditions and indications of use prescribed pursuant to subsection (i)), be considered adulterated within the meaning of clause (1) of section 402(a).

(l) (1) In the case of any new animal drug for which an approval of an application filed pursuant to subsection (b) is in effect, the applicant shall establish and maintain such records, and make such reports to the Secretary, of data relating to experience and other data or information, received or otherwise obtained by such applicant with respect to such drug, or with respect to animal feeds bearing or containing such drug, as the Secretary may by general regulation, or by order with respect to such application, prescribe on the basis of a finding that such records and reports are necessary in order to enable the Secretary to determine, or facilitate a determination, whether there is or may be ground for invoking subsection (e) or subsection (m) (4) of this section. Such regulation or order shall provide, where the Secretary deems it to be appropriate, for the examination, upon request by the persons to whom such regulation or order is applicable, of similar information received or otherwise obtained by the Secretary.

(2) Every person required under this subsection to maintain records, and every person in charge or custody thereof, shall, upon request of an officer or employee designated by the Secretary, permit such officer or employee at all reasonable times to have access to and copy and verify such records.

(m) (1) Any person may file with the Secretary an application with respect to any intended use or uses of an animal feed bearing or containing a new animal drug. Such person shall submit to the Secretary as part of the application (A) a full statement of the composition of such animal feed, (B) an identification of the regulation or regulations (relating to the new animal drug or drugs to be used in such feed), published pursuant to subsection (i), on which he relies as a basis for approval of his application with respect to the use of such drug in such feed, (C) a full description of the methods used in, and the facilities and controls used for, the manufacture, processing, and packing of such animal feed, (D) specimens of the labeling proposed to be used for such animal feed, and (E) if so requested by the Secretary, samples of such animal feed or components thereof.

(2) Within ninety days after the filing of an application pursuant to subsection (m)(1), or such additional period as may be agreed upon by the Secretary and the applicant, the Secretary shall either (A) issue an order approving the application if he then finds that none of the grounds for denying approval specified in paragraph (3) applies, or (B) give the applicant notice of an opportunity for a hearing before the Secretary under paragraph (3) on the question whether such application is approvable. The procedure governing such a hearing shall be the procedure set forth in the last two sentences of subsection (c).

(3) If the Secretary, after due notice to the applicant in accordance with paragraph (2) and giving him an opportunity for a hearing in accordance with such paragraph, finds, on the basis of information submitted to him as part of the application or on the basis of any other information before him—

(A) that there is not in effect a regulation under subsection (i) (identified in such application) on the basis of which such application may be approved;

(B) that such animal feed (including the proposed use of any new animal drug therein or thereon) does not conform to an applicable regulation published pursuant to subsection (i) referred to in the application, or that the purposes and conditions, or indications of use prescribed, recommended, or suggested in the labeling of such feed do not conform to the applicable purposes and conditions or indications of use (including warnings) published pursuant to subsection (i) or such labeling omits or fails to conform to other applicable information published pursuant to subsection (i);

(C) that the methods used in, and the facilities and controls used for, the manufacture, processing, and packing of such animal feed are inadequate to preserve the identity, strength, quality, and purity of the new animal drug therein; or

(D) that, based on a fair evaluation of all material facts, such labeling is false or misleading in any particular;

he shall issue an order refusing to approve the application. If, after such notice and opportunity for hearing, the Secretary finds that subparagraphs (A) through (D) do not apply, he shall issue an order approving the application. An order under this subsection approving an application with respect to an animal feed bearing or containing a new animal drug shall be effective only while there is in effect a regulation pursuant to subsection (i), on the basis of which such application (or a supplement thereto) was approved, relating to the use of such drug in or on such feed.

(4)(A) The Secretary shall, after due notice and opportunity for hearing to the applicant, issue an order withdrawing approval of an application with respect to any animal feed under this subsection if the Secretary finds—

(i) that the application contains any untrue statement of a material fact; or

(ii) that the applicant has made any changes from the standpoint of safety or effectiveness beyond the variations provided for in the application unless he has supplemented the application by filing with the Secretary adequate information respecting all such changes and unless there is in effect an approval of the supplemental application. The supplemental application shall be treated in the same manner as the original application.

If the Secretary (or in his absence the officer acting as Secretary) finds that there is an imminent hazard to the health of man or of the animals for which such animal feed is intended, he may suspend the approval of such application immediately, and give the applicant prompt notice of his action and afford the applicant the opportunity for an expedited hearing under this subsection; but the authority conferred by this sentence shall not be delegated.

(B) The Secretary may also, after due notice and opportunity for hearing to the applicant, issue an order withdrawing the approval of an application with respect to any animal feed under this subsection if the Secretary finds—

(i) that the applicant has failed to establish a system for maintaining required records, or has repeatedly or deliberately failed to maintain such records or to make required reports in accordance with a regulation or order under paragraph (5)(A) of this subsection, or the applicant has refused to permit access to, or copying or verification of, such records as required by subparagraph (B) of such paragraph;

(ii) that on the basis of new information before him, evaluated together with the evidence before him when such application was approved, the methods used in, or the facilities and controls used for, the manufacture, processing, and packing of such animal feed are inadequate to assure and preserve the identity, strength, quality, and purity of the new animal drug therein, and were not made adequate within a reasonable time after receipt of written notice from the Secretary, specifying the matter complained of; or

(iii) that on the basis of new information before him, evaluated together with the evidence before him when the application was approved, the labeling of such animal feed, based on a fair evaluation of all material facts, is false or misleading in any particular and was not corrected within a reasonable time after receipt of written notice from the Secretary specifying the matter complained of.

(C) Any order under paragraph (4) of this subsection shall state the findings upon which it is based.

(5) In the case of any animal feed for which an approval of an application filed pursuant to this subsection is in effect—

(A) the applicant shall establish and maintain such records, and make such reports to the Secretary, or (at the option of the Secretary) to the appropriate person or persons holding an approved application filed under subsection (b), as the Secretary may by general regulation, or by order with respect to such application, prescribe on the basis of a finding that such records and reports are necessary in order to enable the Secretary to determine, or facilitate a determination, whether there is or may be ground for invoking subsection (e) or paragraph (4) of this subsection.

(B) every person required under this subsection to maintain records, and every person in charge or custody thereof, shall, upon request of an officer or employee designated by the Secretary, permit such officer or employee at all reasonable times to have access to and copy and verify such records.

(n) (1) The Secretary, pursuant to regulations promulgated by him, shall provide for the certification of batches of a new animal drug composed wholly or partly of any kind of penicillin, streptomycin, chlortetracycline, chloramphenicol, or bacitracin, or any derivative thereof. A batch of any such drug shall be certified if an approval of an application filed pursuant to subsection (b) is effective with respect to such drug and such drug has the characteristics of identity and such batch has the characteristics of strength, quality, and purity upon the basis of which the application was approved, but shall not otherwise be certified. Prior to the effective date of such regulations the Secretary, in lieu of certification, shall issue a release for any batch which, in his judgment, may be released without risk as to the safety and efficacy of its use. Such release shall prescribe the date of its expiration and other conditions under which it shall cease to be effective as to such batch and as to portions thereof.

(2) Regulations providing for such certifications shall contain such provisions as are necessary to carry out the purposes of this subsection, including provisions prescribing—

(A) tests and methods of assay to determine compliance with applicable standards of identity and of strength, quality, and purity;

(B) effective periods for certificates, and other conditions under which they shall cease to be effective as to certified batches and as to portions thereof;

(C) administration and procedure; and

(D) such fees, specified in such regulations, as are necessary to provide, equip, and maintain an adequate certification service.

Such regulations shall prescribe only such tests and methods of assay as will provide for certification or rejection within the shortest time consistent with the purposes of this subsection.

(3) Whenever, in the judgment of the Secretary, the requirements of this subsection with respect to any drug or class of drugs are not necessary to insure that such drug conforms to the standards of identity, strength, quality, and purity applicable thereto under paragraph (1) of this subsection, the Secretary shall promulgate regulations exempting such drug or class of drugs from such requirements. The provisions of subsection (c) of section 507 of this Act (other than the first sentence thereof) shall apply under this paragraph.

(4) The Secretary shall promulgate regulations exempting from any requirement of this subsection—

(A) drugs which are to be stored, processed, labeled, or repacked at establishments other than those where manufactured, on condition that such drugs comply with all such requirements upon removal from such establishments; and

(B) drugs which conform to applicable standards of identity, strength, quality, and purity prescribed pursuant to this subsection and are intended for use in manufacturing other drugs.

(5) On petition of any interested person for the issuance, amend-

ment, or repeal of any regulation contemplated by this subsection, the procedure shall be in accordance with subsection (f) of section 507 of this Act.

(6) Where any drug is subject to this subsection and not exempted therefrom by regulations, the compliance of such drug with sections 501(b) and 502(g) shall be determined by the application of the standards of strength, quality, and purity applicable under paragraph (1) of this subsection, the tests and methods of assay applicable under provisions of regulations referred to in paragraph (2)(A) of this subsection, and the requirements of packaging and labeling on the basis of which the application with respect to such drug filed under subsection (b) of this section was approved.

Glossary

Administrator: (legal), one appointed by a probate court to settle the estate of a decedent.

Answer: (legal), a defendant's written response to a complaint against him.

Appellee: a party against whom a cause is appealed from a lower to a higher court.

Assault: an intentional force unlawfully directed toward the person of another.

Attachment: (legal), the taking of property into legal custody by an officer of the law, by virtue of a writ of attachment.

Bailee: one who takes another's property into his care and custody.

Bailment: a delivery of personal property by one person to another, in trust for a specific purpose, to be returned when the trust is accomplished.

Battery: (legal), the unlawful touching of the person of another by an aggressor.

Bill of particulars: an itemized statement of accounts or matters, generally pleaded, in a civil action.

Binder: a temporary policy of insurance.

Bona fide: with good faith.

Burden of proof: the duty of establishing the truth of a given proposition by sufficient evidence.

Calendar: (legal), a list of causes of action arranged for trial in court.

Case law: the law as laid down in the cases which have been decided.

Cause: (legal), a suit or action in court.

Caveat emptor: "let the buyer beware."

Certification: a formal attestation of a matter of fact.

Certiorari, writ of: an order commanding the return of the record of a cause pending before the court, so that the party may have a review of the proceedings.

Challenge for cause: a challenge to a juror for some matter which imports bias on his/her part.

Charging lien: a lien which a lawyer has on the judgment, decree or award obtained by him for his client, for his services rendered in obtaining it.

Circumstantial evidence: proof by circumstances surrounding the transaction.

Civil remedy: a remedy obtained as the result of an action brought by an individual for a private right.

Collateral: additional security for the performance of a principal obligation.

Common law: that body of unwritten law founded on custom, natural justice and reason and sanctioned by usage and judicial decisions.

Comparative negligence: the degree of negligence in which each of the parties may be shown to have been responsible for the injury complained of.

Complaint: a legal process charging a party with a wrong done or a crime committed.

Confidential communication: a statement made to a doctor, lawyer or clergyman in confidence and impliedly understood that it shall remain a secret.

Contempt of court: conduct which tends to show disrespect for the judicial process.

Consideration: the benefit as involved in a contract.

Constructive notice: notice imputed to a person not having actual notice.

Contributory negligence: negligence on the part of the plaintiff which results in injury to his person or property.

Conversion: (legal), a wrongful exercise of dominion over the personal property of another.

Count: a declaration; an allegation of an offense in an indictment.

Counterclaim: a cause of action existing in favor of the defendant against the plaintiff.

Culpable negligence: the omission to do something which a reasonable, prudent and honest person would do, or doing something which such a person would not do under all the circumstances in the particular case.

Cy pres doctrine: "as nearly as may be," a rule permitting a court to carry out as may be the intention of a donor to a charitable cause.

Deed: an instrument conveying real property.

Default judgment: a judgment entered after the defendant has failed to appear when properly served with process.

Demonstrative evidence: the object to which testimony relates brought into court and exhibited.

Demurrer: an objection made by one party to his opponent's pleading, alleging that he ought not to answer it for some defect of law in the pleading.

Deposition: an affidavit; the written testimony of a witness in response to interrogatories.

Directed verdict: a verdict which a jury returns as directed by the court.

Duress: an unlawful constraint placed upon a person whereby he is forced to perform an act that he might not otherwise do.

Eleemosynary: charitable.

Emancipated minor: freed from the custody, control and service of the parent during infancy.

Estoppel: a state of affairs which arises when a man's own acts preclude him from averring anything to the contrary.

Evidence, primary: that evidence which suffices for the proof of a particular fact until contradicted or overcome by other evidence.

Evidence, secondary: oral testimony or a copy admitted to prove the contents of a lost original document, or one which the other party can produce but refuses to.

Exception: an objection.

Executor of an estate: a person designated in a will to administer an estate.

Fellow-servant rule: the common law doctrine that if the employer has provided safe and suitable tools, machinery and appliances, in accordance with the duty imposed upon him by law, he is not liable for an injury to an employee resulting from the misuse or nonuse of the instrumentalities by another employee.

Felony: a crime punishable by death or by imprisonment in a state prison.

Fiduciary: one holding a position of trust or confidence with respect to the money or property of another.

Forthwith subpoena: a subpoena calling for the production of records with all reasonable diligence and dispatch.

Guardian ad litem: one appointed by the court to look after the interests of an infant in litigation.

Hearsay: statements made by one not a party in interest, nor a party to the action, and not made under oath.

Habeas corpus, writ of: a writ requiring one detaining another person to produce him and submit to the court's orders.

Hypothetical question: a form of question which is put to an expert witness, in which things which counsel claims to have proved are stated as a supposition and the witness is asked to state and explain the conclusion which in his opinion results.

Independent contractor: one who exercises an independent calling and is subject to the control of no one in his work.

Indictment: an accusation founded on legal testimony of a direct and positive character, and the concurring judgment of at least 12 of the grand jurors that upon the evidence presented to them the defendant is guilty.

Infant: a minor; a person under the age of 21.

Injunction: a restraining order issued by a court in equity.

Interrogatories: written questions propounded to a witness on the taking of his deposition.

Intestate: one who dies leaving no valid will.

Judicial opinion: the reason given by the court for its judgment.

Judgment: the final word in a judicial controversy, entered upon the record.

Judicial notice: the recognition of facts which are deemed to be already known to the court and jury, and which therefore need not be proved.

Jurisdiction: the right to adjudicate concerning the subject matter in a given case.

Landlord: the owner of an estate in land, who has leased it for a term for rent.

Lessee: one to whom the lessor grants the lease.

Lessor: one who grants a lease.

Libel: a malicious writing tending to ruin reputation or expose to ridicule.

Licensee: a person whose presence on the premises of the proprietor thereof is not invited but is tolerated.

Lie: to be sustainable.

Lien: a charge upon property for the payment of a debt or duty.

Malpractice: improper, careless or ignorant treatment.

Mandamus, writ of: a command directed to an inferior court, officer, corporation or person, requiring the performance of a particular duty.

Manslaughter: the unlawful killing of a human being without malice or intent.

Mayhem: maiming of the person.

Misdemeanor: a crime which is punishable neither by death nor by imprisonment in state prison.

Motion: an application made to the court to obtain a rule or order directing some act to be done in favor of the applicant.

Non compos mentis: of unsound mind.

Nonsuit: a judgment given against a plaintiff when he is unable to prove a case or when he neglects to proceed to trial.

Nudum pactum: a voluntary promise without any other consideration than good will.

Offeree: the party to whom an offer is made.

Offeror: one who makes an offer.

Pari delicto: equally at fault.

Per se: by or through itself.

Petition: a complaint; a statement of a cause of action.

Police power: power vested in the legislature to make laws for the health, safety and welfare of the people.

Prima facie evidence: such evidence as is sufficient to establish the fact, and if not rebutted, becomes conclusive of the facts.

Principal: in the law of agency, the employer or constitutor of an agent.

Privity: a mutual relationship between two parties; e.g. an executor is in privity with the testator.

Probate court: a court having jurisdiction of the estates of deceased persons and persons under guardianship.

Process, legal: any means of acquiring jurisdiction of person or property by the court.

Promissee: one to whom a promise is made.

Promissor: one who makes a promise.

Public administrator: a public official who administers the estate of any person dying intestate, without known heirs.

Ratification: giving validity to the act of another.

Rebuttal: testimony intended to deny or to contradict.

Reciprocity of states: full faith and credit given by a state to the acts and judicial decisions of another state.

Release: the surrender of a claim or a right to the person against whom it exists.

Res adjudicata: a thing definitely settled by a judicial decision.

Res gestae: acts and words which are so closely connected to the main fact as to constitute a part of the transaction.

Res ipsa loquitur: the occurrence speaks for itself.

Respondeat superior: the doctrine that the master is responsible for the act of his agent or servant.

Respondent: the defendant in an action.

Siblings: brothers and sisters having the same father and mother.

Slander: the utterance of defamatory words intended to prejudice the reputation or business of another.

Statute of frauds: a statute which requires that certain contracts and transactions affecting realty be in writing.

Statute of limitations: a law limiting the period of time during which an action must be brought.

Subpoena: a process to compel the attendance of a person at court as a witness.

Subpoena duces tecum: a subpoena ordering the witness to bring with him books, documents, or other evidence described in the writ.

Summons: a process served on a defendant in a civil action to secure his appearance in the action.

Surety: one who binds himself with a principal for the performance of an obligation in respect to which the principal is primarily liable.

Testimony: the words heard from a witness in court.

Tort: an injury or wrong committed with or without force to the person or property of another.

Tortfeasor: a wrongdoer.

Undisclosed principal: a principal whose identity is kept a secret.

Unemancipated minor: one who is under 21 years of age and remains under the jurisdiction of the parents. Certain conditions, such as marriage, may emancipate a minor from parental control.

Vacate: (legal), to annul; to make void.

Void: having no legal force or effect.

Waiver: the voluntary relinquishing of a known right.

Ward: (legal), a person over whom or over whose property a guardian has been appointed by the court.

Warranty: a promise that the proposition being made is true.

Writ: a process issued out of a court.

INDEX

(Page numbers in *italics* indicate illustrations.)